Fountain
Lwo – English
Dictionary

Alexander Odonga

Fountain Publishers

Fountain Publishers
P.O. Box 488
Kampala
Tel: 256-(41)259163/251112 Fax: 251160
E-mail: fountain@starcom.co.ug

Distribution in Europe, North America, and Australia by African Books
Collective (ABC), The Jam Factory, 27 Park End Street, Oxford OX 1 1HU,
United Kingdom.
E-mail: orders@africanbookscollective.com
Website: www.africanbookscollective.com

© Alexander Odonga 2005

First published 2005

ISBN 9970 02 487 6

Cataloguing-in-Publication Data
   Odonga, Alexander
      Lwo–English dictionary / Alexander Odonga.– Kampala, Fountain Publishers, 2005
   – p. – cm
   ISBN 9970-02-487-6
   1. Lwo language   I. Author   II. Title

496.53

CONTENTS

ACKNOWLEDGMENTS

I must express my sincere thanks to the many people with whom I discussed this dictionary project individually or in groups. I would, however, particularly like to thank members of the Department of Lwo Language, Makerere University, especially Ms Jane F. Alowo, Head of the Department of Lwo Language, and Dr E.Okello Ogwang, of the Department of Literature, for the useful and very informative discussions I held with them. I am particularly grateful to Mr L. Otika, with whom I had several discussions, for the useful information I obtained from him as well as for making available to me several books written earlier on the Acholi language, which I drew upon a great deal in writing this dictionary. I was greatly encouraged by the enthusiasm that Prof. Muranga showed about the dictionary when he saw the frst draft.

My thanks also go to Mr J. Ocwinyo, and again Mr L. Otika, for editing the English part of the dictionary.

Finally I must express my gratitude to my wife with whom I many times discussed the meanings of certain words, particularly those Acholi words which are not now in common use.

PREFACE

I was compelled to complete the Lwo/Acholi −English Dictionary, which I had started working on in 1996, by my discovery, after writing the two books entitled **Ododo pa Acoli**, that many Acholi, especially the younger generation, did not know much Acholi but a lot of English instead. It therefore became obvious that a dictionary should be made available in which they could fnd the meanings of the words in the **Ododo** that they did not know.

When I started writing this dictionary I found the project very diffcult because the Acholi language has a small vocabulary; consequently one word can have many meanings depending on (1) the tone (intonation) in which it is said and (2) what is being spoken about.

I also found the spellings of the words very diffcult. For example, I had to decide whether, in the process of changing a noun or a verb ending in a consonant into a possessive pronoun, the consonant should be doubled and the appropriate vowel added to it or not. Eventually, I decided that doubling the consonants in such cases would help avoid ambiguity.

I read many of the Acholi books that I could lay my hands on, including the Acholi Bible. The Bible helped me very much concerning whether to double the consonant of a word with which it ends or not. Unfortunately, however, in some parts of the Bible the consonants are not doubled. This was a consequence of the various parts of the Bible being written by different people from various clans.

When I read the books written by Crazzolara and Malandra I found them to be the frst great attempt to write the Acholi dictionary, except that Crazzolara wrote in phonetics which the ordinary people cannot read and understand. Since both of them were non-Acholi, they did not understand some of the words and this led to wrong translation of them.

I discussed the roots of the Acholi words with many Acholi and I found the information they provided very helpful.

From the information I gathered, it became quite clear to me that the only way to write Acholi words with the correct spellings was frst to know the roots of the words −which can be nouns, pronouns, verbs, or adjectives.

I tried to explain in detail how the words should be spelt in the introduction to this dictionary. Therefore, one should frst read the introduction before using the Lwo /Acholi − English Dictionary.

I hope that everyone who uses this dictionary, both old and young, and those who want to learn the Acholi language will fnd it very helpful.

A. M. Odonga
December, 2005

INTRODUCTION

The words dealt with in this dictionary are those spoken and understood by the central Acholi clans. This is because their language is not mixed up with the languages of the surrounding tribes. These central clans are Payira, Patiko, Paico, Bwobo and Alero.

The language of the other clans, such as the Koic, Koro, and Puraŋa is affected by those of Laŋo and Jo pa Lwoo. While that of the Pabo, Lamogi, Pawel and Atiak is influenced by those of the Alur, Jonam, etc. The Palabek, and other East Acholi clans, speak a language that is mixed up with those of the Karimojong, Pajok, Shilluk and other Sudanese tribes.

The Acholi clans who are neighbours to the other tribes have brought into Acholi such letters as **h, f, s, v, x** and **z**, which do not exist in the Acholi alphabet. That is why sometimes one hears someone say **fony** (*teaching*) or **acitto ka fony** (*I am going to teach*), which is not correct. The central clans say **pwony** (*teaching*) or **acitto ka pwony** (*I am going to teach*), which is correct. Others bring in **h,** as in Ocheng or Okech, which should be Oceng or Okec as spoken by the central clans. Some people greet others using **ivutto** (*Did you sleep well?*), which should be **ibutto**.

The Acholi alphabet, which is now considered as standard orthography, and which was devised by Christian missionaries, is as follows: A B C D E G I J K L M N Ŋ NY O P R T U W Y. This shows quite clearly that the letters **f, h, s, v, x** and **z** are not part of the Acholi alphabet.

To know how to write the Acholi language one must first know the root – "**tee lwit lokke**"–of the word to be written. Once the root of the word is known, then it can be written correctly. The root of a word can be a verb, noun, pronoun or an adjective.

NOUNS AND VERBS

Possessive Nouns

To change a noun which is the root of a word into a possessive noun, if its spelling ends with a consonant, the consonant should be doubled and an appropriate vowel added to it to make it a possessive noun as follows:

Noun		Possessive Noun		Normally
buk	*book*	buk-ka	*my book*	bukka
dyaŋ	*cow/cattle*	dyaŋ - e	*his cow/cattle*	dyaŋŋe
dyel	*goat*	dyel-li	*your goat*	dyelli
latin	*child*	latin-na	*my child*	latinna
pany	*mortar*	pany-nye	*his mortar*	panynye

From what is written above it should be clear that **latin**, which is a root word, once it changes into a possessive noun cannot be written as **latina** to mean *my child* because that would refer to a type of grass, for **a** cannot stand for **mera** *(my, mine)*. The best way to write it is **latinna** (*my child*) because **na** stands for **mera**. In normal writing, a hyphen is not put between **latin** and **na** but the word is simply written as **latinna**. Nouns which end with a **c** can be changed to possessive nouns by doubling the **c** and then adding appropriate suffix vowels to them as follows:

Nouns		Possessive Noun	
coc	*writing*	cocc**a**	*my writing*
goc	*beating*	gocc**i**	*your method of beating*
guc	*throwing*	gucc**e**	*his method of throwing*
loc	*rule/governance*	locc**a**	*my governance/ my rule*
roc	*mistake/mistaking*	rocc**i**	*your mistake*
tic	*work/ working*	ticc**e**	*his work*

Nouns / Transitive/Intransitive/Verbal Nouns

Nouns can be derived from the main verbs which are the roots of the words. If any such verb ends with a consonant, **-o** should be added to it to change it into a noun, but if the consonant is first doubled and **-o** is added to it then it becomes a transitive / intransitive verb/ verbal noun as shown below:

Main Verb		Noun		Transitive/ Intransitive/ Verbal Noun	
		only -o added to cons.		*cons. doubled and -o added to it*	
cen	*curse*	ceno	*women's loin dress*	cenno	*to curse / cursing*
dany	*part*	danyo	*rainbow*	danynyo	*to part / parting*
der	*decorate*	dero	*barn / granary*	derro	*to decorate / decorating*
dol	*roll/fold*	dolo	*colobus monkey*	dollo	*to fold / folding/rolling*
gud	*touch*	gudo	*road*	guddo	*to touch / touching*
kan	*hide/save*	kano	*a fruit tree*	kanno	*to hide / hiding/saving*
kor	*praise*	koro	*hen house*	korro	*to praise / praising*
kwok	*carry with*	kwoko	*infection of fruits*	kwokko	*to carry / carrying with*
lar	*dispute/save*	laro	*flat stone*	larro	*to dispute / disputing*
lib	*skim/stalk*	libo	*fresh(milk)*	libbo	*to skim /skimming/stalking*
lim	*visit*	limo	*graveyard*	limmo	*to visit / visiting*
loŋ	*winnow*	loŋo	*hydrocele / loud*	loŋŋo	*to winnow / winnowing*
mal	*fry/grill*	malo	*up*	mallo	*to fry/grill / frying/grilling*
or	*send*	oro	*dry season*	orro	*to send / sending*
riŋ	*run*	riŋo	*meat*	riŋŋo	*to run / running*
tim	*do*	timo	*a long thin drum*	timmo	*to do / doing*

There are some nouns which can be changed into verbs by merely changing one's tone as one pronounces them. Examples of such words are provided below:

Noun		Verb	
bal	*sin/mistake*	bal pii ne woko	*spoil the water*
cam	*food*	cam dekki ducu	*eat all your food / eat all this food*
gen	*trust/hope*	gen lawotti	*trust your friend*
nek	*killing*	nek gweno	*kill the chicken*
pwony	*teaching*	pwony litino	*teach the children*
nyom	*marriage*	nyom dako	*marry a wife*
kwan	*reading*	kwan waraga	*read the letter*
doŋ	*boxing*	doŋ lemme	*box his cheek*

Verbs which end with two vowels can be changed into nouns by removing one vowel and replacing it with –c. For example, in the verb **caa** (*despise*) which is a root word, if one -a is removed and replaced with a suffx **c**, it becomes **cac** (*despising*), which is a noun.

Verbs can also be changed into transitive/intransitive verbs by removing one vowel and replacing it with **–yo.** Examples are provided below:

Main Verb		Noun		Transitive/Intransitive Verb / Verbal Noun		
caa	*despise*	cac	*despising*	cayo	*to despise / despising*	
coo	*write*	coc	*writing*	coyo	*to write / writing*	
yuu	*throw*	yuc	*throwing*	yuyo	*to throw / throwing*	
goo	*beat*	goc	*beating*	goyo	*to beat / beating*	
gwee	*kick*	gwec	*kicking*	gweyo	*to kick / kicking*	
tii	*work*	tic	*working*	tiyo	*to work / working*	

Another way of changing a noun into a transitive verb is to remove the **c** with which the noun ends and to replace it with **–yo.**

The verbs which end with double vowels can also be changed into transitive / intransitive verbs in a different way, i.e. by adding **–no** to the verbs without removing any vowel. This is shown below:

kaa	*bite/cut*	kaano	*to bite/cut/ biting /cutting*
twee	*tie*	tweeno	*to tie / tying*
pii	*induce*	piino	*to induce / inducing*

goo	*beat*	goono	*to beat / beating*	
ywee	*sweep*	yweeno	*to sweep / sweeping*	
gwee	*kick*	gweeno	*to kick / kicking*	
yuu	*throw*	yuuno	*to throw/ throwing*	

There are some nouns ending with **c** that can be changed into noun phrases by adding –**co** to them as shown below.

Noun		**Noun Phrase**	
goc	*beating*	gocco	*way of beating*
gwec	*kicking*	gwecco	*way of kicking*
guc	*throwing*	gucco	*way of throwing*
buc	*plucking*	bucco	*way of plucking*

A monosyllabic verb which ends with a consonant can be changed into a transitive or an intransitive verb by doubling the consonant with which it ends and then adding a suffx **o** vowel to it.

This is the same as in English where monosyllabic verbs ending in a consonant are changed into infnitives. Examples are *cut, cutting; dig, digging; get, getting; log, logging; run, running; quit, quitting;* etc.

Verb		**Transitive/Intransitive/Verbal Noun**			**Normal Writing**
bak	*stab*	bak-ko	*to stab /*	*stabbing*	bakko
cub	*spear*	cub-bo	*to spear /*	*spearing*	cubbo
gen	*trust*	gen-no	*to trust /*	*trusting*	genno
kel	*bring*	kel-lo	*to bring*	*bringing*	kello
nyut	*show*	nyut-to	*to show /*	*showing*	nyutto
ŋol	*cut*	ŋol-lo	*to cut /*	*cutting*	ŋollo
ted	*cook*	ted-do	*to cook /*	*cooking*	teddo
tim	*do*	tim-mo	*to do /*	*doing*	timmo
yeny	*search*	yeny-nyo	*to search /*	*searching*	yenynyo
cit	*go*	cit-to	*to go /*	*going*	citto

The words written above are not necessarily pronounced the way they are written. In words such as **citto** and **mitto,** the **t** has a different quality from its English equivalent. As a result the word **citto** sounds like **cirro** or **cirto**. There are words in English such as *tough, foreign, brought,* which are not pronounced the way they are written either. In the Acholi language also doubling the letters of a word does not mean that the word should be pronounced exactly as it is written.

The doubling of the letters is to show the root of the word and what is being spoken about.

Some other words are pronounced as they are written. Some examples are found among intransitive verbs and possessive pronouns.

Intransitive Verb

camme	*eatable*
timme	*can happen*
kwanynye	*can be removed*
nenne	*can be seen*
wille	*can be bought*
gwokke	*can be kept*

Possessive nouns

timmi	*your action*
dekki	*your food*
ticce	*his work*
tamme	*his idea*
lokka	*my word*
camma	*my food*

Some transitive / intransitive verbs can also be used as nouns. For example:

Transitive / Intransitive		Noun Phrase	
cayo	*despising*	cayo dano pe ber	*despising people is not good*
goyo	*beating*	goyo danone rac	*his way of beating people is bad*
gweyo	*kicking*	gweyo odilone ber	*his way of playing football is good*
tiyo	*aging*	tiyo gin marac mada	*aging is a very bad thing*

Once the root of an Acholi word is known it becomes easy to write the word. Some examples are provided below:

Main Verb		**Verbal Noun/ Intransitive Verb**		**Transitive Verb**	
bal	*sin/mistake*	balle	*can be spoiled*	ballo	*spoiling/ to spoil*
cam	*eat*	camme	*eatable*	cammo	*eating / to eat*
doŋ	*box*	doŋŋe	*can be boxed*	doŋŋo	*boxing / to box*
el	*lift*	elle	*can be lifted*	ello	*lifting / to lift*
gen	*trust*	genne	*can be trusted*	genno	*trusting / to trust*
jak	*pull off*	jakke	*can be pulled off*	jakko	*pulling off / to pull*
kel	*bring*	kelle	*can be brought*	kello	*bringing / to bring*
mak	*hold*	makke	*can be held*	makko	*holding / to hold*
iny	*destroy*	inynye	*destructible*	inynyo	*destroying / to destroy*
nyom	*marry*	nyomme	*marriageable*	nyommo	*marrying / to marry*
pwony	*teach*	pwonynye	*teachable*	pwonynyo	*teaching / to teach*
toŋ	*cut*	toŋŋe	*can be cut*	toŋŋo	*cutting / to cut*
um	*cover*	umme	*can be covered*	ummo	*covering / to cover*
wany	*peel*	wanynye	*can be peeled*	wanynyo	*peeling / to peel*
yab	*open*	yabbe	*can be opened*	yabbo	*opening / to open*

VOWELS

When one of the vowels **a, e, i, o** is prefixed to a word, the word becomes a pronoun, eg

a stands for **an,** *I:* **a**mitto, *I want*; **a**ecam, *I am eating.*

e stands for **en,** *he:* **e**mitto, *he wants*; **e**ecam, *he is eating.*

i stands for **in,** *you,* when it is prefixed to verbs. Thus: **i**mitto, *you want*; **i**mitto ŋoo?

what do you want?; **i**citto kwene? *where are you going*? But when **i** stands by itself then it means **i**, *in*: tye **i** ot, *it is in the house*; *to*: ocitto **i** poto, *he went to the field*; *into*: ocitto **i** ot, *he went into the house*; *inside*: tye **i** canduk, *it is inside the box.*

o stands for **en** *he/she*; but it is spoken in the past tense and the third person; for example, **o**mitto, *he/she wanted*; **o**mitto nenni twatwal, *he/she wanted very much to see you*; ocitto ka lwok, *he went to take a bath.*

The vowels which are suffixes make the words possessive pronouns, thus:

-a stands for **mera,** *my:* latinn**a**, *my child*; kel bukk**a**, *bring my book.*

-e stands for **mere,** *his:* latinn**e**, *his child*; latinn**e** tye kwene? *where is his child*?

xi

-i stands for **meri**, *your*: latinni, *your child*; latinni tye kwene? *where is **your** child*?

TENSES

The simple present tense sometimes may consist of only one word, but most times it is a sentence comprising many words. Below are some examples:

ariŋ ? *may I run?*

lwaŋi cammo gin ma otop	*fies eat rotten things*
amarro pwomo mada	*I like passion fruit very much*
pe amitto kwaŋ	*I do not want to swim*

The present progressive tense is spoken in different ways. For example, to mean *I am going,* some people say **abecitto**, others **aenocitto** or **akacitto** and yet others **aecitto**. The central Acholi prefer **aecitto**; **abecitto** is not appropriate because it can be confused with **abicitto** (*I will go*) which is in the future tense.

The present progressive tense, **e** and **tye ka,** are used as shown below:

e

oecam	*he is eating*
iecam	*you are eating*
aelwokko boŋona	*I am washing my clothes*

tye ka

atye ka cam	*I am eating*
en **tye** ka lok	*he is talking*
itye ka timmo ŋo?	*what are you doing?*
atye ka kwan	*I am reading*

In the present perfect progressive tense, the words used are **beddo** and **onoŋo**. Some examples are provided below:

abeddo ka lwok	*I have been having a bath*
ibeddo ka timmo ŋoo?	*what have you been doing?*
obeddo ka tic	*he has been working*
onoŋo abeddo ka cam	*I was having / eating food*
onoŋo atye ka kwaŋ	*I was swimming*
onoŋo aekwan	*I was reading*

In the present perfect tense, the words used are **tyekko, doŋ**, and **aa**.

Below are some examples:

o**tyekko** citto   *he has gone*

a**tyekko** dwoggo   *I have returned*

i**tyekko** kwan?   *have you fnished reading?*

an **doŋ** abinno   *I have come*

en **doŋ** odwoggo   *he has returned*

in pe **doŋ** ityekko? *haven't you fnished yet?*

i **aa** ki kwene?   *from where have you come?*

a **aa** ki i duka   *I have come from the shop*

o **aa** ki i ot   *he has come from the house*

In the simple past tense the words used are the suffxes –**o** and **a, ceŋ, yaŋ** and vowel prefxes added to the verbs to show pronouns. Some examples are provided below:

ocitto laworo   *he went yesterday*

odwoggo tin   *he returned today*

adwoggo tin   *I came today*

There is an exception to the above rule in that when the verb ends with a vowel then

-**o** is not added to it, as the examples below show:

i**oo** awene?   *when did you arrive?*

i**rii** kwene?   *where have you been ?*

Onoŋo pud, e and **tye ka** are used to indicate the past progressive sense. For example:

onoŋo pud aekatto woko akatta   *I was just coming out*

onoŋo pud oecakko cam acakka   *he was just starting to eat*

onoŋo pud atye ka lwok   *I was still having a bath*

onoŋo pud tye ka wot i ŋet yoo *he was still walking along the side of the road* ono**ŋŋo pud ie**cakko wot acakka   *you were just starting to walk*

In the past perfect progressive tense the words used are **onoŋo ceŋ** and **onoŋo yaŋ** .

onoŋo ceŋ atye ka cam   *I had been eating*

onoŋo ceŋ pe atye ka kwan   *I had not been reading*

onoŋo yaŋ pud atidi   *I was still very young*

Onoŋo doŋ are the words used to denote the past perfect tense. For instance:

onoŋo doŋ acammo woko   *I had eaten already*

onoŋo doŋ otoo woko   *he had already died*

onoŋo doŋ idwoggo ki paco *you had already returned from home*

 From time to time, **nakanen** and **nene** are used before or after verbs to show the past perfect tense.

abinno **nakanen** odiko   *I came this morning*

en **nakanen** ocito ka pur   *he did go to dig*

iwok **nakanen** ki kwene?   *where did you pass through?*

Ceŋ and **nene** are used to refer to past envents as follows:

en ceŋ ocitto Kampala *he did go to Kampala*

ceŋ onekko kwac   *he did kill a leopard*

ceŋ otwoo mada   *he was very ill*

en **nene** ocitto Arua   *he did go to Arua*

in **nene** igoyo Oto   *you did beat Oto*

nene alwoŋŋi kwee   *I did call you in vain / last time I called you in vain*

Yaŋ is also like **ceŋ**,   but it is used for things which took place a long long time ago. Other people use **yam** instead but the central Acholi prefer the former.

kakawa yaŋ o aa ki i tuŋ wok ceŋ   *a long time ago our clan came from the East*

i kare ma yaŋ con *a long time ago*

-bi- is used to indicate the future tense. For example:

ibidwoggo awene? *when will you return?*

abikwannone diki *I will read it tomorrow*

en bicitto Kampala diki maca *he will go to Kampala the day after tomorrow*

Example of adjectives are: **ber, bor, cek, col, kwar, rac** (*plural* **becco, bocco, raccu, cego** etc). In sentences they are used as follows:

bura ma**col**	*a black cat*
boŋone **kwar**	*the clothes are red /his/her clothes are red*
dano mac**ek**	*a short person*
nyako ma**ber twatwal**	*a very beautiful girl*
yat ma bor	*a tall tree*
dano ma**rac**	*a bad person*

Plural Adjectives

gin ducu gi**becco**	*they are all good*
gin ducu gi**raccu**	*they are all bad*
gin ducu gi**bocco**	*they are all tall*

Examples of adverbs are: **dwir, oyot oyot, tek, awene, jwi jwi, yaŋ, tyen adii, laworo, otyeno,** etc. They are used in the following manner:

oriŋŋo **madwir** twatwal	*he ran very fast*
ogoye **matek** mada	*he beat him very much*
cit **oyot oyot**	*go quickly*
obinno awene ?	*when did he come?*
en **jwi jwi** binno kany	*he always comes here*
en **yaŋ** lacan mada	*a long time ago he was very poor*
okello **tyen adii**?	*how many times did he bring?*
adwoggo **laworo**	*I came yesterday*
bin diki **otyeno**	*come tomorrow evening*

Mee is the root of personal possessive pronouns. If one intends to show the owner of a thing, one **e** is removed from **mee,** leaving **me.** To this **r** is added in the case of a singular but **w** in plurals except in third person pronouns, in which case **g** is added. Then to these appropriate vowels are added to show the owner of the thing concerned, except in questions where **mee** is written in full, for example: mee pa aŋaa ? *belonging to whom? / whose things?/ to whom does it belong?*

SINGULAR AND PLURAL FORMS

Singular	**Plural**
mera (meera) *mine*	mewa (meewa) *ours*
meri (meeri) *yours*	mewu (meewu) *yours*
mere (meere) *his*	megi (meegi) *theirs*

Sometimes instead of **r, g** is used and an appropriate vowel is added to it for the singular. For the plural, however, **w** is added to the frst and second person pronouns and appropriate vowels are added to them as follows:

Singular	**Plural**
mega (meega) *mine*	megwa (meegwa) *ours*
megi (meegi) *yours*	megwu (meegwu) *yours*
mege (meege) *his*	meggi (meeggi) *theirs*

g is not commonly spoken.

A word may have a number of different spellings. *F*or example, the equivalent of the English word *very* is said in various ways. Some people say **tutwal, totwal** or **twatwal** while others say **twaltwal**. The central Acholi prefer **twatwal**: ber twatwal, *very beautiful*.

Other spellings which are very different are:

Very different		*Central Acholi prefer*	
lotino	*children*	lutino	lutino gucitto kwene? *where are the children going?*
lodito	*elders*	ludito	ludito gitye ka cam *the elders are eating*
lodwar	*hunters*	ludwar	ludwar doŋ gudwoggo *the hunters have returned*
ubin	*you come*	wubin	wubin kany *you come here*
uriŋ	*you run*	wuriŋ	wuriŋ wudok gaŋ *you run back home*
ib	*tail*	yib	yib ayom bor *a monkey's tail is long*
ito	*smoke*	yito	yito tye ka duny *smoke is billowing*

From the words written above, **ito** for *smoke* is not right because it can be confused with **ito yat**, *climbing a tree*. Therefore **yito** for *smoke* is right.

Ubin is not right because **u** cannot stand for **wun**. When it is written in full,

u will become **un**. Therefore when you say **un bin, un** will have two meanings: 1 *you, 2 torture* or *torment*. **Wubin** is the right word, since **wu** can stand for **wun:** wun bin, *you come*.

The words **li** and **ni** are interchangeable. For example, **oliŋ li cwic** and **oliŋ ni cwic** have exactly the same meaning.

The words **ki-** and **gi-** are also interchangeable; but if **ki-** is prefixed to a noun then it cannot be changed. The examples below show this:

kicaa	cannot be changed to	**gicaa**	*a bag*
kipwola	" "	**gipwola**	*misfortune*
kicika	" "	**gicika**	*a partition of a room*
kitara	" "	**gitara**	*a stretcher*
kigol	" "	**gigol**	*a basket cover for chicken*

When **ki-** is prefixed to a verb, thus making the verb an auxiliary verb, then it can be changeable, as shown below:

kikello	changeable to	**gikello**	*has been brought*
kikwanynyo	" "	**gikwanynyo**	*has been taken*
kibollo	" "	**gibollo**	*has been thrown away*
kitimmo	" "	**gitimmo**	*has been done*
kikwallo	" "	**gikwallo**	*has been stolen*

The central Acholi prefer **gi** to **ki.**

The suffixes **-o** and **–u** are also interchangeable. For example, **Okullo** can be written as **Okullu, kulo** as **kulu, agulo** as **agulu**, etc.

These are spoken by the central Acholi as well as the others.

Verbal nouns, or nouns which are used as verbs, exist in Acholi. For example:

Verbal Noun		**Verb**	
doŋ	*boxing*	doŋ ma tek	*box hard*
gwok	*keeping*	gwok ginne maber	*keep the thing well*
kwany	*taking*	kwany iteer i ot	*take it into the house*
kwer	*refusing*	kwer citto woko	*refuse to go*

PHONETICS

The Acholi language has a limited vocabulary and therefore one word can be spoken in different ways and with different intonations to indicate the root and the meaning of the word. This is exemplified by the word **coo**, which has many meanings depending upon how it is pronounced and the context in which it is spoken. Examples are: **coo**, *men*; **coo**, *porcupine*; **coo**, *guinea worm*; **coo**, *boundary*; **coo**, *wake up*; **coo**, *write*; **coo**, *foul smell*. The various meanings depend upon (1) how they are said, (2) the tone in which they are said, and (3) which things are being spoken about.

Note the following relationship betweeen possessive pronouns and transitive / intransitive verbs regarding how they are formed from the roots.

Root	Posessive Pronoun			Transitive / Intransitive Verb	
tim	timmi	timme	timma	timmo	*to do / doing something*
bal	balli	balle	balla	ballo	*to spoil / spoiling something*
cam	cammi	camme	camma	cammo	*to eat / eating food*
lok	lokki	lokke	lokka	lokko	*to speak / speaking loud*
gen	genni	genne	genna	genno	*to trust / trusting a person*

The above declensions show that unless the consonants with which the roots of the words end are doubled and appropriate vowels added to them, they are meaningless.

The abbreviations used in this book are as follows:

n	noun	*prs*	personal pronoun
prn	pronoun	*poss*	possessive pronoun
adj	adjective	*conj*	conjunction
v	main verb	*Lug*	Luganda
vi	intransitive verb	*inj*	interjection
adv	adverb	*prd*	predicate
A	Arabic	*prp*	preposition
Lang.	Lango	*vn*	verbal noun
Eng.	English	*aux v*	auxiliary verb
lit.	literally	*vp*	verbal phrase
pref.	prefix	*suff*	suffix
c/f	compare with	*pl.*	plural

sing.	singular	*e.g.*	for example
dem	demonstrative	*prov.*	proverb
S	Kiswahili	*sla*	slang
rep	reply	*vt*	transitive verb
con	consonant	*qv*	which read
i.e.	that is	*int*	interrogation

Aa

A, a first letter of the *alphabet*. When **a** is *pref* to other words, it stands for *prs prn* **I** as follows: **amitto, I** want; **acitto, I** went; **adaggi, I** refused; **anenno, I** saw; **acammo, I** ate; **akwanno, I** read; when **-a** is *sff* to other words, it stands for **me, to me, my**, eg. **Okella cam,** he brought **me** some food; **odwogga cen buk ma oterro,** he returned **to me** the book he took; **olwokko boŋona,** he washed **my** clothes.

aa *v* get up; **aa malo icuŋ,** get up and stand.

aa *vn* descendants of; **guaa i kaka me Patiko,** they are the descendants of the Patiko clan.

aa *vi* grows; **ŋomme ber mada nyim aa iye maber mada,** the land is very fertile, simsim grows very well in it; see **ayo.**

aa *injt* exclamations of surprise!

a a *adv* no; **a a pee kitmeno,** no, not like that.

a aa *vi* came from; **a aa bot Okot,** I came from Okot; **a aa ka tic,** I came from work.

a a a pee, *adv.* no, no, not at all; see **pe.**

abaa *n.* father, used more in speech, but **abaana** is used more in writing than in speech, for my father; whereas **abaane,** his father, **abaani,** your father are used both in speech as well as in writing.

abaa baa *n* stupid, foolish, imbecile; see **lagikom, abelu, apoya, gama.**

ababa *n* foolish, stupid; a person who cannot speak well or say any meaningful words and does not understand anything; it is the same as **abaa baa.**

abac abac *adj.* white and black. **komme obeddo abac abac,** its body is striped white and black.

abacala *n A* onion; this is an archaic name. Now it is called **mituŋgulo** or **bituŋgulo.**

abaji *n Lug.* syphilis; introduced from Bunyoro and Buganda; **twoo abaji omakke woko,** he is infected with syphilis.

abakki *vt* I stab you; **koni abakki ki palaa,** I will (soon) stab you with a knife.

aballo *vi* I have sinned, or have spoiled, or have ruined, or have destroyed; **aballo i nyim Lubaŋa,** I have sinned against God; *vt* **aballo caana woko,** I have spoiled my watch; **aballo ticca woko,** I have ruined my work or business; **aballo mutoka mera woko,** I have destroyed my motor car.

Abalo *n* female name (*lit.* I have sinned, I spoiled). Some write it as **Aballo.**

abam *n* platform; **joo madito gubed wii abam ento joo matino gubed piny,** the elders should sit on the platform but the young ones should sit down.

abaŋa baŋa *n* creeping and climbing plant with big edible beans.

abaŋali *n* confused person, someone with unstable mind; **abaŋali en aye doŋ odoŋ paco,** the confused person or person of unstable mind is the one who has remained at home; see **obaŋŋe.**

Abanya *n* female name (**banya** means a debt)

abar-wic-lela *n* severe headache, migraine; **lacoone twoyo abar wic leela twatwal,** the man suffers too much from migraine / severe headache.

abelu *n* restlessness, being mentally ill or weak-minded **abelu omakke,** he has become mental / mad. See also **apoya, gama, gikom.**

abembem *n* male name (*lit.* means very important people. abembem tin gubinno ka legga, very important people came to prayers. *See Oluma* (**Aber** *n* I am good either in manner or physically)

abic n numb five; **miine ciliŋ abic keken,** give him only five shillings.

abicel *n* numb. six.; **dyegi abicel keken aye gitye,** only six goats are present.

abii *n* general name for particular grass for thatching roofs (hut).

abil? *vi* may I taste?; **wek abil,** let me taste.

abila *n* ancestral shrine, usually consisting of the dried wood of a special kind of tree which cannot be destroyed by termites; which are planted in the ground, upon which skulls of killed animals are hung.

abili *n Eng.* Police; **abili obino ka makko dano,** the police has come to arrest the people.

abiliŋ *n* a short thick greenish grasshopper which emits foam from beneath its wings. **abiliŋ ŋullo bwoyo ki i tee bwomme, abiliŋ** makes foam from beneath its wings.

abilla *n* for tasting. **cam me abilla keken,** food for tasting only.

abillo *vi* I have tasted; **abillo dekke mit mada,** I tasted the food, it is very nice.

abillo *vt* I have charmed or hypnotized; **abillo dano ci gunino i ot mape giŋeyo komgi,** I charmed / hypnotized the people so that they slept in the house without knowing where they were.

abino *n* a pot with a narrow neck, usually used for local beer; pitcher.

abinya *n* black magic; **jok abinya,** black magic common among the Alur.

abiro *n* numb seven; **kella gweni abiro,** bring me seven chickens.

aboce *n* a climbing plant with edible tuber; it belongs to a family of yams, and is not normally eaten except in times of famine.

Aboce *n* male name (a child born during famine when people resort to eating this plant because food is scarce.

abok *n* aching, rheumatism which is usually felt by women in their hips and thighs; **abok mwoddo emme,** there is aching pain in her thigh. This is usually felt by women during the last part of their pregnancy; it is thought to be due to the pressure on the pelvic nerves by the descending head of the foetus.

aboke ŋor *n* fully grown cowpea pods containing seeds that are not yet dry. The pods are cooked with seeds in them but later the seeds are taken out from the pods and eaten; sometimes the pods are eaten raw with the seeds in them, when they are still green, by children.

abolbol *n* dewlap, the fold of loose skin hanging down from the neck of a cow or ox.

abollo *vi* I threw, I dropped; **abollo piny kuno,** I threw it down there; **pe aŋeyo kama abollo iye ciliŋ abic,** I do not know where I dropped the five shillings.

Abolo *n* a female name (*lit.* I threw away)

aboŋwen *n* numb. nine; **dano aboŋwen keken aye gubinno,** only nine people came.

abor *n* adultery; **timmo abor,** committing adultery, a married person having sexual intercourse with another person.

abora *n* water lily; **aborane giturro mabecco mada,** the water lily blooms very beautifully.

aboro *n* eight; **litino aboro gin aye gukato peny,** only eight children passed the examination.

abuc *adv* on the brink of something, eg. **omakko abuc,** he held it precariously and it is went about to fall off; **iketto binika abuc mada i wii meja,** you have put the tea pot in a precarious position on the table and it is about to fall down. see **abuny.**

abul? *vi* may I roast / grill?; **wek abul,** let me roast / grill.

abulla *adj* grilled or roasted; **anyogi abulla,** roasted or grilled maize; **dano marro mwoddo anyogi abulla mada,** people like eating grilled maize very much.

abumma *n* swindling; **lim abumma kello can,** swindled money brings misfortune; **labumma,** a swindler; see **labwumma.**

abuno *adj* deep round; **bur abuno,** a deep round hole.

abuny *adj* 1 straight not turned outwards; **dog agulune abuny,** the mouth of the pot is straight, not turned outwards or everted.

abuny *adv* 1 precariously; **imakko atabone abuny, eno gwok koni pot woko,** you have precariously held the bowel, it might fall off; 2 on the brink of; **agulu ma itweyo i ŋee leela doŋ tye abuny mada,** the pot which you have tied to the bicycle carrier is on the brink of falling off; see **abuc.**

abur *n* reedbuck. See **ruda ka lajwa.**

Abur *n* a female name *(lit.* I am a pit or a hole (grave)). The name is usually given to a girl born after the death of some of the children born before her.

aburo *n* a cold. **aburo omakka,** I have a cold /I have caught a cold.

Aburo or **Aburu** *n* a female name (*lit* means I am ash)

aburro *vt* to cheat, to frighten; **aburro ki lim,** I cheated him out of money; **aburro ki odoo,** I frightened him with a stick.

abutida *n* catapult, a Y- shaped stick to which strips of rubber or elastic band have been and which is used for shooting birds.

Abwoc *n* a female name*(lit.* arrogance, insolence).

abwoc *n* arrogance, insolence, sarcasm. **labwoc,** arrogant or sarcastic person; **man lok abwoc mape myero ilokko kany,** this is an arrogant and insolent talk which you should not say / speak here.

abwoga *n.* miscarriage, born before full term: **latinne goro pien latin abwoga,** the child is weak because he was born before full term.

abwol *n.* wristlet, bangle, bracelet, usually made of brass but sometimes made of cut elephant task, which is called also **pogo.**

abworra *adv.* at about 2 to 3 p.m., eg. **ceŋ doŋ tye abwora,** it is now about 2 p.m.

abwora *adj.* part only; **abwora joo ma guriŋŋo,** some of the refugees.

abworre *vn* introduction; **man pudi**

abworre keken, this is just the introduction preliminary information.

abwori *n* eland, an animal which is as big as a cow and in many ways similar to cows.

Abye *n* rocky hill at Patiko near Mt. Guruguru (Palee).

ac! *int* exclammation of disgust or of refusal; get off; **ac, cit teŋŋe kwica,** get away from here.

Acaa *n* correct spelling of Acwaa river.

Acaa *n* a female name, a child borne with the placental membrane covering it.

acac *vn* despising; **lok acac pe ber,** despising words are not good.

acac-acac *adv* despising, thoughtless, careless; **tic acac acac pe konyo ati mo,** thoughtless work does not help anybody; **tim acac acac pe ber,** bad behaviour is not good.

acak acak *adj* whitish in colour; **twol acak acak,** a non-poisonous snake that is white on the belly but greenish brown on the back.

acam *adj* left. **ciŋ lacam** the left hand.

acany *n* chronic ulcer of the skin on the feet or hand; on the hand usually was due to yaws; **acany** is more common on the feet; see **ŋwee.**

acari *n* a particular kind of sorghum which is sweet and is usually eaten raw.

Acayo *n* a female name (*lit.* I despised).

acebe *n* black stork (bird); has air-filled pink pouch which hangs from the front of the neck and a reddish pink fleshy growth at the back of the neck, normally called *marabou stork;* this is different from **arum,** *ground hornbill,* which has casque like or helmet- like structure on top of the large curved long bill; it appears that Acholi call them all **arum.**

acekere *A n* a soldier or a policeman.

acel *n* numb, one. **gicel,** once; **kel gweno acel keken,** bring only one chicken; **timgi ducu lawaŋŋa acel,** do all of them at the same time.

Acen *n* female name, the second of the twin to be born; the first is **Apiyo** if they are both female ; the male are **Opiyo** and **Ocen.**

acikari *n* comes from the Kiswahili word *askari* which means 'soldier'; **acikari tin gumol kany gidok tuŋ potto ceŋ,** many soldiers passed through here today on their way to the west.

acil *n.* very small, thin and long; **acil rec,** very small long fish bones; **acil lum,** sharp seeds of the grass used for thatching roofs and lighting.

Acire *n* male name (*lit.* endured).

aciri *adj* dark grey with bright spots. **komme obedo aciri,** the body has black and white spots.

Acoka *n* a male name (means a woman who got married after she was neglected for a long time by many men) for marriage.

acokko *vt* I have collected; **acokko yenna laworo,** I collected my firewood yesterday.

Acoko *n* a female name. It has the same meaning as **Acoka,** (meaning I have collected for marriage a woman who was neglected for a long time by many men for marriage).

acomma *n* **boŋo acomma,** strip of cloth worn by men in front of their loins.

Acomo *n* a name for females (means I met, usually with trouble).

acula or **alwaya** *adj* oval, partly or completely; **wiye acula**, his head is oval.

acuŋet or **pura** *n* young female hartebeest; see wildebeest, **apoli.**

acurra *adv* plainly, frankly regardless of what other people might think or feel, **curru lok acurra,** speaking frankly without bothering about what other people think or feel.

acuru *adj* pointed; **wiye obedo acuru,** his head is pointed at the back.

acut *n* vulture; a**cut opoŋ kwica, gwok nyo tye lee mo ma otoo kuno,** there are many vultures there, perhaps there is a dead animal there.

acuur cuur *n* rapid or waterfall; the Acholi used to call Murchison Falls **Waŋ Acuur Cuur** or **Pajaa.**

acwa *n* a river flowing from Mount Labala into the Nile between Pakwac and Wodlei. *q.v.* **Acaa.**

acwii *n* a type of beetle which sucks juice out of beans or cowpeas.

acwiny *n* liver; some people pronounce it as **acuny.**

adaa *adj* truth; **lok adaa ma alokkoni,** it is the truth that I said.

adada *adv* truly, really true; **myero iniaŋ adada ni, eno aye yoo ma atir,** you must or should truly understand that, that is the right way.

adada *n* a lion-ant: normally burrows in sand. Their presence in the sand can be noticed by the presence of many shallow little pits on the surface of the sand.

adag *vt* -I refused, I hate, I don't like; **adag citto ka tweyo yen,** I refuse to go to gather firewood; I hate, I don't like; **an pe amitti, adaggi, pe amitto nenno waŋŋi,** I do not like you, I hate you, I do not want to see you; some people say **adeg** but **adag** is the word spoken by the central Acholi.

adagi *n* buttocks; **adagi kwon ŋwiny,** flesh of the buttocks.

adam *n* 1 brain (physical); **Caina marro cammo adam wii dyaŋ,** the Chinese like eating very much ox brain; 2 one's mental condition; **danone adam wiye rac,** the man has a bad head, that is, he is mental.

adanya *n* bungler; **ŋat mape ŋeyo tic mo wacel,** one who does not know how to do any work properly at all.

adek *n* numb. three; **me adek,** third; **kel gweni adek,** bring three chickens; **man dano me adek ma doŋ gubinno,** this is the third person to come.

adet *adj* fresh; **riŋo ma adet,** fresh meat.

adi? *int* how much? how many?; **wel pulle adii?** what is the price of the groundnuts? **ikello kikopo adii?,** how many cups have you brought?

adibu *adv* secretly, corruptly, before; **okwanynyo adibu,** he has taken some corruptly before.

adidadida *n* persistence and insistence with menace; **adidadida pa ominne pi banyane omiyo oriŋŋo woko,** his brother's persistence that he pays his debt made him flee.

adil *vi* let me push in more, normally it is said, **wek adil.**

adila *adj* compressed together or pushed under pressure

adiŋ *n* straining sack made of special grass into which beer is poured and strained leaving dregs behind.

adiŋa *adj* strained , **koŋo adiŋŋa,** strained beer.

adiŋa *n* electric fish; **ka imakko rec adiŋa ci diŋŋo ciŋŋi woko,** if you catch an electric fish **adiŋa**, you get an electric shock which makes your hand numb.

adita *n* little basket, usually made from borassus palm reeds.

aditi *n* a kind of small bird which normally makes its nest on the branches of shrubs.

adiya *adv* constraining oneself regardless of one's wishes or difficulties eg, **abinno adiya,** I came despite the obstacles *or* I came reluctantly *or* I was forced to come.

Adok *n* a female name (*lit* means I return *or* go back)

adola *n* large ulcer on the leg, *tropical ulcer,* which usually comes as a result of a scratch which later is infected.

adomo *n* small gourd bottle for oil; **moo kom latin tye i adomo,** the oil for the child's body is in the **adomo. see kicere**

adoŋ *n* a keloid an excrescence in a scar that can grow to a big size when interfered with and is commonly found around the neck and face.

Adoŋ *n* a name usually given to a female child that is second in line after twins. A female child that is born immediately after twins is named **Akello.**

adoŋ *n* striking with the fist, boxing; **tukko adoŋ**, boxing.

adoŋi *n* cerebral spinal meningitis; it is a very dangerous disease characterized by high fever, severe headache and a stiff neck and causes early death; it is also very infectious; another name, **otel tok.**

aduc *n* small hut made of mud and wattle with thatched roof.

aduku *n* a basket, usually made from the reeds of the borassuss palm.

adul *n* short and blunt ended; **adul yat,** a short piece of cut wood.

Adula *n* pet name for little girls.

aduno *n* heart (physical); **adunone tye ka goone,** i.e. his/her heart is beating very hard / he is having palpitation of his heart.

aduno *n* mind. **adunone rac,** he/she has an evil heart. qv **cwinynye rac.**

aduno *adj* middle, sized and roundish **dako aduno,** a small short roundish woman.

aduŋu *n* a musical instrument consisting of a bow with three small strings made of animal tendons and played by girls or women. *c/f* **opuk** which has a bow with a large oval base, which in the past was of tortoise shell, has many strings and is played by men; the Alur call this **aduŋu.**

adwal *n* a young nearly grown-up female antelope.

adwek *n* small locusts which have not yet developed wings; see **ojede.**

adwii *n* a terrorist, an enemy; *c/f* **merok.**

adwoka *n* yellow cow's milk which comes immediately after it has calved.

adwoggi *n* result, effect, **kwoo tye ki adwoggine** stealing has its effect or result.

adwoŋo *n* very large. **aduku adwoŋo,** very large basket.

adyel adyel *n* ibis hadada (bird). *(hagedashia hagedash)*

adyeny *adj* prominent. **pyere oturro adyeny,** he has prominent buttocks (due to lower back bone bending forward leaving the buttocks protruding backwards or sometimes due to one of the lower vertebrae displacing forward on another below it (*spondylolisthesis*).

adyeri *vt* I leave it to you although I still want it, we should not divide it. I ceded it to you; see **jallo.**

agaba *n* climbing or running plant.

agak *n* crow with white neck and breast (*corvus abus*). **agak caŋa ŋut mon** *n* necklace made from cut ostrich eggs for women.

agara *n* a big spear with long blade; see **toŋ.**

agara *n* a type of fish which is yellowish in colour and has many fine bones it is very difficult to eat, has a strong smell but its soup has a very good taste; its original name is **lacaŋa** but because of the nature of its bones, the people changed its name to **agara**; see **lacaŋa.**

agec *n* backbiting, slandering; **lagec dano,** one who backbites people, **en lalok lok agec twatwal,** he always, backbites people.

agik *n* end, termination; **agiki me wii lobo,** the end of the world. 2 vt. stop, **aegik kany,** I am stopping here.

agii *n* betting; **goyo agii,** betting or taking part in gambling; see **jara.**

agit *n* ring; **agit me ribbe girukko i lwet ciŋ me aŋwen me ciŋ tuŋ lacam,** the

wedding ring is worn on the fourth finger of the left hand.

agobi *n* pain connected with menstruation, felt during menstruation i.e. comes during the time of menstruation seen in girls, and usually disappears with pregnancy and giving birth, *dysmenorrhoea.*

agoga *n* a kind of night bird (nightjar); it is alleged that its cry at night

portends danger or a bad omen.

agola *n* recess for door.

agolgol *n* clavicle.

agona yoo *n* a curve in the road.

agoŋ *adv* left ajar, half-closed; **owekko doggolane agoŋ,** he left the door ajar or he half closed the door.

agor agor *adv* tricky (questions); **penynyo peny agor agor,** asking tricky questions the answers to which he knows.

agoro ŋwen *n* termites or white ants which come at night, about 8-11.00 p.m. **agoro ococce pe, agoro** has no holes (around its hill); see **ŋwen.**

Agucito *n* August, the eighth month of the year.

agulu *n* earthen pot; **agulu deko,** earthens pot for cooking sauce.

aguŋ? *vt* may I bend down?

agura gura *n* horse; **munni gimarro tukko agura gura mada,** the Europeans love horse races very much.

agwata *n* calabash or gourd dish. **agwadeko** n. calabash or gourd cup.

agwaya *n* a fine soft stone for cleaning feet by rubbing with it.

agwaya *n* vegetable; **otigo agwaya,**

edible vegetable which has a slippery feel when cooked.

agwee *n* fresh; **kal agwee,** fresh ripe millet *(eleusine),* which is light brown in colour.

Agwee *n* name of a male person. (*lit* fresh).

agweer *vn* what is left over after the owner has harvested; **ocitto i agweer kal,** she went to harvest the leftover millet after the owner has harvested.

aita *n* ground squirrel; it is also spelt as **ayita, see oneyat.**

ajaa *n* gourd rattles; **ajaa giyeŋŋo kwede jok,** the **ajaa** is shaken for summoning the **jok** or spirit.

ajata *n* 1 the part of game meat put aside for ritual purposes. 2 a muddy place.

Ajing *n a* female name. (*lit.* means' let me recuperate').

ajiya *n* 1 the cooking of maize, beans; etc. in water without mixing it with simsim paste or any other sauce. 2 partial cooking. **riŋo ma okwok koŋ gijiyo ka doŋ gitallo,** bad meat is partially cooked first and then it is smoked dry.

ajog *n* collection; **lajog lim pa gabumente,** a government tax collector.

ajoŋa *n* sauce without simsim paste. **dek ajoŋa,** sauce without simsim; see **akita ka alot; akita** and **ajoŋa** are more commonly spoken than **alot.**

ajoŋa miya *n* mbwa fly, *simulum damnosum;* transmits *onchocerciasis* which leads to river blindness, thickened skin and groin nodules.

ajot jot *n* **otwoŋo ajot jot,** a fattish green grasshopper; see **otwoŋo.**

ajuc *n A* an old man.

Ajulu *n* a mountain, situated twelve kilometres north of Gulu.

Ajulu *n* a female name (*lit.* a 'nursed carefully from death').

ajuru *adv* closely together; **ocitto kwede ajuru,** he went following closely behind him; he went to attack him.

ajut *n* **ajut yat,** short tree stump. **ajut yat oyokko tyenna,** a stump has hurt my foot or I have hurt my foot on a stump.

ajut *adj* stupid; **ajut pa meni,** your mother's stupidity.

dano ma ajut, a stupid person.

ajuu *n* grass used for ritual sprinkling. **oywec ajuu,** broom made of **ajuu.**

ajuu *n* laziness; spoken by the people of north-west of Gulu; see **wac kom.**

ajwaka *n* a spirit's priest, a witch, a sorcerer, a doctor; **ajwaka lami yat,** medicine man, a doctor; **ajwaka latyet ki war,** one who consults spirits with the help of the leather sandals (locally made by the people).

ajwiya lee *n* a place where animals can drink; a pond, river, etc.)

akaa *n* Bengal cane; a stick made from the Bengal cane.

akaa or **akakaa** *adv* wanton, without reason, e.g. **igoye akakaa,** you beat him for no particular reason.

Akado *n* tributary of Onyama river coming from Ajulu mountain.

akanni *n* deposit; **akanni ciliŋ 50 i beŋe,** a deposit of 50 shillings in the bank.

akanyaŋo *n* a small crawling insect that carries a lot of things on its back.

akara-kara yoo *n* a fork, bifurcation of the road, cross-road;

> **wacirwatte i akara-kara yoo,** we shall meet at the fork of the road *or* where the road bifurcates.

Akec *n* female name *(lit.* I am bitter, I am hunger, usually a child born during famine).

akeca *n* animosity, hatred, grievance, annoyance; **obeddo ki akeca madit mada i komme,** he was very much annoyed with him or he was very much grieved by him; **i kin gi tye iye akeca matek mada,** there is great animosity / hatred between them.

akela *n* a type of fish with a red tail and sharp teeth.

Akelo or **Akello** n. female name, given to a girl born first after twins; see **Adoŋ.**

akemo *n* Lango. anger, not used very much by Acholi. Acholi use **kiniga; akemo omakke twatwal i komme,** he was very much annoyed with him.

aker *n* a patch of field preserved from burning, destined for a new field or newly tilled field.

akera *adv* to behave submissively, **beddo akera,** living with humility or living submissively, timidly.

Akera *n* name male *(lit.* live with humility or submissively).

akero or **wayo akero** n war dance after killing an enemy or fierce beast.

akeyo *n* a slightly bitter vegetable which is very much liked by the people.

akic *n* loin or sirloin or lumber part of the back. **puc akic,** fillet.

Akidi *n* female name given by **ajwaka** whose spirit name is **Akidi.**

akili *adj* without handle; **palaa ma akili,** a knife without a handle.

akinyo *adj* **akinyo-akinyo,** variegated colours.

akita *n* sauce without simsim; see also: **alot, ajoŋa;** **akita** and **ajoŋa** are more commonly spoken.

akol *n* child recovered or delivered by caesarian section.

akoŋ or **akoŋ akoŋ** *adj* rectangular, two or more flat sides; **adukune obeddo akoŋ akoŋ,** the basket has a flat or rectangular side.

Akot *n* female name (*lit.* I am rain).

akuku *n* black sand (iron ore with mica) used for smearing the head and female loin dress (**cip ki ceno**).

akul *n* pen. **akul dyel,** goats' pen; **akul dyaŋ,** cattle pen.

Akumu *n* name for a female; a child who was conceived without the mother having menstruation; **onywallo laboŋo neno dwee,** she conceived and gave birth without previous menses.

akumu *n* money given by the bridegroom's family secretly to the bride's family, besides the legal two cows and two goats, which are not returnable on divorce. In the past, if a married woman left the husband and ran away with another man, the bride's parent's had to return the cows and goats given to them by the bridegroom to the bridegroom's parent.

akura *n* sheath, case, covering. **akura toŋ,** spear's sheath; **akura mupira,** condom.

akuri *n* dove; **akuri tik tik,** turtle dove (coos misery); **akuri tugo,** big dove which is like domestic pigeon; **akuri kibego,** large-sized wild pigeon.

akuri-akuri *adv* in small but repeated quantities. **cammo akuri-akuri,** eats repeatedly like the dove; see **pude pude, benye benye.**

akwalla *adj* 1 secret. **lok akwalla,** secret communication. 2 stealing, **lok akwalla** may also mean stolen communication; **jami akwalla,** 'stolen' things or goods.

akwaani *n* **akwaani kic;** haneycombs normally is chewed, the juice or honey sucked out and the wax spat out; **kella akwaani kic anyam,** bring for me some honeycombs to chew.

akwarra *adj* new; **latin akwarra,** newly born child, baby, neonate.

akwaya *n* the fragment of a calabash, calabash saucer, used by women for dishing food, smoothing lump of millet, bread (**kwon**).

akwaya bad *n* shoulder blade, s*capula*

Akwero *n* female name (*lit.* I refused),

akwerro *vt.* I refused; **akwero citto ka myel,** I refused to go to dance.

akwici *n* wagtail; can be identified by white and black plumage, long tail,black chest band, seen frequently in cotton fields.

akwili *adv* wholly, entirely; **omwonynyo akwili,** he swallowed it wholly, without chewing it.

akwilla *adj* whispering, secret; **gitye kakwillo lok akwilla,** they are whispering to each other.

akwilli *vt* I tell you in secret or in confidence.

akwoo *adv* secretely; **obinno akwoo,** he came secretely.

akwota kom *n* swellings which usually occur in large muscles of the body and cause very large abscesses or pus which must be opened and drained away, *tropical pyomyocitis.*

ala tyen *n* shin or shin bone, *tibia;* **oturro ala tyenne woko,** he broke his *tibia,* that is, the bigger bone of the two bones of the lower leg below the knee.

Akwir *n* female name (means I am bitter like poison).

alaŋ-alaŋ *adv* singly, scattered, dispersed, separately; **doone tye ento tye alaŋ alaŋ,** the weeds are there but they are scattered and separate.

Alanyo *n* female name (*lit.* I wasted, I neglected to suffer).

alanynyo *vt* I I wasted, 2 I worn, 3 I neglected; **alanynyo lim ducu ma gimiina,** I wasted all the money that I was given; 2 **alanynyo i ŋwec ma wariŋŋo,** I won in the race 3 **alanynyo gwokko gwenona,** I neglected rearing my chicken.

alebu *adj* young and soft; **lum alebu,** young soft grass, which grows after the old grass has been burnt.

alene *n* a kind of grass used to make brooms.

aleggi *vt* I request you.

alegi *n* **ŋor alegi,** a large kind of cowpea.

aleŋa *adv* not straight on the line; not upright; **oketto bukke aleŋa,** he has put the book obliquely; **oyeyo agulu aleŋa,** she carried the pot not upright on the head.

Alero *n* small clan about 20 miles west of Gulu.

Ali *n* A male name.

aliboro *n* a kind of bird *(lanius collaris fiscal or shrikes)*

aligo *n* a rope tied at both ends to a branch of a tree used by children for swinging, a swing; **wacittu ka lyerre i aligo ligo,** let us go to swing on the hanging rope.

alii *n* discord, hostility, enmity, hatred; **erro alii,** starting discord or hostility; **won alii,** the person who started hostility or war; **waŋ alii gi yaŋ tye con,** their enmity existed between them before.

Alii *n* name *(lit. enmity).*

alii adv secretly; **otimmo alii,** he did it secretly;

Aliker *n.* male name *(lit. kingdom enmity, or animosity).*

alili *n* chicken disease *(Newcastle disease).*

alimma *n* slave; this is a person who has been obtained by buying; **latin alimma,** a child who has been bought not born in the clan; see **opii.**

alip *S n* thousand; **alip aryo,** two thousand; **alip miya acel,** one hundred thousand; any number above that is called **million** which comes from the English million; **alip** has come from the Kiswahili word **elfu;** the word was brought by the soldiers returning from the Second World war; see **tutumiya.**

alipere *n* hymen, covering of the entrance to the vagina; it is intact in virgins.

aloŋo *n* fish eagle; **kokone giloo giloo,** its cry **giloo giloo.** Some people call it **aluya**

alot *n* sauce without simsim; **alot** has got the same meaning as **ajoŋa** and **akita;** the last two words are more commonly used than **alot.**

alugulugu *n* 1 tassel; 2 goitre.

alula or **alwaya** *adj* long, protracted, oblong, oval.

alulo *adj* 1 long and round; **komme obedo alulo,** its body is long and round (stick). 2 *adv* undivided; **oterro alulu,** he took it whole without dividing it.

Alur *n* large tribe to the north-west of Lake Albert, who speak a language which is similar to that of the Acholi except in respect to certain dialects; their dialect is near to Luo of Kenya.

Alur *n* female name *(lit.* I am barren).

aluru *n* quail, see **ayulu, jwil, ayweri ka aweno.**

alwak alwak *adv* in groups, clusters. **gin wotto alwak alwak,** they walk in groups; **orudi wotto alwak alwak,** wolves move about in groups / packs.

alwala *n* small red monkey; see **oŋera.**

alwaya *adj* oblong, oval and longish; **okono mukene obedo alwaya,** some pumpkins are oblong oval; see **alula.**

alwete *n* a finger ring-knife; **alwete girukko i lwet ciŋ me kayo kal, alwete** is worn on one of the fingers for cutting the millet.

alwinya *n* snake bird *(anhinga).*

alwiri *n* tall; **bye alwiri ococce pe,** a tall termite hill has no holes.

alwiri *n* **toŋ alwiri,** a spear with a short blade but long neck made of metal; see **toŋ.**

alwokka *adv* 1 charm made on request by a sorcerer to be used against somebody; **man twoo alwokka,** this is a disease which has been brought by the sorcerer; 2 things which are formally sent to the husband of one's daughter after marriage to start their new home.

alwor *vi* I am afraid, I fear; **alwor me binno kuno,** I am afraid of coming there *or* I fear coming there.

Alworo *n* female name *(lit.* means I feared)

alworro *vt* I feared; **alworro citto kuno,** I feared going there.

amacak or twol amacak *n* a snake which is green on the back but white on the belly, it is usually harmless, not poisonous.

amal *n* various small pieces of meat from various parts of an animal as fixed by custom, cooked quickly as stew and eaten by elders in a ritual ceremony.

amam *n* pigeon.

amara ic *n* large intestine; see **cin tino ki labul.**

amayo amayo *vt* I snatched; **amayo lim ki i ciŋŋe,** I snatched money from his hand.

Amayo *n* a female name *(lit.* I robbed him *or* I snatched from him).

amida *n* a special kind of sorghum, its seeds are roasted and eaten eagerly, sometimes eaten without roasting.

amiina or amiira *n.* a tree which shuts up when its leaves are touched *(mimosa pudica).*

amiŋ amiŋ *n* a kind of white ants (termites) that come out in the evening and sometimes during the afternoon,

not eaten; see other termites, such as **okuba, oyala, naka, agoro and aribu.**

amir *adj* dark greyish brown.

amir amir *adj* tending to be dark greyish brown.

amo *n* a tree whose juice is usually rubbed on the itching parts (scabies) during the dry season when scabies is rampant.

amokka *adv* eaten dry; **cukari amokka,** the sugar for eating dry.

amoko moko toŋ gweno *n* egg yolk; see **latuny toŋgweno,** common name for it.

amor *n.* **waŋ amor,** site of great noise (due to waterfalls), Murchison Falls.

amor *n.* sponge *(luffa cylindrica).*

amu *n* yawning, (old language) now **ŋamu** is used instead.

amuka *n* rhinoceros; there are two types of them, the black and the white.

amuli *n* traitor, scandal-monger, double-dealer; **danone obeddo amuli, myero wugwokke ka wutye ka lok kwede,** be careful when talking to him, he is a traitor / a double-dealer / double speaker.

amuli *n* ŋ*or* **amuli** large kind of cowpeas which usually runs along the ground, while the others stand erect.

amur *n.* duiker; **amur-amur** *adj* ash grey. (common name **abur**), see **ruda.**

Amuru *n* hot water spring found about 90 Km west of Gulu .

amuu amuu *adj* blurred, faint, not clear; **calle doŋ nen amuu amuu,** the picture looks blurred, faint, or not clear.

amwoda *n* body aching, in the past used to be due to yaws and syphilis.

amwoda ic, colicky abdominal pain or stomach-ache.

amwodda. *vi* chewing; **kella anyogi nyo pul amwodda,** bring for me some maize (grilled) or groundnuts (roasted) for eating (*lit*. for me to chew).

amwodda *adv* equally at the same time. **gupotto amwodda i tukko me rette, ŋati mo pe ma oloyo lawotte,** they equally fell together, i.e. at the same time in the game of wrestling, neither defeated the other / his competitor.

an *prn prs* I, me; **okello ki an,** he brought it for me; **an amitto,** I want.

Anena *n* female name (*lit*. to be seen *or* something to be watched or seen).

aniino *n* a whip (made from hippopotamus hide). **gupwoddo ŋwiny dano ki aniino,** they beat the people's buttocks with the whip.

aniino *n* sleeping sickness; **twoo ma otoŋtoŋ en aye kobbo,** it is a disease which is transmitted by the tsetse flies.

anok *n* part of a room reserved for goats or sheep, in the house.

anuno *n* creeping plant, its fibres are bitter and not eaten by termites and so used for tying poles. It is also used extensively for washing utensils.

aŋaa? *Int prn*. same as **ŋaa?** who?; **pa aŋaa?** whose?; **pi aŋaa?** for whom?; **aŋaa nyo ŋaa ma owacci,** who told you?

aŋaci/ *or* **koŋo aŋaci,** *n* millet beer which has not yet been strained; beer with its dregs.

aŋaka *prd/ adj* coarsely ground; **moko aŋaka,** the flour is coarse, not fine.

aŋaki yoo nyo aŋaka ŋaka yoo *n* a crossroad; **ka ioo i aŋaki nyo aŋaka ŋaka yoo ci kwany yoo ma odok i ciŋŋi tuŋ lacam,** when you reach the cross roads, take the road which is on your left arm.

aŋec *adv* behind, later; **obinno aŋec,** he came later.

aŋec aŋec *adj* speckled; **komme obeddo aŋec aŋec,** its body is speckled like that of the alligator / monitor lizard.

aŋeca *n* slave; see **opii;** usually **opii** is for men while **aŋeca** for women, a person who has been captured during war; see **guci, lamiru, jane, alimma.**

aŋet aŋet *adv* on the sides / sideways. **oketto agulu aŋet,** she has put the pot sideways not upright; **but aŋet aŋet,** lie on the side.

Aŋeyo *n* female name (means I know),

aŋoo? *inter. prn*. what? **aŋoo?** what is it?

aŋola ŋola *n* obstacle, hindrance, difficulty, unforeseen problem; **aŋola ŋola mogo doki onen en aye ogeŋa binno,** there were some problems which prevented me from coming.

aŋoli *n* skin disease of goats, sheep and calves characterized by loss of hair and ulceration and weeping of the skin of the animal.

aŋulŋul *n* swellings (usually found in the neck, armpit (*axilla*) and in the groins); these are small discrete swellings which sometimes swell up and become painful, *lymph nodes*; see **awaŋ mac.**

aŋwen *n* num. four; **dyel aŋweŋ,** four goats; **dano me aŋwen,** the fourth person.

Aŋwen *n* female name; (*lit*. I am four *or* a white ant).

anyai *n* all kinds of wild animals which

women and girls are prohibited from eating. predators, examples: **anyara, bura, cwiiny, giliri, kak, kworo, oculi, too,** see **ogwaŋ**

anyanya *n* a dangerous poison used against persons.

anyara *n* a skunk, a kind of animal reputed for its stinking body smell.

Anyayo *n* a female name (*lit*. I have increased or multiplied).

anyeda 1 *adv* unfirmly, unsafely, **ocuŋ anyeda,** it is standing unsafely (can fall any time); 2 disdain; **makko jami anyeda,** holds things with disdain.

anyeeri *n* an edible rat; it is also known as reed rat; **anyeeri atuya,** a small edible rat with short tail; **anyeeri telle**, a big edible rat with a long tail.

anyena *n* a bride, a newly wed or married woman; **anyena en aye matye ka teddo,** the bride is the one who is cooking.

anyerri *n* I laughed at you.

anyim 1 *adv* in front, at the head, before the rest; **wot anyim,** walk in front; 2. *adj* **anyim anyim,** grey or greyish.

anyiŋ *n* tin strip wound up spirally into a small tube as ornament and apparel that women wear arround the back.

Anyiŋ *n* a female name.

anyira *n* girls; **anyira gucitto katweyo yen,** the girls have gone to gather firewood.

Anyoda *n* a female name.

anyogi or anywagi *n*. maize; **anyogi** is the one which is normally spoken.

anyoo *n* measles; **twoo ma makko litino kare ki kare,** the disease that frequently attacks the children.

anyuba nyuba *n* confusion; **Oto en aye okello anyuba nyuba i paco man,** Oto is the one who brought confusion in this home.

anywalla *adj* begotten; **latin anywalla,** a begotten child, not adopted.

anywaŋ *n* sticky kind of clay or soil.

Anywar *n* a male name (*lit*. abuse, naughtiness, insult).

anywar *n* abuse, naughtiness, insult; **anywarre,** his insult or abuse.

Aol *n* a female name (*lit*. I am tired), the third child born after twin; a man is called **Oola.**

aona *n* cough, **aona yello twatwal,** coughing troubles him very much; **ŋullo aona ma obedo remo,** he spits sputum which is mixed with blood.

aonya *n* remains (left-overs from a meal); **mon gucokko aonya pa lwak guterro ki litinogi,** the women collected the food left-over, after the people had eaten and took them to their children.

aor or **aor yen** *n* a raised place for piling firewood in a hut; **aor tye wii anok**, a raised place for firewood is above the place for goats; see **kigoŋ**.

apacca *adv* superficially, aside; **cubbo leene opacco apacca,** he speared the animal superficially but the spear only grazed the animal's skin.

Apaco *n* a female name (*lit*. I am always at home).

apal pal ceŋ. *adj* time from 3-5 p.m., not much used by the Acholi.

apano *adj* wide and long; **dano ma apano,** a person with wide chest and waist, in women the waist is said to be *gynaecoid* shaped pelvis; wide and flat pelvis; see **pyerre opette.**

apar *n* ten; **gipar,** ten times.

Aparo *n* a female name (*lit.* means yearning for or longing for).

aparro *vt* yearning, longing, worrying; **aparro mada me cammo kic, I** yearn very much to eat honey; **aparro citto i Amerika,** I long to go to America; **aparro mada pi litino,** I do worry very much about the children.

apata *adj* flat. **ŋwinynye apata,** his buttocks are flat.

apee intj bless you (normally said to a baby when it has sneezed).

apededede or **labaa** *n.* 'a large brown-coloured grasshopper; see **awiny awiny.**

Apele *n* a female name (*lit.* means troublesome or restless.)

aperu *adv* lying open and unprotected; **doggola obutto aperu,** the door was left wide open throughout the night; **gaŋ tye aperu,** the home is wide open without a fence.

apidiŋ *n* secret and narrow entry to a compound or village; a narrow entrance.

apika *n* the stomach of an animal.

apil *n Eng* appeal; **kokko apil i kot ma malo,** appealed to the High Court.

apili lyaŋ *n* simsim soup only without vegetables or **toki, malakwaŋ** soup only without vegetables.

apim *adj* flattened; **wiye apim,** his head is flattened and large at the top.

apim *n* chronic swelling of the leg characterised by a big leg with thickened and cracked skin due to filariasis, *elephantiasis* of the leg.

apip *adj* low but large in size; **wiye apip,** his head is flattened but large; **ot ma wiye apip,** a house with a low roof but a wide base.

Apiril *n* April, the fourth month of the year.

Apiyo *n* a female name. first of twins; second of the twins is **Acen.**

apodo *n* the great bustard (a bird); family of cranes and rails (crested crane).

apoka *n* the bark of a tree, the rind or shell of a fruit.

apoka poka oro ki cwir *n* The Milky Way (seen in sky at night; *lit.* the division between the dry and wet seasons).

apokko *vi* I distributed, I divided.

Apoko *n* a female name (*lit.* I distributed, I divided).

apoli *n* wildebeest.

apoŋ poŋ nyo obaŋ cet *n* an insect or a kind of grasshopper which emits a foul-smelling fluid when disturbed; see **ajot jot, and otwoŋo mukene.**

apora bot *n* imitation, copying, counterfeiting; prov **apora bot onekko apwoyo,** imitation killed the hare.

apotti pir *vn* imitation, copying; **apotti pir terri i pekko,** imitation or copying gets you into trouble.

apoya *n* madness, weak-mindedness, mental case; see **abelu, gama, gikom.**

apudu *n* kind of grass of the **abii** group.

apulu *n* same as **apwa,** dust; **apwa** is the one which is now commonly used.

apuk puk *n* smaller bustard (a bird); see **apodo.**

apuru *n* boys and girls between 14-17 years, teenagers, youth; see **poi , poyi.**

apurru or **apurro** *vt.* I tilled or cultivated; **apurro poto,** I tilled or cultivated the field.

apwa, *n* dust, dust storm; **yamo koddo** tukko **apwa,** the wind blows and stirs up dust; see **apulu.**

apwoyo *n* a rabbit, hare; hares live in the jungle, whereas rabbits sometimes are kept at home.

apwoyo *vt* thanks; **apwoyo mot ma icwalla,** thank you for the gift which you sent me.

Arac *n* a female name (*lit.* I am bad).

aram tala *n* a white and black stork.

arany *adv* talking without regard; **ŋadi dok lokko lok arany twatwal mape parro ŋati mo,** so and so talks bad words without regard to anybody; see **ranynyo lok.**

arara *n* **lalur arara,** the spotted hyena.

arege *n* waragi, local gin; **dano gumer mada ki arege,** the people were very drunk on the local gin.

aremu *n* a creeper, whose roots are red and used as medicine against dysentery (**yat cado remu).**

ari *adv* crosswise; **waŋŋe ari,** his eyes are crosswise i.e. he has a squint.

ari ari *n* **komme oŋollo ari ari,** its body is cross-striped, like that of the zebra.

aribu *n* a kind of white ant (termite) which comes out in the early hours of the night at about 5-6.00 a.m. in large numbers see, **amiŋ amiŋ, agoro, naka, okuba, oyala.**

aribe *n* a weaverbird (smaller than **ocwak);** finches or seed eaters. (*Srinus atrogularis or s. strialatus*).

aridi *n* silk; **boŋo aridi,** silk cloth or clothes.

arii ! *intj* exclamation to express surprise **arii! in dok ilokko kitmeno iya!** I am surprised! Do you really speak like that!

arocile or **arokile** *n* puttee, a long strip of wool which the police or the army used to wind round and round on their legs to protect them from injury of any kind.

arododo *n* working for chiefs instead of paying taxes in cash, it is simillar to **luwalo.**

aroma *n* great misery, distress, suffering; **aroma me tiyo tic pakaca pe doŋ weko acwee,** the suffering of working as a porter does not make me put on weight.

aromo-ki-ŋuu *n* a thorny plant which yields good fibre.

arony *n* abuse, impertinence; **jalle marro lok arony mada,** the man always likes abusive / impertinent words.

arudo yat *n* 1 young shoots from the stump of a tree. 2 I rubbed the tree.

aruk dyaŋ *n* hump of cattle; **aruk dyaŋ riŋo mayom maber mada,** cow's hump is very soft and nice.

arum *n* a great hunt in which an area where there are many animals is surrounded by the people and the animals are killed for food.

arum *n* ground hornbill (*bucorvus leadbeateri*); general plumage black with white feathers which are noticeable when it is flying; skin of face and neck is unfeathered and it is bright red. At a distance it looks like turkey; it is different from **acebe,** marabou stork, by having a casque which looks like a military helmet on top of its long beak.

arut or **arut arut** *prd* narrow with flattened sides; **arut** is the same as **akoŋ.**

arut *prd* double-dealing, ambiguous.

arwaa *n* pieces of meat that remain when the fat on meat has mealted off after frying.

arwii *n* in the wrong way; **en dok tiyo jami arwii twatwal,** he always does things in the wrong way / awkwardly.

arwit *adv* **tweyo arwit,** to tie with a running knot, i.e. a granny knot.

aryebba *adv* turned downwards, upside down; **but aryebba ic,** lie face down.

aryec *n* deep narrow oblong hole (for trapping animals).

aryo num. two; **dano aryo,** two people; **tyen giryo,** twice.

ata or **atata** *adj* common, of no value, ordinary; **jami atata mogo,** worthless things; **i lokko lok atata,** you talk nonsense; **man boŋo atata,** this is an ordinary dress of no value.

atabo *n* an earthenware or metal bowl; **atabo en aye gigetto iye dek me acamma, atabo** is where sauce for eating is put.

ataca *prd* shallow, flat; **iye ataca,** it is shallow; **wii derone ataca,** the roof of the barn is flat.

ataca-taŋalaro *prd* open and unprotected against the weather.

ataka *n* beads made of tin; a string of the beads that are worn by women; *prov.* **obinno ma ataka pyerre pudi opoŋ,**

she came with her waist still full of beads, **ento pi kare manok ataka doŋ oo kene,** but soon the beads will fall away-in other words, she came with pride and happiness but soon the pride and happiness will disappear.

ataŋŋo ciŋŋa *n* 1 a small greasy shrub. 2 I open my hand. Words used for pleading.

atanya *adv* **wotto atanya,** walks improperly, indecently.

ataro *adv* upward; **but ataro nyo but atataro,** lie face upwards.

Ataro *n* a female name (*lit.* lying face upwards; name given by a mother to her daughther who feels that she has been neglected; see **tarro.**

atego *n* a metal wire made into an armlet, bangle, anklet, wristlet, and usually worn by women.

atego *n* a very strong tree, whose timber lasts for a long time and that is very good for building and not easily eaten by termites.

Atek *n* a female name (*lit.* I am strong)

atenna *adv* intimately; **giwotto atenna nyo gibeddo atenna,** they walk / live together with great intimacy (a husband and wife who love each other very much).

ateŋŋa *adv* far-reaching; **oteŋŋo ŋwec ateŋŋa matek mada,** he took off at high speed; **litino guteŋŋo wot ateŋŋa gucitto wa Gulu,** the children took off and went as far as Gulu.

atero *n* arrow, lancet; **nyig atero,** arrows, bullets, cartridges; **atero balibali,** the arrow with many barbs on its blade.

atii *adv* beginning, first, starting; **ŋa ma oo wii atii?** who arrived first? **wii atii Lubaŋa oketto dano,** God created people at the beginning; **ŋaa ma okwoŋo ŋwec wii atii?** who started running first.

Atii *n* a female name (*lit*. I am old); **an doŋ atii woko,** I am very old.

atii 1 *vt* may I pour (water) or 2 *adv* I am old.

atika *adv* really; **otimmo maber atikatika,** he did it really very well.

atiko *n* the blue bottlefly; a large green hay-hopper; the red locust.

Atiko *n* a male name.

atinna *n* economy, thriftiness, prudence; **jami ducu myero doŋ gitin atinna,** there must be thriftiness in the use of things.

atir *adv* straight, true, just; **lokke atir,** his words are true; **oŋollo lokke atir mada,** he made a just judgement / his judgement was very just; **yatte atir,** the pole is straight.

atoŋŋo ten *vt* let us stop and rest - **kibole,** let us go (words used in hunting).

Atoo *n* female name (*lit*. I am dead), a name given following the loss of many children.

atota *adj* pleated; **ot atota,** ahut thatched in rows of grass that looks like a terrace.

atubu, latubutubu *n.* the dragonfly; other people call it **latugutugu;** the latter is the name that is commonly used.

atudu *n* wild goose, duck; see, **aweno, ayweri, jwil, aluru, amam, akuri.**

atum *n* a bow; **atum koo tek me cello ki jami,** the bamboo bow is strong for shooting things.

atuna *n* proud flesh; **atuna waŋ gwok,** a stye or painful swelling on the eyelid.

atunya *n* another name for lion; see **labwor.**

ature n flowers, **ature man gin becco mada,** These flowes are very beautiful, see **gin anena.**

ature *n* whitish discharge from the eyes. **waŋ latinni dok opoŋ ki ature twatwal** this childs eyes are full of the white discharge.

atuya *n* a small kind of edible rat with a short tail; see **anyeeri telle.**

Atuya *n* a male name (*lit*. small like the little edible rat).

atwat *n* mucus, filthy discharge on genitals, whitish discharge from genitals.

atwom *n* suffering, persecution, torture; **oneno atwom mada i gaŋ pa rwot,** he suffered very much from torture at the chief's place.

atworo *adj* green, greenish; **boŋone obeddo atworo,** the garment was green.

atyer *adv* publicly, openly, frankly; **olokko atyer ma dano ducu guwinynyo,** he spoke openly / frankly and all the people heard it.

atyer- wek- aywee, *n* a kind of insect of the grasshopper family, which has a greatly distended abdomen which is believed to burst to let out the young ones after which the insect dies; this is believed to be their ways of giving birth.

aula *n* a giraffe, zebra or buffalo tail tied to the arm for dancing.

Awac *n* name of a Payira district, called after a river flowing into river Abera which itself flows into river Acaa.

awak poto *n* field work done by many invited people whose payment is a good meal (meat, chicken, etc.) and beer, a kind of communal work.

awal *n* a calabash or gourd dish / plate.

awaŋ mac *n* painful little swellings which may be in the groin or armpit, following an infection in the leg or arm; the little swellings are *lymph nodes*; sometimes the swellings may arise from a disease of the genital organs which then may involve the glands in the groin, this is *bubo*.

awar me dako *n* reclamation of bride price for a divorced wife.

awar bad *n* pieces of meat cut from the foreleg and cooked quickly for the elders to eat during some traditional ceremonies.

awara kic *n* honeycombs of bees; **miya awara kic anyam,** give me some honey-combs to chew; *c/f* **akwani kic.**

awara taa *n* dried tobacco leaves. **miya awara taa meeri wek amatti,** give me some of your dried tobacco leaves to smoke.

awaro *adj* **awaro tyen** the webbed toes of swimming birds.

awene *inter/ prp* when?; **otimme awene?** when did it happen?

aweno *n* the guinea fowl; see **ayweri, jwil, atudu, aluru, ayulu, amam, akuri.**

Aweri *n a* female name (*lit.* I sing for you / I made a song about you).

Awili *n* a female name which is much used in Acholi fables.

Awilo *n* a female name (*lit.* I bought)

awiny awiny *n* a kind of grasshopper which is brownish in colour; see **labaa, apededede, lakaibona, abiliŋ, obaŋ cet, ajot jot, ka ocene.**

awira *adv* turning round, curved.

awira wira *n* a game which children play by turning round and round until they are giddy.

awiya *n* children under twelve; spoken very much by the Alur; see **apuro, poi, bulu.**

awiya nyo wii awiya coŋ *n* a tendon above the patella. *(quadriceps tendon).*

awobi *n* a boy; pl. **awobe,** boys.

awola *n* poison; **takko awola,** removing poison by magical traditional treatment.

Awoko *n* a female name (*lit.* I am out, i.e. always going out).

Awor *n* a female name, (*lit.* I am a night, i.e. born at night).

awuka *n* the stomach of an animal; it is also called **apika.**

Awuka *n* male name.

awula *n* an armlet made of giraffe's hair.

Ayaa *n* a female name (one girl born among many boys in the family; compare with **Okeny** where one boy is born among many girls).

aya or **aya do!** *Intj* exclamation of grief.

Ayago *n* a river coming from Mt Keyo and flowing into the Victoria Nile.

ayal *n* presents required to be given to girls and young women who have accompanied a bride to her new home, before they can take any food.

Ayat *n* a female name (*lit.* means I am medicine) a child kept alive by medicine.

aye *adv* I agree, it is so, it is; **aye binno,** I agree to come, **aye i kom lok ducu ma waloko iye,** I agree to all the matters that we discussed.

ayella *n* persecution, trouble; **lapidi oriŋŋo woko pi ayella yella pa min latin**, the child's nurse or baby sitter ran away because of mistreatment by the child's mother; **pi ayella ma litino pa Icarel gulimmo i Miciri omiyo guaa woko ki kunno**, the children of Israel left Egypt because of the persecution which they suffered there.

ayila jok or **laa dog jok** *n*. skin disease; among the Acholi any disease that cannot be explained is always regarded as caused by **jok,** hence the name **ayila jok.**

ayila *n* itching of the skin.

ayo *vt* 1 producing in abundance; **ŋom man ayo nyim mada,** this field is so fertile that it makes simsim give high yields; see **aa.**

Ayoo *n* a female name (*lit.* I am a path or road, i.e. always walking about).

ayol *adv* quite loosely; **otweyo paline ayol,** he tied his trousers loosely.

Ayoli *n* a male name (lit. loose).

ayom *n* a small red monkey; see **oŋera, dolo, gunya, bim, puno.**

Ayugi *n* a river coming from Mt. Keyo and flowing through Pabo and Attiak and joining the Nile in Sudan.

Ayulu *n* a female name.

ayulu *n* a small kind of partridge; see **aluru, jwil, ayweri, aweno** .

ayuru *adj* sloping down; **ŋwinynye ayuru,** his buttocks slope down.

aywac *n* the last ceremony for a time of voluntary taboos which was started to show public disgust for and hatred of some disgraceful crime of an individual.

ayweri *n* the partridge; see **aluru, aweno, ayulu, jwil.**

aywica *n* a creeping plant with black fruit eaten by children.

B b

B b the second letter of the English alphabet.

baa *adv.* please, **cikella pii baa,** please bring me some water; **titta baa,** please explain to me / tell me.

baa *v* throw, cast away; **baa karatac magi woko,** throw these papers outside; see **bac, bayo.**

bab *vi* to distort, to contract, to deform; **odilone obab woko,** the ball has deflated; see **otoo, ojoo; awal ma dyak ka otwoo ci bab woko,** a wet gourd bowl shrivels when it dries.

bab *v* distort, deform, deflate; **bab dog cupuriane wooko** , distort / deform the edge of the saucepan; **bab odilone,** deflate the football.

baba *n* father; this is the name that young children who are beginning to talk call their father.

babbe *vi* becoming foolish, imbecilic; **latinni obabbe woko,** this child has become mental an imbecile; see **abelu ki apoya.**

babbo *vt* distorting, deformimg; 1 **babbo dog,** contracting one side of the mouth. 2 **babbo cupuria,** pressing and deforming an aluminium saucepan. **babu** *n Eng* bath; **cit ka lwok i babu,** go to take bath in the bath.

bac *n* throwing. **tuko bac me bayo toŋ kama bor,** a javelin throwing game, throwing the javelin a long distance; not commonly spoken; see **baa, bayo.**

bac *n Eng* bus, **wacitto Kampala ki bac.** we went to Kampala by bus.

bad *n* arm; **turro bad,** breaking of the arm; prov **ginoŋŋo ki bad Awana,** meaning they get it from other people's sweat or work.

bai or **bayi** *adv* blank; **nenno piny ni bai,** stares blankly / aimlessly.

Baibul *n* Bible

bayioloji *n Eng* biology; the study of the science of physical life concerned with human beings, animals, plants - their morphology, physiology, origin and distribution.

bak *v* 1 stab; **bak ki toŋ,** stab with a spear; 2 accumulate, heap; **bak moo madwoŋ i dek,** put plenty of oil in the sauce; **bak kal madwoŋ i dero me kurro kec i mwaka mabinno,** store a large amount of millet in the barn for use during the famine next year; **bak moko me tobi,** put flour mixed with water to ferment to form leaven / yeast.

bakacic *A n* payment or a reward for some good work done; **acokko jamini mapol aterro gaŋ ci pee imiya iye bakacic mo,** I collected many of your things and I took them home; could you not give me something to say thank you?

bakala *A n* a mule; a cross between an horse and an ass.

bakke *vi* collected, assembled; **dano gubakke madwoŋ mada i bar odilo,** people have assembled in large numbers in the football field; **dye kal doŋ obakke mada ki lum,** the compound is now overgrown with grass.

bakko *vt* 1 accumulating, putting something in a container; **bakko jami mapol i aduku,** putting many things in the basket 2 **bakko moko,** putting wet flour into a pot, covering it and leaving it for some time to ferment; 3 **bakko dog,** apologizing, pleading (for mercy or forgiveness); 4 **bakko lok,** speaking too much; 5 **bakko tutuno layata / kiyata,** making sweet potato mounds; 6 stabbing or spearing; **bakko ki toŋ,** stabbing with spear.

bal *n* sin, transgression, mistake; **Yecu otoo pi bal mewa,** Jesus died for our transgressions.

bal *v* spoil; **bal jamine woko,** spoil the things / spoil his things; *prov.* **pe ibal oraa ki oboko,** don't waste your grass torch for a small number of white ants, meaning wait for a large number of white ants which will come later when you will need more of the torch.

balaturu *n* a shy animal which closes its eyes and remains motionless when it sees a man; *provb.* **lewic omakko 'balaturu,' 'balaturu'** should not be shy when one meet people whom one not know.

balibali *adj* usually this is spoken of an arrow; **atero balibali,** the arrow with many barbs or spikes

balle *vi* 1 can be spoiled; **cak balle woko ka pe giketto i canduk me ŋicco,** the milk can go bad if it is not put in the refrigerator; **kompwutane oballe woko,**

his computer has broken down; 2 died; **Ben oballe laworo,** Ben passed away yesterday; 3 bad behaviour; **latinne kitte oballe woko,** the child's behaviour is now very bad; 4 jealousy; **waŋŋe oballe woko ka onenno ni gimiyo luwotte jami madwoŋ ma katto mere,** he became annoyed / jealous when he saw that his companions were given more things than himself.

ballo *vt* 1 to spoil, squander; **ballo lim,** squandering money / wealth; **litino man doki giballo cam twatwal,** these children do waste a lot of food; **ballo lok,** spoiling the evidence; *prov* **ogwal acel ballo waŋ pii,** one frog spoils the water well, meaning, one bad act is enough to spoil things; **ballo oraa ki oboko,** wasting the grass torch for a small number (of white ants), meaning, you wasted your grass torch on a small number of white ants, now you will have no torch when a large number of white ants come and that is the time when you should have the torch.

ballo *vn* to sin, transgress, err, commit sin; **dano ka oballo myero otuc balle,** when a man has sinned he should confess his sin.

bam *n* pelvis; **bam me lee ka ginekko gimiyo ki anyira,** when an animal is killed, the hip is given to girls who have been married from the home.

bam *v* chew lightly; **ka imitti pe ikaa kweyo i kwon ci bam abamma,** if you do not want to bite sand in the **kwon** then chew it lightly without allowing your upper teeth to meet the lower ones.

bam *vn* 1 blunt; **lak latoŋ obam woko,** the edge of the axe is blunt; **nyany** is normally used instead of **bam,** eg **lak**

latoŋ onyany woko, the edge of the axe is blunt. 2. trodden down; **dano omol i lum li bam,** people marched over the grass, leaving it trodden.

bam *v* add to; **bam yec man imed ki meeri,** add this load to yours; see **dod.**

bamme *vi* can be added to; **guniya man twerro bamme i wii meeri,** this bag can be added to yours.

bammo *vn.* to bite lightly (a baby or one without teeth bites lightly) **okayo abamma,** it bit it lightly not penetrated.

bammo *vt* making something carelessly and not nicely; **bammo agulu,** making the pot anyhow, not nicely.

bammo *vt* 1 to take another person's goods and add them to one's own; swindle to. 2 add something to others; **okwanynyo cukari mogo pa ominne ci obammo i kom meere,** he took some of is brother's sugar and added it to his.

ban *v* fold; **ban woko,** fold it up.

bani *n* a piece of hide (usually buffalo hide) used as a shield.

banne *vi* be foldable, be folded, can be folded; **bataniya man twerro banne ma rommo donynyo i canduk,** this blanket can be folded so that it can get into the box; **tyenne obanne,** he is knock-kneed.

banno *vt* folding up; **banno boŋo woko,** folding up the cloth.

baŋ *v* eat without sauce, **baŋ layata man,** eat this potato without sauce.

baŋ baŋ *adv* trembling all over, confusion, **komme myel li baŋ baŋ,** he is shaking all over. (usually from fear or embarrassment).

baŋgili *n* a wristlet made of celluloid material

baŋŋi *n* twins, (this name was given because they eat a lot); **min baŋŋi,** the twin's mother; see **rudi.**

baŋŋo lok *vt* speaking in a muddled way, because of fear.

baŋŋo *vt* 1 taming; **baŋŋo lee ki yat,** taming the animal with medicine; 2 charming; **baŋŋo dano ki yat,** making people foolish and senseless with medicine.

baŋŋo *vt* eating potatoes, bread, millet bread, etc. without sauce; **baŋŋo layata nono,** eating the potatoes without sauce; **baŋŋo odii,** eating simsim paste (not mixed with water to make it into sauce).

bany *v* to peel, to remove the skin, **bany pok labolone ka doŋ icam,** peel off / remove the skin of the ripe banana and then eat it; see **wany, pok, ka daŋ.**

Banya *n* a male name (*lit.* debt).

banya *n* debt; **en tye ki banya madit mada ki i beŋe,** he has a large debt in the bank; **tye ka piddo banyane bot Otto,** he is demanding payment of his debt from Otto.

banynye *vi* be peeled; **labolo pokke banynye,** banana skin can be peeled.

banynyo *vt* separating; **banynyo labolo me acamma,** removing / peeling off the skin of the ripe banana for eating; **banynyo wic,** separating / parting the hair making a line on the head; **banynyo kwok ki i waŋ,** wiping sweat from the face with the hand; **yamo obanynyo wii ot,** the wind has blown off some grass from the roof of the hut; **banynyo waŋ coo,** separating / drawing the boundary by parting grass.

bao *A n* a plank of wood, board, wood.

bap *n s* target; **acekere gitye ka cello bap,** the police are shooting at the target.

bap *v* slap; **bap lemme,** slap his cheek; *c/f* **pal.**

bappo *vt* slapping, smacking; **gidotte pi bappo lem latin,** he was accused of slapping the child's cheek. (used mainly by Langi). Acholi call it **pallo.**

bar *n* 1 large piece of ground cleared for dancing or for football.

bar *v* split, crack, eg, **bar yen man me teddo,** split this firewood for cooking; **bar akwota matye i emmeni woko,** open / incise the swelling in his thigh; **bar kany wek laleele omol iye,** open / make a trench here for the rain water to flow easily through it; see **kak.**

baraja *n* verandah; **gitye kabeddo woko i tee baraja,** they are sitting out on the verandah;

Baraja *n s* Monday, the first day of the week; **gin bidwoggo i ceŋ me Baraja,** they will return on Monday.

barre *vi* separating, moving away from the other; turning away from one's direction; **obarre woko ki i kom luwotte ci ocitto mere kamukene,** he turned away suddenly from his companions and went to another place; **yen man twerro barre,** this wood can be split; pain *n;* **wiye tye ka barre mada,** he is having a severe headache.

barro *vt* splitting; **barro yen,** splitting wood; **barro i dyel,** splitting /cutting the goat's abdomen open; **wiye barro mada,** he has a splitting severe headache; **leny barro korre,** he is having heartburn; **barro akwota,** incising or opening an abscess or swelling; see **kakko.**

barru *v* to split open, crack; **kiyata obarru,** the potatoes have cracked / split open the ground.

baru *n* the shell of a bullet which has been fired.

bat *n* same as **bad** *n.* arm; foreleg of an animal; **bad dero,** stand of wood upon which a granary stands.

bataniya *A n* a blanket; see **bulaŋgiti.**

bayo *vt* throwing; **bayo lakidi,** throwing stones; **en ŋeyo bayo atero maber mada,** he is very good at shooting; **bayo it,** not to hear well; **lokke obayo itta,** I did not hear the words well / I missed hearing the words.

bebbo *vt* twisting one's mouth through weeping.

bebbo *vt* **bebbo yec,** carrying a heavy load; **bebbo latin iŋec,** carrying the baby on the back; see **byello** which is preferred.

becen *Eng n* basin; **kel becen me lwok,** bring the basin for bathing.

becco *adj pl* good, nice, beautiful; **gin ducu gibecco,** they are all very good / they are all beautiful; **ticgi becco mada,** their work is very good / excellent.

bed *v* sit **bed piny,** sit down; **bed botwa tin,** stay with us today; **bed mot,** be quiet; **bed rwot,** be a chief.

beddo *vt* sitting, staying, being; **beddo piny,** sitting down; **beddo ki jami,** having things; **beddo ki dako,** having sexual intercourse with a woman / having a wife; **beddo mot,** sitting quietly / causing no problem; **beddo latel wii dano gin matek mada,** being a leader of the people is a very difficult thing.

begga *n S* a detective, an investigator.

bei or **beyi** *n S* price; **nyutwa beiy me kadoni,** show us the price of your salt; **beyi me pul doki rac mada i mwaka man,** the price of groundnuts is very bad this year.

bek *v* pick, peck. **citti ibek anyogi ma pudi odoŋ i poto ni,** go and pick up the maize remaining in the field; **ryam gweno pe obek pul ma gipito ni,** drive away the chicken from pecking the groundnuts which have just been planted.

bekke *vi* can be picked or pecked; **anyogi ma odoŋ i poto pudi romo bekke,** the maize remaining in the field can still be picked.

bekko *vt* 1 pecking; **gweno gitye ka bekko kwidi ki i wii odur,** chickens are pecking grub at the rubbish heap; 2 picking; **mon gitye ka bekko lapena ma otop woko,** the women are picking up the rotten pigeon peas from picking the good ones; **lapoya bekko cam ki i wii odur,** a mad person picks food from the rubbish heaps; c/f **yerro.**

bekko *vt* to roam; **latin man doki bekko piny twatwal,** this child roams /wanders / roves about too much.

bel *n* cereal, corn, normally a collective name for millet and sorghum.

bel *prd* wrinkle; **komme obedo bel bel,** his body is wrinkled all over.

belle *vr* moving hither and thither in anger; **tye ka belle abella i odde ki kiniga pi rweny pa cawane,** he is moving hither and thither in his house with anger over the loss of his watch.

belle belle *adv* hanging, ragged and swinging about; **dako doŋ wotto ki boŋo ma oyec ma beddi belle belle**

i ŋeye, the woman walks about in old clothes with some torn parts swinging about behind her.

bello...

bello vt to open and throwing away, **yemone tek turro belo wii dero wako,** the wind is very strong, it blow away the granary

bel-winyo n a plant whose seeds are eaten by birds and sometimes by children. used as medicine for sore throat; it causes an allergic reaction to animal skins.

bem prn charm; **labem dano,** a man who charms people; c/f **bil.**

bemmo vt charming somebody with magic and ruining him physically and mentally; bewitching somebody; **gidotte ni en bemmo dano,** he was accused of bewitching or charming people.

bendera n flag; **yar bendera malo,** hoïst the flag.

bene cnj also, too; **en bene myero obin,** he should also come / he too should come.

bene bene... adv. throughout, continuously; **orem ki iye malit bene bene i dyewor piny omeddo ki ruu,** he suffered from his abdominal pain throughout the night.

beŋe n Eng bank; **okanno limme i beŋe,** he saved his money in the bank.

benye benye adv eating bit by bit; **cammo cam benye benye pe ber,** eating food bit by bit is not good; see **pude pude, akuri akuri,** the latter two are the ones which are commonly used.

ber adj good, nice, beautiful, charming; **nyako maber mada,** a beautiful and charming girl.

berro lok vt talking too much; **Otto tye ka berro lok kwica wiye doŋ owil woko i kommi,** Otto is talking too much there and has forgotten you.

beyo n a large tree used for making chairs and other furniture.

-bi- pref or sufix particles of future tense eg. **citto,** going, **abicitto,** I will go / I shall be going; **binno,** coming; **abibinno,** I shall be coming / I shall come.

bi- v when it is pref it is imperative; **kadi okwer kombedi, lacen en bitimmone,** although he has refused now, in the end he will have to do it; **ka latin dag cam kombedi koni bicammone,** if the child does not like to eat now, he will have to eat it later.

bi amwonynyi (lit. **bin amwonynyi**) n waves in water or seas; **bi amwonynyi** lit. means come let me swallow you.

bic adv full to the brim; **ojubbo nyim poŋ aduko li bic,** he filled the basket to the brim with simsim.

bic vn squeezing, compressing; not commonly spoken; see **bii, biyo.**

bicu n cave, den, a hole in the ground; during slave trade it was a cave in which people used to hide their corn to prevent it from being taken by the slave traders.

bid v wet, soak. **bid i pii,** soak it water; **bid boŋone ki pii kadoŋ igoo ki pac,** wet the clothes in water and then iron them.

bidde vi can be soaked, or can be softened; **laane twerro bidde ci doko ma yom,** the hide can be softened by soaking in water; **olutto boŋine i pii wek obidde ka doŋ elwokgi,** he diped his clothes in the water to be soaked so as to wash them.

biddo *vt* soaking in water; softening something with fluid; **tye ka biddo boŋine ka doŋ elwokgi,** .he is soaking his clothes in water so that he may wash them.

bii *v* squeeze, press, compress; **bii lemun man me amatta,** squeeze this lemon for drinking; **bii nyim wek inoŋ iye moo,** squeeze / press the simsim in order to extract oil (from it); see **bic ki biyo.**

bikibiki *adv* a kind of noise made; **oriŋŋo ki yen ni bikibiki,** he ran with the firewood on her head making the noise **bikibiki.**

bil *n* 1 tasting 2 hypnotism, taming.

bil *v* taste, **bil ka cukari tye i caine,** taste whether there is sugar in the tea.

bil *v.* hypnotise, **bil dano-**hypnotise the people

bila *n* whistle (usually made of animal horns) used in dancing or hunting.

billo *vt* tasting (with tongue); **obillo dekke ci onoŋŋoni kado kec iye mada,** she tasted the sauce and found that there was too much salt in it.

billo *vt* to tame, charm with magic, domesticate wild animals, make them stupid, hypnotize; **obillo dano gunino woko ci okwwallo jami mapol,** he hypnotized the people and therefore he stole a lot of things; **obillo latin oweko doŋ odoko miŋ woko,** he charmed the child and made him become foolish; see **bemmo.**

bilo *n* charcoal; **bilo ber me teddo woko,** the charcoal is good for cooking outside.

bim *n* baboon; **bim marro labolo mada,** baboon is fond of bananas / likes bananas very much; **bim wotto nyonno ŋom ki ciŋŋe ma oyarro dok ŋwinynye otal,** the baboon walks on the palms of its hands, and has callocitis on its buttocks.see **gunya, puno, oŋera, dolo, ayom.**

bim *v* flatten; **bim wii latin maber,** flatten the hair on the child's head well.

bimmo *vt* flattening; **bimmo yer wic,** smoothing hair usually with the palm or hand.

bin *v* come; **bin kany,** come here; **bin botta,** come to me; **bin cok kany,** come near here.

binika *n s* teapot, kettle.

binno *vi* coming; **binno diki,** will be coming tomorrow; **binno ka tukko odilo,** coming to play football.

binjali *n s turmeric,* the yellow tuber of a plant which is ground and mixed with other spices to form curry powder which is used very much for cooking food to make it tasty.

binynyo *vt* twisting; **binynyo yer wic,** twisting hair into numerous curls by adding chemicals to make it permanent, perming of the hair; *c /f* **keddo.**

binynyo waro *vt* twisting cotton into thread; **tye ka binynyo waro me tol me cikko aweno,** he is twisting cotton wool into thread for trapping guinea fowls.

bir *vi* sprout, germinate, **kal obir woko,** the millet has germinated.

bir *v* fill up to the brim, **bir pii i agulu,** fill the pot up to the brim with water.

birigedia *n* Eng brigadier, a military

rank above colonel but below brigadier general; **birigedia jeneral,** brigadier general is a military rank above brigadier but below major general; see **meja jeneral** and **pil macul** (field-marshal.)

birro *vi* to germinate with a spike, e.g. **geya ki kal gibirro abirra,** sorghum and millet germinate with spikes *or* send out their shoots with spike when germinating; **kal doŋ obirro me tobi,** millet has germinated and now is ready for leaven.

bit *adj* sharp, pointed; **palaa ne lakke bit mada,** the knife is very sharp (*lit.*the tooth of the knife is very sharp). 2 **kado i dekke bit,** the food is bitter because it has too much salt. 3 **dogge bit,** he uses bad language, he is very abusive / has sharp tongue; 4 very good; **ciŋŋe bit mada,** he is very good at shooting, i.e. he is a marksman. 5 **waŋŋe bit,** has sharp sight.

bit *v* entice, decoy, lure; **bit gwok ki riŋo wek imak woko,** entice / lure the dog with a piece of meat in order to catch it.

bit *v* shell, hull, split open; **bit pul ma i atabo ityek woko,** shell all the groundnuts in the bowl.

bit *n* 1 shelling, hulling, splitting open; 2 enticing, decoying, luring.

bit *n Eng* beat, guard, watch; **tye ka kurro bit,** he is on the beat, i.e. he is guarding / keeping watch,.

bito *n* royalty, **latin bito,** the child of the royal family; according to the legend of the Lwoo people, **bito** is the group of people who came from the North following the River Nile and formed the present kingdom of Bunyoro.

bitte *vr* 1 can be lured, be decoyed etc; **twero bitte,** can be lured or decoyed; 2

v **bitte ki gin mo,** lure or entice him with something; 3 *n* **bitte pe ber,** luring, / decoying / enticing is not good.

bitte *vi* can be split open or shelled; **pulle bitte maber mada,** the groundnuts are easy to shell.

bitto *vt* enticing, luring, decoying, tempting, baiting; **bitto gwok ki cam,** luring a dog with food; **bitto rec ki otwol kot ma girwakko i wii goli,** bating the fish with an earthworm fixed to a hook.

bitto *vt* shelling, hulling, splitting open; **bitto pul,** shelling / hulling groundnuts.

biyo *vt* squeezing, pressing; **biyo lemun me amatta,** squeezing lemon for drinking; see **bii, bic.**

blaŋket *n Eng* blanket; **blaŋkette ber mada,** the blanket is very good; see **bataniya, bulaŋgiti.**

bo *adv* when placed at the end of a sentence, it means will; **ibikella bo?** will you bring it to me? **abikelli,** I will / I shall bring it to you.

boc *vn* wrapping, packet; **man boc pa aŋaa?,** whose packet is this?; see **boo, boyo.**

bocco *n pl* of **bor** *n* lengths; **yadine bocco mada,** the trees are very tall; **gin ducu gibocco,** they are all very tall.

bod *v* distract, entice; **in labod wii mon pa dano,** you are a man who entices other people's women; **pe i bod wii latin woko ki kwan,** do not distract the child from schooling /study.

boda boda *n Eng* a carrier which is either a bicycle or a motorcycle; the name is a distortion from the

English word "border border"; this came about because people were being carried across the border of Uganda and Kenya on a bicycle or a motorcyle and so the name of the carrier became "border border".

bodde *vi* be distracted, enticed; **litino ma tino wigi twerro bodde oyot mada,** little children can easily be distracted from doing what they are expected to do; **abodda wic,** distraction, taking the mind away from doing what one should do.

boddo *vt* distracting or drawing away attention, enticing; **boddo wii dako pa lawotti,** enticing away your friend's wife; **boddo wii ŋati mo,** distracting somebody from doing his normal work; **latinna boddo wiya, miyo pe abeddo kena,** my child keeps me busy and prevents me from being lonely.

bok *vn* becoming brown or red, reddening, browning, **bok pa pot yat aa pi ceŋ,** redness of leaves depends upon the sun.

bok *v* narrate, tell, converse; **bok ki wan gin ma inenno ki i Japan,** tell us what you saw in Japan; **bok anyogi wek wamwoddi,** cook / steam the maize so that we may eat it.

bokke *vi* 1 becoming brown; **i kare me oro pot yadi mapol gibokke ci gioo woko,** in the dry season most of the leaves turn brown and later fall off. 2 **lokke pe twerro bokke tum,** the story cannot be completely narrated; **anyogine pud ber twerro bokke,** the maize is still good, it can be steamed.

bokko *vt* to stain red, to colour red;

bwino bokko lak litino woko, mulberry tree fruits colour / stain the children's teeth red.

bokko *vt* cooking; **bokko ŋor, anyogi nyo pul ma gulo,** cooking / steaming cowpeas, maize, unshelled groundnuts in water, when they are still not dry.

bokko *vt* beating freshly cut wood in order to remove its bark.

bokko lok *vt* narrating, conversing, talking, telling; **bokko lok ododo,** telling the fables / narrating the fables.

bol *n* shaft or handle; **bol toŋ,** the shaft of a spear; **bol kweri,** the handle of a hoe; **bol cun, the** shaft of the penis (this is usually spoken figuratively)

bol *v* 1 throw; **bol kany,** throw here.

bolle *n/adj/vn* alert; can be thrown; **bolle ma komme mit,** moves in a lively and alert / a gile manner; **ŋutte obolle mabor,** she has a very long neck; **nyako ma ŋutte obolle,** a girl with a long neck; **adilone twerro bolle,** the ball can be thrown.

bollo, *vt* throwing away; **bollo obwoo me lee nyo me rec,** casting / spreading a net for catching animals or fish; **bollo lok,** giving an example; **bollo cuma,** giving a byword to decide a question indicating a precedent; **bollo nyerro,** bursting into laughter; **bollo kidulle,** tumbling head over heels; **bollo dog,** repeating remarks about what one has done for someone; **gweno obollo toŋŋe,** the hen has laid its eggs; **obeddo obollo ŋutte caa,** he is sitting there with his long neck; **bollo cam ki gwok,** throwing food to a dog / feeding the dog; **bollo**

kwir, casting votes; **bollo kwir atyer,** general election.

bollo *vt* causes blisters; **pii malyet bollo ciŋ,** hot water causes blisters; **tello tol bollo ciŋ,** pulling the rope in a game of tug-of-war causes blisters.

bolo *n* a shelter constructed with grass especially during a festivity or funeral ceremony in which people sit during the day or sleep at night.

bolo bolo *adv* loosely 1 **gutweyo bolo bolo,** they tied it loosely; **ocek bolo bolo,** it has ripened well and is soft; **lyet bolo bolo,** lukewarm; see also **bulu bulu, dedee, dem dem, mor mor.**

bomo *n* a creeper which is usually tied round the waist, wrist or head by mourners of dead twins.

boma *s n* town; **waecitto i boma,** we are going to the town.

boni *n euphorbia a* family type of tree whose leaves are truncated and its milky juice causes blindness when it gets into the eyes.

bono wic *n* a high forehead with corners; a partially bald head with receded hair above the temple.

boŋ *n* 1 **boŋ kic,** beehive; **boŋ kic gilyerro i jaŋ yat,** a beehive is suspended on the branches of a tree; **kic kanno moo gi i boŋ,** the bees store their honey in the bee-hive.

boŋ *v* not; **en boŋ ocitto,** he did not go; this is not normally spoken by the central Acholi, it is usually spoken by the people from west of Gulu.

boŋ *or* **laboŋo** *adv* not or without; **obino laboŋo tok wiye,** he came without his hat; **boŋ iteer boŋona,** don't take my

clothes; this is spoken mostly by people from Pabo, etc.

boŋ *v* touch; **boŋ umme,** touch his nose; **boŋ boŋone wek iniaŋ kitte ma ber kwede,** feel the clothes in order to appreciate how very fine it is.

boŋŋe *vi* can be touched. **ginne twerro boŋŋe;** the thing can be touched, 2 *prn* his beehive, **boŋŋe tye kwene?** (a) where is his beehive? (b) where is the beehive?

boŋŋo *vt* touching; **boŋŋo dog dano pe ber,** touching people's lips is not good.

boŋo *n* cloth, clothes; **boŋo aridi,** silk cloth; **boŋo yer lee,** woollen cloth.

bonyaka *adv* **bedo ni bonyaka,** she sat carelessly / indecently naked (woman).

bonyo *n* migratory locust; they are of two types: **abwum,** greyish brown and moving in large swarms; **atiko,** red, having sharp spikes on their feet but rarely coming and not in large swarms.

boo *n* tender leaves of cowpeas which are much used as vegetables; **boo nyak ngor, boo** are the leaves of cowpeas which produce the peas.

boo *v* wrap or cover; **boo buk man,** wrap this book; see **boc, boyo.**

booŋ nyo lubooŋ *n* a clan other than the royal clan, commoner; **gin lubooŋ,** they are commoners, that is, they will not become the chief of a tribe.

bor *adj* long, tall, far, distant; **bor ni lul,** very tall and round; **bor ni cwac,** very tall and beautiful; **oa kama bor mada,** he came from far away.

boro *n* cave; **boro beddo i got,** a cave is found in the mountain; **olik marro**

nywal mada i boro, bats like breeding very much in caves.

boro *n* the fat layer; **boro i dyaŋ,** the fat layer on entrails, i.e. on the intestines of cattle.

borro *vt* praising; **oborro en ki wer,** he praised him with songs.

bot *prp.* from, to, on one's or a thing's, at one's ; **tye bot Okot,** he is with Okot; **oa bot wonne,** he came from his father; **tye ki botti,** it is up to you.

bot *n a* freshly, roughly tilled field; **man poto ma pud gipurro bot,** this is the field which has just been cultivated (roughly).

bot *adj* tasteless, insipid, saltless; **dek ma bot,** saltless or unsavoury food; **labot bot,** without salt; **romo rut giteddo labot bot,** sheep for twins' ceremony is cooked without salt; 2 **labot,** a bachelor.

bot *v* scoop with the fingers and lap up; **bot cak,** scoop the milk with the fingers and lap up.

boto *adv* 1. big and fat; **obeddo li boto,** it is there big and fat; 2 clumsy and soft; **komme yom ni boto,** the chair is big and very soft / his body is fat and flabby.

botte *adv* can be lapped 2 *vn* can be cultivated roughly. 3 to; **cak man twerro naŋŋe,** the milk can be lapped **poto man twerro botte maber,** this field can easily be roughly cultivated. **teer caa man botte,** take this watch to him.

botto *vt* 1 to cultivate roughly and leave it to rot; **wacittu ka botto poto,** let us go to roughly cultivate the field.

botto *vt* taking with three or four fingers and lapping up.

botto *vt* eating of the leaves of freshly grown maize or cowpeas; **gweni tye ka botto pot anyogi ma pudi gutwii atwiya,** the chickens are eating the leaves of the freshly grown maize.

boyi *n Eng* a houseboy; **an pe amitto tic me boyi,** I do not want to work as a houseboy / I do not like the work of a houseboy.

boyo *vt* wrapping, covering; **boyo buk,** wrapping the book; see **boo, boc.**

buc *v* pluck, remove feathers; **buc gweno man me atedda,** pluck this chicken for cooking; see **bucco.**

buc or **mabuc,** *n* prison.

buc *vi* slipping; **buc ki i ciŋ,** slipped off from the hand. see **but, bwot.**

bucce *vi* can be plucked, be scraped; **yec gwenoni twerro bucce,** the feathers of this chick can be plucked; **laa man komme twerro bucce,** this leather can be scraped.

bucco *vt.* plucking feathers from a chicken; scraping off hair from fresh skin, eg **bucco gweno,** and **bucco del,** plucking the feathers from a chicken and scraping off hair from leather.

buk *v* blow; **buk mac,** blow the fire.

buk *Eng n* book; **buk me akwanna,** a book for reading.

buk *n* place where blacksmiths forge their metals.

bukke *vi* bathing; **gweno bukke i kweyo,** chicken take bathe by fluttering in sand; **opego bukke ki daba,** pigs mud-bathe by swimming in muddy water.

bukko *vt* blowing; **bukko mac,** blowing the fire very hot.

bukko *vt* whirling a fluttering fowl; **bukko gweno me kwer**, whirling a fluttering hen / chicken for ritual purposes.

bukko *vt* dusting; **bukko kom gwok ki yat,** dusting the dog with medicinal powder.

bukko *vt* **bukko ot aita,** smoking a ground squirrel out of its hole.

bul *n* drum; **min bul,** the large drum; **opiri bul,** a middle-sized drum, **lakel bul,** a smaller drum; **nyig bul,** a very small drum.

bul *v* 1 broil, grill; **bul riŋo gimwodi,** grill / broil the meat for eating (*lit.* meat for chewing).

bul apwoyo *n* a toadstool.

bulle *vi* can be grilled; **anyogine twerro bulle,** the maize can be grilled.

bullo *vt* grilling, broiling, barbecuing; **bullo kiyata,** broiling the potatoes; **bullo riŋo,** grilling, broiling the meat.

bulu *n* *Eng* youth (male); comes from the word bull; see **poi, apuru.**

bulu bulu *adj* lukewarm; **pii ma bulu bulu,** lukewarm water; see also, **bol bol, de dee, dem dem, mor mor.**

bulu bulu *adj* smooth and shining; **komme bulu bulu mada,** his skin is very smooth and shining.

bum *n* swindling, **bum pe ber,** swindling is not good; *vt* **pe i bum lawotti;** don't swindle your friend / don't cheat your friend.

bumma *n* swindling, corruption; see **bwumma.**

bumme *vi* can be swindled, cheated; **danone twerro bumme oyot mada,** the man can easily be swindled; **gubumme ki gweno aryo,** they cheated him out of two chickens.

bummo *v* 1 to honour, give importance; **luremme gubummo ladit me binno ka nyomme,** his friends honoured him by coming to his wedding. 2 swindling; **bummo dano pe ber,** swindling people is not good.

buŋa *n* forest; **gucitto i buŋa ka barro yen,** they went into the forest to split firewood.

Buŋatira *n* a village about five kilometres north of Gulu. This is the place to which, according to legend, a mysterious man came with his dog and lodged on a rock where his foot prints and those of his dog were left on the rock and it is said that these footprints can still be seen even up today.

Buŋgereja *n S* England; **joo me Buŋgereja,** the English people.

buŋo *n* **ot buŋo**, a grass hut for temporary use.

buny *v* smile; **buny ki wan ba,** please smile at us.

bunynyo *vi* smiling; **en tye ka bunynyo,** he is smiling.

bur *v* threaten, frighten; **bur Okot wek imaa jamine woko,** frighten / threaten Okot so that you may take his things; 2 *v* **bur Onen ento pe an,** frighten Onen but not me; cheat Onen but not me.

bur *vn* threatening, frightening; **bur pe gin maber,** threatening / frightening is not good;

bur *n* hole, pit; **bur coron,** a pit latrine; **bur lyel,** a grave.

bur *n* sore, ulcer; **bur tye i tyenne,** he has sore or ulcer on his leg; the

word **bur,** ulcer, comes from the word, **bur,** hole, because an ulcer makes a hole in the skin; **bur adola, a** tropical ulcer which sometimes may be very big and deep down to the bones.

bura *n* cat; **bura makko oyoo ki gweni,** a cat catches rats and chicken. see **cwiiny, giliri, kak, kworo, oculi, and too.**

bure *S adv* for nothing; **ogoyi bure,** he beat you for nothing.

bure *n* roan antelope.

burre *prn* his ulcer; **burre rac mada,** his ulcer is very bad.

burre *vi* can be frightened or intimidated; **danone twerro burre,** the man can be intimidated / frightened / cheated.

burro *vt* 1 to intimidate, frighten, threaten; **burrɔ dano ki luduku,** threatens people with the gun. 2 to cheat; **burro lawotte ki cam,** puts aside part of the food for himself and shares the food left with his friend, therefore, he eats more than his friend; taking a bigger share of the food than his friend.

buroji *n Eng* bugle, or horn; **tye ka kutto burogi,** he is blowing the bugle.

buru *n* ash. **keno doŋ opoŋ ki buru twatwal,** the hearth is now full of ash; **buru cet dyaŋŋi en aye gitwonno me kado atwonna,** the ash from the cattle dung is strained for lye / alkali salt.

buryaŋa *n* a cow with long horns; the Ankole type of cow.

but *v* lie; **but piny,** lie down; **but aŋet,** lie sideways; **but ataro,** lie, face upwards.

but *n* side, flank; **obollo kicaa i butte,** he hung the bag on his flank / side; **ka icubbo lee i butte ci pe nekko,** if you spear the animal through its flank, you will not kill it.

but *n* the sound produced by beating often, giving blows in quick succession.

but *vp* falling out or slipping from; **tol ma gitweyo marac but woko,** the rope that has been badly knotted slips easily; see **buc, bwot.**

butta *vn* boasting or pretending to be what one is not; **butta mitto nekke woko,** boasting or pretending to be what he is not, is making him mad; **butta rac,** boasting or pretending to be what one is not, or showing off, is bad; see **nyatte, wakke.**

butto *vi* lying down; to sleep, sleeping with a women; **cit ka butto piny,** go to lie down; vt **butto ki dako,** sleeping with a woman i.e. having sexual intercourse with her, **gidotte pi butto ki nyako,** he was accused of sleeping with a girl, having sexual intercourse with a girl.

buuk *vn* heating the metal very hot in a blacksmith's workshop.

buut *n Eng* canvas shoes (this has come from the word 'boot'); **kella war buutta arukki,** bring for me the canvas shoes to wear.

buyu *vt* attempting but failing to kill; **bura obuyu gwenone abuya pe onekko,** the cat only mauled the hen but did not kill it.

bwac *vp* laceration, coming off of skin; **tyenne tye ka bwac abbwaca,** the skin of his leg is ulcerating ; **opotto ci obwacco coŋŋe,** he fell and lacerated his knee; c/f **pok.**

bwac bwac *adv* crushing sound; **wotto wii bonyo kun nyono ni bwac bwac,** walking on the locusts and crushing them beneath his feet.

bwami *n* swindling, corruption; **bwami terro dano i can,** swindling leads people to disaster.

bwaŋ *n* terrifying, overwhelming.

bwaŋŋo *vt* to terrify, overwhelm; **bwaŋŋo dano ki tek komme ci kwanynyo jamigi woko,** he terrifies the people with his strength and takes their things; **bwaŋŋo lamerok ci nekko woko,** he terrifies the enemy and then kills him; hence the name **bwaŋŋomoi.**

bwarro lok *vt* talking lots of nonsense.

bwoc *vn* winning, defeating, overcoming; **onoŋo kikopo pi bwoc me doŋŋe,** he got a cup for winning in the boxing competition; see **bwoo, bwoyo.**

bwoc *adj* 1 difficult, failure; **waŋŋe bwoc,** he has difficulty in recognizing something. 2 unstable; **ciŋŋe bwoc,** his hand is unsteady (in shooting), he is clumsy. 3 insolent, insulting, **labwoc,** an insolent / insulting person.

bwog *n* miscarriage.

bwogge *vn* can be aborted / can about; **i dako ni caa twerro bwogge ka pe gimiyo yat maber;** that woman's pregnency can abort if not well treated.

bwoggo *vt* 1 miscarrying; **bwoggo latin gin marac mada,** miscarrying is a very bad thing.

bwogo *n* butter which has not yet been processed, still has some water and whey; **moo dyaŋ mabwogo,** fresh butter which still has water in it.

bwol *v* deceive, lie; **bwol Okot ento an pe itwerro bwolla,** deceive Okot but you cannot deceive me.

bwol *n* deception, lie; **bwolla** *vn.* deceiving, lying.

bwola *n.* **myel bwola,** royal dance; usually at installation of a chief or a king or on any royal ceremony.

bwolle *vi/n* deceived, deception; **latinne waŋŋe tek pe bwolle,** the child is smart and sound in mind, and therefore cannot be deceived; **bwolle meri ni pe teeri kamo,** your deception takes you nowhere / deceiving yourself takes you nowhere.

bwollo *vn* deceiving; **bwollo dano pe ber,** deceiving people is not good; **bwollo gin marac mada,** deceiving is a very bad thing.

bwom *n.* wing, **bwom winyo tek miyo gituk,** birds have strong wings, that is why they fly.

bwon *vn* thinking that something is not enough; **bwon pe ber,** thinking that what one was given is not enough is not good.

bwonno *vt* thinks that (something) is not enough; **bwonno lim ma gimiine woko, mitto ma katto eno,** he thinks that the money given to him is not enough, he wants more; **en obwonno gin ma gimiine,** he thought that what he is given is not enough / he thinks that he has been cheated.

bwoŋ *adj* young; **bwoŋ dyel,** a young she-goat; **bwoŋ dyaŋ,** a heifer.

bwop dyaŋ *n* 1 the loose skin between belly and leg of a cow 2 the flank.

bwop ot *n* a small piece of wall added to a house, to form a recess for the door.

bwoo *v* win, defeat, overcome; **bwoo i tukko rette matin,** win in the wrestling competition today; see **bwoc, bwoyo.**

bwot *vp* escape, get off; **otemmo bwot kwee ki i jero,** he tried very hard, in vain, to escape from jail;

bwot *v* leave; **bwot lokke obedi,** leave the case alone.

bwoto n skill, expert, person experienced in a certain skill; **labwoto maber ada i yubo motoka,** he is very skilful / experienced in repairing cars / he is an expert in repairing cars.

bwotte *vi* left; **ticce pe twerro bwotte?** can the work not be left?; **jamine twerro bwotte kany,** the things can be left here.

bwotto *vt* 1 leaving, stopping, **bwotto tic,** stopping working / leaving work; 2 **bwotto dog,** repeating remarks for what one has done for somebody before.

bwoyo *vt* defeating, overcoming, conquering; **olimmo mot pi bwoyo lawotte woko i tuku doŋŋe,** he got a prize for defeating his friend in boxing; **dano ma twoo bwoyo oyot oyot,** a man who is sent down easily by disease; **man dano ma kec bwoyo oyot oyot pe twerro wot,** this is a man who is easily overwhelmed by hunger and cannot walk; see **bwoo, bwoc.**

bwoyo *n* foam, froth, bubble of air; **bwoyo tye i dog latin,** the child has foams / froth in his mouth; **waar bwoyo ki i wii cak ka doŋ itii,** remove the foams from the top of the milk and then pour it; **bwoyo poŋ i wii koŋo ka gitiyo,** the beer bubbles when it is poured.

bwum *n* swindling, cheating; **labwumma,** swindler, cheat, conman.

bwummo *vt* swindling, cheating, holding back part of goods at delivery for oneself; see **bumma.**

byee *n* termite mound or anthill; **ŋwen gicwee giaa ki i byee,** the white ants fly out of the anthill.

byek *v* guess; **byek gin matye i ciŋŋa,** guess what I have in my hand; estimate, budget.

byek *n* estimate, budget; **byek me lim me mwaka man,** the estimate / budget for this year.

byekke *vi* guessed, estimated, budgeted, **lim ma watiyo kwede me nino ducu pe twerro byekke,** the money that we spend every day cannot be estimated / budgeted for.

byekko *vt* guessing, estimating; budgeting, **byekko lim me mwaka manyen me tic mewa oloyo karan mewa woko,** our secretary has failed to budget / estimate money for work for next year.

byel *v* carry on the back; **byel latin i ŋeyi,** carry the child on your back.

byelle *vi* carried; **latinni twerro byelle i ŋeyi,** the child can be carried on your back.

byello *vt* to carry on the back; **en pe ŋeyo byello latin i ŋeye,** she does not know how to carry a child on her back.

byen waŋ *n.* eyebrow, eyelid.

byeny *adv.* missing the mark; **toŋ okatto ni byeny,** the spear passed without hitting the mark.

byero *n* placenta, afterbirth; see **pel.**

C c

caa *adv* there; **latin tye caa,** the child is over there; **nen malo caa,** look up there; **en tye piny caa,** he is down there.

caa nyo cawa, *n s* 1 a watch; **amarro caa ma komme tye iye jabu,** I like a watch coated with gold; 2. hour or time; **caa / cawa adi?** what is the time?

caa *v* despise, look down upon, **myero pe icaa ŋati mo,** do not despise anybody; *vi* **caane,** despising onself; see **cac, cayo.**

caano n despising, looking down upon; **caano dano pe ber,** despising / looking down upon people is not good; see **cayo.**

caar *adj* careless, clumsy, disorderly, loose; **nyako ma caar en aye timme ki awobe atata,** it is only a loose girl that runs around with boys; **dakone caar pe ŋeyo gwoko ot maleŋ,** she is a careless / disorderly woman, she does not know how to look after the house.

caar *v* dazzle; **caar waŋŋe ki toc,** dazzle his eyes with the torch.

caaro *n* carelessness, looseness; **caaro ballo ot,** carelessness and looseness breaks the home; **caarro lok,** speaking meaningless words.

caarro *vt* to dazzle; **ceŋ caarro waŋ,** the sun dazzles the eyes.

caat *v* 1 sell; **caat ruc matye i gunia ni,** sell the rice which is in the gunny bag; 2 *n* **en pe ŋeyo caat,** he does not know how to sell things.

caatto *vt* to trade, sell; **en caatto war mabecco mada,** he sells very good shoes; see **tunno.**

cab *n* defamation, solicitation, humiliation; **lacab nyiŋ dano,** a man who speaks ill of other people, a defamer.

cab *v* defame, humiliate, speak ill of; **cab nyiŋŋe woko wek pe onoŋ tic,** defame / spoil his name so that he may not get a job.

cabbe *vt* 1 being ruined in the eyes of other men by unbecoming behaviour. 2 troubling onself looking for something or not knowing what to do; solicitation; **ocabbe woko pi lac i ot i kare ma omer,** he was ruined and humilated by urinating in the house when he was drunk.

cabbo *vt* defaming, damaging of one's good name, e.g. calling somebody a thief when one is not a thief; **cabbo nyiŋ,** defaming / slandering someone.

cabbu *vt* frequent changing of occupations or words; **cabbu lok,** changing words or statement so easily. 2. noise caused by an object falling into water; **got opotto i pii ni cabu,** the stone fell into the water making the noise **cabu.**

cabidiket *n Eng* certificate, some people now call it **catipiket.**

cabit *n S* Sunday;

cabun *n* soap; **walwokko boŋowa ki cabun,** we wash our clothes with soap.

cac *n* disdain, despise, scorn, looking down upon; **cac pe terro ŋatimo kamo,** despising / scorning takes no one anywhere; see **caa, cayo.**

cac *adv* swiftly; **otiŋo agulu pii i wiye woko ni cac,** she lifted the pot straight away to her head; **pino cwinynyo dano ni cac,** the wasp stings people suddenly and effectively.

cac cac *adv* the sound produced by people when walking or grinding simsim (*sesame*).

cacce *vt* struggling;. **cacce kwede in keni,** struggle with it / fight with it alone; see **tutte**

cacco *vt* grinding; **latin nyako tye ka cacco nyim,** the little girl is grinding the sesame.

cadat *n s* a washing place which is usually covered by reeds; **cit ka lwokke i cadat,** go to wash in the **cadat.**

caden *A n* witness; **kel caden meeri oyot oyot,** bring your witness quickly.

caden *A n* testimony.

caddo *vi* passin running stool; **caddo riŋriŋ** passing mucus; **caddo remo** passing blood (having dysentery). 2 **cado twoo marac mada,** diarrhoea is a very bad illness.

cado *vn* diarrhoea; running stool.

cagin *n Eng* sergeant; **cagin meja,** sergeant-major (a military or police rank above sergeant).

cai *n s* tea; **wacittu ka matto cai,** let us go to take tea.

cai *n Eng* sign; **an doŋ adiyo cai meera woko,** I have already signed it or put my thumb print to it.

cak *n* 1 milk 2 starting, commencing, beginning.

cak *v* start, commence, begin; **cak gerro ot,** start building the house; **cak kwan,** commence studying; **cak wot,** start walking; **cak cam,** begin eating.

cakka *n* to beg or borrow; **ocitto ka cakka me nyim bot laminne,** she went to beg for simsim from her sister because she has none.

cakke *vt vi* can be started; **gerro otte twerro cakke,** building the house can

start; **kot ocakke woko doŋ,** the rain has started already; **lweny ocakke woko i kin Jeremel ki Italiano,** war broke out between Germany and Italy.

cakko *vt* starting, commencing, beginning something; **cakko tic pe yot,** starting working is not easy; **cakko lweny,** declaring war; **cakko cam, cakko wot, etc,** beginning / commencing eating, walking, etc.

cakko or **cakka,** to beg, ask for help; **ocitto ka cakko** *vt* / **cakka bel bot luremme,** she went to beg / ask her friends to help her with some millet because she has none.

cakko nyiŋ *vn* to name, baptize; **gicakko nyiŋ latin tin i kanica,** the child has been baptized today in the church.

cal *n* picture, photograph; **calle gibecco mada,** they are very good pictures.

cal *vt.* resemble, look like; **Otto cal mada ki nerone.** Otto very much resembles his uncle / Otto looks very much like his uncle.

callo *cnj* like, as if; **ilokko callo winyo,** you speak like birds; **ilokko callo pe iŋeyo ginne,** you speak as if you don't know it; 2 *conj* as if **Otto nen callo pe mitto citto,** it looks as if Otto does not want to go; **Otto nen callo wonne kikomme,** Otto looks exactly like his father.

cam *n* food; **cam tye kwene?** where is the food?

cam *v* eat; **cam dek en,** eat this food; **cam** is a general name, **dek** is food which has been cooked and is ready for eating.

camanini *n S* white sheeting made of cotton.

camme *vi* eatable; **camme ken ken-gi calo rec,** they eat themselves like fish do; **camme pe mit,** the food is not nice / his food is not nice / good.

cammo *vt* 1 eating; **cammo dek,** eating food; 2 costly; **ginni cammo lim mada,** this thing is very costly; 3 borrowing; **cammo banya,** borrowing, taking on credit. 3 false pretence; **cammo me goba,** obtaining something by false pretence; 4 becoming; **cammo ker,** becoming a chief.

can *n* poverty, need, misery; **can lim omakke mada,** he is in great need of money; **can opotto i komme matek,** great misfortune fell upon him.

can *v* pile, arrange; **can yen maber,** pile stack up the firewood.

can *n A* a plate, other people call it **cwan, or cuwan; kel can me tokko cam iye,** bring plates into which the food will be served.

canduk *n a* box, trunk; **canduk ŋico,** refrigerator.

canne *prn* 1. his poverty or misery. 2. *v* to struggle; **canne matek wek iwil dyaŋ,** struggle very hard so that you may buy a cow.

canno *vt* setting in order, or piling up or arranging in order; **tye ka canno buk i wii meja,** he is piling up books on the table.

caŋ *v n* healing, cure; **burre pe caŋ,** his ulcer does not heal; **twoone pe caŋ,** his disease does not cure or heal; or does not get cured or healed.

caŋa *n* small discs made of ostrich eggs with holes in them arranged on a string; **caŋa ŋut** *n* a necklace made of discs of ostrich egg shell.

caŋŋe *vi* cured; **twoone pe caŋŋe,** the disease cannot be cured.

caŋŋo *vt* to heal, cure; **kwinini en aye caŋŋo maleria,** malaria is cured by quinine.

cany *adv* heavily; **yer wiye odin ni cany,** his hair has grown heavily;

cany *v* stone, hit; **cany wiye ki lakidi,** hit his head with a stone; **cany gwok,** hit the dog (with something); **cany lobo me agulu,** beat clay for pottery; **cany lak kweri,** hammer the edge of a hoe, i.e. sharpen; **cany wii kom,** sit on the chair and make yourself comfortable.

canynyo *vt* stoning or hurling something against; **canynyo dano pe ber,** itting / stoning people is not good.

cap cap *adv* the sound made by a stone falling in water or by somebody jumping into water.

caran *n s* a sewing machine; **caran me kwoyo boŋo,** sewing machine for making clothes.

caro *n Lug* a rural area; **gibeddo i caro,** they live in a rural area.

caro-caro *prd* rotten, watery, insipid.

caro-dano *n* a queer human appearance, human specimen, robot, spoken in a sarcastic way; **ŋadigi doŋ gicaro dano,** so and so is a poor human specimen; see **akanyaŋo, jwee.**

carolok *n* parable, proverb; **Acoli gitye ki caro lok mapol mada,** the Acholi have many rich parables or proverbs.

cat *v* sell; **cat cukari ma tye i kicaa man,** sell the sugar in this bag.

cat *n* trade; **cat ma tye i kin Jeremel ki Uganda pudi tidi mo,** trade between Germany and Uganda is still little; **lacat wil,** a trader.

cati *n Eng* a shirt; **amarro rukko cati matar twatwal,** I like wearing / putting on white shirts.

catto *vn* staggering, reeling; **catto ni kato kato,** vacillating / staggering about as though drunk.

catte *vi* sold; **jami man ducu twerro catte maber mada,** all these things can sell well.

catto *vt* selling; **tye ka catto pul i cuk,** she is selling groundnuts in the martket.

catto wil *n* trading; **catto wil gin mape yot,** trading is not an easy thing.

cayanci *n Eng* science; knowledge obtained by observation and testing of facts by experiments; **gikwanno cayanci,** they are studying science.

cayo *vt* despising, looking down upon; **cayo dano pe ber,** despising people is not good, see **caa, cac.**

cedde *inj* despising remark; **cedde, imiŋ do ya,** (to express surprise) oh, you are stupid.

ceddo *n* roasting; **ceddo me pul tin omakkogi mada,** today they are fully occupied with roasting groundnuts; **ceddo me riŋo,** roasting meat.

ce, ce ka, ka ce *cnj* if, then; **ce ka mitto,** if he wants; **ce oye balle,** if he accepts his faults; **kace pe ibinno,** if you do not come; **doŋ pe citto ce?** is he not going then?

cec *vn* 1.snatching; **cec pa olwit pat ki pa okwata,** snatching of the hawk is different from that of the kite; see **cee, ceyo.**

ce cee *inj* despising remarks, surprise; **ce cee ki wun bene, wubinno ka cunna!** oh dear, even you, you do come for courtship!

cee *v* snatch, catch suddenly; **gwok okwata pe ocee latin gwenoni,** watch the kite so that it does not snatch the chick, **cee layab ma aebolli eno,** catch the key, which I am throwing to you; see **cec, ceyo.**

ceeg *n.* wife; a general name; the other names are as follows: sing **ceegga, ceeggi, ceegge,** my, your, his wife; *pl* **ceegwa, ceegwu, ceeggi,** our, your, their wives, but if the wife is not closely related but still belong to the same clan than they are called as follows: **ceegiwa, ceegiwu, ceegigi,** our, your, their wives, spoken mainly by? Langi.

ceer *vn* 1 to slip, 2 to lose one's balance; **ceer dogga omiyo alokko lok marac,** a slip of the tongue made me say bad words. 2 **piny ma dyak miyo dano ceer ci potto piny;** wet ground makes people slip and fall down; 3. **ceer dogga okello peko,** slipping of my tongue brought trouble.

ceer *n* rising from the dead; **nino me ceer pa Yecu,** the day Jesus rose from the dead, Easter.

ceer *vn* 1 row; *v* **ceer yeya,** row the boat; 2 stir or spread; **ceer i kal wek otwoo maber,** stir or spread the millet so that it may dry properly; 3 raise the matter; **ceer tyen lok ma laworoni tin doki,** raise the matter / case of yesterday today; 4 *vn* rise from the dead; **Yecu oceer i nino me adek,** Jesus rose from the dead on the third day.

ceere *vn* 1 meddling or interfering; **tye ka ceere i kom boŋo pa lawotte ni meno meere,** he is contesting ownership of the clothes that belong to his friend, 2 thrusting onself forward to do what one is unable to do or trying to do what one is unable to do; **oceere ni eŋeyo**

riŋŋo ki leela ci oriŋŋo ki leela opotto kwede marac oturro badde woko, he insisted / that he knows how to ride a bicycle and as a result he rode it and he fell badly, breaking his arm; **laceere,** one who always wants to do something which he cannot do.

ceerro *vt* 1 raising from the dead; **Yecu oceerro omin Maria,** Jesus raised Mary's brother from the dead; 2. rowing; **tye ka ceerro yeya,** he is rowing a boat; 3 insistng or meddling; **tye ka ceerro lok mape atir,** he is insisting on matter which is not right; 4 stirring the animals from under the grass so that they may come out; **tye ka ceerro lee wek gukatti woko ki i tee lum,** he is stirring the animals from under the grass so that they may come out.

ceg *v* close, shut; **ceg doggola woko,** close or shut the door.

ceggi *pron* near; **kama ceggi ceggi,** near (places not commonly spoken).

ceggo *vt* 1 closing, covering over, locking; **ceggo doggola,** shutting the door; **oa ka ceggo dog canduk,** he came from locking the box; 2 hurting **ceggo waŋ bur,** knocking the ulcer making it painful;

ceggo *adj pl* shortness; **dano ma ceggo,** short people.

cek *adj* short; **dano ma cek,** a short person.

cek *vi* 1 ripe. **labolo cek oyot oyot mada,** a banana ripens very quickly 2 **cam cek awene?** when will the food be ready? 3 **koŋo tye ka cek,** the beer is fermenting.

cekko *vi* ripening, finishing cooking, fermenting; **cekko me paipai nen ka**

komme ducu doŋ obeddo ocwak ocwak, the ripening of a pawpaw seen when it is completely yellow; **cekko me koŋo kal terro nino aryo,** fermenting millet beer takes twoo days.

cekko *vt* producing, **cekko ŋyim madwoŋ,** producing much simsim.

cekko *vt* to entertain, **ŋadi cekko lok mada,** so and so is a great humorist.

cel *n* string net for suspending a bowl under the ceiling of a house.

cel *n* fence; **gurummo otgi ki cel nyonyo,** they surrounded their house with an iron fence.

cel *v* 1 fence; **cel gaŋŋi ki cel matapali,** fence your home with a brick fence.

2 shoot; **cel winyo ki luduko aweno,** shoot the birds with a shortgun for shooting guinea fowls. 3 roast; **cel pul me amwodda,** roast the groundnuts for eating.

cele *adj* poor, bad (taste); **dogge cele,** he has poor appetite / food does not taste well to him.

celo *n* a sparrow (*passer griseus or p. motitensis*)

celle *vn* 1 hitting one another with stones. 2 shooting or fighting one another with guns.

cello *vt* 1 shooting, **cello atum, luduku, lagweŋ;** shooting an arrow, gun and 2. throwing stones.

cello *vt* to roast (meat, simsim, etc), fry (meat); **dakone cello gweno maber mada,** his wife roasts chicken very well.

cello *vt* to surround with a fence; **gucello gaŋgi ki gogo,** they fenced their home with big logs of wood.

cello mwoc *vn* a sudden outburst or expression of happiness with particular words, some of which may be abusive.

cen *adv* behind, in the background; **odoŋ cen,** he remained behind; **ocitto ki i cen ŋeggi,** he went after them; **ocammo ki cen,** he ate elsewhere; **cit cen,** go away; **dirre cen,** move away.

cen *n* a departed spirit, ghost, apparition, which is feared for vengeful actions;

cen opotto i komme omiyo opoo woko, the spirit has fallen upon him, which has made him mad.

cen *v* curse; **cen Orac kace itwerro,** curse Orac if you can.

cenno *vt* to curse, inflicting punishment; **latinne miŋ twatwal calo dano ma gicenno,** the child is very stupid, like a person who has been cursed.

ceno *n* a woman's loin dressing.

ceno mon-pa Lema *n* the name given to a kind of weed whose leaves are used for cleaning a neonate's stool, or dressing for covering the women's back part.

cente *n Eng* cents, shillings.

ceŋ *n* sun; **ceŋ okatti** or **ceŋ opuk. (cenŋ opuk** is spoken mainly by the Lamogi and others from west of Gulu), the sun has risen; **ceŋ otto,** the sun has set.

ceŋ con *prep* a long time ago; in the past; **ceŋ mo,** some day, one day; **ceŋ ma,** when.

cenynye *vi* withdrawing; **cenynye cen,** keeping aloof, in the background.

cenynyo *vt* to walk on tiptoe, or on the edge of your foot because of a bad foot; **wot kun icenynyo tyeni acenynya,** walk on tiptoe.

cep cep *adv* (to walk) softly, imperceptibly.

Ceptemba *n Eng.* September, the ninth month of the year.

cere *n* 1 a hill or rising ground, 2 the spine; **cere ŋec,** back spine.

ceregel *adj* small; **gweno eregel en ayice gweno matino mape gipito maber,** small chickens are the local ones which are not well bred.

cerro lee *vt* beating the grass so that animals which may be either hidden or sleeping under it, may come out so that they can be killed.

cerro lok *vt* insisting on; **en doki cerro lok twatwal,** he insists too much; see **diddo lok, riddo lok, and kwer ka lok.**

cerro *vt* 1 rowing; **cerro yeya,** rowing the boat; 2 strirring; **cerro kaal ma gimoyo,** stiring up the millet which is spread in the compound so that it can dry.

ceru *n* 1. bright star. 2 a cataract in the eye; **waŋŋe tye iye ceru, pieno doŋ pe twero nenno piny maber,** he has cataracts in his eyes, therefore, he cannot see well.

cet *n* 1 dung, excrement, stool, faeces; **cet dano,** human faeces, stool, excrement 2 **cet tiŋ, mo nyim, etc.,** dregs of millet beer after squeezing and straining, and of simsim oil, etc.; 3 **cet leela** metal dross; 4 **cet gweno,** chicken droppings; 5 **cet dyaŋ,** cow dung; 6 **cet oyoo,** rats' droppings.

ceyo *vt* snatching; **okwata ceyo litino gweno,** kites snatch chicks; see **cee, cec.**

ci *cnj* then, but; **oito malo ci onenno maber,** he climbed up and then saw it well; **obeddo ka goyo odilo ci ool**

twatwal, he was playing football but got very tired.

cib *v* put or place; **cib wii meja,** put on top of the table; **cib i tee baraja,** place / put on the verandah.

cibbe *vn* can be placed or put; **twerro kette i wii meja,** can be placed or put on top of the table.

cibbo *vt* putting; **cibbo piny,** putting down on the ground; **cibbo wii meja,** putting up on top of the table.

cid *v* 1 blacken; **cid kom agulu,** blacken the body of the pot with the black dye; 2 clean; **cid wii kidi,** clean the grinding stone (with your fingers).

cida *n* bedstead (usually made of wood fixed on the ground); see **kitanda.**

ciddu *vt* wipe with fingers; 2. **litino ciddu dek ma i atabu,** children wipe out / clean (with their fingers) the food which is left in the bowl.

cii *n* wife; **cii woddi,** your son's wife (its use is limited, it can occasionally be used as **cii Omara**).

cik *v* trap, snare; **cik wino me makko winyo,** lay down the trap for catching the birds.

cik *n* 1 law; **cik me lobo man,** the law of this country; 2 agreement, **cik ma nene guye,** the agreement which they had accepted.

cikko *vt* 1 to warn, admonish 2 to commission, command, order 3 to promise 4 to bid goodbye; 1 **ocikko Olobo ni myero oŋutti,** he warned Olobo to reform; 2 **ocikko lumony ni myero diki gubin con,** he commanded / ordered the army to come very early tomorrow 3 **ocikko ni ebimiinigi mot,** he promised that he would give them

gifts 4 **gucikko won gi ni owot maber,** they bid farewell to their father.

cikko *vt* trapping, catching; **cikko wino ki kek,** setting snares for trapping birds and fish; **cikko obwoo.** setting nets for trapping animals; **cikko layuttta, odiŋ, owic, ka agwak nyo kwakala,** setting those traps and snares for snaring, trapping or catching small animals or big birds such as guinea fowls, patridges and others; see **teero owic.**

cil *adj* bright, clean (not very much used by the Acholi but used very much by the Langi).

cili *n* wire; **cili me lyerro boŋo,** wire for hanging clothes.

cilil *vt* go and tell your lies; this is the name given to spies; see **lureka.**

cilo *n* filth, dirt; **latini komme kicilo,** the child is very dirty.

cim *v* point, indicate; **cim ŋat ma lakwoo,** point at the thief.

cim *n s* telephone, wireless, telegraph, fax etc.

cim *n* epilepsy; a disease whose sufferer, suddenly becomes unconscious and falls down with convulsions and froth coming out   from the mouth; **en tye ki twoo cim,** he has *epilepsy*; **latinni doki potto cim twatwal,** the child gets frequent attacks of epilepsy.

cimmo *vt* pointing, **itye ka cimmo gin aŋoo?** what are you pointing at?

cin *n* 1 bowels, intestines; **cin tino,** small intestines. 2 **cin togo,** bast of papyrus stalk.

cinu *n* stomach, **cinu me lum,** the stomach of ruminants (not commonly spoken); see **apika.**

ciŋ *n* hand; **opany ciŋ**, the palm of the hand; **lwet ciŋ**, fingernails; **nyig ciŋ**, fingers.

cip. *n* the women's loin dress; **cip waŋ kwanynyo**, a string with a couple of small chains, young women's loin dress (*fig.* called so because it exposes women's private parts).

cir *v* endure, bear, struggle against odds; **cir ticce pe iwekki**, endure the work, don't give up; **lacir mada**, he has endured a lot.

cirikali *s* a soldier. **cirikali tin dwoŋ kany mada**, there are many soldiers today here.

cirre *vi* tolerated, endured; **lokke cirre**, his words can be tolerated / endured / the matter or the case can be tolerated or endured.

cirro *vn* to endure, bear, struggle against; **ŋadi ocirro yet pa Okema mada ma yette kwede jwii**, so and so has endured the daily abusive words of Okema.

cirro *vn* overcome, overwhelmed; **two ocirro Akello woko**, Akelo is overcome / overwhelmed / exhausted by the disease.

cit *v* go, **cit ka kwan oyotoyot**, go to the school quickly; **cit i kella book**, go and get me a book.

citam *n Eng* stamp; **kella citam me bollo waraga**, bring for me the stamp for posting the letters.

citecen *n Eng* station; **ocitto i polici citecen**, he went to the police station.

citto *n* going, **citto kakwan**, going to school; **citto ni tye awene Gulu?** when are you going to Gulu?

cob *v* finish; **cob tic man ka doŋ icitti**, finish this work and then go.

cobbo *vn.* finishing; **cobbo dog tic**, finishing or completing the work.

cod *n* illicit sexual intercourse; here **cot** is the word preferred; **gimakke ka cot**, he was caught having sexual intercourse.

coddo *vt* to break the string; **tolle ŋao dyaŋ twero coddone woko**, the rope is weak, the cows can break it.

coddo *vt* to have illicit sexual intercourse; **en coddo dako pa ŋadi**, he has frequent sexual affairs with so and so's wife.

coc *n* 1 writing 2 sowing; **latin ma ŋeyo coc ber mada**, a child who knows how to write is very good; see **coo, coyo.**

coga *n* castor oil tree *(ricinus communis)*; **moo coga**, castor oil.

cogi *n* extraordinarily big; **cogi twon dyaŋi**, very big bulls; **cogi mon**, very big women; **cogi lyec / lyeci**, very big elephants.

cogo *n* **1** bone 2 the last born; **latin cogo**, the last born child.

cok *v* collect, gather; **cok kiyata kacel**, collect / gather the potatoes together.

cok *adv* near, shallow; **gaŋ cok kany**, the home is near here; **pii ne teere cok**, the water pond is shallow; **cwinynye cok**, he cannot keep secrets; **cok cok**, very near; **gaŋŋe tye cok cok kany**, his home is very near here; **cok cokki**, shortly, very soon; **cok cokki wabicito i London**, shortly / very soon we shall be going to London; **cokki**, one day; **cokki wabigerro otwa**, one day we shall build our house; **nyik cok kany**, draw near here; **bin cok kany**, come near here.

cok *vp* about; **Okot doŋ cok ka dwoggo,** Okot is about to return.

cok *vn* ceasing, stopping, coming to an end **kot cok ka cok,** the rain is about to stop; **kot man cok awene?** when is the rain stopping?

cokci *n Eng* socks, stockings; **kella cokci arukki,** bring me socks to wear; **kella cokci mabocco arukki,** bring for me stockings to wear; see **roc.**

cokke *vi* assembly, gathering; **gitye kacokke kwene?** where are they gathering / assembling? **kacokke madit,** a big assembly, parliament; **kacokke Madit,** Parliament; **gucokke laworo i bar odilo,** they assembled yesterdy in the footbal field.

cokko *vt* 1 collecting, gathering, assembling; **cokko yen me teddo,** gathering / collecting firewood for cooking 2 false accusation; **cokko lok i kom dano,** accusing people falsely (lit.collecting words against a person). 3 pretending; **cokko koko acokka,** pretending to weep.

cokko *v* shouting to stop something; **cokko gweno pe gucam nyim,** shouting to chase the chickens away to stop them from eating simsim.

cokko *vn* joining together, fitting into one another, eg joining two pieces or more of a pole to make a long one.

col *n* black, dark, dirty; **col li cuc,** pitch black; **col lamir lamir,** dark grey.

2 disapproval, stinginess; **waŋŋe col,** he is stingy, not happy; **cwinynye col,** he dislikes other people, is cold hearted.

col *v* deliver, assist a woman to deliver; **col dako matye ka nywal,** deliver or assist the woman who is delivering.

cola *n* a state of mourning; **cola me too pa wodde oballo komme mada,** mourning of his son has affected him very badly.

colle *vi* pushing, bearing down; **dakone pe ŋeyo colle,** the woman does not know how to bear down / push. (during birth).

collo *vt* to bear down, push down; **dako man pe ŋeyo collo,** this woman does not know how to bear / push / exert herself to push.

com *v* 1 fix; **com kweri i bolle,** fix the hoe to its handle.

com *vn* meet unexpectedly, **acom i komme i dye Kampala,** I met him unexpectedly in Kampala.

com *v* pour; **com pii maŋic wek okwee,** pour cold water into it to cool it.

commo *vt* coming upon; **commo i kom Okot acomma,** meeting Okot unexpectedly; **kommi gum mada ka commo i komwa ma watye ka cam,** you are very lucky to come unexpectedly upon us while we are eating .

commo *vt* fixing; **commo kweri i bolle,** fixing the hoe to its handle.

comogo *n* kind of grass whose stem is used as a tube for sucking.

comogo *n* a skin disease, ringworms or *allergic* reaction; in the past the people sometimes got the disease after wearing the new clothes bought from the shops.

comoro *n* a rare tree whose leaves have a rough surface used as sandpaper for polishing wood.

con *adv* formally, already, a long time ago; **yaŋ con,** a long time ago; **obinno**

odiko con, he came early in the morning; **jo ma con,** the ancestors.

cono *n* a swelling, usually of the knee, which is usually due to infection of the knee, *septic arthritis* of the knee; see **toko.**

coŋ *n* knee; **coŋŋe orwomme,** he is knock-kneed.

coŋ *n* a great desire for something; **coŋ riŋo nekke,** he has a great desire for meat.

coŋlum *n* stalks of grass.

cony *n* bent; **onyoŋo ni cony,** he squatted on his knees.

cony *v* dent a piece of **kwon** with the thumb; **cony kwon ka wek igwee ki dek,** make a dent in the **kwon** in order that you may scoop the sauce with it.

conynya *n* 1 bending, curving.

conynya *n* abuse, scorn; **laconya,** one who always abuses people.

conynyo *vt* 1 bending 2 pressing, eg, **conynyo kwon me gweyo dek,** pressing **kwon** with thumb making a dent with which to scoop the sauce.

coo *v* write; **coo waraga ki omero,** write to your brother; see **coc coyo.**

coo *v* sow; **coo kal doŋ i poto,** sow the millet now in the field.

coo *v* wake up; **coo latin woko cawa doŋ oromo me citto ka kwan,** wake the child up, it is time to go to school.

coo *n* 1. guinea worm (*dracontiasis*); *dracunculus medinensis.*

coo *n* a porcupine; **okuto coo,** porcupine's quill; see **ococ.**

coo *adj* a particular smell; **ŋwece coo calo ŋwec rec, remo nyo nyac,** smells like fish, blood or a yaws sore.

coo *n* men, husband; **coo gi,** their husbands, sometimes called **coggi.**

coo *n* sound uttered for driving or chasing away cattle fowls, etc.

coo *n* boundary; **waŋ coo me poto tye kwene?** where is the boundary of the field?

cor *v* 1 push; **cor canduk odok kwica,** push the box there; **cor dano guleŋ yoo,** push the people out of the way.

cor *vn* daring, doing or trying to do what one cannot do; **latin man lacor mada me temmo riŋo ki mutoka,** this child is very daring in trying to drive the car **danone lacor mada ocitto ka beddo kama pe romo beddo iye,** he is very bold and daring to go and sit in a place where he is not qualified to sit.

coro *n* a game with four rows of holes on a board or the ground in which stones or a kind of seed are placed and played with.

coro-coro *adv.* coming in a quantity; **bonyo binoni coro-coro,** the locusts are flying in large numbers around.

corre *vt* 1 arrival or coming of too many; **dano gucorre i bar odilo mape wacce,** the people came in large numbers to the footbal field.

corre *vt* trying to fight or compete with somebody who is stronger than oneself, boldness; **danone lacorre,** he is a man who always tries to do what he cannot do, he is a daring person.

corro *vt* 1 pushing; **corro motoka,** pushing the car; 2 **corro lum,** pushing your way through thick grass.

corro *vt* suddenly, unexpectedly; **corro mon ma tye ka lwok pe ber,** coming suddenly upon women who are bathing is not good.

corro *vt* wasting; **corro lim madwoŋ me willo gin mo,** paying too much money on something.

cot *n* 1 illicit sexual intercourse; **gimakke ka cot,** he was caught having illicit intercourse; 2 *adj* unripe, bad tasting; **labolone pudi cot pien peya ocek,** the banana tastes bad because it is not yet ripe.

cot *vn* 1 breaking off. 2 remove something; **cot daba woko,** remove the mud.

cot *v n* reaching puberty; a**wobi doŋ ocot,** he has reached puberty as characterized by having monthly night discharges through the penis, testes have become pendulous and there is a change in his voice; *c/f* **tuur**

coto *n* mud; **gol coto woko ki i waŋ pii,** remove the mud from the water well.

cotto *v* 1 pounding a wet substance, e.g. undried groundnuts or cassava; **cotto gwana ma dyak i pany,** pounding wet cassava in a mortar 2 **cotto poto acotta ma pe giteŋŋo,** cultivation only of a fresh field without preparing it.

cotto *vt* removing; **cotto lobo woko ki i waŋ pii,** removing mud from a well with the hand.

cotto *vt* scornful and sarcastic; **cotto lok,** speaking scornfully and sarcastically.

coyo *vt* 1 waking, reviving, 2 **caa ma coyo dano,** alarm clock; 3 **pe ber me coyo daa ma laworo,** it is not good to revive the quarrel of yesterday.

coyo *vt* writing; **coyo waraga,** writing a letter, see **coo, coc** .

coyo *vt* sowing seeds; **ocitto ka coyo geya,** he went to sow sorghum.

cub *v* stab, spear; **cub lee ma riŋŋo caa,** spear the animal which is running over there *or* **cub ki toŋ,** spear it.

cubbe *vi* can be stabbed, stabbing one another.

cubbo *vt* spearing, stabbing; **cubbo ki toŋ,** spearing with a spear; **okuto cubbbo tyen,** thorns prick the foot.

cubu *adv* fall into water; **opotto ni cubu i pii,** he/she/it splashed into the water.

cuc *adj* very; **col ni cuc,** very dark / black.

cucce *vi* lingering or hanging around for something; **latinni tye ka cucce pi kic ma gitye ka cammone i ot,** the child is hanging around for the honey which is being eaten in the house.

cuci *n* husks or chaff; **cuci kal,** millet chaff; see **cwici.**

cuco cuco *adj* velvety, not smooth; it is normally spoken of a hairy substance.

cud *v* to kill someone who is dying already.

cudde *vi* assisted death; **latoo doŋ ocudde woko,** the dying person killed himself / commited suicide.

cuddo *vt* killing one who is dying already; **cuddo lee madoŋ gicubbo,** spearing and killing an animal which is dying from an earlier spear wound.

cudu *adv* 1 protruding, jutting out 2 exceeding in size; **ot man dok ocuddu katto maca,** this house is bigger than the other one.

cugu or **cugo lun**; various kinds of black ants which bite people.

cuk v encourage, urge; **cuk cwiny latin wek omak kwan matek,** encourage the child so that he may work hard at his studies.

cuk *n A* market; **ocitto ka wil i cuk,** she went to buy things from the market.

cuka *n A* a sheet of cloth, a bedsheet; **miine cuka wek ocit oumme kwede,** give him the sheet of cloth / bedsheet so that he may cover himself wth.

cukari *n A* sugar; **om cukari me cai**, get the sugar for tea.

cukke *vn* try; **kadi beddi ticce tek cukke i tii kwede kit meno,** even though the work is very difficult try hard to do it just the same.

cukku *vt* changing from one (occupation) to another; doing nothing, e.g. **cukko tic** changing work; **ŋadi doki cukku tic twatwal,** so and so changes occupations too frequently.

cukku *vt* 1 urging; **cukku litino ka kwan,** urging the children to study.

2 doing somethingrepeatedly; **cukku kwac ki toŋ** stabbing or spearing the leopard with a spear repeatedly.

cuku cuku *adv* repeatedly; **jwa meja ni cuku cuku,** rub the table repeatedly; **ŋollo riŋo ni cuku cuku,** cutting the meat with a blunt knife.

cukuleke *n Lug* (*soka oleke*) pants, knickers (no longer used).

cul *v* pay, block; **cul banyani,** pay your debt; **cul bur man ,** block this hole.

cul *n* 1 payment (debt, fine) 2 block (holes); **giŋolle cul me dyel aryo,** he was fined or ask to pay two goats.

cula *n* an island.

cula *n* alone; **ŋadi gi doŋ gibeddo i cula,** so and so lives alone.

culla, culle, etc. *vt* pay me, pay him, etc.; **culle lim ma imakko,** pay him the money which you borrowed.

culle *adj* rising above, overlooking, exceeding; **otte oculle katto mukene ducu,** the house is taller and bigger than the others 2 drop into; **oculle i pii,** he dived / jumped into the water.

cullo *vt* 1 paying; **cullo banya,** paying debt; 2 blocking; **cullo waŋ pii man,** blocking this water (so that it does not flow).

cullu pii *vn* adding water; **cullu pii i dek madoŋ gityekko piyone pe ber,** adding more water to the sauce after it has already been mixed with simsim is not good.

cullu *adv* fall into water or liquid; **opotto i pii ni cullu,** fell into the water with a loud plop.

cuma *n* a proverb, by-word, axiom, maxim.

cun *n* 1 penis. 2 **cun kic,** the sting of a bee. 3 courtship.

cun *v* court, befriend, make love; **cun anyira,** court / befriend girls.

cunna *n* courtship, flirtation, insinuating talk, befriending; **ocitto ka cunna,** he went to court, befriend, induce, flirt with the girls.

cunne *vi* be courted, befriended; **nyanne tika cunne,** can the girl really be befriended?

cunno *vt* to court; **ocitto ka cunno anyira,** he went to court, persuade, induce, befriend, or flirt with girls.

cuŋ *v* 1 stop, stand; **cuŋ pee icitti,** stop, don't go; **cuŋ kenyo,** stand there; 2 *vt* fixed; **waŋŋe ocuŋ i komme,**

his/her eyes were fixed on him; 3 *vi* doubtful; **cwinynye ocuŋ acuŋa,** he was doubtful.

cuŋ kal *n* millet chaff; **cok cuŋ kal wek iwaŋgi woko,** gather the millet chaff / and then burn it.

cuŋŋe *vi* can be pressed into; **pamba man ducu twerro cuŋŋe i gunia man,** all this cotton can be pushed into this gunny sack.

cuŋŋo *vt* 1 pushing something; **cuŋŋo pamba i kicaa,** pushing cotton into the sack. 2 forcing; **pe ber me cuŋŋo dano mo me tiyo gin mo,** it is not right to force a perrson to do anything.

cuny *v* build; **cuny latin ot mo piri,** build a small house for yourself.

cunynyo *vt* building a small hut; **tye ka cunynyo latin otte moni en do,** he is erecting his small hut here.

cupa *A n* bottle; **kel cupa me pikko yat,** bring a bottle for putting medicine into.

cupuria or **cibiria** *n S* saucepan, metal cooking pot, usually of aluminium.

cur *v* 1 pound; **cur kal,** pound the millet; 2 pour a large amount of; **cur pii i lobone ka doŋ inyon me mwonno ot,** pour a large quantitive of water on the clay and then knead / mix it with your feet for building the house.

cura *n A* chapter; **yab cura adek me jiri pa Matayo,** open the third chapter of the gospel of St Matthew.

cura *n A* mathematics, the study or science of numbers and sizes including arithmetics, algebra, geometry and trigonometry.

curre *vi* pounded; **kal man twerro curre maber,** this millet can be easily pounded.

curru *vt* 1 pounding in a mortar; **curru kal,** pounding millet (in a mortar); 2 acting rashly, inconsiderately, frankly; **curru lok atyer,** speaking frankly and openly; 3 **curru pii i dek,** pouring much water into sauce.

curu buk *n* bellows (as used by a blacksmith).

curu tet *n* bellows for making fire very hot.

curuwal *n S* a pair of trousers; **curuwal macek,** a pair of short trousers; **curuwal mabor,** a pair of long trousers; see **pali.**

cut *v* take (into the mouth); **cut cam i muny,** take the food (into the mouth) and swallow it.

cuti *n* suit; **an amitto cuti me yer keken,** I want only woollen suits.

cutte *vi* can be taken (in the mouth) and swallowed; **yatte twerro cutte ka munynye,** the medicine can be taken and swallowed.

cutto *vt* taking something into the mouth; **cutto cam i dog,** taking food into the mouth.

cuur *v* groaning, sighing, murmuring, making noise while breathing; **latin tye ka cuur mada,** the child is groaning very much ; *vt* noise, **ŋaa matye ka cuur?** who is making noise? **cuur doki pat ki twarro; cuur noŋŋo ŋat ma komme lit ento twarro** (snoring**) meno ŋat mape ywee maber ka onino,** **cuur** is different from **twarro, cuur** is noise made by a sick person, whereas **twarro** is a noise made by a person while sleeping.

cuur *adv* noises; **iye tye ka cuur,** his stomach is making noises, / rumbling; **piny woo ki koko ni cuur,** the people are wailing / weeping loudly; **opye i pii ni cuur,** he plopped into the water.

cwaa *n* the tamarind tree and fruit; the fruit has a sour taste but is very much liked.

cwaa or **kwidi cwaa** *n* thread-worms; **kwidi cwaa mako litino mapol,** many children are infected with thread-worms.

cwaar *n* husband; **cwaar Anek ber mada,** Anek's husband is very good;

the relations here are as follows: *sing* **cwaarra, cwaarri, cwaarre,** my, your, her husband; *pl* **cwaarwa, cwaarwu, cwaargi,** our, your, their husbands; if the relatives are not close but still of the same clan, then they are called: **cwaariwa, cwaariwu, cwaarigi,** our, your, their husbands.

cwac *adj* very long; **bor li cwac,** very tall / long; **nyako ma oputte ni cwac,** a girl who has grown up tall and slender.

cwak *n* jaw; **doŋŋe tyen mapol turro cwak dano,** frequently jaws are broken in boxing.

cwak *v* 1 defend, back, support; **man doŋ cwak ot,** this is really a parochial defence; 2 cook for a long time; **cwak mac matek pi kare ma lac ka wek del raa ocekki,** keep on poking the fire for a long time in order to make the hippopotamus hide soft 3 breathe in; **cwak ummi,** breathe in hard / draw in air through your nose; see **cwik.**

cwak obwoo *n* a pole to which a hunting net is tied.

cwakke *vi* can be defended; **lokke twerro cwakke i kot,** the case can be defended in court.

cwakko *vt* defending, supporting, backing, making something work well; in **itye ka cwakko dano ma lakwoo ni?** are you defending the thief? **cit ka cwakko laremmi i kot,** go to defend your friend who is in court.

cwakko mac i tee agulu, poking the fire under the cooking pot; **cwakko um,** drawing in air through the nose; **cwakko lok i kin dano aryo wek gulweny,** urging the two people to fight.

cwal *v* push, send; **bin wunu wucwal mutokana,** come and push my car; **cwal waraga obin diki,** send the letter so that it comes tomorrow; **cwal kany,** push here / send here.

cwalle *vi* can be sent, pushed; **jami man mere twerro cwalle botti,** these things can be sent to you.

cwallo *vt* sending, handing over; **cwallo Oto ka willo kado,** sending Oto to buy some salt; **ocwallo kwena boti,** he has sent you a message.

cwari, cware *n* bedbugs **cware dwoŋ mada i kom kitanda man,** there are many bedbugs in this bed.

cwee *v* create, make, knit; **cwee mukeka ki an,** knit a mat for me; see **cwec, cweyo.**

cwee *n* meat soup, **myero ocam cwee madwoŋ ka wek okel komme maber,** should eat more meat soup in order to make him put on weight; see **cwec, cweyo.**

cwee *adj* fat; **dyaŋŋine gucwee mada,** the cows are very fat.

cwec *vn* fatness; **cwec pe myero ki dano macek,** fatness is not good for a short person; see **cwee, cweyo.**

cwec *vn* creating, forming, making, shaping, knitting.

cweer *vn* bleeding; **remo tye ka cweer i tyenne,** he is bleeding from his leg.

cweer *v* scrape, plane; **cweer bao man,** scrape / plane this wood.

cweerro *vt* scrapping, smoothing, removing; **cwerro bao,** planing a plank/ board of timber; **cweerro laa,** scrapping off hairs from the skin / hide; **cweerro tee agulu,** scraping the bottom of a pot. (usually to remove millet crust which is like chips, and which the children like to eat).

cweta *n Eng* sweater; **cweta me yer en aye lyet me arukka ka piny ŋic,** woollen sweaters are the ones which are warm for wearing when it is cold.

cwet cwet *adv* a sound made by a razor when being whetted; **opakko lyedi ni cwet cwet,** he sharpened the razor on the stone and it went **cwet cwet.**

cweyo *vn* fatness; **cweyo kello twoo kor,** fatness brings heart disease.

cweyo *vt* making **cweyo agulu,** making a pot; **Lubaŋa ocweyo dano,** God created man.

cwic *adv* quite, completely; **orukko tok ma orommo wiye ni cwic,** he put on a hat which fitted him quite well.

cwic *vn* sucking; **cwic pa latin,** sucking of a child; see **cwii, cwiyo.**

cwici *n* chaff, husks. *q.v.* **cuci; cwici kaal,** millet chaff or husks.

cwi cwii *prn* nagging, tormenting; **lacoo ma la cwi cwii,** a man who is a tormenter, / always nagging.

cwid *v* suck; **wek latin ocwid cak kadi nok kwede kumeno,** let the child suck the breast even though there is little milk in it.

cwidde *vi* can still be sucked; **cakke pudi twerro cwidde, wek latin ocwid,** the milk can still be sucked, let the child suck.

cwiddo *vt* sucking milk from a breast which is about to dry up; **cwiddo acwidda,** continue sucking though it is drying up.

cwi-cwi *adv* narrowly escaped **oloyo cwi-cwi kono gicelo wako,** he narrowly estaped from being shot.

cwii *vt* suck with force, **cwii lemun en,** suck this lemon; see **cwiic, cwiyo.**

cwiic *vn* sucking; see **cwii, cwiiyo.**

cwik *v* the standard word for it is **cwak;** draw breath in, **cwik / cwak ummi,** draw breath in through your nose.

cwikko *vt* drawing in breath through the nose while crying or weeping softly; **cwakko um** and **cwikko um** are the same.

cwiine *vt* put sticking, adhering to, clinging to; **latin ocwiine kom minne,** the child clung to her mother 2 *vi* sucked; **lemunne twerro cwiine,** the lemon can be sucked.

cwiiny *n* a small carnivore ground squirrel; see **bura, kak, oculi.**

cwiit *n Eng* sweet; **kella cwiit anaŋ,** bring for me some sweets to suck.

cwiiyo or **cwiino** *vt* 1 sucking; **cwiiyo remo ki lacwii,** sucking blood with a sucker; **gucitto ka cwiiyo tiŋ,** they went to suck leftover millet brew / dregs with a tube from a pot. 2 annoying, troublesome, vexing; **lokke cwiiyo cwinynye mada,** he is very much annoyed about the matter / the matter is annoying him very much, or very much affected by the matter; see, **cwii, cwiic.**

cwiny *vn* drying up, evaporating; **waŋ it doŋ tye ka cwiny woko;** the water well is drying up.

cwiny *v* 1 touch with something; **cwiny kadone ki kwon,** touch the salt with millet bread **(kwon);** 2 kindle, light up; **cwiny mac tara,** light the lamp.

cwiny *n* mind, temper, heart, sentiments, mental disposition; **dano ma ocwiny,** a person with an intelligent, sound mind; **tye ki cwiny maber,** he has a good heart, mind, and temper;

cwinynye *prn* his mind, heart; **cwinynye cweer,** he is aggrieved, distressed and offended; **cwinynye kec, nyo cwinynye rac,** he is very bitter, not friendly, does not like people; **cwinynye kwar,** he hates people; **cwnynye leŋ, ber,** he is very friendly, kind, likes people and is trustworthy; **cwinynye yom,** he is happy, contented and friendly; **cwinynye oyee dok opwoyo,** he has approved and consented to it; **cwinynye pe iye,** he does not want to think of it; **cwinynye tek i kom lokke,** he is very doubtful and not certain about the matter; **cwinynye daggi, okwerro, pe mitto,** he has refused, does not like and want it; **cwinynye myel, potoo,** he is excited, alarmed; **cwinynye tek,** he is brave / courageous; **cwinynye oaa iye woko,** he has lost interest in it; **cwinynye doŋ opye,** he has now calmed down; **cwinynye odiŋ ki kec,** hunger does not affect him he is used to hunger; **cwinynye lemme,** feels like vomiting, **cwinynye doŋ otum,** he has died / passed away; **cwinynye yot,** he his light headed and a man who cannot keep secret, light hearted.

cwinynyo *vt* 1 kindling / lighting a fire; **cwinynyo mac i tee agulu nyo**

cwinynyo mac tara, kindling fire under a pot or lighting a lamp.

cwinynyo *vt* stinging; **kic ocwinynyo dye wiye,** the bee stung his head.

cwinynyo *vt* cooking; **cwiny'nyo boo nyo akeyo,** cooking a green vegetable with simsim or groundnuts in a certain way which makes it thick and very tasty.

cwir *n* the rainy season; in Uganda there are two seasons only, the wet and the dry.

cwit *adv* narrowly; **oloyo cwit cwit mada kono motoka oyokko woko,** he narrowly escaped from being knocked by a car; c/f **jwit jwit.**

D d

daa *vn* quarrel; **gin tye ka daa mada,** they are quarrelling very much; **daa i wii dano,** scolding people.

daa *n* my grandmother, my husband's mother; **dayo,** grandmother (a general name); the other names are as follows: *sing.* **daa, daani, daane,** my, your, his grandmother; *pl* **daawa, daawu, daagi,** our, your, their grandmothers; other grandmothers who are not closely related but from the same clan, are called as follows: **daaniwa, daaniwu, daanigi,** our, your, their grandmothers; **daa Okeny konynyo litino mada,** Okeny's grandmother helps the children very much; see **dayo.**

daa *vt* widen, enlarge; **daa ot beddo obed malac,** widen / enlarge the sitting room; see **dac, ki dayo.**

daa-abila *n* an old lady looking after an ancestral shrine.

daa-ker *n* a queen or chief's wife.

daa-lakko *n* inherited widow, a woman taken by the deceased's brother or his close relative.

daa-marru, daa cwiny *n* the favourite wife.

daa mon *adv* continuously; **kotte cweer calo daa mon,** the rain falls unceasingly like the women's quarrel.

daan *n* palate; **bur tye i daan latin,** there is an ulcer in the child's palate.

daan *n* ceiling; **daan ot,** the ceiling of a house; **daan agulu,** the point below the neck of a pot. **daan pii,** river bank; **laromo ot tye i daan ot,** the gecko is under the ceiling.

daa too *n* widow; **teer cam ki daa too,** take the food to the widow.

dab *v* mend roughly; **dab kicaa eno,** mend the bag roughly.

daba *n* mud; **nyonno daba me gerro ot,** treading mud for building the hut.

daba daba *adv prd* 1 muddy. 2 soft, not inflated hard; **mupirane pe gipiko oyeŋ, obeddo daba daba,** the ball is not inflated hard.

dabbo *vt.* mending. roughly 1 **dabbo boŋo,** mending clothes roughly;

2 **dabbo adabba,** superficial; **ocubbo odabbo adabba,** he hit it superficially (with a spear).

dac *vn.* 1 bulging 2 sound of falling down; **kicaane tye ka dac pi kado ma opoŋ iiye,** the sack is bulging on the side because it is full of salt. 2 *adv* **opotto ni dac,** he fell down on his buttocks.

dad *v* 1 open wide; **bar recce ci idad iye woko,** cut and open wide the inside of the fish; 2 open with force; **dad ogul**

ma i ciŋŋe ka wek iwotti, force open her wristlet in oder to pull it off; see **ded.**

daddo *vt* opening wide, e.g. cutting the fish along its length and opening it wide (in order for it to dry well); **daddo ogul,** opening a wristlet with force; see **deddo.**

dag *vi* refusal, hatred; **Ocan dag citto,** Ocan has refused to go / Ocan does not want to go; **Ocan dag Otto mada,** Ocan hates Otto very much; **camme dag dog,** the food does not taste nice / the taste of the food is not agreeable / the food is tasteless.

daga daga *prd* soft and yielding over a larger area; marshy.

dagaryo - dogaryo *n* slow-worm; see **obwol mon**

daggo *vn* hating; **daggo dano pe gin maber,** hating people is not good. **dago** *n* a marsh, swamp.

dak *adj* 1 large; **dak kwon,** a large pot for cooking **kwon.** 2 *n* **dak kor** sternum.

dak *n* emigration, immigration; **dak rac,** emigration is not good.

dak *v* immigrate, emigrate; **dak woko ki kany,** emigrate from here; **dak ibin kany,** immigrate here.

dako *n* a woman, wife; **latin dako,** a young woman, / a young wife; **dako** is always single in name not plural as follows: **dakona, dakoni, dakone,** my, your, his wife; women who are closely related are called as follows: *pl* **monwa, monwu, mongi,** our, your, their women, but the women who are not closely related but belong to the same clan are named as follows: **mon mewa, mon mewu, mon meggi,** our, your, their women; see **ceege.**

da miya pii *n* lion ant which burrows in the sand.

dano *n* men, people; a human being, person.

daŋ *adv* 1 very much; **oryeene ni daŋ**, he streched himself very much. 2 convulsing; **ryeene ni daŋ daŋ**, convulsing (somebody dying); 3 shining; **boŋone ryeny ni daŋ daŋ**, his clothe are shining very brightly.

daŋ *v* tear, peel; **daŋ riŋo ki i kom del**, peel the meat from the skin.

daŋŋe *vn* 1 shouting; **daŋŋe wii lapwony rac**, shouting at the teacher is very bad.

daŋŋo *vt* tearing, peeling, ripping up (the surface of); **daŋŋo apoka yat**, peeling or detaching the bark from a tree; **atero odaŋŋo but lee ne adaŋŋa**, the arrow only ripped the skin on the side of the animal.

dany *vi* spread out; **dano gudany ki ŋwec**, people ran in all directions.

dany *v* open / part a way; **dany yer wii**, part your hair; **dany kora yoo kany**, open the way here by parting the grass.

danyo *n* rainbow.

danynyo *vt/vn* 1to separate, part e.g. **labwor ka obino ci danynyo dano ki ŋwec**, the lion scatters people when it comes; **lapiru danynyo wii ot**, the whirlwind blows out the grass from the roof of the hut 2 unfolding, parting, opening; **latin ma danynyo nyimme kitte rac**, a child who opens her thighs has bad habits 3 **danynyo waŋ**, opening wide the eyes; **Ocen doki marro danynyo waŋŋe twatwal**, Ocen likes very much opening his eyes wide; **ŋat ma marro danynyo waŋŋe lalworo**, someone who is fond of opening his eyes wide is a coward.

dar *v* pick out; **dar gweŋ ki i ruc man**, pick out stones from this rice.

darabin n microscope.

darre *vi* can be picked out; **gweŋ ma tye i nyim tika twerro darre?** can the stones in the simsim be picked out?

darro *vt* separating mixed-up things, picking out unwanted things from a mixture; **darro kweyo ki i kal**, picking out stones from the millet.

dat *v* stab or spear many times.

datto *vt* 1 *q.v.* **nyatto**, making a mass of something; spearing or stabbing many times; **gudatto kwac man mape wacce**, they speared this leopard many times and made a mass of it. 2 to massacre, kill many; **lumony gudatto lumeroko mada**, the soldiers massacred the enemies.

dawa *S n* medicine.

daayo *n* grandmother *qv* **daa**

daayo *vt* widening, broadening an opening; **daayo dog agulu obed malac ka gitye ka cweyone**, widening the mouth of the pot when making it; **daayo dog poto**, widening the field; see **daa** and **dac**.

debe *n S* tin can, pail, bucket.

debe debe *prd* soft, flexible, malleable; **yom debe debe**, very soft.

debbo *vt S* to adjust, adapt, repair; also **dabbo; odabbo boŋo i korre**, she has adjusted her clothe at the breast or amended the clothes at his chest.

dec *vn* 1 retching; **tye ka dec**, he is retching 2 strangulation, **otoo too dec**, died of strangulation; see **dee** and **deyo**.

Decemba *n Eng* December, the twelfth month of the year.

ded *v* to open by force; **ded agit ma omakko i ciŋŋe wek i wot woko,** forcibly open the tight ring on her finger in order that you may pull it off; see **dad.**

dedee *adj* lukewarm; **pii ne dedee pe lyet,** the water is lukewarm, not hot; see also **bol bol, bulu bulu, dem dem,** and **mor mor.**

deddee *vi* open or loosen; **dog kicaa ma gitweyoni odeddee woko,** the mouth of the sack which was tied has become loose.

deddo *vt* separating by force the joined ends of; **deddo abwol ma i ŋut ciŋŋe oloye woko,** opening her wristlet / defeated him / he failed to open the wristlet from her on; see **daddo.**

dee *vn* 1 to adorn oneself; to dress up; **Aceng odee mape wacce,** Aceng has adorned herself very much, or she has dressed herself superfluously 2 **dee i kom lim pa wonne,** proud of his father's wealth; **dec** and **deyo.**

dee *adv* flatly; **oryeyo tyenne ni dee,** she stretched out her legs flat on the ground, lazily.

dee *v* strangulate; **pe idee latin ki boŋo ma itweyo marac i ŋutteni,** do not strangle the child with the piece of cloth which you tied badly on his neck; see **dec** and **deyo.**

deene *vn* . adorn onself; **odeene ki lwak jami mada i komme, caŋa i ŋutte, ogul i ciŋŋe ki agit i iciŋŋe,** she adorned herself very much, ostritch egg

necklace on her neck, copper bangle on her wrist and a ring on her finger.

deene *vi* commit suicide; **ginoŋŋo odeene i odde,** he was found hanged in his house; **deene gin marac mada,** hanging onself is a terrible thing.

deeno *vt* strangliing; **giŋolle twec me mwaka pyeraryo pi deeno dano,** he was sentenced to twenty years in prison for strangling a person.

deer *n* commiting suicide; see **dee**

deer *n* a meteorite, lightning, thunder; see **oyeŋ yeŋ**.

deer *vn* tiredness; exhaustion, fatigue; **en doŋ odeer woko ki tiyo tic boyi,** he is tired of working as a houseboy.

deerre *vi* hanging onself, commiting suicide, **ginoŋo odeerre i ot;** he was found hanging in the house; **odeerre i odde,** he commited suicide in his house; see **deene.**

dek *n.* a savoury sauce, a dish of food, vegetables etc.

del *n* skin; **del kom,** body's skin; **del dog ma malo ki ma piny,** the upper lip and lower lip; **del lak,** gums; **del cuun,** prepuce; **del latwe ic,** belt or girdle; **del anino,** rhinoceros whip or lash.

del *v* 1 watch, concentrate on; **del waŋŋi ikomme matek,** watch him very carefully /closely 2 **del waŋŋi matek ka week inen,** open wide your eyes in order to see; see **deŋ, ped, col, ŋwel.**

dem *vn.* tired, fatigued, enfeebled; **kom Atoo doŋ odem mada ki yacone ni,** Ato is now very much fatigued by her pregnancy.

dem dem *adj* lukewarm; see **bol bol, bolo bolo, bulu bulu de de, mor mor.**

dem *v* cut a big chunk; **dem riŋo em dyaŋ**, cut a big cunk of meat from the thigh of a cow.

demmo *vt.* cutting a big piece, **demmo riŋo em dyaŋ oterro ire**, cutting a big chunk of meat from a cow's thigh for himself; **demmo lok**, exaggerating facts.

den *n* borrowing; **den pe gin ma yot**, borrowing is not an easy thing; **makko den pe gin maber**, borrowing is not good.

den *v* borrow; **den lim ki bot Oneka**, borrow the money from Oneka.

denne *vi* can be borrowed; **lim twerro denne ki i beŋe**, the money can be borrowed from the bank; **doŋ otyekko cullo denne woko**, he has refunded or paid the money he borrowed.

denno *vt* to borrow; **ocitto ka denno lim bot ominne**, he went to borrow some money from his brother.

denno can *vi* suffering (*lit* it can be translated as 'he borrowed suffering') **odenno can mada**, he suffered very much.

deŋ *v* open wide; **deŋ waŋŋi ikome**, look at him seriously with wide open eyes; **del, ped, dany.**

deŋ *n* distend; **odec en aye kello deŋ ic**, enlargement of the spleen is the cause of a large abdomen; **cam madwoŋ twatwal bene kello deŋ ic**, too much eating also brings about a large abdomen; **iye odeŋ**, his abdomen is distended / very big; 2 **odeŋ iŋetta en**, he is clearly visible besides me here.

deŋ deŋ *adj.* unsteadily; **latin wotto ni deŋ deŋ**, the child walks unsteadily with its big belly.

deŋŋo *vt* 1 filling up with water or blowing air into something until it swells up or distended, 2 **deŋŋo waŋ i kom ŋati mo**, staring at somebody 3 **odec en aye deŋŋo i litino**, enlargement of the spleen is responsible for the large abdomen in children.

denynye *adv/vp.* idly; **latin obeddo li denynye**, the child is sitting idly.

der *n* meteorite, a piece of rock from outer space that falls and hits the earths surface.

der. *v* decorate; **der boŋo man maber**, decorate this clothes very well.

dero *n* light, shine, rays; **dero ceŋ**, the sun's rays; **dero mac**, rays of fire; **dero ceŋ carro waŋ**, the sun's rays dazzle the eye.

dero *n* a granary for storing millet, groundnuts etc, barn.

derro *vt* to inlay with something ornamental; **giderro kwot ki atego**, the shield was inlaid with ornamental metal; **bol latek giderro ki mola**, the pipe's handle is inlaid with brass / copper.

det *adj* fresh; **riŋo ma det**, fresh meat.

det *adv* widening; **bur tye ka det i tyenne mada**, the ulcer on his foot is very bad and getting bigger.

det *adv* increasing very much; **mac tye ka det mada**, the fire is getting intensely hot.

deyo *n* ornament, honour, decoration; **jami me deyo tye botte**, he has many ornaments.

deyo *vt* 1 adorning, decorating, embellishing; **deyo ki lalukana me jabu**, adorning with a golden crown.

deyo *vt* strangulating, hanging, choking; **gitweye pi deyo dano**, he was jailed for strangulating a man; **gitye ka deyo dano tin i jero,** they are hanging people in jail; **uno ma gitweyo i ŋut dyel tye ka deyone,** the rope tied around the neck of the goat is choking / strangulating it; see **dee, ka dec.**

dibi dibi *prd* 1 depressed, having malaise, weak, unwell; **komme obedo dibi dibi;** he feels unwell, weak, depressed or have malaise. 2 dullness; **piny tin obeddo dibi dibi,** the weather is dull today.

dic *vn* compression, pressure; **oketto dic matek mada i komme ni pe ocit ka mo,** he put a lot of pressure on him not to go anywhere; see **dii ki diyo.**

did *v* persist, insist; **did kor lokke matek,** insist obstinately on the matter.

diddo *v* urging, persisting in questioning; **ididdo lok i komme twatwal,** you exceedingly insisted on implicating him.

digiri *n Eng* degree; **Oryem doŋ ononŋo digirine i tic me pur, agirikalca,** Oryem has obtained his degree in Agriculture.

didii *n* stinginess; **pi didiine owekko pe gikonynye i kare ma opotto i can,** because of his stinginess, he was not helped when he got into trouble.

dii *v* squeeze, compress, press down; **dii matek ka wek igur maber,** press / push hard in order to nail it well; see **dic,** and **diyo.**

dii *v* be patient; **dii cwinynyi manok ci inoŋŋo,** be patient and you will get.

dik dik *adj* slightly wet or moist, half smoked; **riŋo ma dik dik,** meat which is not yet completely dried, which is half smoked.

dik dik *adv* always, regularly, daily; **en dik dik bino ka tic,** he comes to work daily (spoken mainly by Langi).

dik *v* wait, hold back; **dik cwinynyi manok,** wait a bit or wait for a moment.

diki *adv* tomorrow; **diki maca,** the day after tomorrow.

dikke *vi* delaying, keeping back, slowing down something; **Ocen nino ducu dikke twatwal,** Ocen is always late, delaying; see **dokke, galle, myenne, mine, ŋinynye.**

dikko *vt* holding back, restraining oneself; **dikko cwiny,** restraining oneself, holding back; **dikko tyen,** delaying a bit; **pi dikko tyenne omiyo ginoŋŋe,** because of delayting a bit, he was found.

dikko *vt* writing; **dikko coc maber,** writing very well / writes very well.

diin *vn* (of grass) together wildly, overgrowing; **yoo odiin woko,** the path is overgrown with grass; **diin wic pe ber,** long dense hair on the head is not good.

diiŋ *n* cheek, joint between the lower and upper jaw.

dil *v* stuff, press, compress; **dil waro i goniya en,** push hard or stuff the cotton into this bag.

dillo *vt* stuffing something into container; **dillo pamba i guniya,** stuffing cotton into a gunny bag.

dim *n* spit or spike; **dim toŋ,** the sharp lower end of a spear

din *v* thresh; **din bel,** thresh the millet.

dini *A n* religion

dinne *vi* can be threshed, **kale twerro dinne maber mada,** the millet can be very well threshed.

dinno *vt* 1 threshing; **miya dul me dinno bel,** give me a flail for threshing the corn. 2 beating, making soft; **dinno laa dyaŋ**, beating the hide to make it soft. **3 dinno man dyel,** castrating a goat by smashing its testicles.

diŋ *v* coerce, force, frighten, threaten; **diŋ latin matek ci tucco kama jami gikanno iye**, frighten / threaten the child and he will reveal where the things have been hidden.

diŋ *vn* numb, insensitive, very cold 1 **lemun kello diŋ lak ka i inaŋŋo**, a lemon make, your teeth humb when you suck it; 2 **pinynye tin odiŋ mada**, the weather is very cold today. 3 **cwinynye odiŋ woko ki kec**, he has lost appetite (because of being constantly hungry).

diŋ. *n* deafness; **diŋ it gin marac mada**, deafness is a terrible thing.

diŋ *adj.* narrow; **doggolane diŋ mada**, it's door is very narrow.

diŋ *v* strain; **diŋ koŋo wek gimatti**, strain the beer so that it may be drunk.

diŋŋe *vi* can be strained; **koŋo man me kal twero diŋŋe maber mada**, the millet beer can be strained very well.

diŋŋo *vt* 1 straining under pressure; **diŋŋo koŋo**, straining the beer in a strainer by squeezing it. 2 coercing; **diŋŋo ŋat mo ki lok**, coercing / forcing somebody with words / cornering somebody.

diŋŋo *vt* speaking through one's nose; **lokko ma odiŋŋo umme**, he speaks with a nasal voice / he speaks through his nose.

diŋŋo *vi.* pretending; **diŋŋo it,** pretending not to hear.

diŋŋo *vt* enduring; **diŋŋo kec mada,** endures hunger very much.

diŋŋo *vt* freezing; **diŋŋo kom dano,** freezes the body.

diŋŋo *vt* making numb; **diŋŋo ciŋ dano,** making the fingers numb.

dipoloma *n Eng* diploma; **Otto onoŋŋo dipoloma i tic me pac,** Otto has obtained a diploma in carpentry.

dir *v* push away, move away a little; **dir kom cen ,** move / push away the chair; **dirre cen,** move away; **dirre kany,** move here.

dira *n* work done by people, especially women to help another woman, for which they will be given a good meal or beer on another day; **gucitto ka kayo kal dira,** they went to harvest the millet for future reward; c/f **awak.**

dirica *n S* window; **yab waŋ dirica,** open the window.

diro *n* 1 craftsmanship, skill, art, dexterity; **ŋadi ladiro mada,** so and so is very skilful / works with great skill or dexterity.

dirro *vt* persisting; **dirro waŋ i kom ŋati mo,** persisting in annoying or blaming somebody.

dit *n* art, skill, dexterity **ladit** *n* an artist; see **dirro.**

dit *adj* 1 great quantity or size, much; **otte dit mada,** the house is very big. 2 old; **dano ma dit,** an old man; 3 great or important, **ladit,** a great man, an important person.

diyo *vt* 1 pressing, forcing; **diyo dano ka tic matek,** forcing / exerting pressure on people to work very hard; 2 pressing, squeezing; **warre diŋ diyo tyen,** the shoes are too small, they pinch the feet; see **dii ki dic.**

do *adv* a word used to show assurance; **tye kany do,** it is here; **akello do,** I have brought it.

dob *v* betray, treachery; **pe idob dano,** do not betray people; **en ladob dano,** he is a man who betrays people, a traitor.

dobbo *vt* betraying; **gigoye pi dobbo Ojok,** he was beaten for betraying Ojok.

dobo *n* leprosy. **ladobo,** a leper.

dobo - dobo *adv* overripe, soft, **muyembene doŋ ocek ni dobo dobo,** the mango is too ripe and is too soft.

doc *vn* weeding, (not frequently spoken); see **doo, doyo.**

docco *vi* hindered, prevented; **gin aŋoo ma doki odocco binnoni laworo,** what hindered or prevented you from coming yesterday?

dod *v* pile, **dod buk magi i wii wadigi,** pile these books on top of the others. . **dod** *v* entangle, tie; **dod dyel i mwodo,** tie the goat in the grass.

dodde *vi* 1 get entangled; **tol ododde woko,** the rope is entangled. 2 growing on top of another; **lakke ododde,** his tooth has grown on top of another.

doddo *vt* 1 tying; **doddo dyel ki ogwil,** tying the goats with a long rope for grazing; see **lwoddo, lwobbo, koddo, dwoddo.**

doddo *vt* piling on top; **doddo buk i wii wadigi,** piling the books on top of the others; 3 crossing; **doddo tyen,** crossing the legs.

dog *n.* mouth, opening, beak, brim, language etc. 1 **dog winyo,** a bird's beak. 2 **dog buŋa,** the beginning of the forest. 3 **dog agulu,** the brim of a pot. 4 **dog Lwo,** the Lwo language. 5 **dog poto,** the beginning of the field. 6 **dog kulo,** the bank of the river 7 **dog lum,** the beginning of the grass. **dog rwot,** message from the chief or his command. 9 **dog cel,** the gate of a fence.

dogaryo *n* a slow-worm; c/f **obwol mon.**

dogge *prn* his lips, mouth, words; **dogge olabbe,** his lips are turned outwards; **dogge bit, or dogge kec** (a) his mouth is pointed like that of shrew mouse or (b) he has a sharp and foul tongue; **dogge odut,** his lips are red (as if inflamed); *vt* **dogge oonyo bur,** there is an eruption of rashes around his lips; **dogge cele, or dogge kec,** food does not taste nice to him, in other words, he has lost appetite; **dogge lim,** he has a good appetite, eats very well; **dogge dwoŋ,** he talks too much; **dogge pek,** he is slow in speaking, dull; **dogge mit,** speaks freely and sometimes not correctly; **dogge okatto or oceer,** slip of the tongue; **dogge aryo,** a traitor, informer, double-dealer / double-speaker; **dogge mit ka cam,** he has a good appetite.

dogi *n* poorly developed, eg seeds, **dogi pul, dogi ŋor / muraŋa,** poorly developed groundnuts, cowpeas, or beans.

dogo *n* the bark of a tree. **boŋo dogo** bark cloth.

doggola *n* a door an opening.

dok or doki *adv* else, again; **otimmo aŋŋoo doki ?** what else did he do?

dok *v* 1 return; **dok tuggi awene?** when will he return to their home? 2. following a road, direction, *vt* **odok tuŋ poto ceŋ,** he went towards the west; **odok tuŋkwene?** which direction did he take? *vn* **dok gaŋ nono pe ber,** returning home with nothing without anything is not good; **dok i lokke awene**? when will he reply?

dokke *vn* busying oneself constantly with trifles and losing time; **ladokke** *n* one who is always bustling about and never makes progress; see **galle, dike, ŋinynye, nywenne, myenne.**

dokko *vt* 1 going round from place to place; **tic mewu me dokko dog duka keken?** is your work going round from shop to shop only? 2 going round idly; **dokko piny,** roaming about idly; 3 delaying; **odokka nono,** he delayed me for nothing.

dokko *vn* to become; **ka gilwokko ki cabun ci dokko tar,** if washed with soap it will become white.

dol *v* roll; **dol mukeka woko,** roll up the palm mat.

dollo *vt* making a border, edge, brim; **dollo dog agulu,** moulding the mouth of the pot; **dollo dog boŋo, aduku,** making the edge of the cloth / brim of a basket.

dollo *vt* rolling up; **dollo mukeka,** rolling up the mat; **dollo otac,** weaving a circular head pad; **dollo ciŋ,** clenching the hand; **dollo tyen,** drawing in or pulling in the legs.

dolo *n* colobus monkey

doŋ *cnj* then, after *adv* now, after all; **otyekko cam ka doŋ obinno,** he finished eating then he came; **ci doŋ otimmo ŋoo i kare ma en doŋ odwoggo?** what did he do after he had returned?

doŋ *vn* remaining behind, be left over; **ŋati mo pe ma mitto doŋ cen,** no one / nobody wants to remain behind.

doŋ *v* box; **doŋ lemme,** box his cheek.

doŋŋe *vn* boxing; **doŋŋe en aye tukko ma mitto tek cwiny,** boxing requires determination, stamina and bravery.

doŋŋo *vt* 1 striking with the hand; **doŋŋo bul,** beating the drum with the hand. 2 **doŋŋo nyim,** striking one's private parts for cursing severely; it is a tradition among the Acholi that if a woman wants to curse a person, she strikes her private parts when cursing; 3 to box; **odoŋŋo lem lawotte marac mada,** he boxed his friends cheek very hard.

doŋŋo. *vt* to sound / sounding; **doŋŋo oduru,** to sound / sounding the alarm, or uttering a sound of joy.

doŋŋo *vi* to grow / growing up, becoming big; **doŋŋo maber,** to grow / growing up well.

dony *v* enter; **dony i ot,** enter the house.

dony *vi* surrender; **lumeroko myero koŋ gudony,** the enemy must first surrender.

donynyo *vt* to enter / entering; **donynyo i ot,** entering the house. starting a proper home together after marriage; **nyako doŋ donynyo i odde awene?** when will the girl join her husband to start a home?

donynyo *vt* to understand; **ka i ketto cwinynyi i gin ma gititti ci lokke donynyo i itti,** if you listen carefully to what you are being told, you will understand.

donynyo *vn* to surrender / surrendering; **donynyo pa jo ma gujemo bot gabumenti obeddo laworo,** the surrender of the rebels to the government took place yesterday.

doo *n* weeds; **doo tye i poto madwoŋ,** there are plenty of weeds in the field.

doo n weed; **doo poto man maleŋ,** weed this field very well; see **doc, doyo.**

dor *v* drill; **dor litino ma guryeyo i tyeŋ caa,** drill those children who are lined up there.

dorre *vn* drilling, marching; *v* **citto ka dorre,** go for drilling / marching.

dorro *vt* drilling, marching; **ŋa amatye ka dorro litino?** who is drilling the children?

dot *vi* 1 suck; **latin tye ka dot,** the child is sucking. 2 suckle; **mon myero gudot litinogi,** women must suckle their babies.

dot *v* kiss; **dot lem cwarri / lem latinni,** kiss your husband / your child's cheek; see **not.**

dot *v* accuse, **dot lamoneni keken,** accuse only your enemy.

dotto *vi* 1 sucking; **latin tye ka dotto minne,** the child is sucking his mother's breast. 2 suckling; **min latin tye ka dotto latinne,** the mother is suckling her child.

dotto *vi* to kiss; **min latin dotto lem latinne ka ketto ka butto piny,** the mother kisses her child's cheek and then lays her down to sleep; see **notto**

dotto *vi* accusing; **dotto dano,** accusing the people.

dotto *vt* betraying; **dotto dano i kom gin ma gulokko kacel,** betraying the people on what they discussed together.

doyo *vt* to weed; **gucitto ka doyo doo,** they went to weed; see **doo, doc.**

ducu *adj* all, the whole, e.g. **dano ducu,** all the people.

dud *n* posterior, back, buttocks.

dugu *n* swelling; **dugu kom** 1 small swellings on the body caused by insect bites. 2 skin diseases of various causes, infections, allergic reaction to some foreign proteins or chemicals.

duka *S n* merchant shop.

dul *v* coarce; **dul latin wek otuc lokke,** coarce the child to reveal the case.

dul *v* 1 stuff, push a lot; **dul cam madit i doggi,** stuff your mouth with food;

2 plug; **dul pamba i umme,** plug his nose with cotton wool.

dul *n* club, cudgel; 1 **dul yat,** a piece of wood; 2 **dul mac** *n* pieces of wood leftover from a fire. 3 **dul ladin kaal,** a club for threshing millet (*eleusine*). 4 **dul laten wic;** wooden pillow. 5 **dul dano mogo gucitto Gulu,** a group of people went to Gulu. 6 **dul buk mukwoŋo,** first volume of the book.

dula *n* a kind of granary made of mud for storing simsim etc.

dullo cam *vt* to push a large amount (of food into one's mouth); **latin man dullo mugati madwoŋ mada i dogge, koni gwok bideye,** the child pushes too much bread into his mouth, it might choke him.

dullu (ŋwiny) *vt* turning one's buttocks very prominently backward when lying down.

dum *vn* 1 interpretation, foreign language; **dummo lok,** speaking a foreign language, interpreting, 2 **dum Patiko,** the metaphorical, ambiguous language used by the Patiko 3. **odumma dum,** he deceived me / used ambiguous words. **ladum,** an interpreter.

dume *n* a kind of sorghum which grows quite tall and has whitish seeds.

dummu *vt* cutting a large piece; **dummu riŋo,** cutting a large piece of meat.

duŋ *v* load with many words or frighten with too much talk; **duŋ latin ki lok matek ci bitucco gin ma otimme,** frighten the child by talking a lot to him and he will reveal what has happened; see **diŋŋo.**

duŋŋo *vi* to load with many words; **oduŋŋo dano matek ni o ka gumeddo ki yee,** he loaded them with many words until they all agreed.

duny *v* blow; **duny yito i ot wek oryam obee woko,** blow the smoke into the house in order to chase away the mosquitoes.

duny *v* wipe, clean; **duny apwa woko ki wii meja,** wipe dust off the top of the table.

duny *vi* rise, fly; 1 **apwa duny ni luu,** dust rises up alike a cloud 2 **ŋwen duny ki i bye,** the termites rise out of the anthill and fly out 3 **pii malyet tye ka duny yito,** the steam is rising out of the hot water 4 **lapwopwo, ki kic gitye ka duny,** swarms of butterflies and bees are flying around.

duny *vi* smells; **ŋwec camme tye ka duny ma mit mada,** the food is smelling very nice.

dunynyu *vt* smoking, causing to rise; **dunynyu yito i boŋ,** smoking the beehive; **dunynyu apwa kom dano,** smothering people with dust / blowing the dust on people; **tye ka dunynyu taa,** he is smoking

dunynyu *vt* to wipe / wiping dry, to clean / cleaning; **dunynyu pii ki i wic,** to mop / mopping water on the head; **dunynyu kwok ki i waŋ,** to wipe / wiping perspiration from the face.

dur *n* 1 stinginess. **ladur** one who does not want to spend any money at all, a miser.

dur *v* heap; **dur yugi i bur caa,** heap the rubbish in that pit.

dura *n* a piece of cloth which the youths or young men used to wrap around their waist as a loin dress.

Dure *n* the name of an individual mentioned in **ododo** and in some songs; a person who always wants. to be with the mother even when she is cooking.

durre *vi* collected together, gathered together, assembled; **apwa doŋ odurre wii meja mada,** too much dust has collected on top of the table; **dano gudurre mada ka nenno tuko,** very many people have assembled to watch the sport.

durro *vt* to assemble in large numbers, collect in great quantity; **gudurro riŋo poŋ aduku,** they filled a basket with a large quantity of meat; **gudurro dano i bar odilo,** they collected a great number of people in the football field.

duru *vn* being pregnant (in animal). **dyaŋ man oduru,** this cow is in calf.

duru pii *n* silt or sand, found at the bottom of a pot of water after the clean water has been removed.

dwad *v* entangle; **dwad tyenne woko wekki opot piny,** entangle his leg to make him fall down; see **dwal.**

dwaddo *vt* entangling; **dwaddo tyen dano ka tukko odilo rac mada,** entangling the leg of a man in a game of football is very bad; see **dwallo.**

dwal *v* 1 entangle, this is spoken more frequently than **dwad; dwal tyenne wekki opotti,** entangle his leg to make him fall 2 confusion.

dwal *v n* confuse, confusion; **cit idwal tee lokke woko,** go and confuse the case; **en ladwal lok mada,** he is the one who always causes confusion, he is a confusing agent.

dwal *v* prepare or make; **dwal kwon me acamma,** prepare or make **kwon** for eating; see **myen.**

dwalla *n* 1 entanglement; **dwalla i tuko odilo pe ber,** entanglement in football is not good.

dwalla *n* confusion; **en ladwalla mada,** he is a confusing agent. / he is the one who always causes confusion.

dwalle *vn* stammering or stuttering; **tee lebbe odwalle woko,** he stammers / stutters.

dwallo *vt* entangling; **dwallo tyen i tuko odilo pe ber,** entangling of legs in football is not good.

dwallo *vt* to implicate; **en dwallo dano i piddo,** he implicates people in court cases; **odwallo Owor i lok me kwoo,** he implicated Owor in a case of theft.

dwallo *vt* confusing; **dwallo lok woko i piddo,** confusing his statements. **dwallo** *vi* 1 to prevent (not usually spoken), **lok ma gaŋ pudi odwallo woko,** the home affairs have so far prevented him; 2 preoccupied; **tic odwallo tyenne woko,** he is very much preoccupied with work.

dwallo *vt* preparing by stirring with a special wooden stick with one flattened end; **tye ka dwallo kwon me acamma,** he is preparing a small amount of **kwon** for eating; see **myenno.**

dwan *n* throat, voice, sound, 1 **dwanne lit,** he has a sore throat 2 **dwanne orwee,** he has a hoarse voice.

dwan *n* sound; **dwan burogi winynye kama bor,** the sound of the bugle is heard from far away.

dwany *v* retort sarcastically, confuse; **dwany lokke woko,** confuse the statement.

dwanya dwanya. *adv* wriggling, the way a snake moves; **twol wotto ni dwanya dwanya,** the snake moves by wriggling.

dwanynye *vi* twisting; **tye ka dwanynye ki arem,** it is writhing / convulsing with pain.

dwanynye *vn* twisting; **twol dwanynye ka tye ka riŋŋo,** a snake twists when moving fast **twol tye ka dwanynye ki arem,** the snake is writhing / convulsing with pain.

dwanynyo *vt* to retort ironically or sarcastically; to confuse the meaning of words intentionally, **nino ducu dwanynyo lok,** always retorts sarcastically to confuse the meaning of words.

dwanynyo *vt* 1 mixing; **dwanynyo akeyo ki nyim,** mixing the **akeyo** vegetable with simsim. 2 twisting; **dwanynyo tol,** twisting the rope.

dwar *n* hunting, hunt; this is where many people gather and go to hunt the animals in the jungles; **tye yoo mapol me dwar,** there are many ways of hunting animals; 1 **dwar arum,** this is where the animals are surrounded in jungle in two ways, i.e. either by men or by fire; 2 **dwar obwoo,** this is where the animals are partially surrounded by nets; c/f **cikko.**

dwarro *vt* 1 to hunt; **ludito gucitto ka dwarro lee,** the elders went to hunt animals. 2 seeking, searching for; **dwarro gin mo i ot,** searching or looking for something in the house (not spoken now).

dwatte *n* discharge from the vagina after coitus or sexual intercourse.

dwee *n* 1 moon, month; **por dwee** or **dwee opor ni pere,** first appearance

of the moon; **dwee odoko ogwec,** the moon in its last phase or quarter; **dwee oguddo kidi,** the moon is seen on the horizon; **latin dwee,** the last part of the moon; **muttu dwee,** darkness, i.e. during the period of absence of the moon; **lak dwee nyo derro dwee,** moonshine. 2 n menstruation; **dako tye ki dwee,** the woman is having menstruation; **dwee wirro wiye,** menstrual bleeding (is excessive and so it) is making her giddy. 3 months; **dwee tye apar wiye aryo i mwaka acel,** there are twelve moths in a year; **dwee ne gin ego: Januari, Pwebwari, Mac, Apiril, Meyi, Jun, Julai, Agucito, Ceptemba, Oktoba, Nobwemba, ka Decemba,** the months are as follows: January, February, March, April, May, June, July, August, September, October, November, and December.

dwee *adv* quietly at once; **gitugge i komme ci obeddo ni dwee,** he was shouted at and he sat down quietly at once.

dwelle *vi* climbing up; **odwelle wii ot malo kuno,** he climbed to the top of a house.

dweŋŋo *vt* 1 to speak fluently, entertainingly; **latin man dweŋŋo lok mada,** this child speaks fluently and

entertainingly; **tweŋŋo lok** is preferred; 2 **dweŋŋo wot,** walking or travelling very much.

dwerre *adv* irritability, fretfulness; **latin man ladwerre mada,** this child is very irritable / fretful; see **giŋŋi.**

dwet *vi* to water; **latin man tee waŋŋe doki dwet mada,** the eyes of this child waters very much; **nen waŋŋe ma odwet,** look at his eyes which are watering (abusive words)!

dwiny *v* crush; **dwiny ladeppe ki lwetti,** crush the flea with your nails.

dwinynyo *vt* crushing (between fingers); **dwinynyo kaal,** crushing the millet grain between the fingers (to see whether it is ripe for harvesting); see **ŋinynyo.**

dwir *vp* swift, fast, quick; **awobine dwir mada i ŋwec,** the boy can run very fast.

dwirro *n* swiftness, fastness; **dwirro ŋwec,** running very fast.

dwirro *vt* throwing very far; **dwirro toŋ,** throwing a spear very far.

dwoc *vn* driving, turning, twisting; **dwoc me motoka oloye,** he failed to drive the motor car; see **dwoo, dwoyo.**

dwod *v* pile things up on top of one another; **dwod candukke i wii lawotte,** put the box on top of the other; **dwod dyel i lyek,** tie the goat in a grazing area; see **dod, lwob, lwod.**

dwoddo *vt* tying, harnessing; **dwoddo dyel,** tying a goat with a long rope to allow it to graze; see **doddo, lwobbo, lwoddo,** but **dwoddo jami** means piling things on top of one another and **dodo** sometimes mean, two, for example, **obayo winyo ki laduk ci laduk ododdo / odwoddo winyo aryo,** he threw a short stick at the birds and two birds were hit and killed.

dwog 1 *v* 1 return, bring back; **dwog kalamme cen,** return the pen or bring back the pen. 2 **dwog cwinynyi i kom lok ma i wacco,** recosinder what you said

dwogge *vi* can be returned; **kalamme doŋ pe twerro dwogge,** the pen cannot be returned.

dwoggo *vt* returning, coming back; **en dwoggo paco awene?** when is he returning home?

dwok *v* return, take back; **dwok waarre cen,** return his shoes / take back his shoes.

dwokke *vi* 1 can be returned or restored or put back; **leb kalam ma owot twerro dwokke cen,** the nib of the pen which has come out can be put back / restored to its original position. 2 return to him; **dwokke kalamme cen,** return his pen to him.

dwokko *vt* replacing, returning, restoring; 1 **dwokko cen ki rwode,** returning to the owner 2 **dwokko iye cen,** calming down or forgiving. 3 **dwokko dog,** answering or replying 4 **dwokko wiye piny,** turning it's head upside down or preventing its growth.

dwokko *vt* doing again; **dwokko nyim / moko,** grinding simsim / flour again.

dwol *n* pen; **dwol dyaŋ,** a cattle pen, where cattle are tied to pegs at night.

dwolo *n* fat from the bone marrow; **dwolo moo ma ginoŋŋo i cogo,** fat which is found in the bone marrow.

dwon *v* feel bitter; **pe i dwon cwinynyi i kom latinni,** do not feel bitter against your child.

dwon *vi* dried up, drying up; **dwon pa it man okello can pii mada,** drying up of this water well has caused a serious water problem.

dwonno *vt* obtaining something by evaporating; **dwonno kado,** evaporating salt water to make salt; c/f **twonno.**

dwonno *vi* to make one feel bitter; **lokke dwonno cwinynye mada,** the matter makes him feel very bitter; see **tonno cwiny.**

dwoŋ *v* to knock or hit with the fingers; **dwoŋ doggola,** knock at the door.

dwoŋ *adj* big, large, plenty; **dyaŋi dwoŋ mada kany,** there are plenty of cattle here.

dwoŋo *adj* very large; **aduko dwoŋo,** a very large basket.

dwoŋŋo *vt* knocking, hitting with the fingers; **dwoŋŋo doggola,** knocking at the door; **dwoŋŋo wii latin,** knocking the child's head .

dwoo *v* turn, drive, twist; **dwoo motoka man,** drive this car; see **dwoc, dwoyo.**

dwor *v* coddle, pamper; **dwor cwarri,** coddle / pamper your husband.

dwor *vn* overindulgence, coddling, pampering.

dworro *vt* overindulging, spoiling, pampering by excusing from work, giving good treatment, food etc.; **dako dworro dog cwarre ki cam,** a wife pampers her husband with good food; **dworro wii latin,** spoiling the child by pampering; **dako man doki dworro cwarre twatwal,** this woman pampers her husband too much; see **kerro.**

dwoyo *vt* turning, driving, twisting 1 **dwoyo mutoka,** driving the car. 2 **cam**

man dwoyo cwinynya, this food gives me stomach-ache or colicky abdominal pain and makes me want to vomit; comes from **dwoo, dwoc.**

dyaba dyaba *adv* long, soft and swinging; **yatte ka gitiŋo ci beddi dyaba dyaba,** when the pole is carried it swings up and down.

dyac *adv* the sound made by sliding or slipping on wet ground.

dyacco *vt* grinding; **dyacco odii** grinding simsim peste.

dyak *adj* wet, moistened.

dyaka dyaka *adj* soft, viscous; **kwon gura obedo dyaka dyaka, kwon** made from cassava is viscous.

dyala dyala *adv* **ceno mon madoŋo bor obeddo dyala dyala,** the elderly women's loin dress is long and swings about.

dyaŋ *n* cattle, cow (pl. **dyaŋi**); cattle; **min dyaŋ** a cow; **twon dyaŋ**, a bull; **dyaŋ malur,** a sterile cow.

dyaŋ apwoyo *n* a red mid-sized centipedes; see **okolok.**

dye *n* middle; **dye tyen,** sole of foot; **dye wic,** top of the hand; **dye ot**, floor; **dye ciŋ,** palm of hand.

dyeb *n* diarrhoea (not commonly spoken now)

dyeba dyeba *adv* long and swinging up and down (like a pole when balanced on a shoulder).

dyebbo *vt* having diarrhoea; **dyebbo remo,** having dysentery (this is spoken by people close to Langi and the Langi); see **cado.**

dyed *v* balance; **dyed agulu i wii,** balance the pot on your head.

dyeddo *vt* balancing free on one's head (water pot etc).

dyeddo dyeddo *inj* words of encouragement to make baby stand.

dyel *n* a goat pl. **dyegi,** goats.

dyeny *v* 1 insist. 2 be angry; **Ojok tye ka dyeny ki lokkeni,** Ojok is still insisting on his words. 2 **lapwony odyeny i kom latin kwan,** the teacher was very angry with the pupil.

dyenynyo *vt* protruding, projecting, sprouting upwords; **tye ka dyenynyo dudde,** she is pushing back / protruding her buttocks. or back; see also **dullu dudde.**

dyer *v* although you also want it, leave it; **dyer cam ma odoŋ ki litino,** although you also want it, leave the leftover food for the children; **dyer lim ma kakari ki omeru,** although you also need the money, leave your share for your brother.

dyer *v* offer; **dyer lim me konynyo kanica,** offer some money to help the church.

dyerre *vr* 1 offering oneself to support some cause, pleading, defending; **Yecu odyerre me too pi bal mewa,** Jesus offered to die for our sins / transgressions. 2 in the middle; **tye i dyerre,** he is in the middle.

dyerro *vt* to leave something over, cede; **gudyerro riŋo ki litino,** they left the meat for the children; **dyerro boŋo ki lawotte,** offering the clothes to his friend.

E e

e *prn prf* he, she, it, **openynye ka emitto,** he asked him whether he likes it; here in **e - mitto, e-** stands for he; **lanyutte mapol egi: ecitto kwene?** where is he going?; **etimmo ŋoo?** what is he doing?; **eriŋŋo ŋoo?** what is he running from?; this is rarely spoken now unless the word is preceeded by **ka** as follows: **ka etimmo gin mo, or ka eriŋŋo gin mo,** if he had done something, or if he has run away from something; it is also spoken now as **ka en etimmo gin mo or ka en eriŋŋo gin mo,** if he had done something, or if he had run away from something.

-e *prn sff* him, it, to him, her, to her, to it; **ocelle ki lakidi;** he stoned him; **obolle buk**, he threw a book to him; **odwogge cen,** he returned to him; **omiine cabun**, he gave her a picece of soap; **ocwallo cati ki cwaarre,** she sent a shirt to her husband.

- e *poss. sff* his, her, its; **man jami meere,** this is his/her thing or, this thing is his or hers; **jamine gidwoggo tin,** his/her things were returned today.

ee boŋ wacce, no it cannot be expressed; the central Acholi says **ee pe wacce.**

ee do or **ee do ya** *adv* yes, certainly.

ee wu do ya, *adv* oh yes certainly, oh yes it is so.

eee *intj* of surprise **eee, wu, do ya,** expression of surprise.

e e e *intj* expression of surprise and disapproval.

e e e pe kitmeno, no no no not that way.

ego *prn dem pl* here; **gin ego,** here they are.

Ejipti *n Eng* Egypt; see **Misiri.**

ekcireyi *n Eng* x-ray; **ekcireyi en aye nyonyo ma gimakko kwede cal pa cogo,** an x-ray is the machine for photographing bones.

el *v* lift up, raise; **el dog candukke,** lift up the lid of the box.

elektriciti *n Eng* electricity, the study of electrons and protons and how they produce power, current to supply light, fire, energy etc.

ello *vt* lifting up; **ello wii jami,** lifting lid off something 2 **ello wic ki i wii kitanda,** raising the head from the bed. 3 Opening; **wuel jiri karatac tyeŋ abic, o**pen the Gospels page five; / turn to the Gospels page number five.

ello *vt* rebelling, feeling bad against; **ello wiye i kom ladit tic,** rebelling against the headman or being insurbodinate to his headman by using rude words and not obeying him.

em *n* thigh; **cogo em,** the thigh bone.

em *vt* carry, take; **en oem mere ki ŋut,** he took the neck.

en *prs* he, she, it; **en caa,** he is there; **en aye ma okwallo,** he is the one who stole.

en *adv* here, there; **an aen,** here I am; **en tye eno,** he is there.

enoba *intj* look here, pay attention, take care; **enoba labwor doŋ binno caa,** look out the lion is coming there / take care / be careful the lion is coming there; see **eroba.**

ento *cnj* 1 but; **an onoŋo amitto citto ento lim pee,** I wanted to go but there is no money. 2 as far as, as for, with reference to; **en la Uganda pien ginywalle kany ento en la Nigeria,** he is a Ugandan as far as his birth is concerned but he is a Nigerian.

enni *prn* this one; **en ni enni aye okwallo,** this is the one who stole.

er *vn* provoke, incite, instigate; **laer lokki aŋaa?** who provoked or instigated the trouble; **en laer lok,** he is the one who instigated trouble / quarrel.

ero ba *in* the same as **eno ba, ero ba, gwok tye ka binno piri,** take care the dog is coming for you.

erro *vt* provoking, causing, starting; **erro lok,** provoking or starting trouble; **erro ali,** starting enmity; **erro lweny,** causing or starting a fight or war.

ette *vi* daring, trying to do things which one obviously cannot do; **ette me riŋŋo ki leela kun pe ŋeyo;** daring to ride a bicycle while one does not know how to ride it.

eyo or **eyo do ya** *adv intj* yes, that is it, of course. It is also the best way to answer when one is called; **ka nyiŋŋi gilwoŋŋo ci in idok iye ni, eyo,** when your name is called, you answer **eyo.**

G g

gaa *n* goods, belongings, things; **lakur gaa,** a guardian of goods it is archaic (therefore not very much used)

gaa *vt* looking out of the corner of the eye; **en lagaa dano mada,** she always looks at people out of the corner of her eye; see **gac, gayo.**

gab *v* 1 suspend or hang; **gab boŋo kom yat eno,** hang / suspend the clothes from

the tree; 2 mend; **gab waŋ guniya ma oyecci,** mend the rent in the gunny bag; see **lyeer.**

gaba *adv* tall, long; **odoŋŋo ni gaba,** he grew up tall with long legs.

gabbo *vt* to suspend, hang 1 **obworo pyen gabbo obwoone i jaŋ yat,** the spider hangs or suspends its web from the branches of trees. 2 **tye ka gabbo waŋ boŋone,** he is mending his torn clothing roughly 3 **ocubbo ogabbo agabba,** he speared it superficially.

gabbe *vt* suspending, floating; **pol ogabbe malo,** clouds are floating in the sky; **toŋ ogwal ogabbe wii pii,** frogs' spawn is floating on the water.

gabument *n Eng* government; see **miri.**

gabuna *n Eng* governor.

gac *vn* looking at out of the corner of the eye, see **gaa, gayo.**

gad *v* to eat excessively; **in lagat / gad,** you are a glutton.

gaddo *vt* to eating excessively, **latinne gaddo cam twatwal calo tye ki kwidi iiye,** the child eats too much / excessively as though he has worms in his stomach.

gadi gadi *n* a carriage / coach / wheelbarrow for carrying things or people.

gagi *n* cowrie shells.

gak *v* 1 remain; **gak ki kuno pe doŋ dwoggi,** remain there, do not return; 2 remained behind, lost; **en pudi ogak woko kakonye,** he has just gone out to relieve himself; remain; **ŋadi doŋ ogak Paico,** so and so has remained behind at Paico.

gakko *vt* grinding coarsely, badly; **gakko ŋor me agurra,** grinding coarsely cowpeas for making into soup; **en gakko kal agakka,** he does not know how to grind millet, he grinds it badly.

gako gako *n* the turaco; see **go go.**

gal *v* entertain , delay; **gal wiigi pi tutuno,** entertain them for the time being; **en lagal dano,** he always delays people.

gala, *n*, white people, in the past white people were called **gala** while Nubians and Arabs were called **muno.**

galle *vi* delayng; **ogalle bot laremme,** he delayed at his friend's; **galle ballo tic,** delaying / coming late spoils work; see **dikke, dokke, minne, joŋŋe, etc.**

gallo *vt* delaying; 1 **gallo tic,** delaying work. 2 **gallo waŋ latwoo nyo latoo,** comforting or cheering a sick person or one who has lost a relative; 3 entertaining; **gallo wii welo ki tukko mogo,** entertaining the guests with some plays.

gam *v* receive, accept; **gam wello ka gubino,** recieve or welcome the guests when they arrive; **gam mot meri ene,** accept / receive your gift here; **bin igam giri,** come and take / receive what is yours; **gam buk en icikwan,** receive this book and go and read it.

gam *v* reply, answer; **gam lok ma acooni ni,** reply to what I wrote to you.

gama, *n* impetuosity, impulsiveness; **lok gama meeri ceŋ mo biterri i can;** your impetuous remark will one day get you into trouble; **tim gamani ceŋ mo biterri i can,** your impulsiveness will one day put you in trouble; see **abelu, apoya, gikom.**

gammo *vt* conceiving, being pregnant; **gammo ic;** conceiving, being pregnant; **dako doŋ ogammo,** the woman has conceived / is now pregnant.

gammo *vt* receiving, accepting; 1 **en gammo cam ki bot minne,** he gets / receives food from his mother 2 joining; **gammo lok pe ber,** joining in a conversation which one does not kunderstand is bad; **gammo wer,** joining in a song; 3 replying; **en ogammo ni ŋoo i kom lok ma gicoone?** what was his reply to what was written to him? **en onoŋo gammo ni ŋoo?** how was he responding?

gan *adj* marvel, wonder; **man gin me gan mada / gin aganna mada,** this is a thing of wonder / this is a wonderful thing.

ganno *vt* to marvel, to wonder; **oganno jami maca mape wacce,** he marvelled very much at those things.

gaŋ *n* home or village; **i kin gaŋ,** within the village; **ŋee gaŋ,** behind the village or privy; **ocitto ŋee gaŋ,** he went to ease himself into the bush; **Lagaŋ or Lugaŋ;** a nickname for Acholi used by Laŋi (*lit* means a home dweller).

gaŋŋo *vt* enclosing, fencing the home; **gaŋŋo dwol dyel ki okuto,** fencing the goat pen with thorns.

gaŋo *n* ancestral shrine which consists of some dried pieces of a special kind of wood planted in the ground upon which animal skulls are hung.

gaŋo *n* the last funeral ceremony for deceased person (concluding mourning time); **giputto gaŋo / gitimmo gaŋo,** the last funeral ceremony when shelters (**bolo**) which were constructed for the mourners are now removed; it is also the time when the heir to the deceased is declared.

ganya ganya *adv* badly done; **timmo ganya ganya,** doing it badly.

gar *v* look for; **gar kama libira tye iye,** look for the needle; 2 **gar kama palaa tye iye,** find out where the knife is (not normally spoken now).

gar *n S* train; **gar tye kakatto caa,** the train is passing over there.

gara *n* small ankle bells or rattles (usually for dancing or for encouraging children to walk).

gara *n* hen house made in the form of a large basket used for covering them at night; see **koro.**

gari *S n* bicycle; **tuŋ gari,** bicycle's handled bars; see **leela.**

garro *vt* seeking for, looking for, finding; 1 **tye ka garro libira ne i ot,** looking for his needle in the house. 2 **garro tee lok,** investigating the meaning of, seeking an explanation for.

garro *vt* spearing. **garro lee ki toŋ,** spearing an animal with a spear going through its body; **twoo ogarro korre woko,** the chest pain seems to have pierced through his chest.

gaya or **geya** *n* sorghum; **geya ber mada me koŋo,** sorghum is good for beer.

gayi *n* Bengal cane (used for beating).

gayi *n* a cow with long horns curving upwards, the Ankole type; see **laburyaŋa.**

gayo *vt* to look at someone out of the corner of the eyes, usually angrily; **igaya ki tee waŋŋi piŋoo?** why do you look at me out of the corner of your eyes? see **gaa, gac.**

gebbe *n* with all teeth still intact not with some already uprooted traditionally; **lakki ogebbe, y**our teeth is not yet uprooted; according to tradition, the two lower incisors are removed, something which was thought made lips look beautiful.

gec *vn* 1 insinuating, alluding to; **lok agec,** insinuating talk, alluding talk; **wer agec,** songs which are normally used for abusing someone; 2 vn wiping, cleaning; see **gee, geyo (geyo cet,** clearing away faeces).

gecco *vt* speaking insinuatingly, alluding to; **gecco ŋaa i lokke ni?** to whom is he alluding in his speech.

ged *v* build; **ged ot meri kany,** build your house here, but it is normally said: **ger ot merri kany,** build your house here; **ged nyuka ki litino,** prepare a lot of gruel for the children.

geddo *vt* 1 building, construction; **ka geddo maber ene,** here is a good place for building; **geddo nyuka,** making / preparing much porridge or gruel; 2 *n* **geddo gin matek mada,** building is a very difficult task .

gee *v* clean, remove; **gee cet,** clean the faeces; see **gec, geyo.**

gek *n* hiccough; **gek omakke,** he is having hiccoughs.

gek *n* gecko (a kind of lizard which normally lives in the house), some people call it **laromo ot.**

gek *adv* 2 suddenly; **ocom i komme ni gek,** he met him suddenly.

gem *vi* caught up in something, entangled in something; **odilo ogem woko i wii yat,** the football got caught up in the branchs of a tree.

gem *n* greed, miserliness, avarice, stinginess; **gem pe miyi lonyo,** greediness or stinginess does not make you rich; **gem geŋogi binno ka cam kacel ki dano,** greediness prevents them from coming to share food with other people.

gemo *n* an infectious or contagious disease such as **odyer** (small pox), **kampuli,** (plague); **anyoo** (measles) and other epidemic diseases; **twoo gemo omakko woko,** he is infected with one of the infectious diseases. In the past, it was believed that those diseases were in the form of ghosts which would come and fall on some unfortunate people, hence the word **twoo gemo omakko woko** which literally means, he has been caught or arrested by the disease **gemo.**

gemmo *vt* to take up a large quantity; **ka gicwallo ka ommo cukari ci gemmo madwoŋ mada,** when he is sent to get the sugar he takes a large amount.

gen *v* trust, confide in, have hope in; **gen lawotti,** trust your friend.

gen *n* trust; **gen gin maber mada,** trust is a very good thing.

genno *vt* trusting, confiding in, hoping in; **gennoni limme en aye bilarre,** trusting that his money will save him; **gennoni en pe twerro bwolle,** trusts that he will not deceive him / trusting that he will not be deceived; **gennoni bidwogo diki,** hoping that he will come tomorrow; .**gennoni pe ibititto ki ŋati mo gin ma otitti,** trusting that you will not tell anybody what he confided to you.

geŋ *v* 1 prevent, hinder, prohibit, stop; **geŋ litino pe gubed ka tukko i ot,** prevent the children from playing in the house; 2 **geŋ dano pe guwok ki kany,** stop the people from passing here.

geŋ *vn* strongly or powerfully built; **kor labwor ogeŋ,** a lion's chest is strongly built.

geŋ *n* wasting; **geŋ dyel,** meat from a wasted or sickly goat.

geŋŋe *vi* prevented, stopped; **litino man gudiŋ pe gitwerro geŋŋe me binno ka tukko i bar odilo,** these children are stubborn, they cannot be prevented from coming to play in the football field.

geŋŋo *vt* preventing, hindering, prohibiting; **geŋŋo litino citto ka legga pe ber,** preventing the children from going for prayers is not good; **geŋŋo citto gaŋ,** preventing from going home.

geŋŋo *vt* protecting, assisting; **geŋŋo ŋee Otto,** assisting Otto in extricating himself / protecting Otto.

ger *adv* ferocious, cruel, fierce; **labwor ger mada,** the lion is very ferocious; **dano ma ger,** a cruel person; **labwor ma ger mada,** a very fierce lion.

ger *vi* 1 sexual intercourse; **gimakkogi ka ger,** they were caught having sex.

ger *n* marriage, union; **ger pa Opio gi pe ber,** the marriage of Opio and his wife is not good.

ger *v* 1 dig; **ger dyekal maleŋ,** dig and clean the compound properly; 2 build; **ger oddi,** build your house here /build houses here.

gerre *vi* sexual intercourse; **gimakkogi ka gerre,** they were caught having sexual intercourse.

gerre *adj* bow-legged; **tyenne ogerre,** he is bow legged; **gerre-pa tyenne geŋŋe nyonno leela,** his being bow-legged prevent him from riding bicycles.

gerro *n* ferocity, cruelty, rage; **gerro pa Ongom oryammo dano woko ki kaŋette,** Ongom's rage / cruelty has chased people away from him.

gerro *vt* clearing away the surrounding grass by digging; **gerro dyekal,** clearing away the grass from the compound; 2 building; **gerro ot,** building a house.

gerro *vt* marrying; **gerro dako,** marrying a woman ((but it also means having sexual intercourse with a woman).

get *v* stand in the way; **get woko i doggola wek pe gukatti,** stand in the doorway so that they may not pass.

getto *vt* to stick fast in a narrow way or space or passage; **canduk ogetto woko i doggola,** the box is stuck in the door and cannot be removed; **getto i tic,** sticking to the job; **getto i wii yat,** sticking up the tree.

geya *n* sorghum; **geya amida,** a sweet type of sorghum which can be eaten unground and raw; **geya lawera,** a white type of sorghum; *c/f* **dura.**

geyo *vt* wiping, cleaning; **geyo kwok ki i waŋ,** wiping perspiration from the face; see **gec, gee.**

gi *prs prn prf* they; '**gitye ka tic,** they are working; **gitye ka cam,** they are eating.

-gi *pro prs poss sff* them, to them, theirs; **omiyogi cam,** he gave them food; **man jamigi,** this is their goods; **ocwallogi waraga,** he posted letters to them.

gi *prn/n/vn* sometimes exchanged with -**ki-** eg when it is *prf* to a *verb* as in **gikello,** it was brought, some call it **kikello**. The central Acholi prefer

gikello but when it is *prf* to a noun such as **gicaa,** a bag , **kicaa** is preferred by the central Acholi people; read about it in the introduction.

gicere *n* a small gourd bottle in which oil is kept for use on children; **kicere** is however preferred; see **adomo,** another name for it.

gici gici or **kici kici** *adv* the sound which rain makes when it is falling; **kot cwer ni gicigici / kici kici,** the rain falls **gici gici / kici kici.**

gicika, usually **kicika** *n* a wall separating two rooms in a house.

gicol *adj* black; **dyaŋ gicol,** black cattle.

gicu *n* the spinal cord, the brain substance which runs down from the brain to the second lumber vertebra.

gid *v* tickle; **gid but latin,** tickle the flank of the child; see **giny.**

gid *vn* tickling; **litino gimarro gid mada,** children like very much to be tickled.

gidii? *v* how many times? **gicel,** once; **giryo,** twice.

gidiŋ gidiŋ *n* a small bird with a red tail (thrush, wheat eater); other Acholi prefer to call it **kidiŋ kidiŋ.**

giddo *vt* tickling; **tye ka giddo latin,** he is tickling the child; see **ginynyo.**

gigi *prs prn* theirs; **man gigi meegi,** these are theirs; **gigi tye kany,** their goods are here.

gikebe *s n* a small tin box ; the word which is now more commonly used is **kikebe.**

gigu *n* things; **gigu ducu** everything.

gik *v* stop, short, end; **gik tic pa awobi ni,** stop the work of the boy;

vi **ocitto i Rome ci ogik iye pe doŋ omedde ki wotte,** he wnt to to Rome and stopped there, he did not continue with his journey.

gikko *vt* ending, putting an end to; stopping; **gikko tic diki,** stopping / ending work tomorrow; **gikko tic mere ocakke laworo,** ending of his work started yesterday.

gikoba or **kikoba,** *n* a patch or piece of cloth used for mending a garment.

gikun or **kikun,** *n* fowl flea or bug; others call it **gikuny** or **kikuny.**

giliri, ogwaŋ giliri n civet cat; see **kworo, too, and bura.**

gin *prs prn* they; **gin eno ,** there they are.

gin *n* things; **gin cam,** things for eating; **gin alaka / gin aleya** things to be inherited; **gin anenna,** flowers or works of art, nice things meant to be looked at.

ginne *inj* the thing; this is said when one is trying to find what to say.

giŋ *adv* tightly, firmly; **twee matek li giŋ,** tie it firmly / tightly.

giŋŋi *n* peevishness, petulance; **latin man doki lagiŋŋi twatwal,** this child is very peevish or petulant; see **dwere.**

giŋŋi *n* grudge, rancour; **ketto giŋŋi i kome,** having a grudge against him.

giny *v* 1 tickle; **giny tee ywat latin,** tickle the child's armpit. 2 rubbing hard; **giny ŋeye kama yil,** rub hard the back where it is itching; **litino gimarro giny mada,** children like tickling very much; see **gid.**

ginynye *vi* being tickled; **litino gimarro ginynye mada,** the children like to be tickled very much.

ginynyo *vt* 1 irritating; **aburo ginynyo umme,** the cold in the head is irritating his nose.

ginynyo *vt* 1 stimulate, excite; **bul myel man ginynyo kom mada,** the sound of this dance drum stimulates / excites very much the body; 2 rubbing, scratching; **ginynyo kama yil,** scratching where it itches; see **giddo.**

gipiny *n* things, belongings; **kella gipinynya kany,** bring all my belongings here.

gipwola *n* normally **kipwola** is used; misfortune, mishap, calamity, atrocity; see **kipwola.**

git *v* peel or tear off; **git tyaŋ eno ka wek inyam,** peel off the hard part of the sugarcane and then chew it.

gitaŋa *prd* (**kitaŋa** is preferred) speckle; **komme obeddo kitaŋa,** the body is speckled; see **kitaŋa.**

gitara *n* **kitara** is preferred; stretcher, litter; see **kitara.**

gitele *n* **kitele** is preferred / kind of a tree with a long straight stem for making door shutters or granaries; it is used also for making arrows or arrow shafts; see **kitele.**

gitem tem *adv* slightly better; others say **kitem tem;** see **gitwora twora.**

gitoga *n* a kind of grass used for making granaries.

gitogo *n* placenta, after birth; see **byero , pel.**

gituti *n* (**kituti** is preferred a raised) place for lying down.

gitworra tworra *adj.* slightly better, better than; others say **kitworra tworra;** see **gitem tem.**

giwic or **gin wic** *n* a hat, headgear, head cover; **gin wicca tye kwene?** where is my hat? see **otaŋ, tok wiya.**

gob *v* scrape; **gob cet gweno iciony i bur,** scrape the chicken droppings and pour them into a pit

goba *n* lie; **lagoba,** a liar; **in doki lagoba twatwal,** you are a great liar. .

gobbo *vt* scraping, rasping, planing or grating; tilling , cultivating; **gobbo kor ot ma latuk opoŋ iye tek mada,** scraping the wall of a house which is covered with soot is very difficult; **gobbo bao,** planing / rasping wood; **wacito ka gobbo ŋom,** we went to till / cultivate / dig; see **cwerro.**

goc *vn* beating, striking; **goc matek i kom litino pe ber,** beating the children severely is not good; see **goo, goyo.**

gocogoco or **kocokoco** *n* a type of bird.

goga *n* a temporary small hut built with grass only used as a barn or granary though sometimes people sleep in it; **lapena tye i goga,** the pigeon peas are in the barn.

goga *n* concert, jest, joke, comedy; **en lagoga mada,** he is a great jester / comedian / joker.

gogo *n* turaco. Sometimes called **gakogako.**

gogo *adv* hanging all around; **muyembe onyak ni gogo,** the mangoes are fully ripe and hanging all around; **olik gulyerre ni gogo i wii yat caa,** the bats are hanging all over the trees over there.

gogo *n* **cel gogo,** a fence made of big dried logs, a stockade.

gok, gok kor *n* brisket the breast of animal with ribs cut crosswise.

gol *v* remove, clear; **gol waŋ otul man wek omol maber,** clear the channel so that it may run well; **gol waŋ it maleŋ,** dig and clean up the water well.

gol *v* hook the hands together; **gol ciŋwu,** hook your hands together

gola *n* snake; **twol gola,** cobra 2 double, informer, turncoat; **danone twol gola,** he is an informer / a double

goli *n* a fish hook.

gollo *vt* digging, hollowing, burrowing, scratching; **gollo i dul yat madit,** hollowing out a big log of wood; in other words, making the log of wood into a small canoe; **gollo / gullo i kwon;** shaping a morsel of **kwon** like a spoon; **gweno gollo ŋom,** the hen scratches the ground; **oyoo gollo odde,** the rat burrows the hole in the ground.

gollo *vt* inquiry, investigation; **gollo lok / gollo lok ki ii dano,** drawing out words or statements out of people by investigation or enquiry.

gollo *adj* sunken; **waŋŋi ogollo,** your eyes are sunken (abusive words); **gollo** *vt* hooking; **gollo ciŋ,** hooking hands.

gom *v* bend; **gom nyonyo man,** bend this metal rod; **coo atir ma pe ogom,** draw it straight, without a curve.

gomeci *n Eng* a woman's long dress which is made with up-raised sleeves, the Baganda women's traditional dress; the name was derived from that of a Goan Gomes, who used to make the clothes for women; at the beginning the dress was named **kinagayaza,** after the place where it was first designed and made, i.e Gayaza High School; now the name is **busuti,** meaning a woman's suit.

gomme *vi* can be easily bent, bending easily; **ciline twerro gomme,** the wire can be bent.

gommo *vi* yearning or craving for something; **gommo me beddo ki leela,** yearning very much of having a bicycle, not commonly spoken; see **parro.**

gommo *vt* bending, curving; **gommo yat me odoo,** bending a piece of wood into a stick cane.

gon *v* change direction; **gon wii leela odok tuŋ lacam,** turn the bicycle to the left.

gon wii *adv.* full of; **bonyo ogon wii yat caa,** that tree is full of locust.

gonno *vn* changing direction, turning aside; **gonno yoo,** walking in a zigzag way; **gonno wii leela,** turning the bicycle into another road.

goŋ *n* partially shut; **goŋ doggolane woko,** partially shut the door.

goŋ *adj* wasted and thin; **lacoone obeddo ni goŋ,** the man is wasted and thin.

goŋ goŋ *n* ants which eat honey and sugar.

goŋŋo *vt* partially shutting 1 **goŋŋo doggola,** partially shutting the door. 2 concealing or hiding part of; **goŋŋo lok,** concealing / hiding part of the information.

goŋŋo *vt* to deform; **nyac ogoŋŋo badde woko,** yaws has deformed / caused bowing of his arm.

goŋo *n* spine 1 **goŋo ŋee nyaŋ gwa,** the spine of the crocodile is rough. 2 **goŋo kor,** sternum; **goŋo owoo,** the stalk of a borassus palm leaf 3 **goŋo awal,** a big calabash bowl.

goŋoŋwee *n* the praying mantis.

gony *n* a resting place, lodge; **ot gony,** a rest house, inn, lodge; *vt* **welo tin gugony kwene?** where have the visitors lodged today?

gony *v* untie, release; **gony dyel woko,** untie the goats and leave them free; **gony jo ma gimakkogi woko,** release all those who have been arrested.

gonynye *vi* released, delivered; **dako ogonynye nyako,** the woman has delivered a girl; **gonynye pa mabuc tye ki bot gabuna,** the release of the prisoners depends upon the governor.

gonynyo *vt* to take accommodation, lodge, camp; **welo tin ogonynyo botato** guests have lodged in my house.

gonynyo *vt* 1 untying, releasing, relaxing; **gonynyo pii,** opening of the water tap; **Okot doŋ gigonynyo woko ki i jero,** Okot has been released from jail; **pii ma lyet gonynyo kom dano ka i lwokke kwede,** hot water relaxes the body when you bathe with it.

goo *v* beat; **goo gwok wek oriŋ woko,** beat the dog so as to make it run away; see **goc, goyo, goone.**

goone *vi* beating one another; **joone tin gugoone mada,** today they beat one another severely, in other words, they fought one anothetr with sticks.

gor *n* the ground squirrel; the central Acholi call it **ayita** which is still spelt as **aita** by some other people.

gor *vt* decorate by cutting; **gor awal man maber,** decorate this gourd plate properly.

goro *vn* feeble, disabled, crippled, ill; **lagoro,** a weak, disabled person, an invalid; **dyelle goro,** a weak sickly goat.

goro *n* a poultry pen. It is normally called **koro,** which name which is preferred; see **gara.**

goro-goro *n* a large and old very ferocious leopard.

goroto *n* a plant with good fibre, with leaves sometimes used as a vegetable.

gorre *vi* can be decorated; **kom awal man twerro gorre maber mada,** the back of this calabash plate can be very well decorated, **gorre kama dano cammo iye,** walking around where people are eating (expecting to be called to eat).

gorro *vt* making superficial incisions, scarifying, making superficial cuts; 1 **gorro awal maber,** decorating the calabash bowl very nicely by carefully making small cuts 2 **gorro ŋee agulo,** making ornamental cuts on a wet earthen pot before it is dried and fired 3 **gorro wii pal gwok,** making cuts on the shoulders (usually as evidence of bravery in killing either a man or a wild beast).

got *n* a stone, rock, mountain (rocky); **pyer got,** the lower flank of the mountain; **tee got,** the foot of the mountain; **kor got,** the higher flank of the mountain; **wii got,** tthe top of the mountain.

gotogoto *adv* staggering; **wotto ni gotogoto,** walks on long legs with a staggering gait.

goyo *vt* striking, beating; 1 **goyo wii dakone lero,** striking his wife's head and causing bleeding; 2 **goyo bul,** beating the drum; 3 **goyo olaŋ,** ringing the bell 4 **lutkot ogoyo dano,** people

have been struck by lightning; see **goo, goone, goc.**

goyo *vt* constructing; 1 **goyo cel,** making a fence 2 **goyo dero,** constructing a granary; 3 **goyo cal,** drawing pictures.

goyo *vi* delivering; **goyo rut,** giving birth to twins.

goyo *vt* sounding, making sound; 1 **goyo kijira,** making of ululations by women 2 **goyo oduro wuk wuk,** sounding alarm of danger from a fierce animal or enemy.

goyo *vt* to acuse; **goyo oduro bot rwot,** accusing a person to the chief / bringing an action against a person before the chief.

goyo *vt* blessing; 1 **goyo laa / olwedo,** blessing an action; 2 **goyo taŋa i wii lee i nyim abila,** sprinkling of water mixed with flour on the head of a game animal or beast in front of the shrine, in other words blessing the action of killing the animals.

Grik *n Gr* Greek; **Grik yaŋ guloyo lobo madwoŋ mada,** a long time ago the Greeks ruled many countries.

gub *v* sip, drink little by little; **gub cai ne agubba,** take the tea a little at a time.

gubbe *vi* can be sipped, taken little by little; **nyukane pe lyet twatwal twerro gubbe,** the gruel is not too hot, it can be taken little by little.

gubbo *vt* sipping; **gubbo cak,** sipping the milk or taking it little by little.

guc *v* throw, hurl or fling; **guc odoone kany,** throw the stick here.

guci *n* a slave, a person captured during war; see **opii, aŋeca, jane** and **lamiru.**

guccu or **gucco** *vt* hurling, flinging at, throwing. 1 **guccu dyegi ki odoo,**

throwing or flinging a stick at the goats 2 **gucco ŋwec,** running very fast.

gud *v* touch, feel; **gud boŋone ki ciŋŋi ka wek iniaŋ berre,** touch / feel the cloth/garment with your fingers in order to appreciate its quality.

gudo *n* road; **dano pe marro gerro odigi i ŋet gudo,** people do not like building their homes near the road; **gudo opoŋ ki pony pony keken,** the road is full of potholes.

gudde *vi* touched; **twerro gudde,** can be touched; **tuko gudde** a game of touching one another.

guddo *vt* touching; 1 **guddo toŋ waŋ ki ciŋ pe ber,** touching the eyeball with the finger is not good; 2 **guddo jami ki ciŋ ka wek i niaŋ berre,** touching / feeling things with the fingers so as to appreciate their qualities.

guddo *vt* to affect, disturb; **lokke oguddo cwinynye marac mada,** the matter disturbed him / affected him very badly.

guk *vi* unsteadiness; **laguk tic aguka,** unsteady in any work.

gukku *vt* unsteady, undecided, unsettled; **gukko tic,** starting work and soon leaving it; and then starting again and leaving it not steady for any work.

gul *n* recess, nook; **gul ot, gul kulo,** corner of a room or the house; the corner of a river, bay.

gul *v* dent; **gul kwon ki ciŋŋi,** dent the **kwon** with your fingers.

gulle *vi* can be dented; **ruc pe twerro gulle macalo kwon me gweyo dek,** rice cannot be dented like **kwon** for scooping the sauce.

gullo *vn* to germinate, sprout by raising the earth covering it **pul ki muraŋa**

doŋ gugullo, the groundnuts and the beans have sprouted 2 appearing; **lak latin doŋ ogullo,** the child's teeth have appeared / come out 3 **tuŋ dyaŋ ogullo,** the horn of the calf has protruded out; 4 **tuno ne ogullo,** her breasts have started forming.

gullo *vt* germinating **pul doŋ ogullo,** the groundnuts are now germinating.

gullo *vi* 1 protruding; **dudde ogullo,** his buttocks are protuberant 2 **korre ogullo,** he has a humpback or *kyphosis*.

gullo *vt* denting with the fingers; **gullo kwon me gweyo dek,** denting **kwon** with the fingers into a spoon with which to scoop the sauce.

Gulu *n* a town, the name Gulu came from the small river running under the forest situated half a kilometre west of the present town centre, to join river Oitino. This river had a small fall which people used to call **gulu gulu** because of the kind of noise that it makes. The Europeans came and shortened it to **gulu.**

gum *vn* blessing, good luck; **jo ma yee Lubaŋa gibimiinigi gum,** those who believe in God will be blessed; **gitye ki gum jo ducu ma mwol,** blessed are those who are meek; **komme gum mada motoka omitto yokkone woko,** he is very lucky the motor car nearly knocked him; **komme gum pien obeddo ŋat acel ma okatto peny,** he was lucky because he was one of those who passed the examinations.

gun *vn* crowding, weighing down; **gun pa lwak winyo i wii yat, onallo jaŋ yat piny,** the crowding of so many birds have weighed down the branches of the tree.

guna *n* a hollow (for keeping part of things aside for oneself); *prov* **lapok ciŋŋe guna,** a distributor has a hollow hand (in which things remain in its depth for himself).

gunia *n* sack; **gunia me piko pamba,** a sack into which cotton is put.

guŋ 1 *v* stoop down, kneel down or bow down; **guŋ piny ka i mitto legga,** kneel down if you want to pray.

guŋ *vn* doubtful, suspicious; **iye guŋ i kom lok meeri,** he is suspicious of your words.

guŋŋe *vn* bending down; **ka pyerri lit guŋŋe piny tek,** it is very hard to bend down when you have backache.

guŋŋo *vn* kneeling, bowing, stooping, bending down; **guŋŋo piny tek ki jo ma pyergi lit,** it is very hard kneeling or bending down for those who have backache.

guny *v* smoke; **guny yito,** smoke.

guny *vn* boiling, bubbling, simmering; 1 **pii tye ka guny i cupuria,** the water is boiling in the aluminium saucepan; 2 **guny pa koŋo nyutto ni koŋone doŋ ocek maber me amatta,** bubling of the beer shows that the beer is now mature enough for drinking.

gunya *n* chimpanzee; **gunya wotto nyonno piny ki ŋee ciŋŋe, ŋwinynye bene pe otal calo pa bim,** a chimpanzee walks on the back of its closed fists, it has also no callositis on its buttock; **gunya cal mada ki puno nyo kono tidi,** a chimpanzee looks very much like a gorilla except it is small; see **bim, gorilla.**

gunynye *vt* bubbling, rushing out; **pii ma lyet gunynye,** hot water bubbles while boiling; **waŋ it gunynye,** spring water bubbles or water keeps on coming out from underneath; **pii yenynyo gunynye,** boiling water bubbles, simmers; **pii gunynye i keno,** the water is boiling over the fire; **mac tye ka gunynye i wii cere caa,** the fire is burning fiercely on the hill over there.

gunynye *vi* serious, increased; **lokke ogunynye ki kwica matek mada,** he matter has become quite serious over there.

gunynyo *vn* exciting; **lok man gunynyo iye mada,** this matter is angering him or causing him indignation. 2 smoking; **gunynyo yito,** blowing out smoke, in other words, smoking.

gura *n* (another name **gwana,** which is preferred), cassava, tapioca.

guramma *n Eng* grammar; the study of rules of construction or combination of words into sentences and forms of words.

guru guru *adv* **ocek guru guru;** it is undercooked, therefore not soft.

Guruguru *A n* a mountain with caves situated 9 miles west of Gulu

gut *vn* to accumulate, collect, increased by swelling; 1 **tut ogut woko iiye,** the pus has failed to flow out and so there is a swelling 2 **lapene ogut caa,** over there is a person with a protruding navel (*umbilical hernia*).

gut *vn* hiding or remaining; **ogut woko i ot,** he is hiding or remaining in the house.

gutte *vn* hiding; **gutte i ot pe konynye,** hiding in the house does not help him.

guti *n* poles; **guti me gerro ot,** poles for building the hut.

guu *n* laterite, volcanic stone.

guur *n* Nile perch, a very large fish found in the River Nile.

guur *v* 1 assemble, gather; **guur yugi kacel,** collect the rubbish together; **guur litino i bar odilo,** assemble the children in the football field.

guur *v* fix, nail, hammer; **guur loc,** fix the peg in the ground upon which either the goats or cattle are tied; **guur mucumar man matek,** hammer this nail hard; **guur ki yat,** nail / pierce with a stick.

guurre *vi* assembling, coming together, meeting; **dano gugurre madwoŋ mada i bar odilo ka kwerro nino me Loc Ken,** people assembled in large numbers to celebrate the Independence Day; **tin pe gugurre kany,** they did not assemble here; *n* **gurre meegi pe okonynyo gin mo,** their assembling did not help / their coming together was useless.

guurro *vn* 1 rubbing; **guurro awal i wii lyel,** rubbing the calabash on the ground to make noise for the music at a funeral ceremony 2 mashing; **guurro dek ki ogwec,** mashing, usually cowpeas, with a stick which has one end shaped like a half moon; this half moon shaped end mashes the cowpeas into thick sauce 3 nailing; **guurro canduk,** nailing the box; 4 fixing; **guurro loc,** fixing a peg in the ground to which either goats or cattle are tied; 5 collecting or gathering; **guurro kakka kacel,** gathering the clan members together 6 collecting; **guurro yugi,** collecting rubbish or garbage.

guurro *vt* smashing , mashing, crushing; **dek ŋor giguurro ki ogwec,** cowpea sauce is made by mashing it with a pestle.

gwaa *adj* coarse, uneven, rough; **wii meja ne gwaa,** the top of the table is rough (not properly sand papered) 2 **dano ma komme gwaa,** a man with a rough skin; **gwaa kom a pi tic ki cabun marac,** roughness of the skin comes as a result of using bad soaps 3 **dano ne gwaa,** the man is rough and fierce.

gwaa *v* smear or plaster; **gwaa kor ot ki opuyo,** plaster the wall of the house with clay; see **gwac, gwayo.**

gwac *vn* smearing or plastering; see **gwaa, gwayo.**

gwad *v* remove with the hand; **gwad lobo woko ki i waŋ it,** remove the mud from the well.

gwadde *vi* removed; **daba ma opoŋŋo waŋ it twerro gwadde,** the mud that has filled up the water well can be removed.

gwaddo *vt* getting out or removing with the fingers, usually mud; **gwaddo lobo ki i waŋ it wek pii omol,** removing the mud from the spring well with fingers so as to make it flow; **gwaddo um, gollo um,** scratching the nostrils or picking the nose.

gwak *v* embrace, hold; **cit i gwak korre,** go and embrace him; **gwak latin ene,** here, hold the child.

gwakke *vi* 1 folding arms across the front of the body at the waist; **iparro ŋoo ma omiyo igwakke kitmeno?** what is worrying you that is making you fold your arms? 2 embracing one another; **gwakke pe rac,** embracing one another is not bad (but it could also mean folding the arms across the front of the body is not bad).

gwakko *vt* embracing, clasping; **gwakko kor,** embracing, folding arms around the chest; **gwakko wic,** clasping the head.

gwana *n* cassava, tapioca; qv **gura.**

gwana gwana *prd* long and feeble, tottering; **tyen latin gwana gwana,** the child's legs are feeble, long and bending; sometimes **gwaŋa gwaŋa** is used for **gwana gwana.**

gwanno *vt* distorting; **gwanno lok,** distorting words, statements or information; 2 entangling; **tol ogwanno tyenne omiyo opotto,** his legs got entangled in a rope which made him fall.

gwaŋ *v* spoil, confuse; **gwaŋ lokke woko,** give a confused statement.

gwaŋŋe *vi* incoherent; **lebbe ogwaŋŋe,** he speaks incoherently, he speaks with a poor pronunciation.

gwaŋŋe *vi* not straight; **yoone ogwaŋŋe,** the road is not straight.

gwaŋŋo *vt* 1 speaking incoherently; 2 speaking evasively, dragging in desperate questions; **gwaŋŋo lok,** speaking evasively or scornfully.

gwanya *n* a vegetable which has a sour taste when cooked; see **malakwaŋ**.

gwar *v* gather; **gwar yugi man iony woko,** gather this rubbish and throw it away.

gwara *n* a kind of calabash with a small bowl and long neck, prepared as a horn and blown for entertainment and dances at the courts of the chiefs.

gwarre *vi* 1 gathered; **litino pa Icarel gugwarre ci gucitto woko,** the children of Israel gathered together and went away 2 can be gathered; **yugi matye i dyekal twerro gwarre,** the rubbish in the compound can be gathered together.

gwarro *vt* 1 gathering; **gwarro kal i aduku,** gathering the millet into the basket; **gwarro pul ki i poto,** gathering groundnuts with hands from the field; **gwarro yugi,** gathering the rubbish together / raking the rubbish.

gwarro *vt* scratching; **gwarro waŋ dano,** scratching a person's face; **gwarro wii dano,** scratching someone's head.

gwarro *vt* bearing; **gwarro rudi,** bearing twins, normally said of animals; **dyel man ogwarro rudi or rut,** this goat has given birth to twins; **gwayo** *vt* plastering; **gwayo kom ot,** plastering the wall with clay; see **gwaa, gwac.**

gwec *vn* 1 coming off where it has been fixed; e.g. a rat trap going off before catching the rat. 2 slip off; **waŋ bao ma giribbo ni ogwec woko,** the joint of the wood plank has come off / slipped off.

gwec *n* the kicking of a horse or a cow; **gwokke ka itye ka nyetto cak pi gwec pa dyaŋ,** take care, when milking, watch out for a kick by the cow.

gwec *vn* taking some food with the fingers; see **gweyo, gwee.**

gwee *v* take with your fingers; **gwee dek icam,** take some food with your fingers and eat it; see **gwec, gweyo.**

gwee *n.* swelling due to an abdominal disease, a bitter taste; **gwee** is actually a distension of the abdomen due to gas; **jerro gwee,** belching foul-smelling gas which usually is due to indigestion; bitter; **nyig yatte obeddo kigwee gwee,** the fruit has a rather bitter acidic taste.

gwee *v* kick; **gwee odilo matek,** kick the ball hard; *adj* a good player; **en lagwee odilo maber mada,** he is a very good football player; see **gweyo.**

gwed *v* remove with force, get with force; see **gwen, gwad.**

gweddo *vt* 1 removing with force; **gweddo shillings woko ki i ciŋ,** removing shillings from a hand by force; 2 obtaining information through coercion; **gweddo lok ki bot dano,** getting information from someone though coercion or luring to give the information; See **gwaddo.**

gwegwe *prd.* a bitter-sweet taste, quite bitter.

gwel *v* beckon; **gwel Ojok obin kany,** beckon to Ojok to come here.

gwel *v* take a little; **gwel wek i bil,** take a little with your finger and taste it.

gwele *n* bedstead, scaffold for sitting, bedstead made of wood; *see* **cida**

gwelle *vi* a little can be taken, **odiine twerro gwelle ki ciŋ,** a little of the simsim paste can be taken with the finger.

gwello *vt* 1 beckoning with the fingers from a distance or touching somebody lightly with the fingers; **gwello ŋati obin,** beckoning somebody to come 2 **gwello nyuka,** scooping porridge with the fingers.

gwen *v* peel, scrape; **gwen pok yatti,** peel the bark from this tree; **gwen riŋo ki i kom cogo man,** scrape the meat from this bone.

gwenne *vi* peeled off, scraped; **karatac ma giwmonno i kor ot twerro gwenne,** the papers plastered on the wall can be peeled off.

gwenno *vt.* 1 scraping with the teeth; **dako tye ka gwenno cogo ca ki lakke,** the woman is scrapping the bone with her teeth; **twoo ogwenno komme woko,** the illness has made her very thin and weak 2 peeling or removing with the

fingers; **gwenno placita ki i kom tyen,** peeling the plaster from the leg.

gweno *n* hen, fowl; chicken; **min gweno,** hen; **twon gweno,** cock; **latin gweno,** chick.

gweŋ *n* pebble; **gweŋ ala,** quartz pebble.

gweny *v* sacratch or rub; **gweny kama yil,** scratch the itching part.

gweny *v* alternate; **gweny kin dyegi matar ki macol,** alternate the white and the black goats.

gweny *vn* dislocate, displace; **coŋŋe ogweny woko ka gweyo odilo,** his knee dislocated during the playing of the football match.

gwenynye *vi* can be scratched; **dye ŋeye kama yilli twerro gwenynye,** the itching part in the back can be scratched.

gwenynye *vi* displaced, dislocated; **coŋŋe ogwenynye woko ka gweyo odilo,** his knee became dislocated whilehe was playing football.

gwenynye *vi* alternated; **dyegi twerro gwenynye ki romi,** the goats can be alternated with the sheep.

gwenynyo *vn* 1 passing in opposite directions without meeting, e.g. **gwenynyo yoo.**

gwenynyo *vi* alternating; **gwenynyo jami,** alternating things.

gwenynyo *vt* changing; **gwenynyo lok,** changing statements or words.

gwenynyo *vt* to dislocate; **ogwenynyo coŋŋe woko ka gweyo odilo,** he dislocated his knee in playing football.

gwenynyo *vt* to scratch with fingers; **en gwenynyo komme mada pien tye ki gwinyo,** he scratches his body very much because he has scabies.

gwenyo *n* scabies; itch; the name **gwinyo** is preferred; the name **gwenyo** has come from **gwenynyo,** scratching, this is because scabies causes much itching so that it has to be scratched

gwer *vn* looking for food; **min latin ocitto i agwer,** the mother has gone to look for food, i.e. to harvest from the field of corn after the owner has harvested already.

gwer *v* to make small cuts, to scratch; **gwer badda me odyer,** vaccinate me against smallpox (by making small cuts and putting small-pox vaccine into them.)

gwer *vn* vaccinate, decorate; **gwer me odyer geŋŋo dano noŋŋo twoo odyer,** vaccination against small pox prevents people from getting smallpox.

gwerre *vn* vaccinated; **dano myerro gugwerre,** people should be vaccinated; vaccination, **gwerre gin maber mada,** vaccination is a very good thing; **kibiritine pe gwerre,** the box of matches cannot be struck to produce fire.

gwerro *vt* 1 scarifying, vaccinating, looking for (food); **gwerro kom pi twoo odyer,** vaccination against smallpox 2 **gwerro mac kibiriti,** striking a match 3 **gwerro cam,** looking for food.

gwet *v* knock down with a pole; **gwet muyembe ki tal gupot piny wek wacam,** knock down the mangoes with the pole so that we may eat them.

gwet *vi* displacement, dislocation; **tyen meja ogwet woko,** the leg of the table has slipped out of place. *qv* **gwec.**

gwette *vn* slipped, displaced, dislocated; **waŋ bao ma giribboni ogwette woko,** the joint of the plank of wood has come / slipped out; c/f **gwec.**

gwetto *vt* getting something down with a long stick; **gwetto muyembe opot piny,** a mango from a mango tree with a stick so as to make it fall down.

gwetto *vt* .diverting, turning away; **gwetto wii ŋati mo,** diverting someone or dissuading, turning someone away.

gweyo *vt* 1 scooping sauce with **kwon** 2 taking home for one's children part of the food given, to you to eat, by a host; c/f **dek aonynya;** see **gwee, gwec.**

gweyo *vi* barking; **gwok tye ka gweyo,** the dog is barking.

gweyo *vt* kicking; **gweyo odilo,** playing or kicking football; see **gwee and gwec.**

gwic *adv* swallowing quickly; **omunyo yat ni gwic,** swallowed the medicine quickly.

gwic / gwica *n* interior, corner, nook, bay; **gwica nam,** a bay in the sea; **gwica ot,** inside / corner of the room.

gwin *vn* eat bit by bit; **latinni dok lagwin riŋo twatwal,** this child likes to eat meat bit by bit.

gwinne *vi* can be eaten bit by bit; **riŋŋone twerro gwinne,** the meat can be eaten bit by bit.

gwinno *vt* to eat pieces of meat bit by bit; **marro gwinno riŋo,** he/she likes to eat meat bit by bit.

gwok *n* a dog.

gwok *n* shoulder; **gwok bad,** the shoulder blade.

gwok *adj* incapable, having no idea about; **en gwok tiyo tic man,** he is incapable of doing this work; **gwok lok,** not tactful, tactless.

gwok *prd* misfortune; **tula kok gwok,** the cry of the owl foretells misfortune or a mishap.

gwok *adv* not; **gwok icit kuno,** do not go there.

gwok *v* 1 protect; **gwok litino gweni okwata pe omakgi,** protect the chickens against kites; **gwok litino ki kec,** prevent the children from hunger. 2 **gwok lok paco,** look after the affairs of the family according to the traditional laws and customs; **gwok otti maber,** look after the affairs of your house very well.

gwokke *vi* 1 be very careful, **gwokke mada ka itye ka lok kwede pien dogge aryo,** when you are talking to him, be very careful, because he is a double-dealer / speaker; 2 **gweno twerro gwokke maber, ka gimatto pii madwoŋ,** chickens can be easly to looked after if they take plenty of water.

gwokko *vt* protecting; looking after, **gwokko ot pe gin ma yot,** looking after the house (that is, looking after your family) is not easy; **ŋat ma gwokko gaŋ,** one who guards the home or looks after the home; **ŋaa ma gwokko latin man?** who looks after this child? **ladit ma gwokko gaŋ,** the elder who looks after the affairs of the family.

gwok-i-guda *n* chicken pox (*lit* do not touch me; presumably the people believed that one could get the disease through being touched by an infected person).

gwok nyo *cnj* perhaps; **gwok nyo bibin diki pe aŋeyo,** perhaps he might be coming tomorrow, I don't know.

gwoŋ *n* stammering, stuttering; **en lagwoŋ / lagwom,** he is a stammerer.

gwor *v* make wide; **gwor bur man wek obed malac,** make this hole wide by digging.

gworro *vt* making wider; **gworro bur wek obed malac,** digging more in order to make the hole wider.

gworro *vt* prejudice against somebody; fixing one's mind against someone; **gworro cwinynye me kello ayella i kom lawotte,** determined to bring trouble on his friend.

I i

i- *prs prn pref* means you; before an adjective or a noun, it means you are e.g. **icol,** you are black; before a noun, **imuno,** you are a European; **iryek,** you are clever; when **i** is *prf* to a *verb,* it means you doing something, **icitto kwene?** where are you going? **icammo ŋoo?** what are you eating?

-i *prs prn suff* means to you, your; **okello botti,** he brought it to you; **tye ki botti me binno kany,** it is up to you to come here; 2 **meni,** your mother; **tyenni,** your leg.

i *prp* in; **tye i dero,** it is in the barn; can also be on; **i yoo,** on the road.

i i *prp* in, within, from within; **tye i i canduk,** it is in the box; **en tye i i ot kuno,** he is within the house there; **oa ki i i ot kuno,** he came from within the house there; the above is to emphasise the presence there

ii *vn* **ii ki,** making effort, trying hard, struggling, striving; **an a ii kwede kumeno me tiŋŋo teerra,** I will struggle alone to carry all my luggage; **ii ki tic,** struggling with work or striving with work; c/f **iyo.**

81

ic *n* belly, abdomen; **ic ma odeŋ pe ber,** a big abdomen is not good (healthy).

ic *n* pregnancy; **tye ki ic,** she is pregnant; see **iye.**

iddo *vi* excitement, possessed; **jok oiddo i komme,** he is possessed with demon, that is why he is trembling. 2 **kolo oiddo i komme,** he is seized with anger and wants to fight.

il *v* lift, raise; **il kom malo,** lift up the chair; **il wii malo,** raise or lift up your head; **tii matek wek iil nyiŋ kakani,** work very hard so that you may lift the name of your clan; **il bendera malo,** raise up the flag.

ille *vi* 1 can be lifted / raised; **motoka ma opottoni twerro ille?** can the overturned car be lifted / raised? 2 growing well; **anyogi doŋ oille mabecco mada i poto,** the maize is growing very well in the field 3 rose against; **dano guille i komgi ci gugoyogi mada,** the people rose up against, them and beat them thoroughly.

illo *vt* lifting; raising; **illo mutoka ma opotto piny,** lifting the car which overturned; **tic matek illo wic,** hard work makes one famous; **litino myero gitiyo gin ma illo wii paco,** children should do something that gives the family a good name.

in *prs prn* you; **in itimmo ŋoo kany?** what are you doing here? **en biwotto ki in,** he will go with you; **in idano marac,** you are a bad person.

ir *prn* for; **ir aŋaa?** for whom? **irra, irri, irre;** for me, for you, for him in *pl* **r** is removed from **ir** and replaced with **w** and appropriate *vowel* put except in third *prn* **gi** is used and the word becomes **iwa, iwu, igi; prs prn** for

me, for you, for him; for us, for you, for them.

it *n* scorpion, the common name is called **oton,** used by the people where the scorpion is very common.

it *n* ear, leaf; **itte lit,** he has an earache; **min it,** eardrum; *prn* **itte operre calo it olik,** his ears are wide like those of a bat; *prn* **itte opoŋ ki odok,** his ears are full of wax; **itte odiŋ,** he is partially deaf; **itte otoo,** he is deaf mute; **odiŋŋo itte woko,** he decided not to listen or he pretended not to have heard; **odok ma i itte myerro gigol woko,** the wax in his ear should be removed; **pwon it yat man i teer me yat,** pluck a leaf from this tree and take it for medicine; **it geyane tino,** the ears of the sorghum produced are small.

it *n* spring water, water well; **twommo pii ki i waŋ it,** collecting water from a spring; **waŋ it myerro gigollo beddo maleŋ,** the spring water or water well should be kept clean by removing any obstruction from it; *prov* **ogwal acel ballo waŋ it,** one frog can spoil the water well, meaning one bad person can spoil things for everyone else.

it *v* climb, ascend; **it wii ot,** climb up on top of the house; **it wii aguragura man wek iriŋ kwede,** mount this horse so that you may ride it.

itoŋŋo ten *v* (other people call it, **atoŋŋo ten**) when hunters are tired one of the elders will call out **itoŋŋo ten!** which actually means let us rest; when they have rested the elder will say, **kibole** which means 'let us go'.

itte *vn* his ear; **itte operre calo it olik,** his ears are large as those of a bat.

itte *adj* can be climbed; **yatte pe twero**

itte, the tree cannot be climbed / it is impossible to climb the tree.

itte *vi* mounting; **gwogi gitye ka itte,** the dogs are mounting one another.

itto *vn* climbing, ascending, mounting; **itto yat,** climbing the tree; **dege tuk itto wii pol,** the aeroplane flies and ascends above the clouds; **itto wii got,** climbing the mountain; **itto wii leela,** mounting the bicycle.

itto *vt* having coitus, mounting; **nyok dyel tye ka itto min dyel,** a he-goat is having coitus with / mounting a she-goat.

itto *vt* promoted; **oitto malo i rwom me ticce,** he has moved up in his career.

itto *vt* collecting and heaping up in great quantity; **oitto yen madwoŋ mada i odde,** she stacked a large amount of firewood in her house; **oitto yec madwoŋ mada i ŋee kinaga me tiŋŋo ne,** he heaped up a lot of luggage on the back of the camel to carry; **oitto twon kwon mo me acamma,** she made a very big **kwon** for eating.

iye *prn* his abdomen or belly; see **ic.**

iye *prn* pregnancy; **iye tye;** she is pregnant; see **ic.**

iyee *vt* you have agreed or accepted; **iyee miyo lim,** you have agreed to provide / give the money.

iyo *vt* working hard; **iyo ki geddone kene,** working hard building his house alone; see **ii** and **ic.**

iyo *inj* yes, a good response to a call, by well-bred children; **ka gilwoŋŋi ni ŋadi, in igammo ni iyo;** when you are called, you answer **iyo; dano mape opwonynye ka gilwoŋŋe gammoni,**

ee, nyo ni ŋoo, a person who is not well bred when he is called, will answer **ee** or **ŋoo.**

J j

jaa *v* 1 cultivate superficially 2 pass near; **pur poto ne ci ijaa wii lumme ajaaya,** cultvate this field superficially by only cuting the grass; **wot ijaa ŋet paco,** walk close by the home; see **jac** and **jayo.**

jaa *v* take a bit, **jaa ŋet pulle ka itye ka reggone,** eat some of the groundnuts as you grind them; see **jayo.**

jaa or **jaar** *vi* full and powerful; **kulune doŋ ojaar mada,** the river is now very full and forceful; Murchison Falls in the past was called **Pajaa** because of its power and force.

jaar *vt* rise up against, rebel; **lutic gitye kajaar woko i kom joo ma gumiyogi tic,** the workers are using up / rebelling against their employers.

jaar *vi* stand out visibly, accumulate; **kiniga okello jaar ler i ŋutte,** anger made the blood vessels stand out visibly in his neck; **kot tye ka jaar,** the clouds are accumulating and threatening to rain; full of; **waŋŋe ojaar remo,** his eyes are full of blood because they look red; **pig waŋŋe ojaar woko,** tears started running down; **cak jaar madwoŋ i tuno ka min latin cammo cam maber,** much milk is produced by the breast if the mother eats good food.

jab *v* clean with hot water; **jab waŋ bur,** clean the ulcer with hot water (not commonly spoken).

jabbo *vt* cleaning with hot water, disinfecting, **jabbo waŋ bur ki oboke;** cleaning the leg sore with leaves dipped in hot water (not much used now, **maddo** is preferred).

jabu *n* gold; one of the most valuable minerals, it was used to be the base upon which the finance of a country was valued by how much gold bullion a country has.

jabuli *n* psalms, the songs of David in the Bible.

jacco *vt* (old use) grinding, crushing; **jacco nyim** (now **reggo nyim** is preferred for grinding simsim).

jaga *adv* gait; **dako wotto ni jaga jaga ki atego i tyenne,** the woman walks majestically with her ankles full of metal anklets.

jagge *adv* swaggering, **wotto jagge ajaga,** walks swaggering about.

jagi *n* a shrub with edible bitter yellow berries which is a popular vegetable of the Baganda; c/f **ocok.**

jago *n* sub-county chief *pl.* **jagi; gucitto gaŋ pa jago ka piddo,** they went to the sub-county chief's home for a court case to have their case heard.

jai *n* bhang, hashish, marijuana, cannabis; **matto jai,** smoking bhang or hashish.

jak *v* pull off, tear; **jak jaŋ yat caa,** pull off the branch of that tree.

jakke *vi* pulled off; **jaŋ yatti caa twerro jakke,** the branch of that tree can be pulled off.

jakko vt tearing off, pulling off, over-exerting; **jakko jaŋ yat,** pulling or tearing off a branch of a tree; **jakko bad dano,** pulling someone's arm with a jerk 2. **jakko lok,** speaking haughtily or arrogantly; **lok ajakka,** scornful or arrogant speech.

jal *indef prn* fellow or you there, used to draw someone's attention; **jal bin kany,** you fellow come here (used when calling out to a male person; for a woman, **nyani bin kany,** now women also call each other **jal**).

jal *v*1 leave something which you also want for another person; **jal cam ki lawotti doŋ ocam,** leave the food which you also want for your friend to eat.

jal *v* cut; **jal wii lum,** cut the top of the grass.

jallo *vi* leaving; **jallo cam ki latin ocam,** leaving the food to the child to eat.

jallo *vi* 1 cutting; **jallo wii lum,** cutting the top of the grass.

jam *adv.* on a flat foot; **wotto ni jam jam,** walks treading on the ground with his feet.

jami *n.* goods, belongings, things, property, wealth.

jan *n.* slave; see **lamiru, opii, guci, aŋeca.**

jane *n* not born in the clan, a kind of slave.

jantoo or jantoor *n* a square hut or a rectangular house; see **murukuba.**

Januari *n* January, the first month of the year.

jaŋ *n* branch; **jaŋ yat,** the branch of a tree.

jaŋa or jaŋaka *adv* wholly, altogether; **yat opotto ni jaŋa,** the whole tree fell to the ground.

jany *vn* 1 spreading out; **yat tye ka jany maber,** the tree is spreading out very well.

jany *adv* arrogantly; **jany i wii lapwonynye pi potto peny,** contesting arrogantly with his teacher over failure in an examination.

jany *vn* to sit on chair with an air of importance; **jany i wii kom calo rwot,** sitting on the chair with an air of a chief.

jany *v* sit down, **jany piny kany koŋ,** sit here for a moment (vulgar language).

janynye *vt* 1 sat; **gin ducu doŋ gujanynye woko wii kom,** all of them are now have sat properly on the chairs 2 rose against; **litino ducu doŋ wiigi ojanynye woko i kom lapwonygi,** all the children rose up against their teacher.

janynyo *vt* 1 making stand up, sticking out, opening widely ; **janynyo waŋ,** opening the eyes widely; 2 **coo janynyo okuto komme,** the porcupine makes its quills stick up; **labwor janynyo yer komme,** the lion makes its mane stand up.

janynyo *vt* to raise up the hair; **awobi janynyo wiye ki laket,** the boy raises up his hair by combing it.

jara *n* the game of gambling, or of hazards or betting; **goyo jara,** gambling or playing hazard, or betting.

jara jara *adj* not well; **dekke obeddo jara jara,** the sauce is watery and not well cooked; **dakone obeddo jara jara,** the women is a loose person / not well brought up.

jarara *A n* a button.

jayo *vt* to take part of something that does not belong to one publicly or secretly; **ojayo ŋet lim ma gimiye ni oteer,** he took some part of the money that he was given to take.

jayo *vn* 1 came near; **mac owaŋ ojayo**

ŋet gaŋ, the fire burnt very near the home 2 run over; **tyen mutoka ojayo ŋee tyenne,** the wheel of the motor car ran over his foot.

jayo *vt* scraping; **jayo wii ŋom ajaya,** scraping only the surface of the ground; see **jaa** and **jac.**

jec *n Eng.* a disinfectant (Jeyes ?).

jem *v* rebel, strike; **jem woko pe iye,** rebel against it, don't agree.

jeme-jeme *adv.* frayed or ravelled out; **oyec jeme-jeme,** torn leaving the ends frayed or ravelled.

jemmo *vt* striking, rebelling, refusing, rejecting, declining; **gimakkogi pi jemmo,** they were arrested for striking or rebelling.

jeneral *n Eng* general; is the second highest military rank above **leptenant jeneral** (lieutenant general), but below **pil macul** (field marshal).

jeŋ *v* lean, deposit; **jeŋ leela i kom ot,** lean the bicycle against the house; **jeŋ kwot me pyem,** deposit a shield for the competition; **jeŋ dyel pi banya,** deposit a goat for / in payment of the debt.

jeŋŋo *vt* 1 to lean / leaning against; **jeŋŋo leela i kom ot,** to lean / leaning the bicycle against the wall of a house 2 to pledge / pledging, pawning; **jeŋŋo gin mo me ka waŋŋe,** to pledge / pledging or to deposit / depositing something for it; betting or competition.

jeŋŋo *vi* to delay / delaying; **jeŋŋo ki nyom,** to stay / staying unmarried too long. **jeŋŋo doŋŋo,** slow growing; of **jwir, jwik.**

jeny *v* tighten the muscles; **jeny badi,** tighten your arm muscles.

jeny or **jenyeke** *adv* dried completely; **yat**

otwoo ni jeny/ jenyeke, the tree dried completely.

jenynye *vr* to be furious, to rage or to be irritable; **jenynye me lweny,** being furious and wanting to fight; **jenynye ka lweny pe ber,** being furious and wanting to fight is not good.

jenynyo *vt* to tighten / tightening of muscle; **jenynyo bad,** to tighten / tightening of the arm muscles.

jepa *n S* pocket on a pair of trousers, coat or dress; it is sometimes also called **jeba; kwany caana matye i jepa tuŋ lacam me curuwal mera wek ikella,** get the watch from the left pocket of my trousers and bring it to me.

jer *v* move away, withdraw; **jer teŋŋe wek dano gukati,** move away in order to let the people pass; **jer pa mony woko ki i waŋ lweny,** withdrawing the army from the front line.

jer *n* humiliate, despise, abuse; **gulwenynyo pi jer ni en opii mamwa,** they fought because he humiliated him by telling him that he was only a slave.

jero *n Eng* jail, prison; **en tye i jero,** he is in jail /prison.

jerre *vi* humiliated; ashamed, **tim me jerre in dano madit me citto ka butto i kin litino,** it is a shameful / humiliating thing for an adult to sleep among children.

jerro *vt* to humiliate, abuse, shame; **pe ibed ka jerro lawoti i kin dano,** don't humiliate your friend among the people.

jerro gwee *vn* belching a foul smell (seen in people who have overeaten and got indigestion).

jibi-jibi *adv* simmering, bubbling, foaming; **koŋo ocek ma bedi jibi-jibi,** the beer (native brew) is now mature and foaming / bubbling freely.

jibbe *vi* coming out; **kwok tye ka jibbe i nyimme,** beads of sweats are coming out on his face.

jibbo *vt* beads of water coming out, bubbling; **kwok tye ka jibbo i waŋŋe,** beads of sweat are coming out on his face.

jic *vn* half-cooking of the bad meat; see **jii, jiyo.**

jigi-jigi *adj* many and closely together; **cente ma jigi-jigi ni tye kwene?** where are the coins?

jii **or joo** *n* people (of the Lwo tribe)

jii *vt* part cooking of a bad meat; see **jic, jiyo.**

jijima *n* shoes, (archaic name for shoes when they had just come to the country, to differentiate them from the locally made animal-hide sandals).

jik *adv* absolutely; **en pe oo kany jik,** he does not come here at all / he had not come here.

jik-jik *adv* biting without penetration; **kayo ni jik-jik,** bites with no effect (like biting something tough).

jikko *vt* (**gikko** is preferred) stopping, ending; **gikko tic,** stopping working.

jim *vi* close together; **nyim jim mada ka pe gicoyo maber,** simsim grows close together if not well spaced.

jimme *vi* assembled, collected; **dano gubino ci gujimme woko i bar odilo,** people came and assembled in large in the football field numbers.

jimmo *vn.* assembling in great numbers; **dano gujimmo i lukiko,** people assembled in great numbers at the court; **kal ojimmo i poto mape wacce,** the millet has grown lushly.

jin *v* delay or suppress; **jin lokke woko,** delay the case.

jinno *vt* suppressing, hushing up, delaying; **jinno lok me piddo ne,** delaying his court case; **jinno lok ajinna,** delaying the case, not taking it seriously.

jiŋ *v* harden, tighten, invigorate, take courage; **jiŋ baddi,** tighten the muscles of your arm; **cit ka kwaŋ nino ducu wek ojiŋ kommi,** go to swim every day to invigorate you; **jiŋ cwinynyi,** take courage; *c/f* **jeny.**

jiŋ *adj* rigidity, hardness; **riŋone ojiŋ,** the meat is very tough; **komme ojiŋ,** he is strong and stout.

jiŋa *S n* music drum; **jiŋa ker,** royal drum.

jiŋŋo *vt* to make rigid, make muscles tight, invigorate, take courage; **ojiŋŋo badde matek ci tweyo ciŋŋe oloyogi woko,** he tightened his arm muscles and made his arms rigid and consequently they were unable to handicuff him; **jiŋŋo cwiny,** taking courage; **lwokke ki pii ma ŋic nino ducu jiŋŋo kom,** taking a cold bath every day invigorates the body.

jiŋŋo *vi* stunted or very slow growing; **jiŋŋo doŋŋo,** not growing well, stunted.

jiny *v* screw up the eyes; **jiny waŋŋi i komme,** screw your eyes while looking at him.

jinynyo *vt* to screw up the eyes; **ojinynyo waŋŋe matek i komme,** he screwed his eyes as he looked sternly at him.

jir *v* sneeze; **myero ijir ka wek ummi oyabbe,** you should sneeze in order to make your nose open up.

jira *n* tassel.

Jiri *n* the New Testament.

jiri-jiri or **jiriki-jiriki** *adv* to be very small and very delicate; **nyim tin waŋi ottoo woko, gudoŋŋo ma jiri-jiri kenyo,** the simsim this season failed to grow, it was all stunted.

jirro *vn* to sneeze some people prefer **tam,** which is rarely used now; **latinni dok jirro twatwal,** this child sneezes too much.

jit-jit *adv* spurting out of fluid with a hissing noise; **pii nyette ni jit-jit,** the water spurts out with a hissing noise through a small hole.

jiyo *vt* partial boiling or cooking in water of dry beans, maize and spoilt meat; see **jii, jic.**

jiyo *vt* blocking, closing; **jiyo waŋŋa yoo ki okuto,** blocking the road with thorn shrubs; see **jii, jic.**

job *vi* dip; **aecitto ka job,** I am going to dip myself into water.

jobbe *vr* dipping or diving into water; **jobbe i pii mit mada,** diving into water is very pleasurable / enjoyable.

jog *v* collect; **jog cente ki bot dano,** collect the money from the people.

jogge *vr* gathered, collected; **dano gujogge mada i tee kanica,** many people gathered at the church.

joggo *vt* to collect things from various places or people; **gujoggo cente,** they collected the money.

jogo-jogo *adv* in great numbers; **gweno opoŋ i ot gi ma bedi jogo-jogo,** there are large numbers of chickens in their house.

jogorapi *n Eng* geography, science of the earth's surface, physical features, divisions, climate, products, politics and population.

jok *pl* **jogi** *n* god, spirit, demon.

jol *v* receive, welcome, catch; **jol kalam bot Otto,** get the pen from Otto; **cit ijol welo,** go and receive / welcome the visitors; **jol layab, abollo eno,** catch the keys, I am throwing them there; **jol ii ki pul en,** eat some of the groundnuts here, they will keep you going.

jolle *vi* can be collected, can be caught / received; **pii ma aa ki i wii ot twerro jolle,** the water that is flowing from the roof of the house can be collected; **ka wun ducu wubeddo paco ci wii welo twerro jolle maber,** if all of you stay at home the guests can be well received / welcomed.

jollo *vt* 1 to catch a falling object, running fluid; **cit ka jollo pii ma mol ki i wii ot,** go to collect the water that is flowing from the roof of the house 2 welcoming; **wa aa ka jollo wii rwotwa,** we have come from welcoming our chief. 3 to receive; **gujollo wiye ki yom cwiny mada,** they received him with great happiness or joy. 4 tying; **jollo ic ki tol,** tying the abdomen with string (usually because of diarrhoea or hunger due to mourning).

jom *vn* take a bath; **aecitto ka jom,** I am going to take a bath.

jom *adj* sourish or acidulous; **malakwaŋ obeddo jom jom, malakwaŋ** is a vegetable which is sourish in taste.

joŋŋa *n* my friend (term normally used by women to their women friends); **boŋo pa joŋŋa na,** the clothes of my friend.

joŋŋe *vi* delaying, remaining behind; **Okot joŋŋe twatwal,** Okot always delays; see also **dokke, galle, minne, dwalle, dikke** etc.

joŋŋo *vt* to do roughly; **pe tiyo ticce maber, joŋŋo ajoŋŋa,** he does his work roughly not well.

jony *vn* emaciating, wasting, growing small; **tye ka jony ajonya,** is wasting away or getting emaciating.

jony *n* numbness; **jony me tyen a pi beddo nakanaka i kom tyen,** numbness of the leg comes from sitting for a long time on the leg.

jonynyo *vn* to get small, wasting; **two jonyo,** the wasting disease (AIDS); **tic matek jonyo dano,** hard work makes people thin / lose weight.

joo or jii *n.* people (both are used equally).

joo *vi* decrease in size by leaking of fluid or gas; **odilo tye ka joo,** the ball is becoming soft and decreasing in size because of leaking of air; **joo = too; too** is more commonly used nowadays than **joo;** see **joyo.**

jor *n* a robe, insignia of royalty, **jor me ker,** royal robe or gown.

jot *vi* wet, moistened, smeared, dripping; **dog gwok ojot ki remo,** the mouth of the dog is smeared / wet with blood; **dog latin ojot ki dek keken,** the child's mouth is smeared with food.

jotto *vt* wetting, moistening; 1 **jotto dog ki moo,** smearing the mouth with oil / fat. 2 **remo ojotto lak toŋ,** the edge of the spear is smeared with blood. 3 **latin tye ka jotto kome ki toyo,** the child is wetting his body with dew.

joto-joto *Adv* dripping; **boŋone cwer ni joto-joto,** his clothes are dripping.

joyo *vt* deflating, reducing the pressure; **latin tye ka joyo tyen leela woko,** the child is deflating the bicycle tyres; see **joo;** c/f **toyo.**

jub v collect with hands; **jub pul ikella amwoddi,** bring me some groundnuts in your hands for me to eat.

jubi n buffalo; 1 **oluma jubi,** the head bull of a buffalo herd; 2 **okoc jubi** n an old single buffalo bull; **nyako jubi,** heifer of buffalo.

jubbe vi collected; **kal ma otorre i dye ot jubbe maber,** the millet which is heaped up on the floor can be easily collected.

jubbo vt collecting or taking up with both hands; **jubbo kal,** scooping millet with hands.

juc vn reprimand, warning; **latin ka pe winynyo juc pa wonne ci pe twerro beddo maber,** if a child does not listen to his father's warning he will not be good; see **juu, juyo.**

jud v pout; **jud doggi,** pout / push out your lips.

juddo vt sulking, pounting, protruding, **juddo dog,** pouting out lips (because one is angry or enraged); **ijuddo piŋoo?** why are you sulky?

juk n restraining, dissuasion, hindrance, prevention; **latin myero owiny juk,** a child must obey or accept to be restrained.

juk v collect with the hands; **juk nyim iterre omwoddi,** collect the simsim with your hands and take it to him to eat (*lit.* to chew).

juk v prevent, stop, restrain; **juk latin pe obal pii,** stop the child from spoiling the water; **juk latin pe obed ka timme atata,** prevent / restrain the child from misbehaving.

jukke vi prevented, stopped; **kit rac pa latinni twerro jukke,** the bad behaviour of the child can be stopped / prevented.

jukke vi taking up with the hand; **nyim ma i koloni twerro jukke ki ciŋ,** the simsim on the papyrus mat can be scooped / taken up with the hands.

jukke vi smearing; **opegogi tye ka jukke ki daba,** the pigs are smearing themselves with the mud.

jukko vt taking up with the hand; **jukko nyim,** taking up simsim with the hand; see **jubbo.**

jukko vt smearing; **jukko kom ki lobo,** smearing with earth; **opego jukko komme ki daba,** the pig smears its body with mud (in other words, the pigs wallow in mud).

jukko vt to dissuade from, advise against, hinder, prevent; **gutemmo jukko latinni ni pe oryam motoka marac,** they tried in vain to dissuade the child from driving the car dangerously.

jukko vt to console; **dano mapol gujukko cwinynye mada,** many people consoled him / comforted him very much.

jukko vt to stop; **yat jukko caddo,** the medicine stops diarrhoea.

jukko vt to control; **ŋat acel acel myero jukko kiniga ne kene pe obed ka daa atata,** everyone should control his anger himself and should not continue quarrelling.

jul v take care; **jul gweno wek gunyaa,** look after the chickens carefully, so that that they may multiply.

jul vn sulkiness, sullenness, being cross or angry, moodiness; **jul pe myero ki nyako,** sulkiness is not appropriate for a girl.

Julai n July, the seventh month of the year.

jullo *n* ill temper , frown, moodiness, sulkiness; **en doki marro jullo twatwal,** he loves sulkiness too much.

jullo *vt* traditional care as directed by an **ajwaka** in order to prevent a child from dying one like before him; **jullo latin,** taking special care the according to **ajwaka's** instructions to prevent the child from dying 2 special care; **jullo gweno wek onyaa,** taking special care in rearing the chickens in order to make them multiply 3 being thrifty; **jullo lim,** being thrifty, watching over one's expenditure. the expenditure.

jum *adv* many at a time; **nyim otwii ni jum**, the simsim germinated all at once.

jum *vi* to dip; **olutto boŋo i pii ni jum,** he dipped the clothes altogether in the water.

jun *n* chin; **jun coo nino ducu beddo yer,** a man's chin always has hairs.

Jun *n* Eng. June, the sixth months of the year.

juŋ *v* squeeze or make small; **juŋ boŋone woko,** squeeze the cloth.

juŋ *vi* 1 shrivel, shrink, shorten. 2 withdrawing frightening 1 **boŋone juŋ oyot oyot,** the clothes shrivel or shrink very easily 2 **pe konynyo me juŋ i ot,** it is no use to withdraw into the house.

juŋŋe *vi.* delaying, remaining behind; **juŋŋe twatwal,** always delaying; see **dikke, dokke, galle, joŋŋe, minne, myenne, niŋŋe.**

juŋŋo *vt* shortening, reducing the size; **tye ka juŋŋo boŋone,** he is reducing the size of his clothes.

juŋŋo *vt* soaking; **tye ka juŋŋo boŋŋine macol i pii pi kare moo ka wek okwany cilo woko,** he is soaking his dirty clothes in water first for some time, in order to remove the dirt.

juŋŋo *vt* doing something badly; **juŋŋo lok,** speaking illogically; **lajuŋ lok, lajuŋ tic,** a bad speaker, a bad worker.

juŋŋo *vt* speaking incoherently, confusedly and embarrassingly, eg. **juŋŋo lok.**

juny *v* build (a small house); **juny latin ot mo,** build a small house; see **cuny.**

juny *adv* 1 abundance; **wiye odin ni juny,** he has an abundance of hair.

junya *n* a jigger or jiggers; the central Acholi people call it **jwinya.**

junyo *n* a kind of tree from which fibre is made for making ropes and used also in ceremonies after birth.

junynyo *vt* building something small; **junynyo ot,** building a small hut.

jur *v* pass urine or pour water; **jur nyo ony pii kany,** pass water / urine or pour water here.

juro *n* a quiver, bag where arrows are stored.

juro kulo *n* wet soil near a river or stream; **i dog oro gipitto layata omuŋi i juro kulo,** at the beginning of the dry season, sweet potatoes are planted on the wet river bank.

jurro nyo curro *vt* passing in large quantity (liquid); **jurro lac i ot,** passing urine in the house (during sleep), wetting the bed.

jurro *vt* storing up goods in the house in large quantities; **jurro kal i dero,** storing millet in the granary.

jut *v* beat; **jut gwok ki odoo,** beat the dog with the big stick.

jut *adv* in great quantity; **dyaŋi opoŋ ni jut i kulo,** there are many cattle at the river.

jut *adj* short; **cek ni jut,** very short.

jutto *vt* striking with a big stick; **jutto ki odoo tyen adek,** striking three times with a big stick.

juune *vi* running swiftly away; **juune ki ŋwec matek mada ka cubbo lee,** running very fast to spear the animal (not spoken now) see; **ywiine.**

juyo *vt* reprimand, tell (somebody) off; **ojuyo litino ni pe gubal pii,** he remanded or ordered the children not to waste water; see **juu, juc.**

jwaa *v* clean, wipe; **jwaa wii meja maleŋ,** clean or wipe the top of the table clean; see **jwac, jwayo.**

jwaano *vt* to wipe, polish; **en pe ŋeyo jwaano jami,** he does not know how to polish things.

jwaane *vi* can be polished, wiped; **wii meja man twerro jwaane maleŋ mada,** the top of this table can be very well polished.

jwaar *vn* growing up tall and beautiful; **anyira gujwaar kany mape wacce,** the girls have grown up here very tall and beautiful.

jwaat *vn* making an exclamation or clicking tongue in grief, pain or sorrow.

jwaat *vi* to click tongue to show annoyance; **ojwat mada ka owinyo lok ma gidotte kwede,** he clicked his tongue and wondered about the matter of which he was accused.

jwac *n* rubbing, ironing, polishing, cleaning, wiping; **pe ngeyo jwac,** does not know good polishing, or good ironing; see **jwaa, jwayo.**

jwan *n* tooth of a boar etc. planted on a headdress: **jwan kul, raa, lyec,** teeth of hog, hippo, and elephant tusk planted on a headdress.

jwan *n* a round hut; **ot jwan,** a round hut with a sharply pointed roof; the pointed is first constructed on the ground and then it is mounted on top of the house.

jwan *v* spoil, confuse; **jwan ka tee lokke woko,** confuse or spoil the case.

jwan *vt* rub or smear; **jwan mugati ki kic ka icam,** dip your bread into honey and smear it with it and then eat it.

jwanne *vi* walking about without purpose, turning this way and that way; **latinne ka giorro pe tikko yoo atir, tikko jwanne i yoo,** when sent on an errand the child does not go straight but turns this way and that way.

jwanno *vt* digressing, deviating, going off, or departing from the right way or direction; **jwanno lok,** talking in a confused way see **dwallo lok, juŋo lok.**

jwaŋŋo *vt* to do something imperfectly; **otweyo tol ojwaŋŋo woko ajwaŋŋa,** he did not fasten the rope properly.

jwat *v* cane, strike, beat; **jwat ŋwinynye ki kedi,** strike her / him (buttockside) with a twig.

jwatte *vn* striking one another; **litino tin gujwatte ki kedi ma pe wacce ki i olet,** today the children beat one another severaly with twigs in the grazing field, in other words, they fought one another with sticks.

jwatto *vt* striking with a small stick or twig; **jwatto latin ma oballo bal ki jaŋ yat,** striking a child who has done something wrong with a stick.

jwatto *vt* to run very swiftly; **ojwatto ŋwec matek mada,** he showed a clean pair of heels.

jwayo - jwaano *vt* wiping; 1 **jwayo coc woko ki i kom bao,** wiping out writings from the blackboard. 2 polishing; **jwayo bao wek obed mapwot,** polishing the board to make it smooth; **jwayo lak,** brushing the teeth, *qv* **jwac, jwaa.**

jwee *n* a strange looking form of humanity, an ugly being; see **akanyaŋo.**

jwer *v* 1 cut away , slash; **jwer mwodo ma i dye kal,** slash the grass in the compound 2 poorly developed; **geya ma ojwer nyo dano ma ojwer,** sorghum which is not well developed or a man who is wasted.

jwerre *vi* can be cut or slashed; **lumme twerro jwerre,** the grass can be slashed.

jwerro *vt* 1 cutting or slashing grass and small trees (with sickle/scythe); **tye ka jwerro dye kal,** is slashing the compound. 2 removing by striking with the hands or broom; **jwerro pii ma omol i dye ot,** sweeping out water which has flowed into the house with a broom; *c/f* **ywerro.**

jwerro *vt;* to kill all; **gujwerro dano woko liweŋ ma i gaŋ**, they killed all the people in the home; see **raddo, rwaddo.**

jwet *vt* run away; **jwet ŋwec i riŋ woko,** take off and run away fast**; jwetto ŋwec,** to take to one's heels or taking to one's heels.

jwetto *vt* to run away; **ojwetto ŋwec matck oriŋŋo woko,** he ran away very fast.

jwic *n* hissing disapproval; **wek jwiyo jwic obedi,** do not go on hissing hatred; see **jwii** and **jwiyo.**

jwii *v* hiss; **jwii doki aye ka itek,** hiss again if you think you are strong.

jwii *n* wet ground near a river, marshy ground.

jwiine *vi* percolated, be imbibed or absorbed by; **pii jwiine i kom agulu ni jwii ci dyako komme woko,** water percolates through the wall of the pot and makes its body wet

jwi jwi *adv* always, continuously, continually; **timmo jwi jwi,** does it all the time / always; **timme kitmeno jwi jwi,** he behaves like that all the time / always.

jwik *n* 1 reduction, decrease; **jwik pa ratiline doŋ beddo awene?** when will the reduction of its weight be? **jwik me cwer pa remo doŋ cok,** the reduction of the bleeding is very close; 2 not growing; **latinne doŋ tye ka jwik ajwikka,** the child is getting stunted.

jwik *v* reduce, decrease; **jwik mol pa piine,** reduce the flow of the water.

jwikke *vi* can be reduced, **mol pa piine twerro jwikke,** the flow of the water can be reduced / decreased.

jwikko *vt* to reduce physically or socially; **matto koŋo twatwal jwikko kom dano,** drinking too much alcohol makes a person thin.

jwil *n* quail, a kind of small partridge;see **aluru, ayweri, and aweno.**

jwir *vi* stunting , withering, failure to grow normally; **rucce tye ka jwir woko,** the rice is withering away.

jwirro *n* withering, stunting; **ceŋ tye ka jwirro kal woko,** the sun is withering the millet.

jwit jwit *adv* narrowly; **oloyo jwit jwit,** he escaped narrowly.

jwiyo *vt* hissing disapproval; **ijwiyo pi ŋoo?** why do you hiss? **pe ber ka**

jwiyo dano, it is not good to hissing at people; see **jwii ki jwic.**

K k

ka used in particle indicates (a) place of **ka cam mewa,** the place where we eat / our eating place; **ka tic, ka butto, ka kwan, ka dwar, ka ot, ka cokke, ka wot, ka tukko, ka kwaŋ, etc,** place of: work, sleep, study, hunting, housing, assembling, walking, playing, swimming, etc. (b) there or somewhere; **ket ka kenyo,** put it there; **ocitto ka moo,** he went somewhere; (c) in place of or in exchange for; **omiyo cukari ka waŋ gweno ma nene oterro,** he gave some sugar in exchange for the chicken which he took; 2 as a *preposition* after a *verb* means, to, at, from; (a) **olokko ka dogga, doggi, dogge,** he spoke according to my, your, his words. (b) **John tye ka tic,** John is at work; (c) **oa pud ka cam kom bedi,** he has just returned from eating 3 *adv phrases*; **ket ka kany, ka kenyo, ka moo, ka acel, ka mukene, ka kwene?** put it here, there, anywhere, together, elsewhere, where? 4. *conj.* followed by the *present* and *past tense* will mean , if, when, then; (a) **ka en mitto citto weki ocitti,** if he wants to go let him go. (b) **en twerro citto ka cam ka doŋ otyekko ticce,** he can go to eat when he has finished his work; (c) **otyekko ticce koŋ ka doŋ ocakko wotte,** he finished his work first then he started on his journey.

kaa *v* harvest, bite; 1 harvest; **kaa kal ma i potoni ityek woko,** harvest all the millet in the field; 2 bite; **kaa tyaŋ ka wek iwiny mitte,** bite the sugarcane in order to taste its sweetness; see **kac and kayo.**

kaa *adv* a particle used in interrogative sentences; **itmmo ŋoo kaa?** excuse me, what are you doing? or what have you done? depending how you pronounced it.

kaba *n* 1. a big spear with a long blade and a short neck; see **toŋ** 2 loin.

kaba *S n* braces, suspenders.

kabad *n Eng* cupboard; **ket ki kopo ki can i kabad,** place the cups and the plates in the cupboard.

kaba kaba or pata pata, *vi* violently moving; **gimakke ci giterre ni kaba kaba,** he was caught and taken away with speed and force, pushing and pulling him along with the rope with which he was tied.

kabaka *n Lug* king; **Kabaka pa Baganda,** the King of Baganda.

kaboni *n Eng* (not used now) company, name for youths, a group of youths.

kabu or **kabi** *n* swelling of the wrist joint which in the past was thought to be due to yaws mainly but which is now known as *synovitis* of the wrist joint due to many causes; *c/f* **tok.**

kabu *S n* overcoat, raincoat (sometimes called **kabut**).

kac *n* an ancestral shrine, usually made up of dry woods which are planted in the ground upon which the skulls of animals killed are hung.

kac *n* 1 harvest. 2 vt biting; **ocitto ka kac,** she went to harvest; **kac pa gwokke rac mada,** the bite of the dog is very bad; see **kaa and kayo.**

ka ce *conj* if; **ka ce pe obino ci doŋ itimo ŋoo,** if he does not come, what will you do?; **ka ce onoŋo ni gwenone**

pe ber ci oyeer mukene, if he finds that the chicken is not good, he can select another one.

kacco *vt* piercing from different sides, affecting in different ways; 1 **lok okacco woko,** problems from all sides have occupied his time 2 **arem okacco korre woko,** his chest is compressed or being pierced by pain from every side.

kad *v* weave, knit; **kad tol,** weave / make the rope.

kadi *conj* although, even if; 1 *prov.* **kadi ibut ki maaru i tee pii ducu biwinynye,** even if you sleep with your mother-in-law under water, it will be known; meaning that whatever you do in secret one day it will become known 2 **kadi beddi okwallo ento okwerro woko,** he denied it, although he stole it 3 *conj* **kadi wa wun bene wubinno ka cunna,** even you, you have come for courting me!

kadde *vi* can be woven; **tolle twerro kadde,** the rope can be woven.

kado *n* salt (may be mineral salt or Acholi salt made by straining of ash various shrubs or cow dung and goat's droppings.)

kaddo *vt* to weave or tie; **wacit ka kaddo wii ot,** let us go to tie the roof of the house.

kago *n* a shrub yielding strong poles for building.

kak *n* a blackish grey *carnivora* type of mongoose; see also **cwiiny, oculi, bura, kworo.**

kak *v* 1 incise or open up; **bur doŋ ocek, kak woko,** the swelling is now ready, incis or open it 2 split; **kak yen man wek gited kwede,** split this wood so that it may be used for cooking; **baone okak woko,** the wood has split.

kaka *n* clan; **kaka tuggi Payira, rokgi Acholi,** their clan is Payira, the tribe Acholi.

kakara *adv* cannot be bent, inflexible; **odwel man doŋ oteŋ ni kakara pe twerro banne,** this hide is so hard that it cannot be folded.

kakarra *prn* my place; **kakarre,** his place etc.

kakena, kakeni etc. *pos prn*, by myself, by yourself etc.

kakke *vi* can be incised or opened; **akwotta emme ni orommo me kakke,** the swelling in his thigh is now ready for incision / opening.

kakko *vt* to split (wood), to cleave; 1 **ocitto ka kakko yen me teddo,** he went to split the firewood; 2 incising; **kakko akwotta bur,** incising a swelling or an abscess; see **barro.**

kakwat *n* pasture, parish (church); **gucitto kakwat i olet,** they went to herd (their animals) in the pasture; **ladit kanica ocitto kakwat meere,** the clergy went to his parish.

kal *n* millet *(eleusine).*

kal *n* a compound enclosed by a fence of any kind, in the past usually logs; it is usually referred to as the compound of a chief; **acitto i kal,** I went to the chief's compound (in other words, I went to the chief's home).

kal *v* jump; **kal yat ma giriyoni,** jump over the pole.

kala kala *adv* quickly, very fast; **dano gukatto ki ŋwec ni kala kala,** people started running quickly away.

kalam *A n* pen; **leb kalam,** nib; **bol kalam,** penhandle, or penholder.

kalaŋ *n* large black biting ant with a sharp smell.

kaliri or kali *n* a kind of groundnuts, looks like beans; it is eaten after it has been cooked unlike groundnuts which can be eaten raw, (scientific name *Voandzeia subterranea).*

kalle *vi* can be jumped across, **kulune twerro kale,** the river can be jumped across.

kallo *vt* jumping over; **kallo malo,** high jump 2 **kallo lok,** leaving outsome words.

ka ma *prp* where; **ka ma ocitto iye,** where he went; some people from East Acholi say **kanya ocitto iye,** where he went.

Kamagili *n* a famous spirit of the Joo-pa-Lwo, where it is said that a cow horn dances during the ceremony.

Kamco *n* a river of Koc county which flows into the Victoria Nile.

kamicion *n Eng* commission.

kamiciona *n Eng* commissioner.

kamlara *n* cayenne pepper; small red pepper.

kampuli *n Lug* the plague, a contagious and infectious disease which is transmitted by fleas from rats.

kan *v* save, hide, store; **kan limmi i beŋe,** save your money in the bank; **kan caa ni i canduk,** hide your watch in the box.

kana *n* donkey; **kana leela,** bicycle; see **agura gura,** horse.

kanica *S n* church; **aecitto ka legga**

i kanica, I am going to pray in the church.

kanne *vi.* hiding; can be hidden; **twerro kanne,** can be hidden or saved; **okanne kwene?** where is he hiding?

kanno *vt* to hide, store up, put by, or save 1 **kanno boŋone i canduk,** locks his clothes in the box / locking his clothes in the box; 2 **kanno limme i beŋe,** saves his money in the bank o/saving his money in the bank; the meanings of the above sentences depend upon the way each sentence is said.

kano *n* a plant which produces small purplish edible fruits.

kaŋ *vn* a sarcastic statement or saying what does not mean anything.

kaŋ *n* being barren (female); **dakone okaŋ woko,** the woman is barren / his wife is barren; this depends upon how the sentence is said.

kaŋ *adv* very tall; **nyakone odoŋŋo atir nikaŋ,** the girl has grown very tall and straight.

kaŋ *n* out of place; **lak ma okaŋ pe nen maber,** protruding teeth are not nice to look at.

kaŋa *n* a kind of gourd from which royal band instruments, **gwarra,** are prepared.

kaŋŋe *vi* projecting outwards; **lakke okaŋŋe,** his teeth project outwards from his mouth.

kaŋŋo *vt* preventing by magic; **kaŋŋo dako,** preventing a woman from bearing by magic through magic or other means.

kaŋŋo lok *vt* talking sarcastically and arrogantly.

kany *adv* here;**bin kany,** come here; **kel kany,** bring here; some people from the

East Acholi use **kany** for **ka ma,** e.g. **kany matye iye instead of ka ma tye iye**, where he is.

kany *v* endure; **kany matek pe i wekki,** endure and do not give up.

kanynye *vi* can be endured; **aremme dit mada mape doŋ twerro kanynye,** the pain is so intense that it cannot be endured.

kanynyo *vt* suffering courageously, confronting difficulties fearlessly, enduring difficulties; **tye ka kanynyo aremme,** he is enduring the pain.

kapbad *n Eng.* cupboard **kapbad en aye kama giketto iye kikopo;** a cupboard is a place where cups are placed.

kapcul *n Eng* cupboard; **kapbad en aye hama giketto nje kikopo,** a cupboard is where cups are placed.

kapcul *n Eng* capsule; **yat kapcul en aye munynyone yot,** medicine in the form of a capsule is easy to swallow.

kapere *n* a daring person, an imitator, a person who wants to do something which he knows he cannot.

kapten *n Eng* captain, the military rank above lieutenant and the third lowest commissioned officer in the army.

kar *n* place of; **bin ka kar Okello,** come in place of Okello.

kar *v* pick; **kar mac iter,** pick the fire and take it.

kara *vp* surprisingly; **in kara ceŋ icitto kunu,** surprisingly you did go there.

kara *prn.* is, are really; **in kara lakwoo!** you are really a thief! **en kara lacan,** he is really a poor man.

karakak *n* maneater a *q.v.* **lakarakak;**

karakap *n* wooden sandals or clogs; see **tarabana.**

kara kara *adv* 1 crawling of a child; **latin mullo ni kara kara,** the child moves by half-walking and half-crawling.

kara kara *adv* hastily and badly; **itiyo ticci kara kara,** you work hastily and badly.

karama *A n* a feast with much food and drink, now refers to Christmas.

kara man *conj* while, whereas; **onoŋo otitto ni en pe ebicitto, kara man ocitto,** he said that he was not going whereas he did go.

karan *A n* a clerk; **amitto karan me konynya ki coc,** I want a clerk to help me with writing.

karatac *S n* a sheet of paper; **kella karatac me coc,** bring me some paper to write on.

kare *n* time; **kare bioo ma piny biyubbe maber,** time will come when conditions will be greatly improved.

karre *vi* being divided into two fork-like prongs; **yoo okarre aryo,** the road is divided into two.

karro *vt* carrying something with two sticks; **karro twol ki yat aryo,** carrying the snake on two sticks.

karro *vt* to straddle; **Atoo pe ŋeyo karro latin,** Atoo does not know how to straddle a child on her side.

kat *v* pass; **kat i citti,** pass and go; **pe doki i kat ki kany aye,** do not pass this way again.

katte *vi* can be passed, **yoone twerro katte,** the road is passable.

katto *vt* 1 going across, passing over; **katto kulu,** going across the river 2 getting out; **katto woko ki i ot,** getting out from the house 3 Entering; **katto i ot,** entering the house 4 going ahead; **katto anyim,** going ahead; 5 gone beyond; **lokke doki okatto kakare woko,** his speech went beyond what was required 6 not properly heard; **lokke doki okatto itta,** I did not properly hear what he said 7 passing over; **latinni oriŋŋo okatto luwotte ducu,** this child has beaten all his friends in running.

kawo kawo *adv* 1 the kind of noise made by somebody walking over grass or dry leaves 2 irritating taste of pepper; **kamlara tye ka royo dogge ni kawo kawo,** the hot pepper is burning / irritating his mouth.

kayo *n* firstborn; **man en aye latin kayo meere,** this is his firstborn child.

kayo *vt* 1 to bite; **gwokke ger kayo dano,** the dog is fierce and bites people 2 causing pain; **mwoddo pul ma numo kayo ic,** eating unroasted groundnuts causes abdominal pain; 3 to harvest; **ocitto ka kayo bel,** he went to harvest the millet. 4 to take courage; **pi kayo cwinynye matek, omiyo odonynyo i ot matye ka waŋ ci olarro latinne,** because of his courage, he entered the burning house and rescued his child 5 persisting in the thought of harming somebody; **kayo cwiny i kom lawotti pe ber,** persisting in thinking of harming your friend is not good; see **kaa, kac.**

kec *n* 1 hunger; **kec nekke,** he is hungry. 2 famine; **kec opotto i Atiak,** there is famine in Atiak.

kec *adj* 1 bitter, biting, pungent; **dek lalaa kec, lalaa** vegetable is bitter; **ceŋŋe tin kec,** the sun is very hot and biting today

2 bad luck; **komme kec, opotto oturro tyenne woko,** he is unfortunate / he is unlucky, he fell and broke his leg. 3 unfriendly; **danone cwinynye kec,** he is an unfriendly person.

kec cwiny *n* bitterness of heart.

kece other people say **kone** *cnj* or; **dano man kece nyo maca?** this man or the other?

kecco *vi* being enraged, being annoyed; **danone kecco oyot oyot twatwal,** he gets annoyed quickly.

ked *v* 1 weave; **ked tol man,** weave this rope; 2 decorate by cutting or tattooing; **ked dye ŋeye,** decorate his/her back by making small cuts or tattooing it.

keda *n* bile, gall; **kec calo keda,** bitter like gall or bile.

kedde *vi* 1 can be decorated by making small cuttings; **dye ŋeye twerro kedde maber,** her back can be well decorated 2 *n* decoration by cutting or tattooing; **kedde mere pe nen maber,** her decoration does not look nice / appear clear.

keddi *vt* weaving; **ka iŋeyo keddone ci keddi,** if you know how to weave it then weave it.

kedi *n* a little rod of stick; **latin man mitto gigoo ki kedi,** this child needs to be beaten with a tender twig.

keddo *vt* 1. tattooing, scrarifying; **keddo waŋ,** scarification or tattooing of the face 2 making ornamental impressions on a pot while it is still soft by marking it with a pattern made of grass.

kee *v* spread, disperse, pass away or disappear; **kee litino i kin ludito,** spread the children among the elders; **dano guŋukko kee woko ma tukko**

pudi peya otum, people dispersed before the end of the game; **kacokke doŋ okee woko,** the gathering has broken up / has dispersed; **lokke doŋ okee woko,** / the matter / is now over; see **kec, keyo.**

kee *n* desire (for food, especially meat,) longing for or yearning for; **kee riŋo nekke mada,** he longs too much for meat or he has a great desire for meat; **kee okwer mada i komme,** he has an unquenchable longing for meat.

keego *n* a creeping plant with good fibre that is used for suturing.

keerre *vi* behaving submissively, humbly, in order to win some favour; **beddo bedo akeerra botgi,** he lives submissively and humbly with them.

kek *n* a fishing basket for trapping fish. It is different from **ogwaa** because it allows the fish to get into it but it will not able to come out.

kek *vn* to split; **pamba ka otwoo ci kek,** when cotton is dry, it splits open.

keken *adv* alone, only; **en keken en aye obinno,** it is he alone who came; **en keken en aye tye,** he is the only one who is here.

kekere *adv* thin and wasted, or dry and hard, e.g. **oteŋ ni kekere,** dried very hard.

kekko *vt.* to deafen **daŋŋegi kekko it.** their shouting is deafening.

kekko *vi* to split open (of seed capsules); **nyim nyo waro kekko,** simsim or cotton splits open.

kel *v* bring; **kel kany,** bring here.

kele *n* cataract in the **waŋŋe opor kele,** he has cataract in his eye.

kele kele *adv* unfirmly, unsteadily, oscillati ng; **yatte gicommo kele kele,** the pole has been fixed loosely; **tyen meja yeŋŋe ni kele kele,** the table's leg is shaky.

keli *n* a small axe carried on the shoulder by a man as ornament but that can be used for defence.

kelle *v* bring him; **kelle kany,** bring him here; *vi* brought himself; **okelle kene kany,** he brought himself here.

kello *vt* bringing ; **aŋa ma twerro kello gweno diki?** who will bring the chicken tomorrow?

kem *adj* bad or pungent (of smell); **riŋone otop, ŋwecce kem,** the meat is rotten, its smell is very bad.

kema *A n* tent; **gucito ka butto i kema,** they went to spend the might in a tent.

kemicitri *n* · chemistry, a science that deals with the compositions of substances and how their elements combine, how they act under different conditions; **lutino gucitto ka kwanno kemicitri,** the children have gone to study chemistry.

kemmo *vt* aiming at, following the straight line, pointing straight to; **wotto kemmo potto ceŋ**, travels straight westwards.

ken *poss sff* 1 alone, personally, self 2 strength, determination.

kendul *n Eng* candle; **kella kendul wek acwiny me mnynyo ot butto,** bring for me a candle so that I may light / to light my bedroom.

kenna, kenni, kenne, *prn* myself, yourself, himself, alone; **abinno kenna,** I came alone; **ibinno kenni,** you came alone, **obinno kenne,** he came alone.

kenne *vi* striving to survive, determined to survive; **tye kakenne kenne ŋat ma konynye pe,** he is striving alone, with no one to help him; **marro kenne kenne mada,** he likes to strive alone.

keni *n* polluted or infected food, dirty food; **cammo keni twatwal,** eating too much polluted food.

keni keni *prd* different, distinct; **dano me rok ma keni keni ducu gubino i kacokene,** people from different nationalities came to the gathering.

kenno *vt* assisting , supporting a weak person (physically or morally); **wacitto ka kenno Otim, en kenne pe twerro,** we went to support Otim, he cannot do it all by himself (the meaning of this sentence depends upon how you say it because it could also mean, let us go to help Otim, he cannt do the work, etc by himself).

keno *n* a fireplace; **ket agulo i keno.** put the pot on the fire.

keno *n* calabash plant or gourd.

keŋ *v* to guard, to watch; **keŋ lukwoo pe gukwal jami,** watch out for the thieves so that they may not steal the things.

keŋ *v* 1 not to have; **iye cwer pi keŋ mot,** he was disappointed about not getting the prize. 2 failed to get; **obino lacen ci doŋ okeŋ neno daktar woko,** he came late therefore he failed to see the doctor. 3 omitting; **gukeŋ kwan tin gibikwano doŋ diki,** they omitted studying today but they will study tomorrow.

keŋ *adv* firmly; **ot ocuŋ ni keŋ,** the house is standing firmly.

keŋ keŋ *adv* unstable, loosely connected;

agulune pi tyerre woko doŋ tye ni keŋ keŋ, the pot is cracked in several places and therefore weak.

keŋŋo *vt* guarding, watching, looking out for; **tye ka keŋŋo lukwoo,** he is looking out for the thieves.

keny *n* marriage; **kollo keny,** taking cattle to the bride's relatives; **toŋŋo keny,** bringing cattle to the bride's parents without her consent.

keny *v* spoil, squander, waste; **keny lim ma gimiini ata,** squander / waste the money which you have been given.

kenya or **atta** *S adv* without hindrance, worthless, at random, a prostitute; **dakone doŋ wotto mere kenya / atta,** the woman is a prostitute, goes freely anywhere she likes.

kenynye *vi* wasted, squandered; **lim man ducu twerro kenynyne woko pi dwee manok keken,** all this money can be squandered in only a few months.

kenynyo *vt* squandering thoughtlessly through too much generosity, scattering; 1 **Okwera tye kakenynyo limme woko ki malaya,** Okwera is squandering his money on prostitutes 2 to scattr; **gweno kenynyo bel,** the chickens scatter the corn.

kenyo *adv* there, nearby; **en tye kenyo,** he is there; **cok kenyo,** nearby.

keo *adv* slight noise; **gin aŋo ma okatto i lum ni keo ni?** what has passed in the grass with thrustling noise / big rustling noise?

ker *n* royalty, power, authority, chieftainship, kingship; **litino ker,** royal children; **luker,** the royal family; **kerre,** his kingdom.

kere *n* gaps, **lakere (lak),** a person with gap between his teeth.

kere kere *adj* 1 transparent, clearly 2 having multiple holes or gaps.

kerro *vn* having energy; **kerro me tic,** the energy to work.

kerro *vt* to pamper, coddle; **dako kerro dog cwarre ki cam,** the woman pampers her husband with food; see **dworro.**

kerro *vn* 1 to have gaps; **wiye okerro,** the hair on his head is patchy usually due to infection by ring worms - *tinea capitis.*

kerro *vi* clucking of hen; **gweno tye ka kerro,** the hen is clucking.

kerro *adv* to pass through and through; **ocubo dyel ki toŋ okato kerro,** he speared the goat and the spear passed right through its body.

ket *v* 1 make; **ket Otto obed rwot,** make Otto a chief 2 put; **ket buk piny,** put the book down; 3 save; **ket lim i beŋe,** save money in the bank.

ket *v* 1 scatter; **ket litino woko ki ii bar odilo,** scatter the children from the football field 2 break; **ket kenynye woko,** break up the marriage 3 comb; **ket wii latin maber,** comb the child's hair well.

kette *vi* 1 can be made; **Onek twerro kette me beddo rwot,** Onek can be made a chief 2 made himself; **Ali okette kene me beddo rwot,** Ali made himself a chief.

ketto *vt* making, putting, laying, placing; **ketto dano,** making a man; **ketto lim i beŋe,** putting money in the bank; **ketto nyeko,** being jealous; **ketto i ker,** enthroning or investing one with authority; **ketto cwiny ka tic,** dedicating oneself to work, applying onself seriously to work; **ketto it ka winynyo lok,** paying attention to what is being said.

ketto *vt* demolishing, scattering, putting asunder, breaking up; 1 **ketto ot,** demolishing the house, 2 **ketto keny,** putting asunder marriage, or breaking up marriage 3 to get; **litino kec kettogi oyot oyot,** children get hungry very quickly 3 to spread **ober ketto two malaria,** the mosquito spreads malaria 4 to comb **ketto wic,** combing the hair; see **kiddo.**

keyi *n* water plant, water lily.

Keyo *n* a village ten kilometres to the West of Gulu.

keyo *vt* to spread, cure, disperse; 1 **ober keyo two malaria,** the mosquito spreads malaria 2 to cure, **yat keyo two,** a drug cures diseases. 3 to disperse **ŋaa ma citto ka keyo litino wek gudok paco?** who is going to disperse the children so that they can go home? see **kec, kee.**

ki- as *prn.* frequently is replaced by **gi-** e.g. **kicammo** is replaced with **gicammo, etc.**

ki *cnj prn* with, and, against; 1 **Otto ki Okello gibicitto,** Otto and Okello will be going. 2 **ocubbe ki toŋ,** he stabbed himself with a spear. 3 **gwok moyo kal ki gweno,** protect the millet which are spread out against the chickens **gwok Owor ki lakworre,** protect Owor from his enemy.

kibego *n* leftover food taken home from where someone was eating for children.

kibeŋ *adv* pretence, pretension; **oporro nino me kibeŋ,** he pretended to be asleep / to be sleeping.

kibira *Lug n* a kind of tree (useful for building).

kiboko *S n* a whip made from hippo hide; see **anino.**

kibogo *n* white and black colour.

kiboo *n* white; **dyaŋ kiboo,** a white cow; **yer wic kiboo or lwaa,** grey hair.

kibworo *adj* tawny hair; **dyel ma kibworo en aye gitummo me abila,** a tawny goat is the one which is sacrificed the shrine.

kic *n* bee, honey; **nyig kic,** a bee; **moo kic,** honey.

kic *n* orphanhood; **latin kic,** an orphan.

kic *vn* watching; guarding; **tye ka tic me kic i duka,** working as a guard in the shop; see **kii and kiyo.**

kica *n* pity, compassion, mercy, forgiveness; **timma kica,** forgive me, have mercy on me; **kica omakke mada i komme,** he took much pity on him.

kicaa *A n* a bag.

kicce *vi* shrinking into onself, withdrawing, humbling; **kicce akica,** he is withdrawn and lives by himself.

kicere moo *n* a very small gourd (bottle) used for keeping oil for children.

kici kici *adv* 1 drizzling of rain; **kot tye ka cwer ni kici kici,** the rain is drizzling. 2 fine, small; **okeddo komme ni kici kici,** he scarified his body finely.

kicika *n* a wall dividing two rooms in a hut or a room divided by a wall; also called **gicika.**

kid *v* tear, split, comb; 1 **kid otit me cweyo mukeka,** split the palm (**otit)** leaves for weaving or making mats 2 **kid wii latin ki laket eno,** comb the child's hair with the comb there; see **jwer, ket, kiny.**

kidi *n* 1 stone, rock; **kidi reggu,** a

grinding stone; **kidi me pakko palaa,** whetstone (stone for sharpening knives) 2 **dwe ocitto kidi nyo oguddu kidi,** the moon is seen in the horizon 3 red-coloured ostrich feather.

kidikdik *adj* moist inside; **riŋo ne pudi kidikdik,** the meat is not yet dry but still contains some moisture.

kidiŋ kidiŋ *n* small bird with a red bill and tail (wax bill).

kidde *vi* combed, split or torn; **yer wiye yom twerro kidde maber,** her hair is soft and therefore it can be well combed; **tyaŋŋe tek pe kille,** the sugar cane is very hard, it cannot be split.

kiddo *vt* to tear or split into small strips, to comb the hair; **tye ka kiddo wiye,** he is combing his hair; **winyo tye ka kiddo komme,** the bird is preening its plumage; **kiddo ottit,** tearing palm tree leaves into small strips; see **ketto.**

kiduu *n* not well developed; **pulle obeddo kiduu keken,** the groundnuts were underdeveloped and very small.

kigiŋŋi *n* an obstacle, an obstruction of wood or stone.

kigol *n* a basket with wide meshes for covering fowls or carrying fowls.

kigoŋ *n* a raised place for stacking split firewood, e.g. **kigoŋ yen;** see **aor.**

kii *v* watch, guard; **kii lukwoo pe gubin i gaŋ,** guard or watch over the home so that thieves do not get in; see **kic ki kiyo.**

kii *v* sieve; **kii moko man ki keyi keyi,** sieve this flour with a wire-gauze sieve.

kii-ne *vi* moving gently and quietly; **okiine mot mot nio ka omeddo ki donynyo kwede wa i ot,** he moved gently and quietly until he entered the house; see **kwille, kwalle.**

kiino *vt* same as **kiyo** *vt* watching, guarding.

kijaŋ *n* flat broad basket-work used for washing **tobi**

kijere *n* a rough wooden chair (used for ritual ceremonies).

kijiko *n S* a spoon; see **malaga, lakologoc.**

kijina dwan *n* a tumour in the throat sometimes due to enlarged tonsils.

kijiŋ *n* a large tree whose bark when pounded is sprinkled on skin burns.

kijiŋ *n* a piece of twisted palm leaves made into a pattern which is used for impressing designs on pots while it is still wet.

kijiŋ kijiŋ *n* the rattling sound made by small bells which are tied round the ankles when shaken during dancing.

kijira *n* a high-pitched shout of joy by women during dancing, wedding, or at a marriage ceremony, e.g. **goyo kijira.**

kijumi *adv* continuous rain from morning; **kot tin ocwer kijumi,** it has rained continuously today without a break from morning.

kijut *n* dragonfly, (not commonly used word); see **latugutugu.**

Kijuu *n* a mountain to the north of Patiko near Ajulu mountain.

kika *n* a door or shutter, usually made of fine twisted stems of a certain tree.

kikiri *adj* short and stout; **Ongom odoŋo oran nikikiri,** Ongom has poorly grown and remained short and stout.

kikoba *A n* a patch of cloth for mending torn clothes.

kikopo or kikobo *Eng.* *n* a cup or mug.

kikopo *n Eng* cups; **kel kikopo me matto cai,** bring the cups for taking tea.

kikun or kikuny *n* a flea of fowls. c/f **ladep**

kikuŋ *n* marabou-stork; see **arum.**

kikuny *n* lion-ant, fowl flea; see **kikun.**

kikwaci *S n* safety pin.

kil *v* peel, tear; **kil tyaŋ ka wek i nyam,** peel the sugar cane with your teeth in order to chew it.

kilau *adj* queer, unpredictable; **dannone obedo kilau,** he is a queer unpredictable person.

kilac *n Eng* class; **tye i kilac abic,** is in class five.

kilajok *n* a kind of *euphobia tree* whose leaves are like needles - long and thin.

Kilak *n* a mountain south of Nimule.

kilaŋ *n* a kind of beans of Indian origin.

kilau *adv* funny, lousy, unpredictable; **danone obeddo kilau, pe niaŋŋo dano,** he is a funny and unpredictable person.

kilega (buk me kilega) *n* a prayer book.

kiletti *n* hornbill *(bucerotidae) (bycanistes brevis);* see **arum**.

kili *adj* without a handle; **palaa ma kili,** a knife without a handle or shaft.

kili *n* quarrelsome, unsociable, bad tempered; **en layeny kili twatwal i kom dano,** he is always making trouble with people (*lit* he always finds a quarrel with people).

kili *adv* painful feeling; **okuto ocubbo tyenne ci rem winynye ni kili ka ocuŋ ki tyenne matye iye,** he has a thorn in his foot, he feels pricking pain when he stands on the foot.

kiliko or kilu *n* a whistle made of the horn of a small animal or the end of a calabash; see **bila.**

kiliŋ mo *adj* very small in quantity; **wacammo dek kiliŋ mo keken,** we ate only a little food.

kiliŋiri *n* a small and short person; the word is used during play by children.

kille *v* peeled; **tyaŋŋe yom twerro kille ki lak,** the sugar cane is soft , it can be peeled with the teeth.

killo *vt* peeling, tearing off bark, removing; **killo tyaŋ,** tearing off the hard part of sugar cane with the teeth, before chewing; **killo tol ki i kom yat,** peeling or stripping off bark fibre.

kiloŋ *adj/adv* the wrong way, upside down, opposite, inverted, inside out.

kiluka *n* a calabash bottle.

kiluŋ kiluŋ *n* black stork (acebe); see **arum.**

kiluu or kiliko *n* a whistle made from the end of a calabash bottle.

kin *prp* between, among; **kin odi,** between the houses; **i kin gaŋ,** among the villages; *v* **pok kin gi woko,** separate them.

kinaga *n* camel.

kincek *n* groin.

kiniga *n* anger; this is preferred to **akemo; kiniga omakke mada,** he was very angry.

kini-kini *adv* 1 moving to and fro, dangling. 2 the wind shaking trees to and fro.

kinno or kinno ŋut *vt* moving the head and neck in a peculiar manner of a shy girls; **nyanne doki kinno ŋutte twatwal ka gilokko kwede,** the girl is very shy, which makes her move her head and neck in a peculier way all the time.

kino-kino *adv* the same as **kini kini;** moving to and fro.

kinu *n* a heavy wooden trap for wild beasts.

kinoŋ *adj* thick; **boŋone kinoŋ mada,** the cloth is very thick.

kiŋ *adv* fixed, immovable; o**mokko woko ni kiŋ,** it is firmly stuck, it cannot be moved.

kiŋa *n* a sharp edge, the corner of a square piece of wood.

kiŋa kiŋa *adv* having edges.

kiny *v* comb, clean; **kiny wii latin ki laket,** comb the child's hair (not commonly spoken); see **jwer, ket, kid.**

kinynyo *vt* the cleaning / preening of plumage by birds. **winyo gitye ka kinynyo komgi,** the birds are cleaning / preening their plumage.

kinyo *n* a needle; **kel kinyo me kwoyo boŋo,** bring a needle for sewing cloth.

kipuŋuo or **kipuŋua** *S n* key.

kipwola *n* calamity, disaster, misfortune, mishap.

Kipwola *n* a female name (*lit.* Calamity)

kir *n* infringement of intimate social customs, mainly family, usually a sheep, depending on the gravity of the infringement is killed as a sacrifice in order to prevent misfortune of some kind from befalling the family.

kir *adv* bad smelling, pungent, the smell of urine; **ŋwec komme kir,** her body smells bad, like the smell of urine.

kir *v* sprinkle, jump; **kir pii i boŋo wek okwee ka doŋ ijwaa ki pac,** sprinkle the water on the cloth so as to make it soft for you to iron it; **daba okir i komme,** mud has splashed on him. *(Prov.* **mac okir i kommi, ceŋ mo ipor ki nyako,** ember has jumped on you, one day you will elope with a girl).

kirre *vn* jumping; **tukko me kirre malo,** high jump.

kiri-kiri *n* annoyance, restlessness.

kirro *vt* sprinkling; **kirro pii i poto,** sprinkling water in the garden.

kirok kirok *n* bee-eater *(merops acreabetes)*, a bird which eats termites, bees and insects.

kiroŋor *n* kingfisher, a bird which lives on fish around rivers and lakes.

kit *n* character, manner, behaviour, customs, way; **kitte ber,** he has a good character, manner, etc.

kitabu *A n* a book.

kitambara or **latam** n *S* a handkerchief **en tye ki kitambara maber** he has very beautiful handkerchief.

kitanda *A n* a bedstead, see cida and **laŋere.**

kitele *n* a tree which is frequently used for making barns; children use them for arrows.

kiteya or kitaya *n* young termites taken out from within the lump of earth where they have been laid, good for chicks to eat; there is a proverb about it which goes: **min gweno bene toŋŋo**

kiteya i kin litinone, the hand also eats the termites which its chicks are eating, in other words, the mother also eats what its chicks eat .

kiteyi teyi *n* 1 a frocks 2 large beads on a string worn as necklace by women.

kiti or **kitiki** *adv* visible, in its entirely; **amuka ocuŋ ni kitiki caa,** the rhino is standing there entirely visible.

kiti-kiti or kiri kiri, kwac kitikiti, cheetah.

kiti-kiti *adj* troublesome, irritable; **in doki la kiti-kiti twatwal,** you are very troublesome; see **lataŋgalo, lapelle.**

kitina *n* 1 burnt stumps of grass left by a fire 2 a short type of grass also known as **alene** which has dense leaves.

kitogo *n* thw afterbirth of an animal (commonly not used); see **byero, pel.**

kituba *n* a large tree, fig tree, its bark is made into barkcloth.

kituti *n* a raised platform in a room.

kiyata *S n* sweet potatoes; also called **layata.**

kiyo *vt* to watch / watching, to guard / guarding, or to lie / lying in wait (for thieves); see **kii kic.**

kiyo *vt* to sieve / sieving; **kiyo moko ki keyikeyi,** to sieve / sieving flour through a gauze sieve; see **kii, kic.**

kiyo *n* mirror; **kella kiyo anen ki waŋŋa,** bring me a mirror so that I may look at my face in it, it is a word that is not much used now.

ko *adv* no, not; **an ko,** not me, not I; **acitto ko,** I did not go.(not commonly spoken now except by people living west of Gulu).

kob *v* translate, transfer, move away; 1 **kob lok man ki dano,** translate this speech to the people 2 **kob ki kany ci icit kamukene,** move away from here and go elsewhere 3 **kob Otto woko Kitgum,** transfer Otto to Kitgum.

kobbe *vi* can be translated, transferred or moved away; **lebbe twerro kobbe i leb muno,** the language can be translated into English; *vt* **Owot twerro kobbe i Nebi,** Owot can be transferred to Nebi; *prn* **kobbe atata pe gin ma yot,** moving frequently is not an easy thing.

kobbo *vn* 1 translating; interpreting. 1 **kobbo lok muno ki dano i lok Acoli,** interpreting English into Acoli to the peolpe 2 move from one place to another; **kobbo woko ki i ot,** moving away from the house 3 reporting, revealing; **gwokke ki Otto, en kobbo dog dano,** be careful about Otto, he does not keep secretes.

koc *n* tin, aluminium.

koc *vn* to separate oneself from others, staying alone; **okoc jubi,** a big old lone buffalo, eating by itself and separated from the others; **dano ma koc kene kitte rac,** a person who lives by himself is bad; see **koo, koyo.**

koc *n* a riddle; usually one says **koc** and another '**lit**'. It means 'I have a riddle' and another responds by saying, bring it'.

Koc *n* (sometimes written as **Koich**) a county in southwestern Gulu.

koc *n* a stupid fellow who passes faeces just anywhere; **latinne lakoc,** the child is stupid and always passes faeces anywhere (not commonly used now).

koco-koco *adj* 1 wet all over; **boŋone odyak ni koco koco,** her dress is soaked all over with water. 2 well cooked; **riŋone ocek koco koco,** the meat is well cooked, it is very soft.

kod *v* tether; **kod dyel** , tether the goat; see also **dod, dwod.**

kodi *n* seed; **kodi pul,** groundnut seeds.

kodi *n* kind; **kodi boŋo macalo man pe ber,** kind of clothes like this is not good; **kodi gin aŋoo ma ikello,** what kind of things have you brought?

kodo *vn* the blowing of wind; **yamo tye ka kodo,** the wind is blowing.

koddo *vt* to bind / binding together; **koddo dyel,** to tether / tethering the goats together; see also **doddo, dwoddo.**

koddo lok *vt* talking too much, conversing excessively; **koddo nyiŋ dano,** backbiting people.

koga *n* a large bird, with a black body, beak, feet and red hind part.

kogo *n* (finger) nail; see **lwet ciŋ.**

kok *n* redemption, ransom; **gimitto dyel aryo me kok,** two goats are required for his ransom.

kok *v* 1 weep, cry; **kok matek,** cry loudly. 2 *vi* **latin kok** , the child is crying.

kokke *vi* redeemed, saved; **dyel meri ma gimakkoni twerro kokke ki lim,** your goat which was taken away can be ransomed with money.

kokko *n* lamenting, weeping, crying; 1 **kokko can,** lamenting over poverty; **kokko too,** weeping or mourning for the dead. 2 **kokko,** all sounds made or uttered by animals, such as squealing, squawking, rattling, etc.

kokko *vi* to redeem, to ransom; **Yecu otoo me kokko wa ki i bal mewa,** Jesus died in order to redeem us from our sins;

ocitto ka kokko Ocan ma gimakko pi mucoro, he went to pay poll tax for Ocan who was arrested for failure to pay the tax so that he may be released.

kok-kok kilirokok *n* the crowing of a cock, cock-a-doodle doo.

kokoliro or kok kiliro *n* cockscomb

kol *n* the skin of a few particular animals; **kol kwac,** the skin of a leopard.

kol *v* remove, **kol okuto ki i tyenne,** remove the thorn from his foot 2 **kol waŋŋe wako,** gouge his eyes.

kolle *vi* can be removed out; **okuto twerro kolle ki i tyene,** the thorn can be removed from his foot.

kolej *n Eng* college; **doŋ odonynyo i kolej,** he has entered the college.

kollo *vt* gouging out, removing with a sharp-pointed instrument, 1 **kollo junya ki kikwaci,** removing the jigger with a safety pin. 2 **kollo waŋ,** gouging out the eye. 3 **kollo dyaŋ, dyel, gwok,** castrating a bull, goat, dog by removing their testicles.

kollo keny *vt* taking the bride price - cattle-to the bride's people; see **toŋŋo keny.**

kolo *n* irascibility, quarrelsomeness, hot-temperedness; *proverb* **gaŋ pa lakolo pe poŋ,** the home of a quarrelsome person will never be full of people.

kolo *n* a papyrus mat for sleeping.

kom *n* 1 the body; **kom myero gilwok nino ducu,** the body should be washed daily. 2 **kom lokke tye niŋ niŋ**? what is the nature of the problem/matter 3 **komme pe / komme wac,** he is lazy. 4 **en ki komme,** he himself / personally. 5 **komme lit,** he is ill.

kom *n* chair; **kom obwol,** a round mushroom-shaped chair; **miyo gin mo ki rwot me tee kom pi yee piddo meeri,** giving something as a bribe to the chief for accepting to take up your court case; **komme tye kwene?** where is his chair? **bed we kom,** sit on the chair.

kommo *vi* 1 limping, hobbling; **tye ka kommo pien oturro tyenne woko,** he is limping because he has broken his leg. 2 *vt* **kommo latwoo,** supporting a sick person by holding him while walking with him.

kompwuta *n* computer; **jammi ducu doŋ me coc gitiyo ki kompwuta keken,** everything to do with writing is now done only by computer.

kon *vi* drip; **pii ma i boŋo ma dyak tye ka kon i dye ot,** the water from the wet clothes is dripping on the floor.

kona *n Eng* **kona ot** 1 a corner of the house. 2 term used for those who become obsessed with what they have got; **Aceng kona ki cwarre ni,** Aceng and that husband of hers! is completely obsessed with him; **ŋadi kona doŋ rwot,** so and so and his having become chief! (has become obsessed with his new position status).

kone *n* a castrated animal; **kone dyaŋ**, a bull that has been castrated.

kone *cnj* or; **Ocan kone Otto,** Ocan or Otto; **Otto kone Ocan?** is it Otto or Ocan? see **kece.**

konel *n Eng* colonel, in hierarchy, colonel is above lieutenant colonel in the army.

koni *adv* soon, now; **binno koni,** will come soon after; **kokoni,** just now, immediately; **koni agoyi ka itukko,** I will soon beat you if you fool around.

kono *cnj* 1 if, had; **kono Owor en aye ocitto, kono ayela obeddo pe,** had

Owor gone, there would not have been trouble. 2 or ;**Orac kono Acan,** Orac or Acan.

kono nyo *adv* perhaps; **kono nene ibin con, kono nyo atitti,** had you come early perhaps I would have told you.

kono *n* feather (of ostrich and fowls). **kono alwe lwe / yila,** long and pointed feathers; **kono kidi nyo loŋoloreŋ,** red-coloured ostrich feathers; **kono udu,** ostrich feathers; **kono kica,** small broad feathers.

kontraceptib *n Eng* contraceptives, devices for the prevention of conceptions such as drugs of various types, and intra-uterine devices, intra-cervical cap.

Gladys tye kamunynyo kontraceptib teblet me geŋŋe yaccu, Gladys is taking contraceptive tablets so as not to get pregnant.

kopulo *n S* padlock.

koŋ *prp* first, first of all; **kur koŋ acitti,** first wait till I have left.

koŋ *adv* really, very; **yat ogom ni koŋ,** the tree is really bent; **otii ni koŋ,** he/she is very old.

koŋŋe *adv.* acquiline, i.e. long thin sharp, **Somali gin aye dano ma umgi koŋŋe,** all the people who have acquiline noses, i.e. long, thin and sharp noses are Somali.

koŋŋo *vt* building a barrier around the edge of something, also (**goŋŋo**); **goŋŋo nyo koŋŋo ŋet poto,** building a barrier around the field.

koŋo *n* beer; 1 **koŋo lacoyi,** unfiltered beer prepared from millet, sorghum, etc mixed with hot water and then drunk by sucking through a long tube; 2 **koŋo lukut,** beer made from remains of **kwon** for children and women, and

which is usually sweet 3 **koŋo arege,** a kind of gin.

koŋo ogwal *n* gooseberry.

kony 1 *v* help, save, assist, support; **kony lawotti,** help or assist or support your friend. 2 *n* **kony gin maber,** to help / to assist is a good thing.

Kony *n* a male name, *lit.* means help, assistance.

konynye *vi n* helping, assisting, supporting; **omeego myero gukonynye,** brothers should help one another; **cwiny me konynye en aye gin ma dano ducu myero gubed kwede,** the spirit of helping is the one thing that everyone should have; **konynye kello mer ki kuc i lobo,** helping / supporting one another brings love and peace in the country.

konynye *vi* help oneself; **ocitto ka konynye,** he went to help himself; this is used by well bred people instead of 'he went to toilet or to pass stool'.

konynyo *vt* 1 helping; **konynyo dano ber,** helping people is good 2 assisting against; **konynyo dano ki can,** helping people against poverty. 3 to assist, to support, back up; **komme konynyo pyer dano,** the chair supports the waist; **konynyo lucan,** to support / supporting the poor.

koo *vt* isolate, leave; **koo gweno matar, ter macol keken,** leave the white chickens, take only the black ones; see **koc, koyo.**

koo *n* bamboo tree; some people call **koor.**

kop *n* matter, question, case, dispute; **kop aŋoo?** what is the matter? **kop aŋoo matye i kinwu?** what is the problem or dispute between you? **kop**

oloye, he was defeated in the dispute; c/f **lok aŋoo ?**

kopia *S n* kofia, a hat which is conical in shape, which used to be worn by police and Muslims; see **tarabuc.**

kopolo *n Eng* corporal, the lowest non-commissioned officer in the police or army.

kor *n* 1. chest; **kor labwor ogeŋ,** the lion's chest is big and bulging; **dak kor,** sternum; *c/f* **labana** in animals, **lapok,** breast, in fowls.

kor *n* path, footprint, trace, way, tract; **kor lee tye kany,** the track of the animals are here; **lee gilubbo ki korgi,** the animals are traced by their tracks / footprint **man en aye kor twol,** this is the mark / path of the snake.

kor *v* praise; **kor Lubaŋa,** praise God.

korre *n* his/her chest path; **korre dit,** his chest is broad, /big.

2 assistance, witness; **lakony korre pe,** there is has no witness, no one to corroborate his words 3 one after the other; **can ki korre ki korre,** pile them up one on top of the other.

Koro *n* a small clan near Gulu.

koro-gweno *n* a fowl or chicken house built over four long wooden poles.

koro-koro *adv* the sound made by rats running on hanging mat or cowhide used as a sleeping mat.

korro *vt* sending evil spirits out of someone by shaking a gourd rattle.

korro *vt* praising; **korro Lubaŋa ki wer,** praising God with songs. 3 scraping meat from the bones; **gwok tye kakorro riŋŋo ki kom cogo,** the dog is scraping meat from the bones with its teeth.

koro gweno *n* a hen house.

kot *n* rain; **potto kot,** the beginning of the rainy season; **kot waŋ dyaŋ,** rain from an unusual direction (North-West); **kot oro,** a short drizzle; **kot owoo awooya keken,** it drizzleds only a little.

kot *n Eng* court; **ocitto i kot ka pido,** he went to attend a case at court; see **lukiko.**

koti *n Eng* coat; **kella koti arukki,** bring me the coat to wear.

kotto *vt* exalting or praising oneself; **kotto komme,** playing idly and exalting himself.

koto-koto *adv* weak, emaciated; **ojony ma wotto ni koto-koto,** he is so emaciated, and very weak that he can hardly walks.

koyo *n* cold, cool breeze; **kot ocwer okello koyo,** the rain has brought the cold; **koyo nekke,** he feels cold.

koyo *n* an adze (a carpenter's tool for shaping wood); **koyo me payo kom,** an adze for shaping wood into chairs.

koyo *vt* isolating, leaving some among others; **gubino gukoyowa woko, guyerro jo mukene.** they came and picked other people but left us; **tim man gikoyo me dwar i mwaka ma bino,** this jungle has been preserved from being burnt for hunting next year; **okoyo tee wiye maber mada,** he has trimmed / shaved his hairline very well; see **koo, koc.**

ku *adv* in compounds or joined with other words; **kupiny, kumalo,** in the lower, in the upper; **dok kuŋeya,** go behind me; **cit kuca,** go there; **nen kunyimme caa,** look,m the front is there.

kub *v* join, transmit; **kub tol wek obed**

mabor, join the rope to make it long; **kub lok ocit ki jo ma paco,** transmit the matter to the people at home.

kubbe *vi* to be joined, connected, transmitted; committed; **tolle twerro kubbe,** the rope can be joined; **lok twerro kubbe nio wa Gulu,** the matter can be communicated up to Gulu.

kubbo *vt* 1 joining to; **kubbo tol,** joining the rope. 2 pass or transmit; **kubbo lok pa rwot bot dano,** passing the chief's words onto the people.

kuc *vn* peace; **kuc obed kwedwu,** peace be upon you/ peace be with you.

kuccu *vt* to trample / trampling the ground and turning it into dust; **dyel kuccu piny twatwal,** goats trample the ground heavily and turn it into dust.

kud *v* hold something in the mouth; **kud pii i dogi,** hold water in your mouth.

kudde *vi* hiding; **litino gucitto gukudde woko i ot,** the children went and hid themselves silently in the house; **tye okudde i ot,** he is there hiding silently in the house; **obeddo ka kokko twatwal ci man pud doŋ okudde en,** he has been crying very much but he has just stopped.

kuddo *vt* to hold food or something in the mouth; **latin kuddo cam i dogge,** the child holds the food in her mouth.

kudo *vi* a small swelling or rash; **komme okudo ki gwenyo,** his body is full of / covered with scabies.

kuk *adv* unexpectedly; **oyoko ni kuk,** he knocked it unexpectedly.

kuku kuku 1 *adv* great mass, great force, densely; **kot bino ni kuku kuku ma miyo ayom mitto deere,** the rain is coming with such great force that it

makes the monkey wants to commit suicide 2 struggle, trouble; **jonne doŋ gitye ki kuku kuku i kin gi,** these people are having trouble among them.

kuku oduro *vt* raising the alarm with the mouth; **goyo nyo kuku oduro ŋuu,** raising the alarm for a wild beast; **kuku oduro me mony,** making the alarm for war.

kul, or akul *n* a pen, enclosure; **kul dyaŋ,** a cattle pen; enclosure for cattle; **akul** is prefered.

kul *n* wild pig, warthog.

kul *v* bow, ben, lower down; **kul wii piny,** bow / lower your head.

kula *n* alliance, coalition, conspiration; **gucokko kula i komme,** they have formed an alliance against him / they conspired against him.

kulle *vn* to bow / bowing, to bend / bending; **kulle piny wek akwany lum ki i wii,** bend down so that I may remove a piece of grass from your head (hair).

kullo *vt* to bend / bending down; **kullo wiye piny,** to bow / bowing his head.

kulo *adv* 1 wholly, entirely; **oterro kicaa cukari kulu ire,** he took the whole bag of sugar for himself.

kulu *n* river, brook; **anyira gucitto ka twommo pii i kulo,** the girls have gone / went to draw water from the river.

kuluko *adj* bulky, voluminous; **wiye olorre ni kuluko.** his head is very bulky (big).

kum *n* support, assistance; **kum gin maber mada i can,** support / assistance in times of sadness / grief is very good (important).

kum *v* assist, support, help; **kum lawotti ka tye i pekko,** assist / support your friend when he is in trouble.

kuman or **kumeno** *adv* in this way, thus, so, so it, it is; **lokke tye kitman,** the matter is like this; **lokke otimme kumeno,** the matter happened in that way.

kumme *vn* helping, supporting, assisting one another; **kumme gin maber mada miyo ŋat matye ki pekko pe doŋ bedo marac,** supporting / helping one another makes the one who is in trouble not feel so bad; **omeego myerro gikumme,** brothers should support / assist one another.

kummo *vt* supporting, assisting, helping; **kummo omeegini ber mada,** supporting / assisting your brothers is very good.

kummu *vn* grief, affliction; **tye ka kummu pien orwenynyo minne,** he is in grief because he lost his mother.

kun *vn* refusal, declining (because offended); **kun pe ber,** refusing to do something because one is offended is not good.

kun *cnj* while, whereas, although, notwithstanding; **pi lewic okwerro cam kun mitto,** because of shyness he refused to eat although he wanted to; **ocitto ka tukko kun kono myero ocit ka kwan,** he went to play although he should have gone to study; **kadi bedi pekko obedo tye, litino gutyekko kwan maber,** notwithstanding the problem, the children completed their studies successfully.

kun ... kun *adv* on both sides; **kun coo kun coo,** on both sides there are men of the same strength.

kunno *vt* keeping, preserving, taking good care of; **kunno litino bura, meegigi doŋ otoo woko,** taking care of the kitten, their mother has died.

kunno *vt* refusing, declining and being sulky; **tye ka kunno cam woko pien gigoye,** he is refusing to eat food because he was beaten.

kuno *adv* there, over there, on that side; **tye kuno,** it is there; **gibollo tuŋ kuno,** it was thrown on that side.

kuŋ or **li kuŋ** *adv* clearly visible; **got Ajulu ocuddo li kuŋ,** the Ajulu mountain is standing out prominently.

kuŋ kuŋ *adv* inseparate; **bedo i kor minne ni kuŋ kuŋ,** he follows his mother everywhere.

kupulu *n* a padlock; **kella kupulu wek alor ki dog candukka,** bring me a padlock so that I may lock my box.

kur *adj* 1 pleasant and agreeable in smell; **oteddo rucce ma ngwecce kur mada,** he cooked pleasantly smelling. rice. 2 **lokke okur mada laworo,** the discussion went on very well yesterday and everybody was pleased with it.

kur *vi* burnt to ashes; **mac oyo laworo okur mada,** yesterday the fire for warming, burnt very well and the logs were burnt to ashes.

kur *v* wait, guard; **kur kany nio ka adwogo,** wait here until I come back; **kur ŋati mo pe odony kany,** guard here so that no one enters.

kurre *v* wait for; **kurre kany,** wait for him here.

kurro *vt* 1 waiting for, awaiting, guarding; **tye ka kurro minne,** he is waiting for his mother 2 to guard;

ocitto ka kurro beŋe, he went to guard the bank.

kuru cuk *A n* a chair for lying on; see **rwot ool,** 'the chief is tired'.

kurukuru n **latin gwok,** puppy, small dog.

kuru kuru *adv* doing hastly.

kut *n* a very deep centre of water.

kut kut kut 1 *inj* fowl calling its chicks 2 state of craving after, longing for; **cwinynye bedo ni kut kut,** his heart is incessantly craving.

kut *v* blow; **kut burigi matek,** blow the bugle loud; **kut balun matek,** blow the balloon hard.

kutte *vi* can be blown or inflated; **balun man ducu tika twerro kutte,** can all these balloon be blown full / inflated?

kutto *vt* blowing whistles of various types; **kutto bila,** blowing a whistle made of animal horns.

kutu kutu *adv* muttering, grumbling; **dako bedo ni kutu kutu ki lok i ot,** the woman is grumbling to herself and seems to find fault with everything.

kutyelo *n* a room behind the partition in a hut or a house, inner room.

kwaa *n* descendent; **lakwaa Orac,** the descendant of Orac / Orac's grandchild; **kwaa lu Koich kitgi eno,** that is the character of the Koich people; **kwaaro lu Patiko,** descendents of the Patiko.

kwaa *vt* beg; 1 **kwaa kado ki bot nyekki,** beg for salt from your co- wife; 2 herding, looking after; **kwaa dyeggi man,** look after these goats; see **kwac, kwayo.**

kwaar *adj* red; **boŋo ma kwaar,** a red cloth; see **raŋi.**

kwaara *n* my grandfather; **kwaaro,** grandfather, a general name; the relations here are as follows: sing **kwaara, kwaari, kwaare,** my, your, his granfather; *pl* **kwaarowa, kwaarowu, kwaarogi,** our, your, their granfather or grandfathers; grandfathers who are not closely related but from the same clan are as follows: *pl* **kwaariwa, kwaariwu, kwaarigi,** our, your, their grandfather or grandfathers: *sing* **kwaarina, kwaarini, kwaarine,** my, your, his grandfather.

kwaaro *n* grandfather, husband's father.

kwac *vn* 1 begging; **ocitto ka kwac me kado,** she went to beg for salt 2 herding; **tye ka kwac,** is herding; see **kwaa, kwayo.**

kwac *n* **leopard;** see **kwac kirikiri / kitkiti, kworo,** and **giliri.**

kwac kiti kiti *n* cheetah; some call it **kiri kiri.**

kwadeŋe *n* beetle; also called **kamdeŋe** by other people.

kwaduk *n* part of animal's stomach, *duodenum.*

kwak *v* embrace, hold one another; **kwak korre,** hold his chest (also **gwak korre**) 2 adding something; **kwak labolo man i ciŋŋi imed ki ma i aduku ma iyeyo iwii,** take this banana in your hand to add to the ones in the basket which you are carrying on your head.

kwakala *n* a trap for rats and other animals also called **agwak.**

kwakke *vi* embracing each other; *c/f* **gwakke,** which is the standard Acholi.

kwakko *vt* 1 adding something to what one is taking; **kwakko jami mo i ribbo kom mukene,** adding something to something else. 2 **kwakko /**

gwakko, embracing; kwakko kor lawoti, embracing your friend.

kwal *n* theft, stealing kwal pe gin maber, stealing is not a good thing.

kwal *v* steal; kwal toŋ icit kwede, steal the spear and go with it.

kwalle *vi* moving stealthily away; okwalle odonynyo i ot ka kwoo, he stealthily entered the house to steal; see kwille, kiine.

kwallo *n* to steal / stealing; litino ma kitgi raccu aye gimarro kwallo jami, the children with bad character are the ones who like to steal / stealing things.

kwan 1 *v* read, study; kwan buk aryo tin, read two books today 2 *v* count; kwan maber lim matye i kica kany, count carefully all the money in this bag.

kwan *n* read, study; latin ma marro kwan bedo ryek, a child who likes reading will be clever; tye ka kwan i kilac, he is reading in class.

kwanne 1 *vi* can be read; waragane twerro kwanne, the letter can be read 2 *vi* can be counted; limme twerro kwanne, the money can be counted. 3 latinne kwanne pe tye maber, the child is not studying hard or the studying of the child is not well.

kwanno *vt* to read / reading, to count / counting, to study / studying; kwanno buk, to read / reading a book; kwanno lim, to count / counting the money; kwanno i kilac, to study /studying in the class.

kwaŋ *n* 1 swimming; kwaŋ mere ber mada, swimming is very good 2 heavily; opotto piny ni kwaŋ, he fell heavily down.

kwaŋ *v* swim; kwaŋ iŋol kuloni, swim across this river / the river can be swum.

kwaŋŋe *vn* to swim / swimming; kwaŋŋe me pyem tek mada, a swimming competition is very dfficult; kulone twerro kwaŋŋe, it is possible to swim across the river / the river can be swum.

kwaŋŋo *vt* 1 to swim / swimming; kwaŋŋo pii katto lokka caa, swimming across the water to the other side. 2 ŋeyo kwaŋŋo yeya, knowing how to row a boat / he/she knows how to row a boat 3 transmission of words (or something) from one to another; kwaŋŋo lok, transmitting words; see kubbo lok.

kwany *v* take away, pick up; kwany kom iter i ot, take the chair into the house; kwany cente ki i kom eno, take the cents from that chair there.

kwanynye *vi* it is removable, can be separated, taken away; twerro kwanynye, can be removed or taken away.

kwanynyo *vt* to take / taking away, to pick / picking up; kwanynyo war ki rukkone, to take / taking the shoes and to wear / wearing them; kwanynyo rac kit pa wonne ni, picking up his father's bad manners.

kwar *n* red; kwar lilaŋ, li pac, liraŋ, deep red, scarlet, crimson.

kwar cwiny *n* hatred, bad character, bitterness; kwar cwiny kipwola, hatred / bitterness is a misfortune; see kipwola.

kwar piny *n* early morning, morning flush.

kwar-waŋ *n* firmness of purpose, earnestness, determination; oommo

ki om me kwar waŋ, he brought it with a firmness of purpose; **makko geddo me kwar waŋ,** building with great determination / earnestness.

kwat *n* herding, tending cattle; **lakwat,** a herdsman; **citto ka kwat,** going to herd or look after(cattle).

kwaya *n* spy, emissary for reconnoitring; **bollo kwaya,** sending out an individual for reconnoitring; **lakwaya,** a spy or a hunter searching out game.

kwaya bat *n* the shoulder blade; **waŋ kwaya,** the junction between the arm and the chest.

kwayo *vt* to request, ask, beg; **citto ka kwayo kado bot daane,** going to beg for some salt from her mother-in-law; see **kwaa, kwac.**

kwayo *vt* to herd / herding, to tend / tending cattle; **kwayo dyaŋi,** to herd / herding cattle; **kwayo romi,** to shepherd / shepherding sheep.

kwayo jami *n* varieties of things or species; **kwayo jami ma i wii loboni pol mada,** there are many varieties and species of things in this world.

kwed *vp* with; 1 **cit ki latin,** go with the child 2 search; **kwed tee lum,** search under the grass; **kwed tee lokke maber,** examine the case carefully.

kwed or kwedda *prn* with, with me; **obinno kwedda,** he came with me.

kwedde *vi* 1 can be investigated; **tee lokke twerro kwedde,** the problem can be investigated. 2 with him.

kweddo *vt* to search / searching for (under grass or anything); **kweddo tee lum,** to search / searching under the grass; **kweddo tee lok,** investigating / examining a case very carefully.

kwe *adv* very, extraordinary, extremely; **awaci kwe pe iwinynyo lok omiyo ipotto i can,** I tried very hard to tell you but you refused to listen, that is why you got into trouble.

kwee *vp* 1 to become quiet, calm, cold, compose onself; **piny doŋ tye ka kwee,** the weather is becoming cool, condition in the country is becoming calm; 2 pain is getting better; **arem tye ka kwee,** the pain is subsiding 3 becoming calm; **Ocol doŋ okwee,** Ocol has composed himself and has become quiet or calm.

kwee *vi* comfort, console; **cit icikwee cwinynye,** go and console / comfort him; see **kwec, kweyo.**

kwee *v* cool, freeze; **kwee cai ka doŋ imatti,** cool the tea first and then take.

kwe-kwe *adv* very slowly; **en doki wotto kwe kwe twatwal,** he walks very slowly.

kwek *v* open; **kwek dog latin,** open the child's mouth.

kwekke *vi* be opened; **opuk ka olorro wiye woko i iye, ci dogge pe twerro kwekke,** when the tortoise has shut its head inside, its mouth cannot be opened.

kwekko *vt* 1 to open / opening, to break /breaking open (nuts etc.); 2 opening up; **kwekko lum,** to separate / separating, to open / opening up, to part / parting (grass for passage); **kwekko dog gwok,** to open / opening a dog's mouth.

kwele *n* prostitution, lust; **lakwele,** a prostitute.

kwene? *inter. adv* where? where to? whence? **icitto kwene?** where are you going? **i aa ki kwene?** where have you come from? **yoo man citto kwene?** where does this road lead to?

kwenno *n* to stroll / strolling about, to roam / roaming about, saunter about; **kwenno piny,** to roam / roaming about; see **gwenno piny.**

kwer *v* refuse; **ka in lacoo ada, ci kwer cullo mucoro,** if you are truly a man, then refuse to pay the tax!

kwer *vn* refusing; k**wer me cullo mucoro twerro terri i jero,** refusing to pay the tax may lead you to jail!

kwer *vi* persist, press (on) hard, rage; **kwer i kom lok mape iŋeyo terre twerro terri i can,** persisting on matters which you do not understand may lead you into trouble; **two okwer i komme,** he is badly off with the disease; **kee okwer i komme,** he is having excessive desire for meat; **koyo okwer i komme,** he is feeling very cold.

kwer *n* 1 menstruation; **dako tye ki kwer,** the woman is having her period or is menstruating.

kwer *n* a traditional religious ceremony.

kweri *n* hoe; **kweri man doŋ lakke onyany woko,** the edge of this hoe is now blunt; **wapurro poto ki kweri,** we cultivate the field with the hoe.

kwerre *vi* 1 can be rejected / refused; **lok marac kitmeno twerro kwerre,** such bad news can be refused or rejected 2 ordained; **Onen mere twerro kwerre me bedo ladit kanica,** Onen can be ordained to be a clergy or a priest 3 a traditional ritual ceremony; **tye ka kwerre pi nekko ŋuu,** is having traditional ritual ceremony for killing a wild beast; **pe ikwerre pi too pa lamoneni,** do not hold a ritual ceremony for the death of your enemy.

kwerro *vt* celebrating; **kwerro ketto laker,** celebrating the enthronment /

installation of a king / ruler.

kwerro *vt /n* abstaining from, refusing, objecting, declining, rejecting, giving up, denying; **kwerro koŋo,** abstaining from alcohol; **kwerro cammo okoro,** rejecting / objecting to eating snail; **kwerro citto ka kwaŋ,** refusing to go and swim; **kwerro tic ma gimiine,** declining the offer of the job; **kwerro lok anywar,** objecting to insulting words.

kwet *n* (abusive word) naughty or silly brat; **lakwet pa aŋaa ma okonynye kanynyi?** whose spawn / offspring / breed has defecated here?

kwet-kwet *adv* noise made by the feet when somebody is walking lightly; **wotto ma tyenne gwetto ŋom ni kwet kwet,** walks with the feet making noises as they rub the ground.

kweyo *n* sand; **litino gitye ka tukko i kweyo,** the childreen are playing in the sand.

kweyo *vt* to tranquilize / tranquillizing, to pacify / pacifying, soaking. 2 **kweyo cwiny,** to console / consoling, pacifying the mind 3 to make / making cold; **kweyo cak me amatta pa latin,** making the milk cold for the child to drink see **kwee, kwec.**

kwic *adv* suddenly; **oa ni kwic ci ocitto woko,** he got up suddenly and went away; **okwata oceyo latin gweno ni kwic,** the kite snatched the chick suddenly and flew away with it; see **kwik.**

kwici-kwici *adv* entirely, completely; **ŋinynyo woko ni kwici-kwici,** destroying it completely.

kwici-kwici *adj* spotted all over with various colours; **aweno ki kwac komgi**

obeddo kwici-kwici, the guinea fowl and the leopard have spotted bodies.

kwidi *n* microbe / worm, grub, maggot; **riŋone opoŋ kwidi keken,** the meat is full of maggots; also called **kudi.**

kwik *adv* suddenly and vigorously; **gubinno ci gutugi makke woko ni kwik,** they came and suddenly and vigorously arrested him; see **kwic.**

kwikko *adv* crying, especially of animals; **kana kok ni kwiko kwiko,** the donkey cries **kwiko kwiko.**

kwil *v* whisper; **gitye ka kwillo lokke akwilla,** they are only whispering about the matter; let out a little about a case; **kwil igi lokke mo manok,** whisper to them a little information about the case.

kwil *vp* settled, well adapted; **terro kare me dye ot me kwil,** it takes time for the floor to be fine and smooth; **dye ot doŋ okwil,** the floor is now well and smooth.

kwil *adv* asunder, broken; **otur / oŋun ni kwil,** it is broken completely asunder.

kwille *vn* walking stealthily, gently and quietly; **lukwoo gukwille ci gudonynyo i ot ki dye wor ci gukwallo jami,** the thieves walked stealthily, gently and quietly at night and stole things; see **kwalle, kiine.**

kwillo *vt* whispering; **wun wutye ka kwillo lok aŋoo?** what are you whispering about?

kwillo-kwillo *adv.* 1 walking lazily or lingeringly; **latinne gorro wotto ni kwillo-kwillo,** the child is weak and walks lingeringly / lazily. 2 a slow burning of fire; **mac tye ka lyel ni kwillo kwillo,** the fire is burning slowly.

kwiin *n Eng* queen; **Kwiin me Buŋgereja en aye Elicabet,** the British Queen is Elizabeth 11; see **daker.**

kwiiny *prd* 1 strong, fit, and intelligent; **latin ma kwiiny,** a strong, fit and intelligent child.

kwiny *v* dig up, excavate; **kwiny burre madit,** dig a big hole.

kwinynye *vn* can be dug; **kadi beddi got dwoŋ kany, ento twerro kwinynye,** even though there is much rock here but it can be dug.

kwinynyo *vn* digging up, excavating, unearthing; **kwinynyo bur,** digging a hole.

kwir *n* 1 poison; **yatte kec callo kwir,** the medicine is bitter like poison.

kwir *adv* 1 very painfully, excruciatingly; **okayo ni kwir callo kac pa oton,** bitten him very painfully like the sting of a scorpion 2 dead silent; **gaŋ oliŋ ni kwir,** the village is dead silent.

kwir *n* 1 casting lots, a general election; **bollo kwir atyer,** a general election 2 ordeal; **goyo kwir,** traditional way of finding out who is the wrongdoer, or culprit, was to ask the suspects to lick or hold the white hot blade of a knife with a tongue or hand; the one who is not guilty, his tongue or hand will not be burnt, while the one who is guilty will be burnt.

kwirri *prd* intelligent, very able and talented; **dakone kwirri,** his wife is very intelligent and talented.

kwitte *vi* to move convulsively, unconsciously, to writhe. 1 **twol ka tye ka too kwitte ki yibbe,** when a snake is dying, its body and tail writhe; **dyel tye ka kwitte pien doŋ giŋollo ŋutte woko,** the goat is now convulsing because its neck has been cut 2 to struggle; **ka imitto ni in bene inoŋ ci myero ikwitte pire,** if you want to get it also, you should struggle for it.

kwiya *vt/vn* being ignorant of, not knowing, being unaware; **kwiya gin ma otimme laworo,** unaware of what happened yesterday; **kwiya piny gin marac mada,** ignorance is a very bad thing indeed.

kwoc *vn* tailoring, sewing, stitching; **tye ka kwoc,** he is tailoring / sewing / stitching; **kwoc gin maber mada,** tailoring is a good thing; see **kwoo, kwoyo.**

kwok *v* take with you, **kwok buk man kweddi,** take this book with you.

kwok *n* sweat, perspiration; **kwok tye i waŋŋe,** he has some sweat on his face.

kwok *vi* gone bad (food), spoiled and starting to smell; **riŋo okwok woko, doŋ ŋwe,** the meat has gone bad and is smelly.

kwokke *v* go with also; **kwokke ki buk man ka iecito i laibary,** if you are going to the library take this book also with you.

kwokko *vt* to take / taking with one; **kwokko buk ki mukene,** to take / taking the book in addition to the others.

kwon *n* millet bread; it is made by pouring millet flour in boiling in a pot over a fire while it is being stirred until it becomes very thick and well cooked.

kwoŋ *v* commence, start, begin; **kwoŋ cakko ŋwec,** be the first to start running

kwoŋ *n* swearing, taking an oath; **yat kwoŋ,** medicine taken as a pledge of reconciliation; **tee oput,** a kind of

medicinal plant which is quite bitter, sometimes taken for treating malaria by the people.

kwoŋ *v* swear; **kwoŋ ni in pe ma ikwallo,** swear that it is not you who stole.

kwoŋŋe *vi* to swear / swearing, swearing-in, taking an oath; **dano ma gimitto beddo memba me paliament nyo ot me ketto cik madit, tin gukwoŋŋe,** people who want to be Members of Parliament today took oaths.

kwoŋŋo *vt* 1 to swear / swearing, to take / taking an oath; **kwoŋŋo goba goba,** falsely swearing; **memba adi me paliament ma tin gukwoŋŋo?** how many Members of Parliament took the oaths today?

kwoŋŋo *vt* to start / starting, to commence / commencing, to begin / beginning; **kwoŋŋo pitto pamba i   mwaka man,** to starting planting the cotton this year.

kwoo *v* stitch, sew; **kwoo boŋo man,** stitch this cloth / gament; see **kwoc, kwoyo.**

kwoo *n* theft, stealing; **lakwoo,** a thief; **gimakke ka kwoo,** he was caught stealing.

kwoo *vn* 1 living, being alive 2 life; **kwoone pe ber,** his way of living is not good.

kwooko *n* an insect that lives in stalks of sorghum.

kwor *v* clean by winnowing; **kwor bel,** clean the corn by winnowing it.

kwor *n* enmity (due to murder or manslaughter).

kwor *vn* paleness of skin caused by dust; **kwor kom,** dirty body due to dust.

kworo *n* serval cat see also **giliri, too, bura, oculi, cwiiny and kak.**

kworre *vi* jumping up, leaping over, springing; **kworre loka kulu,** jumping over the river; **kalle okworre maber mada,** the millet was well cleaned by winnowing.

kworre *vi* winnowed and cleaned; **nyim man twerro kworre maleŋ mada,** this simsim can be winnowed and cleaned quite easily.

kworro *vt* to clean / cleaning millet or simsim by winnowing and dropping it from a height so that the wind blows awaythe chaff; **kworro pii, dek nyo ŋor malyet ki agwadeko wekki okwee,** pouring hot sauce or cowpeas soup with a calabash plate from a height to expose it to the wind to cool it.

kwot *n* 1 shield. 2 protector; **wir moo i kom kwot wek pe oteŋ**, smear the shield with oil so that it may not warp; **kwot pa latin en aye wonne,** the child's shield is the father.

kwot *vp* swelling; **kwot ciŋ**, swelling of hand.

kwotto *vt* 1 causing swelling; **twoo olaŋ kwotto kom,** kidney disease causes swelling of the body.

kwotto *vt* backbiting, slandering; **kwotto dano,** backbiting people.

kwotto *vt* breaking wind / passing wind; **kwotto cet ma ŋwee,** breaking wind / passing flatus which smells very bad.

kwoyo *vt* sewing, stitching, tailoring; **kwoyo boŋo,** sewing, stitching, tailoring clothes; **lakwoc,** a tailor; see **kwoc, kwo.**

L l

la *pref* used in combination with other words; when added to a verb, the verb changes into a noun or a pronoun; eg **kwoo,** stealing, **la-kwoo,** a thief; **ŋwec,** running; **la-ŋwec,** a runner; etc. **la** - makes the Acholi language different from Lango and Alur: where Acholi say **latin**, the Langi say **atin.**

laa *n* hide; proverb: **rom-rom ma laa too,** it is all the same like the jackal's skin, it makes no difference, they are the same.

laa *v* urinate, micturate, pass urine; **cit ilaa i coron,** go and urinate in the toilet, see **lac, layo.**

laa *n* spittle, saliva; **pe iŋul laa kany,** do not spit here.

laa dog jok *n* small rashes or swellings on the skin usually due to an *allergy.*

lab *v* remove; **lab gweŋ woko ki i nyim ma girubbo ki pii,** remove the stone from the simsim mixed with water; **lab daba woko ki i waŋ it,** remove the mud from the well.

labaa *n* a fibre plant used for making nets; **obwoo labaa,** a net from the **labaa** plant.

labaa *n* a kind of grasshopper; see **otwoŋo.**

labac labac *adv* partially; **olwokke labac labac,** partially washed.

labac *n* a ramrod; **kel labac me jwayo i luduku,** bring the cleaning rod for cleaning the guns.

labal-aweno *n* **labal, lacik aweno** *n* a trap for guinea fowls.

labala *n* a kind of fish.

labala *n* a dance; **myel labala** a kind of dance in which people dance without striking the drums, and all the drums are put down, part of **bwola** dance.

labalaŋo *n* an enemy; **labalaŋone en aye Olweny,** his enemy is Olweny.

labala-waŋ-odyak *n* a bird.

labana *n* sternum; **labana kor,** meat around the sternum of an animal which elders like to eat because it is soft; *c/f* **lapok, dak kor.**

labarakak *n* a maneater that is thought to be a human being who has changed into a leopard or lion.

Labeja *n* the name of a spirit a male name.

labelu *n* a restless, mentally ill child, an imbecile; see also **lagama, lagikom, lapoya.**

labeno *n* the back loin dress worn by elder women which may be of animal skin or cloth.

labet-bet *n* a dress made of skin for old men.

labika *n* a weed whose seeds have spikes which stick easily to clothes.

labila-wii-ot *n* the peak of a hut, or pinnacle of the hut.

labiri-biri *n* the bumblebee, a big hairy fly which makes great noise when it flies.

labit *n* bait; **gin labit rec en aye otwol kot,** bait for fish is earthworms.

labit *adj S* foolish; **in labit mada,** you are a foolish person (it is obsolete and used to be used in the police).

labbo *vt* skimming; **labbo moo ki i wii cak,** skimming cream off the milk; **labbo lok** or **cotto lok,** *vi* speaking angrily or roughly; **labbo dek,** taking a large amount of sauce

labo *n* a circle described by a bird in the air.

labok *adj* the brownish yellow colour of fowls and birds.

labol *adv* 1 example; **labolle en, lokke yaŋ otimme con,** for example, this happened in the past. 2 **labol dog dano** *qv* **bwotto dog dano,** repeated remarks about what one has done for some-body; **dek mamit en aye labol me teddo maber** good food is evidence of good cooking.

labolo *n* banana or green plantain; **tuga labolo,** a bunch of bananas.

laboŋ *n.* a member who does not belong to the royal clans; a common man.

1 laboŋo *n* thin high shrubs whose barks are used for making ropes.

2 laboŋo *prp* without; **obinno laboŋo bukke,** he came without his book.

Laboŋo *n* a male name (given to one who has no brother).

laboretori *n Eng* laboratory, a place where experiment, research and examinations of things are performed; **gicwallo remone i laboretori ka pimmone,** his blood has been sent to laboratory for examination or the blood has been sent to laboratory for examinaton (under microscope).

labot *n* a spinster, bachelor; **Jon pudi tye labot,** John's still a bachelor.

labot *adj* without; **dek labot bot,** sauce without salt.

labuka *n* a large tree of the *Euphorbia* variety with large leaves, whose leaves some people use as medicine for diarrhoea or intestinal worms.

labul *n* duodenum of cattle and goats etc; *c/f* **lakwaduk, apika.**

labuma *n* swindler, conman; see **labwami nyo labwuma.**

labuta *n* a boaster, a proud fellow, an impostor; **awobine labuta mada,** the boy is a boaster.

labutte *n* an impostor a proud fellow or a boaster; trying to be what he is not; **danone labutte makato ducu,** the man is an imposter, always trying to be what he is not; see **lawakke, lanyatte.**

labututu *n* mumps, a swelling around the ear.

labwami *n* swindler, conman; **gwokke ki William en twon labwami mada,** be careful about William for he is a great swindler; see **labuma.**

labwoc *n* an insolent offensive person; **jalle labwoc mada,** the fellow is an insolent or offensive person.

labwor *n* a lion; **labwor olik** or **labwor ocida,** a big lion which usually does not walk with others in groups but lives alone; this is usually an old lion; **labwor nya oculi,** a small kind of lion which lives with others in groups.

labwori *n* kind of thin tree used very much for building.

labwoto *n* 1 a man who is an expert in opening abscesses and draining them, native surgeon; **en labwoto me barro akwota,** he is an expert in opening / incising abscesses 2 an expert; **labwotto i yubbo caa,** an expert in repairing watches.

lac *vi/n* urine, passing urine; **tye ka lac,** he is passing urine; **lacce tye iye remo,** his urine has blood in it; see **laa, layo.**

lac *adj* broad, wide, spacious; **ot beddone lac ni woŋ,** the sitting room is very broad, and spacious.

lacacar or **lacarro** *n* an extravagant, careless, unaccountable person; **latinne lacacar ki lim,** the child is very extravagant with money.

lacakacaka *n* a sauce which consist of cut cowpeas leaves mixed with fresh groundnuts or simsim paste and then cooked into a thick sauce.

lacam *adj* left-handed, on the left side.

lacan *n* a poor or needy person 2 a bachelor.

lacaŋa *n* a mid-sized yellow fish with many bones, people like it for the delicious taste of its soup; it is now called **agara** because of its bones; see **agara.**

lacara *n* a white foreigner.

Lacara *n* na male name.

lacari *n* a thorn tree *(Acacia albida).*

lacarro *adj* having bad habits, unchaste, loose; **dakone lacarro,** she is a loose woman.

lacat wil *n* a trader sometimes (called simply **lacat) lacat wil oa ka catto jammi ne,** a trader returned from selling his wares.

lacek *n* dik dik; see also, **ruda, lajwa, abur.**

lacele, lalobolobo, oliŋ, larakaraka *n* names for the same kind of dances, without spear, in chronological order, **diŋidiŋi** is the most recent one but only dance for the girls no boys; there is **omok or lamoko moko,** this is a dance which takes place at night for both girls and boys, came during the second world war period.

119

lacen *adv* 1 last; **obinno lacen,** he came last 2 later; **lacen en obinno,** later on he came.

lacen *n* the vengeful ghost of a deceased person.

lacene *n* a type of green grasshopper which comes at night periodically in large number (delicacy to some tribes); the majority call it **ocene.**

lacer *n* a plant used for treating chronic ulcer.

lacerre *n* a tubborn person, one who does not listen to advice; **latinni dok lacerre twatwal pe mitto winynyo lok mo me pwony,** this child is very stubbon, he does not want to listen to any advice.

lacir lok *n* an obstinate person; **latin ma lacir lok mada,** a very obstinate child.

lacoc *n* a writer; **en lacoc maber mada,** he is a good writer.

lacoc *n* a sower; **lacoc ocitto ka coyo kal i poto,** a sower went to sow millet in the field.

lacoco *n* a prostitute, a lustful or adulterous woman; **dako ma lacoco pe myerro beddo i gaŋ pien ballo mon mukene woko,** a woman who is a prostitute should not be in the home because she spoils other women.

laco-codo *n* 1 a game for little girls in which they jump while squatting with heels touching thighs while holding knees 2 snake.

lacoi or **koŋo lacoi** *n* a kind of millet beer drunk through long tubes from a small pot.

lacol got *n* the peak of a mountain often covered with a big flat stone.

lacolla, or lacollo *n* a midwife.

lacoo *n* a man.

lacoor or lacor *prn n* an impostor, **man mere lacor pe ŋeyo yubbo motoka,** this one is just an imposter, he does not know how to repair the car.

lacuc *adj* right; **ciŋa tuŋ lacuc,** my right hand.

lacuko gweno *n* crop of fowl.

lacuko, lacukocuko *n* the dried hard cover of the fruit of a tree which are prepared and in which small stone are put so they can serve as rattles when tied to the legs of dancers; **myel lacuko cuku,** dancing with the rattles tied to the legs to make a rhythmic sound when dancing.

lacuŋ *n* representative, a pleader; **lacuŋ pi Uganda i Amerika,** Uganda's ambassador ito America; **lacuŋ dwarra,** my lawyer, protector, (in a case of a child) my guardian; **lacuŋ dwarra mo peke,** I have nobody to intervene on my behalf such as a lawyer or an intercessor.

lacurubee *n* animals paid for taking someone else's wife, usually cattle or cattle together with goats.

lacuur *n* a stone in a sling which is turned round and round several times and then let loose; used to shoot birds or hit other things.

lacwec *n* potter, maker, creator 1 **lacwec; agulu,** a potter. 2 **Lacwec lobo en aye Lubaŋa,** the maker of the earth is God

lacwii or lacwii remo *n* a sucker, commonly a cowhorn for sucking blood from people who are having pain or severe headache. **Lacwii me cwiiyo remo kama rem,** a horn for sucking the blood from the site where there is much pain on the body; that was the method of treating pain especially headaches, in which the blood was sucked from the head.

lacwi-cwii *n* a tormenter, harassing person, nagger; **dano ma lacwi cwii pe twerro noŋŋo lutic,**.a man who is a great tormentor or a harassing person cannot get workers.

ladeŋ tun *n* inner lip of the vagina (*labia minora*) which normally swells during coition or sexual intercourse; see *labia majora* (the vagina has two lips covering it, the outer lip is called *labia majora*, and the inner lip is called *labia minora*).

ladep *n* flea; **ladep nyaa mada i kom gwok mape gilwokko,** fleas multiply very much on a dog which is not washed.

ladeyo *n* a dandy; **awobine ladeyo mada,** the boy is quire dandy.

ladidii or lagem *n* a miser, a stingy person; **ka ilego ni omiini gin mo miini ma titidi mo pien en ladidii twatwal,** when you ask him to give you something, he will give you very little of it because he is a miser.

ladikke *prn* a person who always comes late or who delays coming; see **ladokke, ladwalle, lagalle, laminne, lajoŋŋe, lajuŋŋe, lanywenne, laŋinynye.**

ladiro *n* an artist, expert, craftsman; **en ladiro yubbo redio mada,** he is an expert in repairing radios.

ladit *n* Mr, old man, big man, authority; **wamitto nenno ladit Oto,** we want to see Mr. Oto; **ladit kanica,** priest, **ladit kom,** chairperson; **ladit tic,** foreman, headman, manager; **ladit gaŋ,** an elder or head of the home; **ladit tic ma loyo ducu,** general manager.

ladoŋo nyim *n* in July; see **nyim lajimu-** which is sown in August.

ladum *n* interpreter; **lwoŋ ladum obin ogony lok,** call the interpreter to come and interpret.

laduk *n* a small short stick thrown at birds or anything else.

laduk - duk *adv* ending in a short tassel - like bush; **yib rii olot laduk-duk,** the tail of a giraffe is long with a bushy end.

laduni *n* a man of Bunyoro (now rarely used).

ladur *n* a miser, a stingy person; **lacoo ma ladur twatwal pe miyo gin mo ki ŋatti,** a stingy person does not give anything to anybody.

Ladur *n* a female name.

laduru (otigo) *n* a vegetable plant, whose leaves and seeds are eaten.

ladwala *n* a stammerer, stutterer; **myerro ibed dano ma lacir nyo ladii cwiny ka wek iwiny lok pa ladwala maber,** you should be a person who has patience in order to clearly hear what the stammerer says.

ladwanya *n* one who twists meanings of words.

ladwar *n* a hunter.

ladwerre *n* an irritable, irascible child, a peevish child; see also **lagiŋŋi.**

ladwoŋ *n* same as **ladit,**

Ladwoŋ *n* a mountain situated between Nimule and Gulu.

lagada *n* reed with flat reed stalks, used extensively in building roofs of huts.

lagal *n* metal rings worn as a necklace; the white colour of clerical vestments.

lagalo or lawaŋŋe otoo *n* a species of fly (*simulum damnosum*) which bites sharply; also called **ajoŋamiya.**

lagam n a mid-sized basket.

lagam *n* a reply, answer; **kella lagam meri i kom gin ma aconi,** bring me your reply or an answer to what I wrote to you; see **dok iye.**

lagama *n* an imbecile, a mentally ill person; see also **labelu, lagikom, lapoya.**

lagara *n* red locusts.

lagara *n* small sets of rings put all round the ear lobes.

Lagara *n* a male name.

lageddo *n* a builder, constructor, contractor.

lagelo *n* a bird, that is said to talk to itself; a parrot.

lagem *n* a miser, a stingy person.

lager *n* a bow legg; **dano ma tyenne lager,** a bow legged person or a person with a bow leg.

lagerro *adv* (animal or human being) ferocious or cruel.

lagikom *n* an imbecile, a mentally ill person; see also **lapoya, labelu, lagama.**

lagilo lak *n* tusk, tooth; **ogilo lak** is the expression currently used for canine tooth.

lagilo lee *n* a piece of meat from the neck and a small part of the chest.

lagiŋi *n* a person who is always grudging, a vexing or quarrelsome person; **lagiŋi callo minne,** he is always grudging like his mother.

lagiri-giri *adj* stunted; **dano ma lagiri giri,** a short and stunted person.

lagit or agit *n* ring; **lagit ciŋ,** a finger ring; **agit** is more commonly used.

laggo *vt* to come / coming to one's assistance, to help; **wucit oyot oyot ka laggo litino ki cam kec nekkogi,** go quickly with food to save the children from hunger.

lagoba *n* liar, deceiver; see **lalilla.**

lagoga *n* joker, clown, jester, comedian.

lagoŋotoo or goŋoŋwe *n* praying mantis the latter is the more common name for it.

lagora ot *n* a circle of reeds made as frames for a hut.

lagot *n* the handle of a hoe which is bent into semi hook form.

lagucu-gucu or **laduk** *n* a short stick thrown at birds or anything else.

lagut *n* a shrike or wagtail.

laguti *n* a special edible kind of mushroom. It sprouts in great numbers at the beginning of the rainy season.

lagwar *n* the zebra

lagwar yugi *n* 1 a rake for collecting weeds 2 person raking weeds.

lagwee *n* a lizard.

lagweno kulu *n* the water rail or water-hen of the *ralleni* family, the crested crane.

lagwok otiŋo riŋone *n.* simsim sauce without meat in it (it is a proverb).

lagwom or **lagwoŋ** *n* a stammerer, stutterer; **danone lagwom pe twerro lok maber,** he cannot speak well because he stammers.

laibreri *n Eng* a library which is a place or a building where books, newspapers etc are kept for reading, study and borrowing.

la-it *n* a ladder; **la-it dero,** a ladder for entering a barn or granary; see **layibi.**

la itte otto or la itte odiŋ *n* a deaf person.

lajaja dog *n S* glass; **ladore, lacan kumu,** straight glass rods filed from pieces of broken bottles and put through the hole made in the lower lip as an ornament (not used now).

lajayi *n* a pudding from ground cowpeas mixed with simsim paste.

lajimo *n* a type of simsim sown in August; see **ladoŋo, reŋe.**

lajire myel or myel lacuku cuku *n* dancing with rattles (on the legs).

lajok *n* an evil man who is supposed to dance at night - night dancer and uses magic, a wizard or a witch.

laju *n* small patches of grass in water.

lajuk *n* a brake; **lajuk leela,** bicycle brake; **cam odiko me lajuk ic,** breakfast.

lajwa *n* oribi, duiker; see **abur, lacek, ruda.**

lajwa jami *n* polish, things for polishing.

lajwa lak *n* a toothbrush.

lajwac *adv* 1 frankly, plainly; **alokki lajwac,** I tell you frankly. 2 Loosely; **wiyo tol lajwac,** twisted the rope loosely 3 unlimited time and length; **ocitto lajwac,** he went for good; **tolle bor lajwac**, it is very long rope.

lak *n* 1 tooth, elephant tusk. 2 **lak kweri** old worn-out hoe. 3 **lak dwe, lak ceŋ, lak nyaŋo,** moonshine, sunshine,

morning sunshine. 4 **lak palaa, lak toŋ,** edge of a knife, spear; **lak palaa oluu, / oligu,** the edge of the knife is blunt.

lak *vi* 1 to crawl, slither; **twol lak alakka ka wotto,** the snake slithers when going about 2 creep; **kiyata twerro lak ummo poto woko,** the potatoes can creep and cover the whole field.

lak *vn* wander, roam; **latini doki lak twatwal i kin duka,** this child wanders aimlessly among the shops.

lak ŋet *n* flank; **ogoyo lak ŋette,** he struck his flank **lakaa bel nyo lakac** *n* harvester.

lakac *n* 1 big white ostrich feathers. 2 a harvester.

lakaibona *n* the female pointed-head green grasshopper, the male is called **lateketeke;** see **labaa, awiny awiny, apededede, ajot jot, obaŋcet, abiliŋ.**

lakaka *n* a lizard; see **lagwee, tokoloŋ.**

lakaka lyec *n* the membrane under the skin of an elephant, hippo.

lakal *prn* one who stays in the palace.

lakalabuk *n* a kind of hat made of hair.

lakalagwec *n* the swift is a bird which leaves on the palm and therefore called palm shift; its wings slender and like scythe or like half moon or **ogwec,** their tail is also forked; they are very swift and can glide for some distance without flapping their wings (*cypsiurus parvus*) see **meda,** swallow.

lakalakidi *n* grass twisted together into a rope that women use for tying firewood.

lakalatwe or latwe *n* a star.

lakalatwe layibbe *n* a shooting star.

lakap *n* 1 diaphragm; **otweyo paline**

wa i lakaap, he tied his trousers right up above the waist; 2 *n Eng* lock-up; **giterro i lakap,** taken to the lock-up.

lakar *n* a y-shaped piece of wood for supporting or on which a granary stands.

lakarac *n* a carved stool with three or more legs; **kom pa ludito,** elders' stool.

lakarakak *n* a man-eater which is believed to be a human being who do change from time to time into beast, when it wants to eat man.

lakele *n* small side drums; see **drum.**

laker *n* a royal person, a chief, a king.

Laker *n* a name that is both male and female.

lakerre *n* latin **lakerre** *n* a newborn baby, neonate.

lakerre *n* a person with a gap between the teeth.

laket wic *n* a comb; **kella laket wic, aket ki wiya,** bring me a comb so I can comb my hair.

lakeya *n* my niece, a daughter of my sister ; **lakeyo,** a niece (a general name); the order for these relations are as follows: sing **lakeya, lakeyu, lakeyone,** my, your, his niece; *pl* **lukeyowa, lukeyowu, lukeyogi,** our, your, their nieces; nieces who are not closely related but belong to the same clan are called as follows: **lakeyiwa, lakeyiwu, lakeyigi,** our, your, their niece.

lakeyo *n* a niece; **lakeyo konynyo daayo mada,** the niece helps grandmother very much.

lakica *n* a kind person who has compassion, who is ready to forgive, or to serve.

lakide *n* a kind of grass with a bushy head.

lakidi *n* a stone.

Lakidi *n* a male name.

lakili *adj* stubborn, quarrelsome, obstinate, (cf. **lagiŋi**)

lakilikili *n* dumplings made from **lamola** seeds used as sauce.

lakiribala, atiko *n* a kind of large (brownish) grasshopper.

lakirikiri *adj* restless, seizes and breaks everything; see **lapele, lataŋgalo, lakiti kiti, waŋŋe pit pit.**

lakko *vt* to inherit , take over from another; **ocitto ka lakko jami pa wonne,** he went to inherit his father's property; **lakko dako ma cwarre otoo,** taking over a woman whose husband has died.

lakko *vt* to rinse / rinsing out, to clean / cleaning by rinsing; **boŋo doŋ gilwokko, teer ka lakkone,** the clothes have been washed, take them to be rinsed.

lakob-dog, lakob-lok *n* an interpreter, mediator, reporter, go-between.

lakobo or lakobe *n* a head ornament (old custom).

lakodo, usually **dero lakodo** *n* a small granary for simsim.

lakok or lakok wii ot *n* a layer of thatch which reaches to the top of the roof; see **nyarabuk.**

lakol *n* a prisoner with a log fixed to the foot (in the days of slavery).

lakologoc *n* a wooden or metal spoon; **kella lakologoc me tokko cam,** bring me a spoon for serving / dishing the food; see **malaga, kijiko.**

lakor tipu *n* one who summons ghosts

or of living people to the bodies appear and talk , thus causing them to die.

Lakor *n* a male name.

lakucel or tuŋ cel *adv* 1 on one side, one-sided; **dogola gilloro lakucel keken,** the door has been closed on one side only 2 **ogoye lakucel,** he beat him without him hitting back.

lakuci *n* the thorns of the acacia tree used against snakes; if put around the holes in a house, they will prevent snakes from entering.

lakucu kucu or **lapuru puru** *n* very small gnats, that swarm around and bite one's head particularly in the evening.

lakur *n* a guard, security; **lakur gaŋ**, a home guard.

lakuru *n* a short leg; **gweno lakuru,** a stunted chicken or short-legged chicken.

lakwaduk *n* stomach of animal; *c/f* **apika, labul.**

lakwal *n* a babbler, bird (*turdoides melanops).*

lakwana *n* red earth used for dressing hair.

lakwaŋ yeya or **lacer yeya** *n* a boatman, the rower of a boat.

lakwaa *n* grandchild; **man lakwaa Okot,** this is Okot's grandchild.

lakwaara *n* my grandchild; **lakwaara tye kwene?** where is my grandchild?

lakwaaro *n* a grandchild; **lakwaaro konynyo daayo,** the granddaughter helps the grandmother.

lakwat *n* a shepherd; **lakwat maber en aye Yecu,** Jesus is a good shepherd.

lakwelle *n* a prostitute, a loose girl; **man lakwele beddo ki coo ata,** this is a prostitute stays with any man.

lakwenna *n* a messenger, envoy, apostle; **lukwenna pa Yecu,** the apostles of Jesus.

lak kweri *n* the edge of a hoe blade; **lak kweri pe bit,** the edge of the blade of the hoe is not sharp.

lakwoo *n* 1 a thief; **lakwoo kwallo jami,** a thief steals things.

lakwoo *n* a survivor; **lakwoo en aye bileyo otte,** a survivor will inherit the house.

lakwor *n* an enemy; **lakwor meeri tye kwene?** where is your enemy? see **lameroko.**

lal *vi* to get lost, disappear, go astray; **latinne doŋ lal ata,** the child is lost, is wandering about.

lala *n* a metal cooking saucepan (in the past it was of brass).

lalaa *n* a bitter vegetable (byword: **ber ber pa lalaa,** it is very nice to look at but has some hidden defect).

lalago *n* a large head ornament of ostrich feathers.

lalakko *n* an heir, inheritor; **lalakko pa Onen tye kwene?** where is Onen's heir?

lala lala *adv* copiously; **lalelee mol ni lala lala,** rain watch flowed down copiously.

lalar *n* a saviour, rescuer; **Yecu lalar,** Jesus the saviour; **lalarra,** my saviour.

lalarra *n* one who disputes or quarrels over something which is not his**; man dano ma lalarra mada, larro jami ma pe mere,** this is a man who always quarrels about things, he disputes ownerships of things which are not his.

lalebbe otoo *n* a dumb person.

lalebbe acel *n* a plant (used by witches) with one point.

lalee-dog-kika *n* roaming aimlessly from door to door; **latin ma lalee dog kika pa dano,** a child who goes from house to house aimlessly.

lalek, lalek pany *n* a pestle for a mortar; **nyim gioddo i pany ki lalek,** simsim is pounded in a mortar with a pestle.

lalekka *n* a herdsman; see **lakwat.**

lalelee *n* one person who passes from one thing to another, picking up anything he finds on his way; see **latoŋtwe, waŋŋe pit pit.**

lalelee *n* rivulets, of any size, caused by rain torrents; **litino gitye ka tukko i lalelee,** the children are playing in the rivulets; **lalelee omukko but ot woko,** the torrent rain has washed away the side of the hut.

lalem *n* **lalem tee kwot**, a ball of ostrich feathers fixed to the bottom of a shield.

lalem *n* without horns; **lalem en aye dyaŋ ma tuŋŋe peke, lalem** is a bull or a cow without horns.

lalilla *n* 1 a blabber, betrayer, 2 a traitor 3 an informer 4 somebody who cannot keep secrets 5 an untrustworthy person; **lalilla pe kanno lok i cwinynye,** an untrustworthy person can not keep secrets; **lalilla titto lok ma giwacce woko,** an untrustworthy will tell what he has been told to another person.

lalilii or la er alii *n* one who frequently causes trouble or one who is always a troublemaker.

lalimu tok or gija *n* a small ball covered with soft ostrich feathers carried as an ornament at the back of head.

laliŋ-liŋ *n* a small round stone used for smoothing pots during their making.

laliŋ-liŋ *adv* silently; **en tiyo jamine laboŋo ayella laliŋ-liŋ,** he does his things quietly without trouble.

laliya *n* a tree, the bark of whose new sprouts yield fibres for strings; its roots are used as medicine.

lallo *vt* to spread / spreading. 1 **lallo bel i kolo,** to spread / spreading millet on the papyrus mat in order to make it dry. 2 **lallo jami,** to squander / squandering things away. 3 **lallo dyee ot ki cet dyaŋ,** plastering the floor with cow dung.

lalobo-lobo *n.* old name for the **lacele** dance; *q.v.* **labala, laliŋoliŋo, larakaraka.**

laloka (*pl* **luloka**) *n* a person from the other side of the river (the name for **Joo- pa-Lwo, Bachope** in northern Bunyoro); but the name now includes Banyoro and Baganda; see **mwaa.**

laloko-lony *n* red sweet potatoes.

laloŋo loŋo *n* a cudgel, a piece of short thick wood used for closing the door of a hut for goats and sheep.

lalonyo *n* a rich or wealthy person.

lalor kika *n* a crossbar bolt or lock / for shutting the door.

lalor *n* a circular headgear, circle with ostrich feathers attached.

laluk *n* **dyaŋ ma laluk**, a cow with its horns bent down.

lalukka *n* a tracker, usually of game; **lalukka lee,** a man who can tell where animals have passed by their tracks.

lalukana *n* a tight cup-shaped head-covering made of hair and beads and worn as an ornament crown; **kwin rukko lalukana me jabu,** the queen wears a golden crown.

lalur *n* a hyena; **lalur orara** or **lawara,** a big hyena; **lalur tindiyo,** a small hyena.

lalur *n* 1 a barren woman; sterile man. 2 impotent man; see **lur.**

lalwee or **lamanne ki lwee** *n* a *monorchid* person, that is, a man with only one testicle, with the other remaining inside as an undescended testicle; **lalwee,** an impotent man, that is, a man whose penis cannot get erect; see **latekke opotto woko i pii.**

lalyer, lyer pa meni *n* angry abusive language (means your mother has a protruding labia minora).

lam *prd* few, not enough, a small amount. 1 **cukari ma ikello lam mada pe romowa ducu,** the sugar you brought is not enough for all of us. 2 **nyimme waŋi lam mada pe ocek maber,** this time the simsim is very poorly developed; **loc pa jago lam mada,** the sub-chief's authority is very little.

lam *n* cursing or blessing.

lam *v* 1 bless; **ogoyo lam maber,** he gave a good blessing 2 curse; **lam latin olaa i ot,** curse the child so that he urinates in the house.

lamal *n* a vagabond, vagrant, loafer 1 **lamal ata,** a vagabond. upward, **ket lamal i wii meja,** put it up on the table.

lamaar *n* a friend; **danone lamaar mera,** he is my friend.

lamaarra *n* my cousin; **lamaarro,** cousin (a general name); *sing* **lamaarra, lmaarru, lamaarre,** my, your, his cousin; *pl* **lumarrowa, lumaarrowu, umaarrogi,** our, your,

their cousins; clan 'cousins' are named thus: **lumaariwa, lumaarriwu, lumaarrigi,** our, your, their cousins; see **lameerra. lamaarra, lamaarri** *prn* my beloved, your beloved; **dako lamaarone,** his beloved wife; sometimes called **damaarro,** beloved darling.

lamaarro *n* a cousin; (a general name) see **lamaarra,** my cousin.

lamaraika *n S* an angel (an old name, now called **lamalaika**).

lamar-lamar *prd* brownish yellow colour; **lemun mape ya ocek obedo lamar lamar,** unripe lemon is yellowish green.

lamat kwir or **lakak kwir** *n* a thing for administering poison as an ordeal to find out an offender or culprit.

lameera *n* my sister; **lameego,** a general name for a sister; *sing* **lameera, lameeru, laminne,** my, your, his sister *sing* sister with many brothers; **lameegiwa, lameegiwu, lameegigi,** our, your, their sister; *pl* sisters with many brothers; **lumeegiwa, lumeegiwu, lumeegigi,** our, your, their sisters; clan 'sisters' call themselves **lumeego, lumeegowa, lumeegowu, lumeegogi,** sister, our, your, their sisters.

lameego *n* a sister; **lameego odok gaŋ,** the sister has returned home.

lamele *n* a small yellowish bird, a finch.

lameer *n* 1 a friend 2 sister; **eni lameer aŋaa?** whose sister is this?

lameroko *n* an enemy; **lameroko acel okatto kany,** one enemy has passed here.

lamerro *n* a drunken person; **lamerro moni opotto en,** a drunkard has fallen here.

lamin *n* a sister, **lamin Orac,** a sister of Orac; **laminne,** his sister.

lamiŋ *n* a stupid person a blockhead, a silly fellow; **lamiŋŋi tye kany,** the stupid fellow is here.

lamir or **lamir-lamir** *adj* dark brown.

lamiru *n* a slave; see, **opii, aŋeca / jane.**

lamme *vi* to curse / cursing one another; **mon tin gudaa ma gulamme mape wacce,** the women quarrelled today and strongly cursed one another.

lammo *vt* 1 to curse / cursing, wishing ill to, casting a spell on; **lammo dano,** cursing people or wishing them ill luck 2 praying; **lammo dog i nyim jok,** praying to **jok.**

lammo *vt* to remove / removing something by soaking in water; **lammo nyim,** to remove / removing grit from simsim by pouring simsim into water, with the grit going under and simsim rising up.

Lamogi *n* an Acholi clan with a dialect close to that of Jonam and Alur.

lamola *n* a kind of plant, similar to simsim grown for its oil.

Lamola *n* the name of a mountain not far from Mt Guruguru.

lamoluny *n* a peculiar ornament worn by one who has killed some big wild beast or man.

lamone *n* an enemy.

lamulo mulu *n* a bright kind of lizard.

lamuro-muro *n* pancreas; **mitto lamuro muro me acamma,** he wants pancreas for eating.

lanam *n* a member of the Alur people inhabiting the banks of the River Nile and the northern shores of Lake Albert.

lanebi *pl* **lunebi** *n* a prophet, one who foretells, predicts the future.

lanedde *n* 1 a slender girl; **mitto nyako ma lanedde,** wants a slender girl. 2 **lanedde yat;** a slender tall tree without branches.

lanek *n* a murderer.

Lanek *n* a male name.

lanekko *n* a madman especially one who is violent.

lanen *n* a sign, token, an example, a distinguishing mark; **lanen tye kwene ma nyutto ni ogoyi mada?** where is the sign / mark which shows that you have been badly beaten?

lano *adj* light brown **awobi ma lano** a boy with a light brown skin.

laŋ, li laŋ *adv* immovable; **ocuŋ li laŋ,** it stood firmly.

laŋabu *adj* long-legged with a short trunk, lofty; **pyerre laŋabo,** his waist is high (and chest short).

laŋalla *n* a proud man who despises or ridicules other people; *prov* **laŋalla cammo boo ki toyo,** a proud man eats vegetable with on it dew (meaning eats unprepared vegetables).

laŋaŋayo *n* a kind of grass whose roots are eaten, usually by children.

laŋatte *vi* a proud man, a boaster; **lacoo ma laŋatte mada,** he is a very proud man.

laŋayo *n* a big green-headed biting fly.

laŋgere *A* a bedstead made of leather and has wooden legs; see **cida, kitanda.**

laŋii *n* a mirror; **kella laŋii wek anen / aŋii ki wiya,** bring me a looking glass so that I may look at my head.

lanin *n* remains of ground simsim on the stone on which it was ground, collected by rubbing with the hand; **lanin kidi,** remains of ground simsim on the grinding stone, used for cleaning the grinding stone.

lanini-nini *n* 1 a very heavy load drawn along by many people 2 a heavy roller for impacting a road.

laninynye *n* one who bustles about and never comes out quickly; see **ladokke, lagalle, ladwalle, ladikke, laminne, lamyenne.**

Lango or Lango Omiro *n* the Lango people who speak the Acholi language mixed with Ateso.

lanne *vi* roaming around without purpose, sauntering about aimlessly; **tye ka lanne Kampala labono tic mo,** roaming about without job in Kampala.

lanno lok *vt* speaking evasively; **danone lanno lok doki twatwal,** .he is a man who always beats about the bush.

lanogo *n* a chameleon.

lanok *n* pimples or acne on the face of a young person; **wanne opon ki lanok,** his face is covered of pimples.

lanollo *n* a cripple.

lanoya, ogwil *n* a long rope.

Langoya *n* a male name.

lanudi *n* a hyena, a coward; p**inynye onono don lyet ma lanudi pe don twero o iye,** the atmosphere was so hot and tense that a coward would not dare come near it.

lanuna *n* a liar, an unreliable reporter, untrustworthy person; see **lanwer lok.**

lanweke-nweke or **lagorlobo** *n* a large comb made either of wood, gourd, or shell for drawing lines on mud painting on the body in preparation for dancing (now obsolete).

lanwer lok *n* one who incorrectly reports the what he has heard by leaving out some facts and sometimes adding his own words; see **lanuna.**

lanwette *n* an impostor, or one who claims to be able to do what he cannot do; see **lacor.**

lagwilo *n* a plants that yield poles.

lany *v* to waste, squander; **pe ilany lim woko,** do not waste / squander the money.

lany *n* wasting, squandering; **lany me lim pe ber,** wasting or squandering of money is not good.

lanyal *n* a small white water insect.

lanyam *n* a point of conjunction of the upper and lower jaws (*fig* **lanyam** means **dog,** mouth).

lanyata *n* an earthworm; see **otwol kot.**

lanyatte *n* a proud fellow; **en lanyatte mada,** he is a proud fellow, show-off; see **labutte, lawakke.**

lanyek nyo lanyekko *n* a jealous person; *prov.* **lanyekko calo gweno, omiyo gipyello i ot,** he is jealous like chickens that is why they deposit their droppings in the house.

lanyiri *n* a kind of wristlet (of celluloid material). see **Bangili**

lanynyo *vt* to outstrip / outstripping, to beat / beating in a running contest; **lanynyo ki nwec,** outstripping or surpassing in running. 2 wasting, squandering; d**ako man lanynyo jami mada,** this woman wastes a lot of things. 3 exhaust; **tiŋŋo kicaa kado lanynyo kom mada,** carrying salt bags is very exhausting. 4 very badly, **olanynyo lawotte mada ki yet,** he insulted his friend very badly.

lanyuro *n* a neonate, a baby; see **lakere.**

lanyut *vt* an example; **lanyutte tye kwene?** where is the example?

laole *prd* a troublesome, vivacious person; **dano ma laole,** a troublesome person.

laor *n* a messenger; **laorra,** my messenger.

laora *n* a river or a brook.

lapaa *n* a kind of pumpkin.

lapaa yat or lapac *n* a carpenter.

lapaco *n* a villager, a countryman, a relative.

laparanat *n* 1 a mid-sized bird, white with black wings and a peculiar uneven beak.

laparanat *n* a severe famine which kills many people; **kec laparanat opotto i Sudan,** a severe famine has occurred in Sudan.

lapaŋ cata *n* a stupid and useless person; **lapaŋ cata en aye dano ma mal ata mape tye ki kama beddo iye nyo tiyo iye,** a stupid and a useless person who roams about helplessly and has no where to stay or does any work anywhere.

lapel *n* patchy, partly white and partly black or not regular; **yamo oputto wii ot odoŋ lapel,** the wind blew off part of the roof and left it partially open.

lapel *n* an insignia.

lapel *n* a large disc with sharp edge , which is protected by a sheath and has a hole in the centre, worn on wrist as an ornament at a dance or as a mean of preventing somebody holding ones hand in fighting.

lapele *n* a restless, active, jolly child who will stop at nothing; see also **latati, lataŋgalo, lakiti kiti.**

lapen *n* a person with umbilical hernia, a projecting navel; sometimes referred to as **lapenne.**

lapena *n* pigeon peas *(cajunus indicus).*

lapero *n* open; **ot lapero,** a hut with an open window and door.

lapiddi *n* children's maid, or nurse.

lapiddo *n* a plaintiff, complainant.

lapil-pil *n* a splinter, sharp splinter from a reed or bamboo.

lapii *n* a messenger of a king or chief who comes for the purpose of obtaining assistance for war.

lapii *n* wood used for drilling or making fire.

lapira *n* an earwig.

lapiru *n* a whirlwind; **lapiru omukko wii school woko,** a whirlwind has blown off the roof of the school building.

lapit *n* a nurse; **lapit latin** one bringing up an orphan.

lapiya *n* an instigator, inciter of people to quarrel or fight, one who pushes others to fight; **danone doki lapiya twatwal,** the man is a great instigater.

lapok *n* a breast; **lapok gweno,** a chicken breast; *c/f* **labana, dak kor.**

lapoti *n* a copier, counterfeiter, copycat, imitator; usually called **lapoti pir.**

lapoya *n* a mentally ill person; see **lagikom, labelu.**

lapuku *n* a weed with big white flowers which, together with the leaves, smell.

laput *n* a malnourished child; sometimes called **aputa.**

laput *n* a small covered tin with a wick into which paraffin is poured and which is then lit to provide light.

laputa *n* cowpea sauce without salt, eaten at breakfast; prepared for a mother of twins to eat.

lapwo-pwo *n* a butterfly; **lapwo-pwo opoŋ mada i kom ature,** there are many butterflies on the flowers.

lapwony *n* a teacher; **lapwony ocitto ka pwonynyo litino,** the teacher has gone / went to teach the children.

lapwonynye *n* a learner, a student, an apostle.

lapyem *n* 1 a protester, challenger, competitor. 2 an argumentative person; **Atoo doki lapyem twatwal,** Atoo is a very argumentative person.

lar *v* save, rescue, assist; **lar latin pe otoo ki cwer remo,** save the child from dying from bleeding; **larwa ki cam kec tye ka nekkowa mada,** save us with food, we are dying of hunger.

laree lok *n* a humorous person, fun-maker, an entertainer; **danone laree lok mada,** the man is a very humorous person.

larem *n* a friend; **laremma,** my friend.

larere *n* one who is impatient, a meddler in other people's affairs.

larere *n* a small red lizard.

larii lok *n* an impatient person, who insists obstinately for something to be done.

larita *n* **larita ŋor,** an oblong structure covered with grass in which cowpeas, dried termites, etc. are put and which is then fixed on a pole and planted in the courtyard or compound as a method of conserving them.

laro *n* a flat stone surface, naturally formed and used for drying and threshing millet or sorghum etc.

larok *n* a foreigner, an enemy.

laromo ot *n* a gecko, lizard which normally is found in houses; see **gek.**

larop *n* one who provokes or annoys others, one who incites.

laroro *n* a scandalous gossip, malicious gossip, double-dealer; **wugwokke mada ka wulokko lok ki laccono pien en laroro mada,** be careful when talking with the man because he is a double-dealer / a malicious gossip.

larot piny *n* an explorer, a spy.

larre *vi* saved; **dano ma olarre,** a person who is saved; **kal matye i koloni twerro larre ka gijubbo oyot oyot ma noŋŋo kot pud peya omollo,** the millet on the papyrus mat can be saved if it is removed quickly before it is swept away by the rain.

larro *vt* 1 to dispute / disputing, to contend / contending, to quarrel / quarrelling about; **gitye ka larro waŋ poto meegi,** they are disputing or quarrelling about the boundary of their fields 2 seeking; **olarro bot rwot ka dot,** he ran to the chief to lodge an accusation.

larro *vt* to save / saving; **larro dano ma opotto i pii,** to rescue / rescuing a person who has fallen into water.

larum lee *n* back part of chest, with half the ribs attached on both sides.

larwece *n* a medium-sized tree, whose bark is pounded and poured into water to stupefy fish; see **ober, obucu, lurogo** (whose leaves are used instead).

Larwodo *n* a small river in Paico, flowing into Acaa River.

latam or kitambara *n S* a handkerchief; **kel kitambara me jwayo waŋŋa,** bring me a handkerchief for mopping my face.

latam *n* a thinker, a philosopher.

latam kwot *n* a concave hand-grip in the centre of a shield.

lataŋgalo *n* an active, restless and careless child; a see **latati, lapele, lakiti kiti, lakiri kiri.**

latati *n* a merry, playful, active and restless child; see **lataŋgalo** above.

lataya *adv* for ever, continuously; **in ibedo kany lataya ce?** are you staying here for ever? **pii pe myero omol lataya,** water must not run continuously.

latebe nyo latebere *n* a creeper with very small succulent leaves that are not eaten.

lated *Adj* for cooking

lateddo *n* a cook; **lateddo tye kwene?** where is the cook? **lated kot,** rain maker, **lated tim me dwar,** one who makes hunting successful and peaceful.

latek *n* a strong man; **latoŋ pa latek ladit en aye ommo,** a strongman's axe is obtained by a big man.

latek *n* a disobedient person who refuses to be sent; *prov* **latek keŋ wii ogwaŋ mutwo,** one who is disobedient will not get the dried head of a fox, i.e, he will get no presents; **latek wic,** a bold person; **latek dog,** one who cannot accept his mistakes, who is always argumentative.

latek *n* a pipe; **latek me matto taa,** a pipe for smoking *prov.* **latekke opotto i pii,** *lit.* his pipe has fallen into water, i.e he is sexually impotent.

lateke teke *n* 1 a male grasshopper; the female is called **lakaibona.**

lateke teke *n* a dance for girls; **piyo lateke teke,** dancing shaking of waist in a special way.

latel wic *n* a guide, leader; **latel yoo,** a guide; **latel wic i odilo,** a football captain.

latemme *n* a wild banana *(Musa ensete).*

laten *n* a support, pillow; **laten wic,** a pillow.

latet *n* a blacksmith.

latin *n* a child, *pl* **litino or lutino; latin kic,** an orphan; **latin dyel,** a kid; **latin gweno,** a chick; **latin dyaŋ,** a calf; **latin ot,** a small hut etc. **latino or lajimu** *n* simsim sown in August.

latiŋ dio *n* 1 a catapult, consisting of a forked stick with rubber bands tied to it, used to hurl a stone 2 a stone put in an open sack which is then swung round and round and let loose.

latok dek *n* a ladle or calabash cup for dishing / serving food.

latoŋ *n* an axe; **kel latoŋ me barro yen,** bring an axe for splitting wood.

latoŋtwe *n* an unruly and disrespectful girl, who does things which she should not do; see **lalelee, waŋŋe pit pit.**

latuk *n* soot; **latuk dwoŋ mada i ot jokon,** there is a lot of / too much soot in the kitchen.

latuŋ–tuŋ-tyen lyec *n* the pad like sole of an elephant's foot.

latuny toŋ gweno *n* egg yolk.

latwee *n* a star.

latwok *n* morning star (Venus).

latwok-lak-lyec *n* a bird; **butto i ogo,** sleeps in tree holes.

latworo *n* a bird with a long white tail, paradise bird, fly-catcher *(Terpsiphone viridis).*

Latworo *n* a female name.

latyet *n* a diviner who works by means of leather sandals which he throws down and 'reads'.

laume-luk *n* 1 small bushy plant with permanently wet leaves; 2 persons with a running nose.

lawac kom, lanyabo *n* a lazy person.

lawala *n* 1 a loop which children use for game 2 wheel made of a tender twig tied in the form of a circle.

lawaŋ acel *adv* uniformly; **wulok lawaŋ acel,** speak using the same words, i.e tell the same story / speak altogether at once.

lawaŋ kal *n* a member of a royal or chief's household, spokesman of a royal or chief's household.

lawaŋŋe arii or lawaŋŋe aŋet *n* a person with a squinted eye.

lawaŋŋe otoo *n* 1 a blind person 2 fly with a mosquito-like snout which has a painful bite *(Simulum damnosum); see* **ajoŋa miya**

lawany *n* one who looks eagerly at people when they are eating, expecting to be invited.

lawara or arara *n* a large hyena.

lawat *n* a friendly relative (one who visits others frequently).

lawii lweny or lawii mony *n* the leader of an army, the commander of an army.

lawil *n* a merchant.

lawinya *n* is a mixture of the following: 1 honey and simsim paste / honey and ground white ant paste 2 ghee and simsim paste / ghee and white ant paste 3 shea nut oil and simsim paste / shea not oil and white ant paste.

lawirre ata *n* a person who roams around.

lawiye otal *n* a bald-headed man.

lawok *n* a person with some missing teeth leaving a large gap.

lawoko *adv* 1 on the surface, superficially; **teer i ket lawoko pe i canduk,** take and put it outside not inside the box 2 one who is always outside and does not stay at home.

Lawoko *n* a male name; *lit* means 'always out'.

lawol *n* a poisoner, usually a bad woman who poisons people.

laworo or lawor *prp* yesterday; **laworo maca,** the day before yesterday;

laworo macaca, the day before the day before yesterday; **laworo kaka onyoni**, yesterday at this time.

laworro *n* an obedient person, a respectful person; **latin ma laworro noŋo gum,** an obedient child always gets blessings or respectful child always gets blessings.

laworro *n* a miser; **laworro cam cammo mere kene,** the miser eats his food alone.

lawot *n* a traveller, a tourist; **lawotta,** a friend or a person with whom we walk together.

layab *n* a key; **miya layab me doggola,** give me the key to the door.

layak *n* a robber.

layata nyo kiyata *n* potatoes.

layer *adj* usually used to refer to a chicken with feather on its legs; **gweno layer,** chicken with feathered legs.

layibi *n* pole for lifting up the roof of a barn or granary in order to get into it.

layido *n* a skin disease affecting particularly the joints, knees, elbows, *allergic* skin diseases.

layi *n Eng* it is a distortion of "lines", a barracks, a group of huts built in a line with a compound where people live together.

layibbe *n* a shooting star.

layir *n* a bewitcher, charmer.

la iye onat *adj* a person with a flat abdomen (usually liked very much by women), slender, slim; **dako la iye onat ber mada,** a slender woman is very beautiful.

layo *vi* to pass / passing urine; **layo i ot dyewor,** passes urine at night in the house, or he wets his bed at night; see **laa, lac.**

layoi or **ladiro cip** *n* the long ends of threads or strings of women's loin dress.

layom *n* a person with a congenitally exposed glans penis; congenitally circumcised.

layoŋ–ŋec *n* three short strings about three inches long, upon which brass is wound, worn behind hanging down from the waist just covering the upper gap between the buttocks, worn by girls in the past.

layuta *n* a trap consisting of a pole and string for trapping birds or rats.

laywaa *n* one who ruins crops through the use of magical powers; **laywaa bel i poto,** one who makes crops fail.

laywe *n* one or two sticks with small dense branches used as a broom.

leb *n* the tongue; **tee lebbe pe,** he is dumb. 2 edge, **leb toŋ,** the edge of a spear, blade of a spear 3 **leb kinyo,** the point of a needle.

leb *n* language, **leb English, or leb munu,** the English language.

leb *v* carry; **leb tuga labolo iteer i ot,** carry the bunch of bananas into the house.

leba *n* swelling of the glands of the groin; **leba omakke nyo en tye ki leba,** he has painful swelling of the glands of the groin (sometimes referred to as **awaŋ mac**), *lymphadenitis.*

lebe-lebe *adv* hanging free, oscillating; **boŋo ma oyec iŋeye doŋ bedi lebe lebe,** the torn pieces of clothes behind him are swinging to and fro.

lebbe *vi* can be carried, **gunia cukari ne twerro lebbe,** the sugar bag can be carried *see* **tiŋŋe**

lebbo *vt* to carry / carrying usually by two people; **lebbo kicaa cukari,** to carry / carrying bags of sugar.

lec *vn* to inherit / inheriting, to receive / receiving; **jami me lec keken pe konyo ŋatimo,** inherited things alone do not help anybody; see **lee, leyo.**

ledde *vi* to speak / speaking continuously;

wek ledde ki nyiŋŋe obedi, stop speaking about him all the time.

leddo *vt* to talk / talking too much about something or somebody; **leddo nyiŋ two pa ŋati mo pe ber,** speaking just to anybody about somebody else's disease is not good.

lee *v* inherit, receive; **cit ilee jami pa worru,** go and inherit your father's property.

lee *n* a game animal, all animals.

lee *n* an axe (the name used by some clans, but not much used).

leg *v* 1 pray, ask, request, beg; **leg Lubaŋa wek otimmi kica,** pray to God to forgive you 2 loosen; **leg tyen mejane woko,** loosen the table leg.

legga *n* prayers, **waecitto ka legga,** we are going to pray.

lege-lege *adv* loosely, not firmly, not fixed; **oketto canduk ma pek i wii meja ma tyenne lege lege ci otur opotto woko,** he put a heavy box on a table with unstable legs, therefore the legs broke and callapsed.

leggo *vt* praying, asking for, begging, requesting; **leggo Lubaŋa,** praying to God.

leggo *vt* loosening, making not firm by moving it about, shaking it about; **pe ibed ka ywayo meja aywaya leggo tyenne woko,** don't drag the table about (because) it loosens its legs.

leja leja *S adv* little by little; **catto leja leja,** selling little by little, retail selling.

lek *n* dream; **tin ilekko niŋo,** what did you dream about today?

lekko *vt* 1 to dream / dreaming; **lekko citto i London,** dreaming about going

to London. 2 herding; **lekko dyaŋ i puno ka cam,** to herd /herding the cattle to the grazing field to graze there.

leela *n* the name of a mountain in Palaro from which in the old days iron (**leela**) was obtained (that is why the mountain is called **leela).**

leela *n* a large flat expause of rock where women spread their millet to dry. and for threshing.

leela *n* a bicycle.

lello *vt* 1 to stir / stirring up; *prov* **ogwal acel lello waŋ pii woko miyo doko col,** one frog can stir up the water and make it dirty; to talk / talking too much, to spread / spreading by talking too much 2 **pee i bed ka lello nyiŋ twoo ma ŋati moni twoyo,** do not spread or talk too much about a disease which a certain individual is suffering from 3 making watery; **pee iony pii madwoŋ i dek miyo lello woko,** do not pour too much water in the sauce because it will make it watery.

lem *n* a cheek.

lem *vi* feeling nauseated, feeling like vomiting; **cwinynye tye ka lem,** he feels like vomiting.

lem *v* lick; **lem cukari ne,** lick the sugar.

lemmo *vt* to make one feel nauseated; **lemmo cwiny dano,** it makes people feel like vomiting; see **ullo cwiny.**

lemmo *vt* licking, lapping up or tasting with the tongue; **otyekko lemmo kadone ki lebbe,** he has tasted the salt by licking it with his tongue.

leŋ *v* make free, clear obstacles 1 **leŋ yoo wek akati,** make way for me.

leŋ *n* clean, pure; **cwinynye leŋ,** he is pure; has a good heart, is kind and friendly. 3 good looking, **waŋŋe leŋ mada,** she is very good looking. 4 bright, **dwe man tin tar nyo leŋ mada,** the moon is very bright today.

leŋŋa *n* a charm, amulet, worn in order to bring or obtain good luck, e.g. **gum me nekko lee,** luck for killing animals during hunting.

leŋŋa *n* white or red lily.

leŋŋo *vt* 1 to make / making free, to clear / clearing obstacles; **leŋŋo yoo wek gikatti,** to make / making way or to clear / clearing an obstacle so that it may be passable; 2 to imput / imputing, ascribing a fault to somebody else; **guleŋŋo ni Orac en aye ma okwallo kwoo, kun en pe okwallo,** they said that Orac was the one who stole something yet he did not 3 to blow / blowing hard; **leŋŋo bila,** blowing hard the whistle; 4 to inflate / inflating; **otyekko leŋŋo odilo matek mada,** he has inflated the ball very hard 5 to kick / kicking high; **leŋŋo odilo citto malo,** kicking the ball very high.

leny *n* heartburn; **ka omatto lemun ci cwinynye leny barro kore mada,** whenever he takes lemon, he feels severe heartburn.

leny *v.* liquidize, melt, liquefy; **leny moo i kel,** melt the ghee / butter and bring it here.

lenynye *vi* can be melted; **moo lenynye woko ka giketto i ŋet keno,** the butter will melt if it is put near the cooking place.

lenynyo *vt* to liquidize / liquidizing, melting; **lenynyo moo dyaŋ,** melting the butter .

leptenant *n Eng* lieutenant, a military rank below captain; **leptenant jeneral,** lieutenant general, a military rank above major general but below general; see **jeneral, pil macul.**

ler *n* artery, vein, tendon, root; **ler yat,** the root of a tree; **ler remo,** artery / vein.

lerro *n* a bleeding scalp wound; **ogoyo wiye lerro,** he struck his head and caused a severe bleeding wound.

lewic *n* shame; **lewic omakke,** he is ashamed *saying* : lewic omakko **balaturu** *lit* the cape monitor feels ashamed, meaning one who feels ashamed is not necessarily bashful or shy; **lalewic,** a shy, timid person.

leyo wic *vt* to humiliate / humiliating, making ashamed; **timme pa latinni leyo wic,** the behaviour of this child is shameful and humiliating.

leyo jami *vt* 1 inheriting; **leyo jami pa wonne,** inheriting his father's property 2 **leyo wii wonne,** succeeding his father; **laleyo, lalee ker,** the successor to the throne or kingship. 3 **leyo boŋo owekko ononŋo twoo midda i komme,** sharing clothes made him get a skin disease (ringworm).

leyo *vt* 1 to search / searching about with the hand in the dark for something; **leyo ciŋ i tee agulu pii ma pii opoŋ iye wek inen ka gin mo opotto iye,** dipping your hand in a pot full of water to see if something has dropped in it and to find out whether there is something there; 2 to snatch something thrown to one; **oleyo ni kwic layab ma gibolle,** he snatched the key thrown to him straightaway 3 missing, **oleyo lemme piny ki ciŋŋe kono odoŋŋe matek,** he aimed a blow at his cheek but narrowly missed it otherwise he would have struck him hard. 4 take somebody's things without permission; **litinoni gubino kany ci gutugi leyo aleya mere labolo matye wii meja,** the children came here and ate the bananas without asking for them; see **lec, lee.**

lib *v* 1 skim, stalk; **lib mo i cak,** skim the cream from the milk 2 **lib kor lee ne mot mot,** stalk the animal slowly.

libbe *vi* 1 can be skimmed; **moo matye i wii cak twerro libbe,** the cream on the surface of the milk can be skimmed 2 walking quietly; **lakwoo libbe mot mot ka citto ka kwal,** a thief walks quietly when going to steal.

libbo *vt* to skim / skimming or to remove / removing carefully substance from another; **libbo pii i kulu ki agwata wek pe gitwom daba,** skimming the water with a gourd cup in order to avoid collecting mud.

libbo *vt* to follow / following carefully and slowly from behind without being seen; **citto ka libbo lee,** going to stalk the animal. 3. lying in waiting; **lalibbo,** one who lies in waiting.

libira *A n* a needle; **kel libira me kwoyo boŋo,** bring the needle for sewing the clothes; see **kinyo.**

libo *adj* fresh; **cak ma libo,** fresh milk.

libo-libo or kwilo-kwilo *adv* cautiously, sneakingly.

lic *vi* liquefy; **papai ka giwekko kama lyet ci lic woko,** when pawpaw is left in a warm place it goes bad and become watery; see **lii, liyo.**

licce *vi* becoming liquid; **nyuka ka okwee ci licce woko,** when gruel becomes cold it becomes watery; **papai ka ocek tatwal ci licce woko,** when a papaw is very ripe, it becomes too soft and watery.

licco *vt* to liquify / liquefying; **cammo mayembe madwoŋ licco i dano woko,** to eat / eating too many mangoes causes diarrhoea.

liggo *vt* to blunt; **pe iŋol paala ki yat pien liggo lakke,** don't use the knife for cutting wood because it blunts it.

li *adv* **li** is interchangable with **ni,** e.g **omakko woko li or ni cwic, omako woko ni cwic,** he caught it suddenly.

lii *v* pour slowly and carefully; **lii pii,** pour water slowly and carefully; **lii pii ki dano me logo,** pour water to the people for washing the hands; see **lic, liyo.**

lik *adj* slow, awkward, disgusting; **latinne lik pe tiyo cura ne oyot oyot,** the child is slow and dull, he does not do his mathematics quickly; **lokke lik pe myero me awacca,** the words are disgusting, they should not be mentioned anywhere; **waŋŋe lik,** he looks awkward and serious. 2 looks serious and frightening; 3 **buŋane lik,** the forest is frightening.

lil *n* charred grass carried by the wind.

lil *v* polish, clean; **lil wii meja maleŋ,** polish and clean the table very well.

lililili *adv* completely, properly; **mucuŋwa ocek ma kwar ni lililili,** the orange has properly ripened into a bright red colour.

lille *vi* to clean themselves; **anyira gucitto ka lillo komgi,** the girls went to clean their bodies.

lillo *vt* 1 to level / levelling, 2 to polish / polishing; **gujwayo gulillo wii meja mapwot mada,** they polished the top of the table into a smooth surface.

lillo *vt* to clean / cleaning; **citto ka lillo**

tyen maleŋ, going to clean the legs.

lillo lok *vt* blabbing or blurting out news; **lillo lok okelle can,** blabbing or blurting news brought him trouble.

lim *n* visiting

limmo *vt* 1 to visit / visiting for inspection, **citto ka limmo ot yat,** going to inspect the hospital 2 **citto ka limmo laremmi** going to visit your friend.

limu *n* a graveyard; **limu en aye kama dano mutoo ducu giyikko iye,** a graveyard is where the bodies of dead people are laid to rest.

limuk *adv* totally, completely; **dano gucorre woko limuk i bar,** people came and filled up the field.

li liŋ *adj* unconscious; **opotto otoo woko li liŋ,** he fell and became unconscious.

liŋ *n* a finger-ring knife for harvesting millet *see* **alwette.**

liŋ *n* **kado liŋ,** mineral salt (whereas **kado atwona,** is salt drained from ashes)

liŋ-liŋ *adv* 1 the sound of steps when one walks; **okatto wotto ni liŋ-liŋ,** he passed here with his feet thumping the ground 2 satisfaction; **oyeŋ ni liŋ-liŋ,** he stuffed himself very much with food. 3 quietly; **timmo liŋ-liŋ,** does it quietly.

liŋŋo *vt* to smooth / smoothing, to polish / polishing; **oliŋŋo kom agulu ma ocweyo maber mada,** he polished very well the pots which he made.

lipim *adv* gathered in large numbers; **dano gudurre lipim i bar odilo,** the people gathered themselves in large numbers in the football field.

lir *v* cut, strip, circumcise; **lir laa man wek i noŋ iye del tol matek,** cut this leather into strips in order to get a strong rope; **lir cuun awobi man,** circumcise this boy's penis.

lirre *vi* to be circumcised; **gucitto ka lirre pien mwaka me lirre doŋ oo,** they went to be circumcised because this is the year for circumcision.

lirro *vt* 1 to cut / cutting, to strip / stripping or making something from the hide, **lirro war,** stripping the leather to make sandals. 2 excision; **lirro del waŋ,** excision of a scared eyelid (*tarsectomy or tarsotomy)* caused by trachoma 3 circumcising; **lirro cuun,** circumcising the foreskin.

lit *adj* painful, aching; **komme lit,** he is ill or sick; **iye lit,** he has abdominal pain a or stomachache.

litto *vn* affliction; **litto man doŋ orommo komme woko,** he is overwhelmed with suffering / he is severely afflicted with body pain.

litto lum *n* itching due to grass scratches.

liyo *adj* fluid, liquid-like, watery; **nyuka man liyo twatwal,** the porridge is too watery.

liyo *vt* 1 to filter / filtering, to pass /passing through the sieve; **liyo pii me amatta,** to filter / filtering water through a sieve for drinking. 2 melting metal; **liyo cet leela me noŋŋo nyonyo maber,** melting iron ore to make iron; see **lii, lic.**

lobele *n* a platform.

lobo *n* earth, clay, land.

lobo-lobo *adv* very soft; **layata ocek lobo-lobo,** the potatoes were cooked very soft.

loc *n* a peg fixed in the ground; **loc ma**

gigurro me tweyo iye dyel, a peg fixed in the ground for tying the goat upon.

loc *n* governance, win, defeat, rule; **loc pa Jeremel onoŋo gwa mada,** German rule was very cruel / the govenance of the Germans was very cruel; see **loo, loyo.**

locco *vt* 1 to alternate / alternatuing; **gulocco dyaŋŋi macol ki matar ka doŋ gucwallo,** the cattle were put in line in alternate colour of black and white before they were sent. 2 pass in the opposite direction; **pe warommo, walocco yoo ki larema,** we did not meet, we went in opposite directions.

locco *vt* to debilitate, weaken; **two doŋ olocco komme woko,** disease has debilitated him.

locco *vn* rule, governance; **locco ma kitmeno pe ber,** that type of rule / governance is not good.

lodi mac *n* glowing charcoal, coal, embers.

log *v* loosen; **log tolle woko,** loosen the rope; see **yog;** wash; **log ciŋi, ki waŋŋi,** wash your hands and face.

loggo *vt* washing; **loggo ciŋ,** washing the hands; **loggo waŋ,** washing the face.

loggo *vt* loosening; **loggo tol,** loosening the knot of a string; see **yoggo.**

logo-logo *adv* loose, slack 1 **otweyo logo-logo,** he tied it loosely, not firmly 2 *v* **twee matek pe itwee logo-logo,** tie it firmly, not loosely.

lok *n* word, speech, case, e.g. **lok tye i komme,** there is a case against him; **lok ma olokko pe ber,** his speech was not good; news, **lok aŋoo?,** what news?; **lok pe,** no news, that is, all is well (this is the greeting and its response during the day).

lok *v* 1 change; **lok pii ma tye i agulo woko,** change the water which is in the pot 2 speak; **lok gin ducu ma imitto,** say all you want to say.

loka or loka caa *adv* on the other side of either a river or valley; **loka caa, loka tuŋŋi,** the other side, this side; **loka,** land of the Joo-pa-Lwo.

loka *n* chief protecting spirit or god of the Koc people.

lokke *vi* change oneself, turn around; **ineno kwene, lokke bota kany!** where are you looking to, turn towards me!

lokko *vi* talking, speaking; **danone lokko twatwal,** the man speaks too much.

lokko *vi* 1 to turn / turning round or about, inside out, upside down 2 *vt* changing; **gucitto ka lokko pii i agulo mukene,** they went to change the water into another pot; **oa ka lokko lokke woko,** he came back from changing his statement.

lok omeru *n* a kind of lily which people chew in order to make them successful in courtship.

loŋ *v* winnow; **cit iciloŋ bel,** go and winnow the millet.

loŋŋe *vi* to move to and fro; **oloŋŋe tin mada i opici pa jago ka limmo waraga me mucoro,** he moved to and fro today in order to get a poll tax ticket from the office of the sub-chief.

loŋŋo bel *vt* 1 to winnow / winnowing; **odero en aye me loŋŋo nyim nyo kal,** odero is the one which is used for winnowing simsim or millet; 2 **loŋŋo piny,** going round and round, surveying.

loŋo *adv* only; **okello dyel acel loŋo,** he brought only one goat.

loŋo *adj* audible, loud; **bulle loŋo mada,** the drum is very loud.

loŋo *n* fluid in the sac containing the testicles called *hydrocele.*

loŋo *n* depression on the surface of the earth, abyss; **tye twon loŋo mo kany ka motoka opotto iye pe kwanynye,** there is a great depression here into which if a car was to fall it would not be possible to lift; abyss; **opotto i twon loŋo mo matut mape twerro kwanynye,** he fell into an abyss out of which he cannot be lifted.

loŋ ramatol *n* a pair of trousers; **pali loŋ** is preferred now.

lony *vi* 1 increase in size; **latin lakere tye ka lony,** the infant has gained weight. 2 become rich; **joo Kenya gitye ka lony ki omen mewa,** the Kenya people are becoming rich from our coffee; **dano ma olony mada,** a very rich man; **coo lony,** *prov* a torn skirt, worn by some women, which allows some parts of the body to be visible.

lonyo *n* wealth, goods and property, riches; **lonyo madwoŋ twatwal nekko dano,** too much wealth kills people.

lonynyo yoo *vt* making a path by continuously following the same way; **oyoo olonynyo ola gi pi riŋŋo iye nino ducu,** rats make their path by running on it every day.

loo *v* to rule, govern; **loo lobo man,** rule / govern this country.

loo *vi* dissolve, melt, dwindle away; **toŋ gweno oloo woko,** the egg has broken; **pee oloo woko,** the ice has melted; see **loc, loyo.**

lor *v* shut; **lor doggola,** shut the door; close , **lor dirica,** close the windows;

lor dul yen man icwal piny kwica, roll this log of wood and push it down there.

lor piny *vn* 1 descending, coming down, gliding down; **gitye ka lor piny,** they are descending 2 *v* **lor piny,** come down.

lorre *vi* can be shut or closed; **doggalani twerro lorre,** the door can be shut / closed; **pipa me moo peterol li twerro lorre,** the petrol drum can be rolled .

lorro *vt* rolling, pushing along on wheels; **gitye ka lorro pipa me moo peterol,** they are rolling a drum of petrol; see **ŋillo.**

lorro *vt* to shut / shutting; **lorro doggola,** to shut / shutting the door; **lorro waŋa yoo,** to close / closing the road; see **puŋ.**

lot *vi* sprout, shoot forth; **jaŋ yat tye ka lot mada,** the tree is sprouting many branches.

loyo *vt* to win, to defeat, to rule; **en nino ducu loyo i ŋwec,** he always wins in running; rule; **en aye ma loyo Albania,** he is the one who rules Albania; see **loo, loc.**

loyo *vt* to escape; **ŋeyo kit me loyo mak me mucoro,** he knows how to escape being arrested for tax evasion 3 dissolving; **kot tye ka loyo matafali ma numo woko,** the rain is dissolving or washing away the sun-dried bricks; see **loc, loo.**

lub *v* follow, pursue, trace; **lub kor laditti,** follow in the footsteps of your father; **lub kor lee ma okatto kany,** pursue the animal which has passed through here.

lubbe *vi* can be followed; **obot tyen lee**

ma gukatto kanynyi twerro lubbe, the tracks of the animals which have passed here can be followed.

Lubaŋa *n* name of a spirit which, was adopted by missionaries as the word for God in Acholi; it came from the Runyoro **Ruhaŋa;** it is called **Rubaŋa** by the Roman Catholics.

lubbo *vt* following, pursuing, tracing; **tye ka lubbo kor dyaŋ meere pien gurweny woko,** he is following the tracks of his cattle because they are lost.

luboo *n* a tick, tick fever.

lucoro *n* a large tree with thorny stems and leaves. It has red flowers which come out at the beginning of the rain and produces red seeds.

ludok *adv* naked; **okatti woko ludok ki ot, laboŋo ruk i komme;** he came out from the house stark naked; see **lunywan, munero.**

luga *n* a type of grass whose tubers have a peculiar smell, which women used to wear as a necklace, its smell like girls smell at puberty.

luga *n* a wild pigeon; **akuri luga,** a large kind of dove.

lugaga *n* a charm buried in one's path which is supposed to harm the person it is intended for if they step on it.

lugogo *n* a small papyrus-like plant found in rivers.

lugora *n* a plant that is cultivated as a vegetable with scarlet berries.

luggu *vi* be depressed; **tye ka luggu alugga pien minne otoo,** he is depressed because of the death of his mother.

lugulugu *adv* the sounds made by something in a container when it shakes.

lujiko *n* gonorrhoea; *c/f* **abaji,** syphilis.

luk *v* follow, find; **luk kor latin ci i kel,** follow the child, find him and bring him; **luk kor gwok ki obot tyenne,** follow the dog by its tracks.

luk *n* 1 a fine paid for illegal sexual intercourse, by the man to the parents of the woman with whom he had the intercourse 2 payment for pregnancy before marriage or for abducting or eloping with a girl.

luk *vi* being wet, dripping, trickling with moisture or liquid; 1 **oboke oluk ki toyo mape wacce,** the leaves are covered in dew 2 **lum ma otwoo pe luk ki toyo,** the dried grass does not get covered with dew 3 **latin ma umme luk ki otwinyo pe ber,** the child whose nose is clogged with mucus is not good.

luk *vi* growing too much; **laconi doki wekko yer tikke luk twatwal,** this man allows his beard to get very bushy.

lukeme (lukembe) *n* a musical instrument of the xylophone type (Alur type).

luker *n* a royal family.

lukiko *n Lug* court; **gucitto i lukiko,** they went to attend the court.

lukile *n* an ornamental axe with the handle with copper or brass wires wound round as a decoration and, which used to be carried on shoulder; it could be used for self-defence when attacked; see **parat, olayo.**

lukoko *n* a kind of common grass.

lukiro *n* commission of an act that goes against tradition such as relatives having sexual intercourse, or a woman opening her private parts when quarelling, which usually requires a goat, a sheep, to be sacrifieced as part of a cleansing rite.

lukke *vi* followed; **kor lee pe twerro lube,** the tracks of the animals cannot be followed.

lukku or lukko *vt* following pursuing; **lukko kor lee.** following the tracks of animals.

lukulo *n* coagulated milk.

lukut *n* beer prepared from the remains of **kwon,** usually sweet and drunk by children.

lukwaa ŋadi *n* the grandchildren of so and so.

lukwaya *n* my grandchildren.

lulibbo *n* terrorists, snipers.

lullu *vt* constructing or setting up in a row, constructing in an oblong shape.

lulu. *n* bright copper and brass bracelets and wristlets.

lum *n* grass

lumalaika *n s* angels; **lamalaika Gaburiel obinno bot Maliam ka titteni ebinywallo lalar,** the angel Gabriel came to Mary to tell her that she would give birth to a saviour (in in the original Acholi Bible the angels were called **lumaraika**).

lumuku *a/adv* work in which every person participates; **anyira ki awobe ducu gucitto ka jwerro bar odilo lumuku,** all the girls and the boys alike went to slash the football field.

lunebi *n s pl* prophets; **lunebi mapol gutittoni gibinywallo lalar,** many prophets predicted that a saviour would be born; see **lanebi.**

luŋ *n* slope, sloping ground, valley; **luŋ pa gotte tuut mada,** the slope of the hill is very steep.

luŋ *v* bend or turn down; **luŋ dog agulu piny,** turn the mouth of the pot down.

luŋŋe 1 *adj* being round; **odilo komme oluŋŋe,** the ball is round 2 *v* bend; **luŋŋe piny,** bend down.

luŋŋo *vt* making round; **tye ka luŋŋo latin otte,** he is building a small round hut; turning; **luŋŋo dog agulu piny,** turning the mouth of the pot downwards; bending; **luŋŋo jaŋ yat piny ka wek gipwon nyigge,** bending the branch of the tree down so that its fruit can be picked or plucked; bending, turning down; **luŋŋo wic piny,** bending the head down.

luŋoi *n* chalk.

luŋoro *n* a red clay.

luŋoro *n* a swelling in the throat, *adenoids*, a common disease of children.

luny *v* undress, take off; **luny boŋo,** undress or take off your dress; **luny war,** remove the shoes; **luny lawotti tin mada i rette,** defeat your friend thoroughly in wrestling today.

lunynye *vi* can be removed or taken off; **boŋone twerro lunynye,** the clothes can be taken off; **war pa latinni twerro lunynye,** the child's shoes can be removed; **tin gulunynye mada i rette,** they threw each other down hard in wrestling today.

lunynyo *vt* To undress / undressing, taking off, **litino noŋo lunynyo boŋo tek,** children find undressing or taking off their clothes very difficult.

lunynyo *vt* thorough defeat; **gulunynyogi**

mada i tuko me rette, they defeated them thoroughly in the game of wrestling; see **luru.**

lunyodo *n* parents; **lunyodo gubinno ka nenno tukko pa litinogi i cukul,** the parents came to school to see the games played by their children.

lunywan *prd* naked; **owotto lunywan,** he walked naked; see **ludok, munero.**

Luo *n* a sub-group of Lwoo who passed on to Kenya.

luporo or kono luporo *n* big white ostrich feather.

lupoya *n* mad people; **ot pa lupoya opoŋ ki cet keken,** the mad people's house is full of feaces; see **lugama, lugikom, abelu.**

lupwony *n* teachers; **lupwony gitye ka pwonyo litino,** the teachers are teaching the children.

lupwonynye *n* learners, disciples; **lupwonynye pa Yecu,** Jesus' disciples.

lupwuu *n* mist, fog; **lupwuu tin omwonno piny woko,** the fog / mist has densely covered the country; some people call it **lupuu**

lur *n* sterility, barrenness; **lur gin marac mada ma mon pe gimitto,** sterility is something very bad which is not wanted by women; **lalur,** a sterile barren person.

lur *v* 1 pour slowly and carefully, filter; **lur pii man maber me amatta,** filter this water carefully for drinking 2 pound; **lur kal en,** pound this millet to remove the chaffs

lure *n* flute; **ŋeyo kutto lure mada,** knows how to play the flute very well.

lureka *n* informers, spies, intelligence agents; **man gin aye lureka ma gitye ka rekko piny kany,** these are the informaers / spies who are going round the various places getting information.

lurogo *n* a plant whose seeds or leaves are pounded and poured into water to make fish drowsy so that they can be caught easily; see **larwece, ober,obucu.**

lurono *n* a creeper whose roots have a very nice smell with a peppermint-like flavour, which is liked very much by children and is supposed to be an appetizer.

luronyo *n* chalk; **dano giwirro komgi i kit yoo ma patpat ki luronyo ka gicitto ka myel,** the people smear their bodies in different ways when they go to dance; see **luŋoi.**

lurre *n* battered, repeated; **tin gulurre mada i rette nio ka guol,** today they battered themselves thoroughly by throwing each other down many times until they were totally exhausted.

lurre *vi* filtered, poured; **cakke pe twerro lurre maber, laboŋo moo wii cak me katto iye,** the milk cannot be poured without some of the cream going with it.

lurro *vt* 1 to throw / throwing each other many times until totally exhausted 2 pouring out slowly and carefully leaving dirt behind, filtering; **tye ka lurro pii me amatta,** he is pourin the water out slowly and carefully, leaving out dirt behind or he is filtering the water for drinking.

lurro *vt* to pour / pouring water; **lurru pii me lwokko ciŋ,** pouring water for washing the hands; see **liyo.**

lurro *vt* to thresh / threshing; **lurro bel,** threshing the millet thoroughly to remove the chaff; **tye ka lurro kal i pany,** he is threshing millet in the mortar.

lurru *vt* 1 to trample / trampling and to destroy / destroying the grass as by cattle. 2 throwing one to the ground several times in a wrestling contest. 3 repeated attacks of illness.

luru *n* remains; **luru pii,** fine dirt in water which normally sinks to the bottom of a pot of water; **luru moko,** the remains of the flour. 2 the last small amount of something which still remains; **luru dwe,** the last trace of menstruation.

luru luru *adv* sickly, weakly; **wotto ni luru luru,** walking sluggishly and sickly.

lut *n* stick; **lut me goyo litino,** a stick for caning children.

lut *v* dip in; **lut i pii,** dip into or immerse in water; push into something; **lut tyenni i war,** push your foot into the shoe; **lut boŋo i pii wek okwany cilone woko,** dip / immerse the clothes in the water to soak them.

lutaci *n* inflammation of the urinary passages, urethritis due usually to gonorrhoea (old name, not used now).

lutkot *n* lightning; **lutkot ogoyo ot,** the house has been struck by lightning.

lutori *n* a plant which grows tall with prickly leaves like those of thistle.

luu *vn* grow very tall; **yadi ma gudoŋo ka maber, luu mada,** trees which have grown or fertile soil, grow very tall indeed.

luu *adv* 1 moving slowly in a big amount; 2 **yito duny ni luu,** smoke rises up densely and slowly; **apwa duny ni luu,** dust rises up slowly.

luut *n* eel.

luwalo *n* work done for chiefs instead of paying tax in cash; this used to be done in the past but not now.

luyolo *n* bright kinds of beads of various sizes for necklaces.

lwada or ni lany *adv* quietly, motionless with a relaxed body as if dead; **obutto ni lwada / ni lany,** he slept quietly and motionless as if dead.

lwaga-lwaga *adv* with infirm movement; **wotto ma badde beddo ni lwaga lwaga,** walks with the arm dangling as if it is broken.

lwak *n* a herd, crowd, group, multitude; **lwak dyang man,** a herd of cattle; *pl* **lwakki; nen lwakki lee man ka gitye ka cam i puno,** look at the very many animals which are grazing in the grazing field (once **lwak** follows a noun, it is not necessary to change the noun into the plural, eg **dyaŋŋi.**)

lwak *n* people; **lwak pa Otto.** the people of Otto. 2 many; **lwak motoka,** many motor cars.

lwal *vi* being gloomy, cheerless and thin; **komme dok lwal mada,** his body gets thin frequently.

lwala *n* red soil; **boŋoni doŋ omakko lwala,** your clothes are staned with red soil.

lwala lwala *adv* slowly and ponderously (the movement of a lion or leopard).

lwalle *vi* contesting with, competing with; **lwalle i myel, i cubbo lawala, i wer ki ŋala,** competing in dancing, in the circle game, in singing and making fun of each other.

lwallo *vt* to defeat / defeating, in a game or contest of any kind; **lwallo** is usually used in the game of **lawala** (circle); see **lunynyo, lurru.**

lwana lwana *adj* thin and weak.

lwaŋo *n* fly; **lwaŋo cammo doki bollo toŋŋe i gin ma otop keken,** a fly eats and lays its eggs on rotten things only.

lwany lwany *adv* informally; **opotto ni lwany,** he fell heavily stretching out at full length; **twol bollo wiye ni lwany lwany ka mitto too,** a snake tosses its head from side to side when it is dying.

lwar *n* greyness, hoariness of hair; **wiye gilwar,** his hair is grey.

lwar *n* getting sufficient, enough; **moo yaa ma watye ka teddoni tye ka lwar kwee mada,** the shea nut oil which we are boiling is coming out very slowly, not sufficiently.

lwata lwata *adj* long and thin; **yip gwokke bor ni lwata lwata,** the dog's tail is very long and swings about.

lwayo *vt* extending in length; **Otto olwayo ot madit mada,** Otto has built a large house; see **oywayo.**

lwe lwe *adv* moving quietly and noiselessly; **bura woto ni lwe lwe,** the cat walks noiselessly.

lweddo *vt* to strike / striking down several things; **olweddo winyo woko ki odoo acel ma oyuyo;** he struck down several birds with the one stick which he threw at them; (a better expression is however **orwaddo winyo).**

lwek *adv* whole; **ocutto ni lwek,** he swallowed it whole.

lweka (otigo lweka) *n* okra, lady's fingers, *hibiscus esculente.*

lwekko *vn* 1 to roam / roaming aimlessly; **lwekko piny,** roaming about aimlessly; 2 **lwekko waŋ,** looking this way and that way aimlessly.

lweny *v* fight; **lweny kwede,** fight him.

lweny *n* fighting; **lweny pe gin maber,** fighting is not a good thing.

lwenynyo *vi* to fight / fighting; **jonni tin lwenynyo piŋoo?** what are they fighting for today?

lwer *v* cut, trim, prune; **lwer jaŋ yadi matino woko,** cut off the small branches of the trees, or prune the trees.

lwer *vi* stripping off leaves and small branches, shedding off; **pot yadi doŋ tye ka lwer woko,** the leaves of the trees are falling off or are being shed off.

lwerro *vt* to strip / stripping off leaves or to prun / pruning of small branches of trees; **cittu ka lwerro pot tyaŋ,** go to strip off the dried leaves of sugar cane.

lwet *n* finger and toe nails; **ŋollo lwet,** trimming the nails.

lwic *n* whistling; **ŋa ma ŋeyo lwic,** who knows whistling? see **lwii, lwiyo.**

lwii *v* whistle; **lwii matek ,** whistle loudly; see **lwic, lwiyo.**

lwii *vi* escape, steal away (some people use **luu** but **lwii** is the word spoken by the central Acholi); **latinne marro lwii woko ki i cukul,** the child likes escaping from school; **tyen mapol latin acel i kom rudi marro lwii woko,** many times one of the twins escapes, i.e., dies; see **lwiyo, lwic; c/o kwalle.**

lwiny *v* dive into water; **citti ilwiny i tee pii,** go and dive into the water.

lwiny *n* dead larvae of beetles which normally are found in dried meat and fish.

lwiny *vn* sink, be submerged, dive into water; **dano myero guŋee lwiny i**

tee pii, people must know how to dive into water.

lwir *n* does not conceive quickly, **dakone lwir,** the woman does not conceive quickly; see **kaŋ.**

lwiro *prd* a prolonged period of child bearing; **dako ma lwiro,** the woman who conceives, at long intervals, see **okaŋ.**

lwit *n* 1 a charm, amulet; **tye ki lwit me nekko lee,** he has an amulet for killing animal 2 parasite, a tree which attaches itself to another tree and grows on it. 3 piles in anus 4 a solitary projecting swelling of skin (*papiloma* on the body).

lwit *n* root; **lwit yat, the** root of a tree; see **lyak.**

lwiyo *vn* whistling; **marro lwiyo twatwal,** likes whistling very much;

comes from **lwii, lwic, lwiyo.**

lwob *v* tie; **lwob dyel i lum kama cammo iye,** tie the goat in the grass where it can eat.

lwobbe *vi* following one another; **dyegi gitye ka lwobbe alwobba,** the goats are following one another.

lwobbo *vt* 1 to tie / tying with a long rope; **lwobbo dyel,** tying the goat with a long rope 2 to pile / piling; **lwobbo agulu i wii lawotte,** to pile / piling the pots on top of one another; see also **doddo, koddo, dwoddo.**

lwoc *n* mist, fog; see **lupwu** which some peole call **lupuu.**

lwodde or lwobbe or kubbe *vi* be connected; **lokke okubbe ki man,** the matter is connected to this (**kubbe** is better than the other two).

lwoddo *vt* to ponder / pondering, to reflect / reflecting, meditating on; **tye ka lwoddo lokke i cwinynye,** he is pondering about the matter.

lwoddo *vt* to fasten / fastening; **lwoddo dyel,** fastening goat to a tree with a rope; see **lwobbo.**

lwok *v* take a bath; **lwok kommi,** take a bath; **cit ka lwok,** go to take a bath.

lwok *n* bathing; **lwok miyo kom yot,** bathing makes the body healthy.

lwokke *vi* to bathe / bathing, to wash / washing; **dano myero lwokke nino ducu,** one must take a bath every day.

lwokko *vt* washing; **lwokko boŋo,** washing clothes; **lwokko kom,** bathing the body.

lwokko *vt* 1 to see / seeing a guest off; **lwokko wello ki terro i ŋee gaŋ,** seeing a guest off the home, or taking the guest outside the home, or escorting the guest outside the home. 2 casting out evil spirits from a person; **lwokko kom dano,** giving an offering to the spirit in order to make it get out / leave someone's body.

lwoŋ *v* call; **lwoŋ Onek obin kany,** call Onek to come here.

lwoŋŋe *vi* calling; **danone pe mitto lwoŋŋe cee,** is he someone who does not want to be called?

lwoŋŋo *vt* to call / calling; **lwoŋŋo Onek wek obin,** calling Onek to come.

Lwoo *n* the name of the largest tribe of the Ji people living along the Nile in the sub-Saharan region & speaking more or less the same language.

lwor *v* respect, fear, go round; **lwor menni ki worru,** respect your mother and your father. **wot i lwor ot,** go round the house.

lworre *vi vn* fear him / her, fear;**lworre en dano madder mada,** fear him (for) he is a cruel person.

lworro *vt* fearing, respecting 1 **lworro too,** fearing death. 2 **lworro ludito,** respecting the elders; **lalworro** *n* a coward.

lworro *vt* to go / going or to walk / walking round, enclosing 1**wotto rummo** or **lworro ot,** walking round the house 2 **goyo cel lworro gaŋ,** building the fence to enclose the home.

lyaa *adv* in long threads; **otigo telle ni lyaa lyaa,** okra sauce is viscous, it stretches into long threads when being eaten.

lyaco or lyatto or lyakko *vt* to grind / grinding simsim or groundnuts until it is like butter or paste; **lyakko** is preferred to the other two.

lyak *n* the root of a tree; see **lwit.**

lyak *v* to grind; **lyak odii ma pwot piwa me acamma,** grind the simsim paste very smooth for us.

lyakke *vi* ground; **nyim tika twerro lyakke i kidi man,** can simsim paste be ground very smooth on this stone?

lyakko *vt* to grind / grinding; **lyakko odii,** grinding simsim paste smooth.

lyak lyak *adv* shines, burns brightly; **jabu ryeny ni lyak lyak** gold shines brightly, fire burns brightly.

lyaŋ-lyaŋ *adv* raging; **mac lyel ni lyaŋ lyaŋ,** the fire is raging.

lyec *n* an elephant; **lyecci,** elephants.

lyedi *n* a razor; **kel lyedi me lyello wic,** bring the razor for shaving the hair.

lyedo *n* shaving the hair.

lyek *n* a patch of land where the grass has been burned.

lyel *n* a tomb, grave.

lyel *v* to shave, **lyel yer tikki ki yer ummi woko,** shave your chin and moustache.

lyel *vi* burning; **mac tye ka lyel,** the fire is burning.

lyelle *n vi* 1 his grave; **lyelle giyubbo ki marble,** his grave is made of marble; shaved 2 shaving; **wii latinni pe twerro lyelle,** the child's hair cannot be shaved.

lyelli *n* the late; **lyelli Oketa yaŋ ber,** the late Oketa was a good man.

lyello *vt* shaving; **lyello tik,** shaving the chin.

lyer *n. labia minora* or the inner small lip of the vagina which protrudes from the vagina in some women; **lyer ma omakko meni,** the inner lip of your mother's vagina protrude, (used as an insult).

lyer dye ŋec *n* the rest of the spine.

lyer nyim *n* a wooden frame on which the simsim is dried.

lyer *v* hang, suspend **lyer boŋo wii tol** hang the cloth on the line.

lyer *v* cook vegetables; **lyer dek oyot oyot wek gicam,** cook the vegetables quickly so that they may be eaten.

lyerre *vi* swinging from a rope; **latin tye ka lyerre,** the child is swinging.

lyerre *n* pretending, **tye ka lyerre ni pe emitto,** he is pretending or disdaining that he does not want; **tye ka lyerre pi kic ma gitye ka cammone,** he is hanging around because of the honey which is being eaten.

lyerro *vt* hanging up, suspending; **lyerro otigo,** cooking okra (suspended in water); **lyerro boŋo wii tol,** hanging the clothes on the clothesline to dry.

lyet *adj* hot; **dekke lyet,** the sauce is hot.

lyono *n* a plant whose tuber is used for playing by children learning to spear.

lyono *n* a running plant which produces big tubers which children shoot with arrows in a kind of a game.

M m

ma *conj* whilst, though, without; 1 **mape oballo,** without committing a crime, without committing sin; **gigoye mape oballo gin mo,** he was beaten though he did not do anything wrong. 2 **ma** which **ma pe larre,** which can not be disputed; **ma pe wacce,** which can not be spoken about.

ma *relative prn* who, that, which: *prefix* to *adj* as **ma-ber**, good, nice. **dano ma-rac mada,** a very bad person; **ma** is usually joined to the *adj*ective which it qualifies. e.g. **maber, marac** instead of the above.

maa *v* take by force, rob, mug; **maa buk woko ki i ciŋŋo,** take away by force the book in his hand; see **mac, mayo.**

maa *n* my mother (my mother's sister, also is called my mother); **meego,** mother, a general name; the word **meego** comes from the word **mee,** meaning love each other; the relationships here is as follows: *sing* **maa, meeni, minne,** my, your, his mother; *pl* many mothers to many children; **meegiwa, meegiwu, meegigi,** our, your, their mothers; *sing* mother to many children; **minwa, minwu, mingi,** our, your, their mother; this is not commonly spoken, now **meegiwa, meegiwu, meegigi** are used as plural.

maar *n* love, favour, liking; **maar gin maber mada,** love is a very good thing.

maar *v* love, like; **maar lawotti macalo in,** love your neighbour as yourself.

maarra *n* my mother-in-law; **maarro,** mother-in-law; **maarru, maarre,** your, his mother-in-law; *pl* **maarrowa, maarrowu, maarrogi;** see below.

maaro *n* comes from the word **maar,** love; hence the name **maaro,** mother-in-law who loves you *pl* **maarri,** which is a general name; the relationships are as follows: *sing* **maarra, maarru, maarrone,** my, your, his mother-in-law; *sing* a mother-in-law with many sons-in-law it will be **maarrowa, maarrowu, maarrogi,** our, your, their mother-in-law; *pl* mothers-in-law with many sons in law this will be **maarriwa, maarriwu, maarrigi,** our your, their mothers-in-law; **maarri** are not close relative are referred to as, **maarri mewa, maari mewu, maarri meegi nyo ni maarri meegwa, maarri meegwu, maari meegi.**

maarro *vt* loving, liking, favouring; **maarro tukko odilo mada,** loves / likes football 2 loves/likes playing football very much; **marro latinne mada,** he/she loves his child very much.

maawe, maa do, aya maa do, etc. *inj,* exclamations of grief, sorrow and pain.

mabuc *n* S prison; see **jero.**

mabur *n* A steamer, ship, boat.

mabura *n* a file; **kel mabura nyonyo leela,** bring the iron file for filing or rubbing metal.

mac *n* fire, **mac tara,** a lamp; **mac tye ka lyel caa,** the fire is burning over there; **mac luduku,** gunfire; **mac luduku tin omakkogi mada,** they were fired at very heavily.

mac *n* robbery, plunder, taking by force; see **maa, mayo.**

mac *n* March, the third month of the year.

maca *dem prn* that, those; **dano maca,** that man; **jami maca,** those things.

macalo *dem* for example, like this; **en onoŋo pe ŋeyo leb lurok, macalo leb muno,** he did not know foreign languages, for example, English; **pe rac, en doŋ otimmo macalo kit meno,** it does not matter, he did it like that.

macak *n* large bluish beads; **orukko otiko macak i ŋutte,** she wore blue beads around her neck.

mad *v* clean the wound, swab the ulcer with hot water; **mad waŋ bur,** swab the ulcer; **mad me waŋ bur oketto awobi woko,** swabbing of the ulcer has overwhelmed the boy *or* the boy is overwhelmed by the swabbing.

madara *A n* mirror, spectacles.

Madi *n* a tribe found north-west of Gulu in West Nile.

madde *vi* can be swabbed; **ocitto ka madde,** he went to have his ulcer cleaned / swabbed with hot water; **dakone madde kene ka onywal,** the woman swabs herself when she has given birth.

maddi *v* clean the ulcer, swab the ulcer with hot water.

maddo *vt* swabbing the ulcer with hot water and dressing it; **gitye ka maddo waŋ bur,** they are swabbing the ulcer; **ŋaa matye ka maddo dako ma onywalli,** who is swabbing the woman who has just delivered?

maga *adv* completely; **opoŋ agulo ni maga,** the pot is completely full; some people use **mara** instead of **maga.**

maikorocikop *n Eng* microscope, **gitye ka pimmo remone ki maikorocikop me neno ka kwidi maleriya tye iye,** they are examining his blood under the microscope to find out whether there are malarial parasites.

mairo *n Eng* mile; **owotto mairo acel,** he walked for one mile.

majan *A n* a balance, weighing scale; **majan gipimmo kwede ki riŋo,** a weighing scale is for weighing meat.

majan cai *n* tea leaves.

mak *v* hold, arrest, apprehend, capture; **mak pe oriŋ,** hold (and) do not let him run; **mak man pi tutuno,** hold this one for the time being; *prov.* **mak tutuno en aye pok,** means what you have been given already and is in your hand, is yours, hold on to it, you may not get any more of the same thing.

ma ka *conj* in place of; **miine cente ma ka boŋo,** give him money instead of clothes; *c/f* **ka waŋ boŋo.**

ma-kare-pe *adv* infinitely, very; **oriŋŋo mabor ma kare pe,** he ran very far indeed.

makaa *n S* charcoal

makatala *n S* punishment; **en oturro cik me cukul myero gimiine makatala,** he boke the school rule, (therefore) he must be punished.

makatap *A n* court; **terro ŋati mo i makatap ka piddo,** taking one to the court to answer a case (no longer spoken).

makke *vi* 1 catch him, arrest him, 2 stick together, to be caught; **buk gumakke**

kacel, the books got stuck together; **danone pe twerro makke,** the person cannot be arrested.

makko *vt* to arrest / arresting, to catch / catching, to hold / holding, to capture / capturing, etc.1 **makko rec,** to catch / catching fish 2 **makko mabuc,** to arrest / arresting the prisoner 3 **bura tye ka makko oyoo,** the cat is catching a rat.

makko *vn* feeling; **makko kiniga i komme,** feeling very angry with him.

makko *vi* to inherit / inheriting; **makko goba pa minne,** to inherit / inheriting the lying habit of his mother.

makko dog *vt* to have a bad sticky taste; **nyig yatte makko dog,** the fruit is bad and has a bad sticky taste.

makko dog *vt* surprised; **lokke omakko dogwa woko,** his words surprised us, (and we were unable to speak) .

mal *vi* to roam about, lose hope; **latinne mal ata,** the child roams about aimlessly.

mal *v* fry; **mal riŋo man oyot oyot,** fry this meat quickly.

malaga *A n* a spoon; see **lakologoc.**

malakwaŋ *n* a popular acid-tasting vegetable, *hibiscus family of* shrubs.

malaya *S n* harlot, prostitute; **dako man doŋ twon malaya mape wacce,** this woman is now a seasoned prostitute.

maleriya *n Eng* malaria; **Onyac otwoyo maleriya twatwal,** Onyac has suffered too much from malaria.

mali *A n* wealth; this word was used very much in the twenties and thirties.

malle *vi* 1 twisting, rolling about; **twol ka tye ka too malle amalla ni dwanya**

dwanya, when a snake is dying it twists about.

malle *vi* become red; **papai ne doŋ Omalle woko,** the pawpaw has now become yellow.

malle *adv* can be fried.

mallo *vt* frying; **mallo riŋo amalla,** frying the meat.

malo *adv* up, above, aloft; **it malo wii yat,** climb up the tree; **nen malo,** look up; **tuk malo i wii yadi,** flies above the trees; **wotto ki wiye malo pe nenno ŋati mo,** walks with his head aloft and does not mind about anybody.

man *demo prn* this; **dano man pe ber,** this man is not good; **man aŋaa,** who is this? **teer man gaŋ,** take this home.

man *n* scrotum, testicle; **nyig manne,** his testicles.

mandara *n A* looking glass.

manne *vi* to go / going round something in order to escape when being pursued; **omanne ki ot ci orweny woko,** he went round the house and disappeared; **en manne ki ot ci rweny woko;** he goes round the house and disappers.

manno *vt* going round something; **manno yat.** going round a tree.

manno *vt* to hide something away; **omanno jami mukene woko ma gimiyo ni okel,** he hid some of the things which he was given to bring for himself.

many *adv* completely, for ever; **ocitto ni many,** he went away for ever.

many *v* looking behind **many ŋeyi** look behind you.

manynyo *vt* turning one's sight toward something, looking through the corners of the eyes; **manynyo ŋec,** looking behind through the corners of his eyes.

mara-mara *adv* vaguely, indistinctly, faintly; **calle obeddo mara mara,** the picture looks blurred / indistinct.

mat *v* 1 drink; **mat pii en,** drink this water 2 smoke; **pe imat taa,** do not smoke.

mat *n* drinking, smoking; **marro mat mukato kare woko,** likes drinking / smoking very much.

matalici *n S* a postman, one who used to take letters by bicycle (not in use now).

matapwali *S n* bricks; **goyo matapwali,** making bricks.

matata *adv S* trouble; **pe ikel matata kany,** don't cause trouble here.

matto *vt* 1 drinking; **matto pii,** drinking water. 2 absorbing, sucking in; **boŋo matto lac pa latin woko,** the cloth absorbs the urine of the child. 3 smoking; **en matto taa twatwal,** he smokes tobacco too much.

mawulu *Lug n* the ground hornbill, normally called **arum.** c/f **acebe.**

mayo *vt* robbing , mugging, preying, plundering, seducing; 1 **mayo jami pa dano,** robbing people of their property 2 **mayo dako pa laremme,** seducing the wife of his friend; see **maa, mac.**

me *prp* for, for the purpose of; 1 **agwata me lamat pii,** gourd bowl for drinking water 2 **me ŋoo?** for what purpose? 3 **me acel, me aryo etc**, the first, the second etc.; **lutic me gudo,** road maintenance workers.

med *v* add, increase; **med moo petrol i motoka,** add more petrol in the car; **med dekke dok manok,** add some

more food please; **med mac wek mutoka oriŋ matek,** increase the fire to make the motor car run fast (increase speed).

meda *n* swallows, forked tail and outer tail *rectrices* elongated (bird); see also **lakalagwec,** swift.

medda *vt* give me some more; **medda dekke dok manok,** give me some more food.

medde *v* to increase, grow bigger or larger, further away; **medde i cit anyim,** go further forward; *vi* **latin tye ka medde mada ki doŋo,** the child is growing very fast; **akwotta emme tye ka medde amedda,** the swelling in his thigh is getting bigger and bigger.

meddo *vt* to add to, to increase; **ter motoka ka meddo moo ne,** take the car to add some petrol into it (for refuelling).

mee *prn* belonging; **mee pa aŋaa?** belonging to whom? / whose / for whom? **jami meera, meeri, meere,** *etc,* my, your, his/her things; *pl* **meewa, meewu, meegi,** ours, yours, theirs.

mee *vn* clandestine friendship; **man mee Ocol,** this is Ocol's secret or clandestine girlfriend; see **meec, mecca** (for poetical, singing purposes).

mee *vi* increase, 1 **mac tye ka mee mada,** the fire is burning more ferociously 2 **twoo tye ka mee mada i komme,** the disease is getting worse in him.

mee *vi* 1 melt, 2 spread; **moo ma oo ca tye ka mee,** the oil that spilt out there is melting; **moo dyaŋ ka pe giketto kama ŋic ci mee woko,** if butter is not put in a cold place, it melts away.

meec *n* secret friendship between a man and a woman; **mecca,** my secret girlfriend (*poetic*, used in singing); see **meer, mecca, meya.**

meego *n* mother; **meego ocitto kwene?** where has mother gone?

meeni *prn* your mother.

meer *vi* 1 being friendly; **jooni gimeer mada,** they are very friendly. 2 friendly and approachable; **danone meer mada ki dano,** he is very friendly and approachable; **anyirane gimeer mada,** the girls love one another very much.

meer *n* friendship; **meer ber,** friendship is good or being friendly is good.

meer *vn* being drunk, intoxicated; **lacoone doki meer twatwal,** the man gets too much intoxicated; **dano ma matto, rubbo koŋo ma patpat, meer twatwal,** a person who drinks, mixing various type of alcohol, gets too drunk.

meerre *vi* boasting; **wek meerre ki jammi ni obeddi,** stop boasting about your things / assets.

meerri, meera, meere *pos prn* yours, mine, his; see **mee pa aŋaa?**

meerro *vt* being drunk, being intoxicated; **koŋo arege meerro dano mada,** waragi makes people very drunk.

meeya, meeye, meeyi *pos prn* my, his, your girlfriend (clandestine).

meja *n S* table; **meja en aye gitiyo kwede me ketto jami iwiye,** a table is used for putting things on.

meja *n Eng* major, a military rank above the captain but below the lieutenant colonel.

meja jeneral *n Eng* major general, a military rank above brigadier general but below lieutenant general; see **jeneral, pil macul.**

mel *n Eng.* mail steamer; in those days there were steamers which used to bring mail, **mel** being a distortion of mail ship; see **mabur.**

mel *adv* without rain; **piny tin dyewor obutto mel,** it did not rain last night.

memba *n Eng* member; **memba adii me paliament ma gubinno?** how many Members of Parliamnt came?

menne? *inter prn* which? **buk mene?** which book?

meno *dem prn* that, those, who? **meno aŋaa gi?** who are those? **gin ma kit meno pe nen kany,** a thing like that is not seen here or a thing like that does not happen here.

meŋŋo *vt* to enervate, debilitate; **yatte meŋŋo kom,** the medicine enervates the body and makes one feel like vomiting; **ceŋ meŋŋo kom,** the sun enervates the body.

meny *v/vi* 1 light, illuminate, **meny wek okwan,** light so that he may read 2 flash, glimmer; **otit meny dyewor,** the firefly glimmers at night; **meny pa kot,** lightning of rain.

menynye *vi* can be litilluminated; **i ot col twatwal pe twerro menynye ki kendal keken,** is too dark inside the house be illuminated by candles only.

menynyo *vt* illuminating, lighting; **menynyo ot,** illuminating the house; **tarane menynyo piny maleŋ mada,** the lamp illuminates very well.

met *adv* very extensive; **opurro poto ni met i ŋet gaŋŋe,** he cultivated a very extensive field around his home.

mette *vi* being extremely fat; **matto koŋo ki cam madwoŋ miyo dano mette mada,** drinking and eating too

much food make people become very
fat.

met met *adv* extremely fat.

mette *vn* increased; **pii opoŋ omette
wa wii tera,** the water has increased
greatly and spread all over the land.

metto *vt* enlarging, making very big;
metto poto twatwal, extending the field
greatly.

meyo *vt* 1 keeping it going; **meyo mac
ki yen matino,** keeping the fire burning
by adding small pieces of firewood or
sticks to the fire 2 melting; **latet meyo
nyonyo me atteta,** the blacksmith melts
the iron for forging.

meyo *vt* 1 liquify; **meyo moo ya,** melting
the shea nut butter.

meyo *vi* feeling sick and disgusted;
**cammo kic twatwal meyo cwiny
woko,** eating too much honey makes
people feel sick of it 3 enervatte,
weaken; **ticce meyo kom dano,** the
work enervates people.

meyo *vt* enervating; **cammo gwana
meyo kom dano,** eating cassava
enervates people.

mic *vn* 1 gift, giving 2 closing; see **mii,
miyo.**

mican or **micon** *n Eng* mission (Church
Missionary Society).

Miciri *n A* Egypt, an old name for it
which is found in the old Bible; see
Ejipt.

mida *n* a skin disease, ringworm,
normally found on the neck, and body,
circular in shape; see **omemelo** which
normally affects the head.

middo *vi* to exude, ooze, percolate; 1
agulu pii ne middo mada, the water
pot oozes too much water. 2 **pii matye**

**ka cwer nia ki i paipo ma otuc middo
oo wa i ot,** the water from the leaking
pipe percolate up to the house 3 **moo
tye ka middo i komme,** the oil is
oozing out of his body.

mii *v* give; **mii pii ki latin,** give water to
the child.

mii *v* close; **mii waŋŋi,** close your eyes;
see **mic, miyo.**

mil *vi* sparkle, glitter, shine; **jabu mil ni
pil pil,** gold sparkles brightly; **jabu mil
amila ni mak mak,** the gold shines
very brightly.

mile *n* a common salt **miya kado mile,**
give me common salt. see **kado
atwona.**

mille *vi* run surpassing others; **mille
amilla ka ŋwec,** running very first in
front; see **wille awilla.**

mil-mil *adv* appearing and disappearing;
twol naŋŋo lebbe ni mil mil, the snake
moves its tongue restlessly in and out.

mim *adv* in large mass; **kweyo ocorre ni
mim ma kot okello,** the sand which the
rain brought came in large mass.

min *n* mother of; **min Orac,** the mother
of Orac. 2 **min** before the common
name of an animal, it it indicates that
it is a female animal; **min dyaŋ,** cow;
min dyel, she-goat, etc.

min *adj* big; **min got, min yat,**
big mountain, big tree (referes to
spirit which are supposed to live in
mountains, trees and rivers); **min kulu
omakko latin woko,** the river or brook
spirit has got hold of the child; **min
kidi,** big base stone for grinding; **min
bul,** the big drum.

min *v* twist, make; **min uno tol tworo
me tweyo dyel,** twist sisal fibres into
ropes for tying goats.

min ic *n* rectum or intestine; **min ic okatto woko ki i ŋwiny,** prolapsed rectum, or excessively long *intussusception* has come out through the rectum;

min it, the eardrum.

minicita *n Eng* minister; **minicita me pwony,** Minister of Education.

minno tol *vt* twisting two or more strands into a rope.

miŋ *adj* 1 stupid, foolish; **dano ma miŋ**, a stupid person, simpleton 2 incompetent, awkward, unfit.

minyo *n* suet; **minyo dyaŋ**, suet of a cow.

miri *n.* government; **jami pa miri,** government property; see **gabument.**

miri *n* charcoal; **miri en aye gitetto kwede nyo giteddo kwede,** charcoal is used for forging and for cooking.

miri-miri *adv* shines brightly; **akuku ryeny ni miri-miri,** when polished mica or iron ore shines very brightly.

miri miri *prd adv* indistinct, vague; **nen miri miri,** not clearly seen, seen vaguely.

mit *n* 1 desire; **en tye ki mit madwoŋ twatwal me jami,** he has excessive desire for things. 2 good taste, or tastes good; **camme mit mada,** the food was very nice 3 **lok pa ladit mit,** the words of the elder were good. 4. entertainer, **lokko mamit mada,** he is an entertainer, very humourous, speaks very well.

mit-mit *adv* closing and opening; **ŋwiny gweno beddo ni mit-mit**, a chicken's anus contracts and relaxes.

mitte *vi* desirable, necessary; **mitte me awilla,** desirable to be bought.

mitto *vt* to desire / desiring, to wish / wishing, to like / liking, to love / loving; **mitto citto,** to desire / desiring or to wish / wishing to go; *vi* **cwinynye mitto,** he likes it.

mitti *n* desire, greediness, gluttony; **tye ki mitti me lim mada,** has excessive desire for wealth.

miya *s n* hundred; **gweno miya acel,** one hundred chickens

miya *vt* give me; **miya cam,** give me food.

miyo *vt* giving; **miyo cam ki dano,** giving food to people; see **mii, mic.**

miyo *vt* closing the hand or eyes; **miyo waŋ,** closing the eyes; see **mii, mic.**

miyo *adj* fatty ; **riŋone miyo,** the meat is fatty and of a high grade;

mo *indef.prn.* some; **ŋatimo,** someone, somebody; **gin mo,** something; **matidi mo,** very small. **mo** *adj* some, **kel gin mo** bring something **kella cam mo** bring me some food.

moc *vn* putting to dry, drying; see **moo, moyo.**

moc *n* nutritional value; **moc riŋo,** the nutritional value of meat; **danone moc kommme pe,** he is thin and wasted.

mok *v* 1 light, kindle; **mok mac,** light or kindle a fire; 2 eating powdered food, **mok** *v* eat dry powder; **mok cukari,** eat granular sugar.

mokke *vi* eaten, lit; **cukarine mokke maber,** the sugar can be easily eaten well. **yenne twerro mokke,** the firewood can be lighted.

mokko *vt* 1 lighting; **mokko mac,** lighting or kindling a fire.

mokko *vn* entangled, caught, sticking fast; **lee omokko i obwoo,** the animal got caught in the net.

mokko *vt* eating (powdered food or taking a mouthfull of food); **dyaŋ mokko puno,** the cows eat the salted earth near the river; **mokko cukari,** eating the sugar.

moko *adv* some; **miya moko,** give me some.

moko *n* flour; **moko me teddo mugati,** flour for making bread.

moko-moko *prd* like powder; **obeddo moko-moko,** it is like powder.

mol *vi* flow, move fast in large numbers; **pii tye ka mol,** water is flowing; **dano tye ka mol,** people are passing by in large numbers or a multitude of people are passing by.

mola *n* metal; **mola makwar,** copper; **mola matar,** silver.

mollo *vt* 1 being carried off by a current of watch. 2 debilitating, enervating; **twoone omollo komme twatwal,** the illness has affected him very much, he is wasted and weak, or the illness has debilitated him very much; 3 **twone mallo kom dano twatwal,** the illness causes much debilitation and wasting of body.

mon *n* women, wives; **monwa, monwu, mon gi,** our, your, their wives.

mono *n* reserve food, put aside in a granary, for future use; **kal monone eno,** that is his reserve millet for hard times.

mono *prd* incapable, unfit; **en mono me beddo rwot,** he is unfit to be a chief; **mono me beddo latel wii dano,** unworthy or incapable of being a leader of the people.

mono *inj* now; **in mono itye katimo ŋoo?** what are you doing now?

mony *n* war, campaign, raid; **mony ocakke laworo i kin lobo aryoni,** the war broke out between the two countries yesterday.

mony *v* attack; **cittu wumonygi,** go and attack them; **cittu ka mony,** go to war.

mony *n* menstruation; **mony omakko laworo,** she started menstruation yesterday.

monynyo *vt* to attack / attacking, to start / starting a war; **jo ma gukwoŋo monynyo Poland gin aye Jeremel,** the Germans were the first people to attack Poland.

monyo *n* menstruation; **dakoni tye ki monyo,** she is menstruating.

moo *v* put to dry; **moo boŋo i ceŋ,** put the clothes out in the sun; see **moc, moyo.**

moo *n* fat, butter, oil; **moo dyaŋ,** fat of cow, ghee; **moo nyim,** simsim oil; **moo ma icogo,** bone marrow; **moo ma bwogo,** freshly made butter before it is processed; **moo tara,** paraffin.

moo *n* pulp; **moo tugu,** the pulp of the *borassus* palm tree; **moo muyembe,** pulp of mango.

moo *n* somewhere **ocitto ka moo,** he went somewhere

moon *vi* being on bad terms with, being enemies; **gimoon ki neru ne,** he is at loggerheads with his uncle; **gin lumoone,** they are enemis of each other.

moono *vt* spreading out in order to dry; **moono kal,** spreading millet out in the sun to dry it.

moono *vt* exposing a secret; **moono lok muŋ pa lawotti pe ber,** to expose the secrets of your friend is not good.

moor *v* look with menace or suspicion; **moor waŋŋi i komme,** watch him carefully; **pe imoor waŋŋi i komma, an pe ma aballo,** don't look at me with suspicion I am not the one who spoilt it.

mooro waŋ *vi lit.* opening the eyes wide and fixing them on something.

morro waŋ *vt* being annoyed with someone; **morro waŋŋe i kom dano mo,** being annoyed with someone.

mor *n* roar, thunder; **mor pa labwor kello lworo,** the roar of a lion causes fear; **polo mor,** rain thunders.

mor-mor *adj* lukewarm; **pii ne mor-mor,** the water is lukewarm; see also **de de, bol bol, dem dem, bulu bulu.**

Moro *n* **got Moro,** Moro mountain near and to the east of Gulu.

moro *n* soldier ants which travel in long lines and biting and carrying anythings they find on their ways.

mot *adv* 1 slowly, gently, quietly; **wot mot mot,** go slowly 2 **bed mot,** be quiet 3 **mak mot,** hold gently.

mot *v* greet; **mot Onen ka inoŋŋe,** greet Onen if you find him.

mot *n* greetings; there are many ways of greeting depending upon the times of the day and the circumstances; they are as follows: 1 **mot me odiko,** morning greeting, **ibutto?,** this is a shorten form, it should be **ibutto niŋniŋ?** how did you sleep? people from Kitgum say **icoo?** which is a shortened form, of **icoo niŋniŋ?** how did you wake up? The central Acholi prefer the former. The answers to the above greetings are: **abutto maber,** I slept well, and **acoo maber,** I woke well; in short you greet as follows: **ibutto,** response **abutto; icoo,** response **acoo** 2 greetings in the street **itye,** response **atye,** meaning, **itye niŋniŋ?** how are you and the response **atye maber,** I am well 3 greetings in the day at home, **wubeddo,** response **wabeddo** or **wurii** response **warii.** The meanings of all these are: **wubeddo niŋniŋ,** how have you been? response **wabeddo maber,** we have been well; **wurii niŋniŋ,** how have you spent the day? response **warii maber,** we have spent the day well 4 greetings in times of grief: hosts the people at home greet the guests; **wun doŋ wukatti,** is short for **wun doŋ wukatti niŋniŋ?** how did you come? response **wan doŋ wakati,** which is a shortened of **wan doŋ wakatti en,** we have now come 5 when the arrival of the guests are expected, the people at home greet the guests who have arrived thus **wun doŋ wuoo,** this is short for **wun doŋ wuoo niŋniŋ?** response **wan doŋ waoo,** short for **wan doŋ waoo en nyo maber,** we have come very well (we have had no problem on the way) 6 greetings at any time of the day; **lok aŋoo? lok pe,** what news? no news; some people greet thus: **kop aŋoo? kop pe,** what matter? no matter; the two greetings have different meanings, but the former is preferred.

motoli *n* serum, serous fluid; **obwacco tyenne ci motoli en aye tye ka cweer,** he lacrated his leg and serum / serous fluid is coming out. **motoli** *n* serous fluid from a wound or burn, serum.

motoka *Eng n* motor car.

motte *vi* greeting; **motte ki luremmi,** greeting each other, you and your friends.

motto *vt* greeting; **motto dano i yoo mape iŋeyogi pe ber,** greeting people in the street whom you don't know is not good; **wamottowu ducu,** greetings to you all.

motto *adv* to settle; **donynyo pa anyena i ot doŋ omotto,** the bride is now settled in her house.

motto *vi* soaking or penetrating; **moo omotto i bataniya,** the oil has penetrated / soaked the blanket.

motto *vi* to enter; **odilo omotto,** the ball has entered the goal.

moyo *vt* drying, putting out to dry; **moyo boŋo i ceŋ,** putting the clothes out in the sun; see **moo, moc.**

mucara *n Lug* wage, salary; **cullo mucara,** paying wage or salary.

mucija *Lug n* a cold in the head, fever (no longer spoken).

mucoro *n s* tax; **cullo mucoro,** paying taxes.

mucumar *n A* nail, **mucumar me gurro bao,** nails for nailing wood.

mucumeni *n A* saw; **mucumeni me ŋollo bao,** a saw for cutting wood.

muduku *A n* gun, rifle; also called **luduku,** with the latter preferred.

muganna *n* a rafter going from the bottom to the roof of a hut.

mugaŋa *n* gunpowder.

mugati *S n* bread; **kel mugati ki latin,** bring some bread for the child.

muindi *S* an Indian.

mujula *n A* a poor man without a wife or hut (not much spoken now).

muk *v.* break off; **muk but mugati wek i cam,** break off a piece of the bread and eat it; uproot; **muk yat man,** uproot this tree; **lak latin doŋ cok ka muk woko,** the child's tooth is about to fall out.

mukene *indf.prn.* another one; **kella boŋo mukene,** bring for me another dress.

mukko *vt.* uprooting, breaking at the bottom in order to pull it away or up.

mukko yat, uprooting a tree.

mukko lak *vi* uprooting the tooth when it is diseased; c/f **nakko lak.**

mukuŋu *n Lug* parish chief; **rwom me loc me Acoli onoŋŋo tye kitman, cakke ki i kom: won paco, mukuŋu, jago ka nio kom rwot,** the administration hierarchy of the Acoli was like this: the head of the village, the parish chief, sub-chief then the chief.

Mulaya *S n* Europe, usually called **Bulaya,** the latter is preferred.

mullo *vi* crawling; **latin tye ka mullo,** the child is crawling.

mullo *vt* touching with the fingers; **mullo komme,** touching his body.

munero *adv* naked; **Okatto woko munero,** he came out stark naked; see **ludok, lunywan.**

muno *n* a white man; origionaly it was a name given to colours other than black, the whites being called **otara,** but later on when the Arabs became known to be different, then only the whites were called **muno.**

muŋ *n* a secret; **pe myero ituc muŋ pa ŋati mo,** do not let out the secrete of somebody; **olokko i muŋ botte,** he spoke in secret to him.

muŋŋe *vi* 1 can be concealed; **lokke twerro muŋŋe,** the matter can be concealed, or the matter can be kept secret. 2 **pe imuŋŋe mo manok,** do not tell or confide in him.

muŋŋo *vt* concealing, keeping secret, confiding; **muŋŋo mo manok,** confiding some points to somebody; **muŋŋo lokke woko,** concealing the matter.

muny *v* 1 swallow; **muny yat,** swallow the medicine 2 **muny i pii,** drown or sink in water.

munynye *vi* can be swallowed; **yatte twerro munynye,** the medicine can be swallowed.

munynyo *vt* swallowing; **twol tye ka munynyo ogwal,** the snake is swallowing the frog; **munynyo yat,** swallowing the medicine.

munyoo *indef adj* of this time; **dano munyoo ni pe giŋeyo ŋati mo,** the people of these days do not know anybody.

mupira *S n* 1 ball 2 a flannel overcoat, or raincoat.

mur *n* 1 vagina 2 socket; **mur toŋ,** socket where the shaft of the spear is inserted; spoken by Langi and Alur mostly.

mur *v* warm or heat; **mur dek wek gicam,** warm the food so that it may be eaten.

muraŋa *n* beans; **muraŋa cam maber pi litino,** beans are good food for children.

murre *vi* warmed; **dekke twerro murre,** the sauce can be warmed.

murro *vt* warming or heating; **ŋa matye ka murro dek me acamma?** who is warming the food for eating?

muttu *n* 1 darkness; **dyewor obeddo muttu,** there was no moonshine and so it was dark. 2 black, **kono muttu,** black ostrich feather.

muut *adv* 1 with one cut; **oŋollo riŋo ni muut,** he cut the meat with one stroke. 2 deeply; **ocubbo ni muut,** he pierced it deeply.

muwu *prn* yours; this is rarely spoken, the standard one is **mewu** *prn.* yours.

Mwaa *n* 1 Muganda. 2 nothing **Baganda** in the past in Acholi were called **Mwaa** while **Banyoro** were called **Luloka** which means the people on the other side of the river. All these now are archaic; Luloka now is used for both Baganda and Banyoro.

mwa *adj* nothing

Mwa *n* a male name

mwaka *n* year; **tin mwaka me abic,** today is the fifth year.

Mwaka *n* a male name (a child born at the end of the year).

mwam *vi* 1 sudden, unexpectedly; **welo ocorre woko li mwam,** the visitors arrived suddenly in large numbers 2 unexpectedly; **ogurro ci otuc woko limwam,** he hammered the nail in and it came out through the surface.

mwam *prn* 2 blurt out a secret; **lamwam lok,** one who does not keep secrets.

mwammo lok *vi* 1 to blurt out secret; **dano ma mwammo lok myero pe beddo i kin dano,** a man who blurts out secretes should not be among people.

mwarro *vt* breaking up or cutting off, leaving a gap; **mwarro kwon madit,** cutting off a great portion of millet bread leaving a small portion.

mwoc *vi* 1 burst with a loud noise; **kot tye ka mwoc,** the rain is thundering.

mwoc *n* shouts expressing joy (each person usually has his words which he says when shouting, by which he is recognised).

mwoc *n* labour pains; **mwoc okayo dako,** the labour pains have started.

mwod *v* eat; **mwod layata ma numo,** eat an uncooked sweet potato; **mwod pul,** eat groundnuts; **mwod riŋo,** eat meat (why eating meat is usually referred to as **mwoddo riŋo,** is not known, perhaps because in the past the meat eaten was mainly smoked ones).

mwodde *vi* having pain; **iye mwodde,** he is having abdominal pain or stomachache; **komme mwodde,** having body-ache; **riŋone twerro mwodde,** the meat can be eaten.

mwoddo *vt* eating something not properly cooked or hard; **mwoddo layata manumo,** eating raw, uncooked potatoes.

mwoddo *vt* cutting off with an axe bit by bit; **mwoddo yen,** cutting off tree with an axe bit by bit for firewood.

mwodo *n* a dense creeping grass (French grass), very useful for compounds, easy to mow.

mwodo *n* yams, tubers of a climbing plant; see **obato, opelo.**

mwok *n* an ant-bear or anteater; see **coo.**

mwol *adj* gentle, meek, humble; **dano ma mwol,** a gentle person; **dano ma lamwolo,** a gentle person.

mwolo *n* gentleness, meekness; **mwollo ber mada,** gentleness is very good.

mwolle *vi* 1 dressing themselves; **anyira gimwolle ki karatac me coron ka gitye ki kwer,** the girls dress themselves with toilet paper when they have menses; 2 humbled themselves **gudonnyo ma gumwolle,** they humbly entered.

mwollo *vt* adjusting well; 1 **beddo ma mwollo boŋone i komme,** sits with the clothes well pushed round the legs to prevent exposure of the private parts 2 **beddo ma omwollo tyenne,** sits with the legs well folded together 3 **gwok mwollo yibbe,** the dog presses its tail between its legs 4 **ŋeyo mwollo dog boŋo maber mada,** knows how to fold the edge of the clothes very well.

mwomme *vr* bursting out, running away suddenly; **lakwoo omwomme ki ŋwec,** the thief suddenly took to his heels.

mwomme ki ŋwee kakatoo, woko ki i ot pe beri, bursting out when coming from the house is not good, bursting out from the house when coming out is not good.

mwonno *vt* to plaster, cover with clay; **ocitto ka mwonno odde,** he went to plaster his house; **mwonno but ot ma otuc,** blocking off the hole in house with clay 3 **kic omwonno komme matek mada,** the bees covered him while biting him.

mwonynya *prd adj* pleasing to the eye, good-looking, fit; **nyaa pa Onek mwonynya mada,** Onek's daughter is very good-looking and intelligent.

mwonyo *n* a kind of medium-sized tree usually found on an anthill with many spreading branches.

mwonynyo *vi* swallowing; **mwonynyo yat,** swallowing medicine; see **munyayo yati.**

mwot *n* joint, articulation; **mwot ciŋ,** wrist joint; **mwot tyen,** ankle joint.

mwut *adv* quite dark; **piny ociddo ni mwut,** it is quite dark.

myel *n* 1 dance; **gucitto ka myel,** they went to dance. 2 trembling; **ciŋŋe myel,** his hands are trembling / shaking; **komme myel ka tic,** he is very eager to work; **komme myel,** he is trembling from fear or excitement.

myello *vt* dancing, trembling, shaking; **gitye ka myello myel bwola,** they are dancing the **bwola** dance; **en myello maber mada,** she dances very well; shaking, **yatte myello kom dano,** the medicine makes the body shake.

myen kwon *v* stir a mixture of millet flour and water in a container under fire until it becomes thick.

myenne *vi* delaying by moving here and there aimlessly; **see minne, dokke, dikke, galle etc.**

myenno *vi* about to weep or to cry; **latin onoŋŋo doŋ omyenno woko ma pud peya onenno minne,** the child was a already about to cry before seeing his mother.

myenno *vt* 1 stirring, mixing; **myenno kwon,** stirring the mixture of millet flour with water on fire until it is thick and well cooked.

myenno *vt* mixing; **myenno lok,** mixing words.

myero *adv* 1 suitable, fit to be tolerable; **en myero mada ki tic ma wamitto iye dano,** he is suitable for the job for which we want a person. 2 should, **in myero icitti,** you should go.

N n

-na *prn sff* my; **boŋona,** my clothe; **me deyona,** for my honour; **pi pacona,** for my home. push/bend slightly **naa manok,** bend slightly.

naa *v* slightly; **naa manok,** push / bend from the top; push a little from the top to the side; see **nayo.**

naba-naba *adv* tall, slender and flexible.

nada-nada *adv* long, thin, and soft.

naga-naga *adv* moving, bending slightly and seriouslyly; **wotto ni naga naga ki agulu pii ma otiŋŋo i wiye,** walks swinging to and fro with water pot on her head.

nak *v* 1 transplant, remove; **nak latin mucuŋgwa iteer icipitti,** remove this orange seedling and take and transplant it; 2 **nak lakke woko,** extract one of her normal tooth

nak *n* shelf or cupboard built on the wall and made of earth.

naka *n* a kind of white ants (which come mostly from a flat gourd) during the afternoon. See also, **amiŋ amiŋ, okuba, oyala, agoro ka aribu.**

naka *conj* not really; **en naka pe olokko kitmeno,** he did not really said so.

naka *conj* until; **obeddo naka nio ka adwoggo,** he stayed on until I returned.

naka, naka - naka *adv* forever, always continually; **Lubaŋa en aye labed naka naka,** God is the one who lives for ever and ever

nakanen *adv* a moment ago; **naka nen onoŋo watye ka kwan,** a moment ago when we were studying.

nakke *vi* bending sideways, turning aside; **kono ogoyo wiye woko ka pe onakke,** he would have struck his head if he did not bend his head away.

nakke *vi* can be transplanted; **litino lemun man twerro nakke;** these lemon seedlings can be transplanted.

nakko *vt* to extract / extracting or to uproot / uprooting; **nakko yat,** extracting or uprooting the trees with roots and transplanting elsewhere

nakko-lak *vi* extracting or uprooting the tooth; long time ago, it was customary to uproot two lower teeth for beauty.

nal *v* bend down; **nal jaŋ lemunne wek apwon,** bend the branch of the lemon so that I may pick or pluck (the seeds) see **naa.**

nalle *vi* can be bent; **jaŋ yatte twerro nalle,** the branch of the tree can be bent

nallo *vi* to bend / bending slightly, to press / pressing, weighing down; **yamo tye ka nallo yat,** the wind is bending the tree down; **bonyo ka dwoŋ ci nallo jaŋ yat piny,** when the locusts are many, they weigh down the branches of the trees.

nam *n* big river or sea, **ocen.**

nam *adv* to lie / lying into mass / massing on the ground; **dano gubutto piny ni nam,** the people have lied down en masse.

namba *n Eng* number; **man namba abic,** this is number five.

nammo *vn* to pass time in conversation, entertainment; **citto ka nammo i waŋ oo,** going to the fireplace to pass time.

naŋ *v* lick; **naŋ cukari en,** lick this sugar.

naŋa *n* a musical instrument with seven strings.

naŋŋo *vt* licking up; laping up; **naŋŋo nyuka,** licking gruel or porridge using fingers as spoon.

naŋ naŋ *adv* through; **gitye ka corro lum ni naŋ naŋ,** they are pushing through the grass.

naŋ naŋ *adv* completely; **naŋŋo woko ni naŋ naŋ,** eating all completely.

nayo *vt* to push / push aside; **dyegi ma guwok kany gunayo lum mada,** the goats which passed here have pushed aside grass; see **naa, nac.**

nedo *n* malnutrition, results from failure of proper winning of a child from sucking.

nek *v* kill, destroy, smash; **nek bura man woko,** kill this cat; **nek mac matye i ot beddo woko,** switch off the light in the sitting room; **nek agulu ki awal ducu matye i ot kany,** destroy all the pots and the calabash in the house; **nek mac woko,** extinguish the fire.

nek *n* killing; **nek gin marac mada,** killing is a very bad thing.

nekke *vi* 1 can be destroyed; **jammi ni ducu twerro nekke,** all thesc things can be destroyed; 2 killing; **onekke kene,** he committed suicide; 3 feeling; **kec tye ka nekke,** he is feeling hungry.

nekko *vt* to kill / killing, to break /breaking; **nekko awal,** to break / breaking the calabash / bowel; **nekko dano,** to kill / killing a man; **nekko mac,** to extinguish / extinguishing the fire or to switch / switching off the light; **kec nekko,** he is hungry.

nen *v* look, see; **nen labwor caa,** look or see the lion there.

nen *vi* visible, appear, seen; **waŋ dwee tin nen maleŋ mada,** the moon is clearly seen today.

nene *adv* sometimes ago; **guwotto nene wa Atiak,** sometimes ago they walked up to Atiak.

nenne *vi* 1 seeing one another; **nenne gicel gicel ber mada,** seeing one another from times to time is very good; **ginne twerro nenne ka i cuŋ ki tuŋ kwica,** the thing can be seen if you stand on the other side.

nenno *vt* 1 to see / seeing, to look / looking at, to look / looking for, **nenno boŋo mo maber me awilla,** to look / looking for a good dress for buying; 2 to choose / choosing; **nenno dyaŋ mene maber ma loyo ducu,** to choose / choosing which cattle which is better than all of them; 3 suffering; **tye ka nenno can mada,** he is suffering very much.

nep *adj* soft, flexible; **yatte nep,** the pole is soft and flexible.

ner *vi* wither; **yat ma apitto oner woko,** the tree I planted has withered away.

neera *n* my uncle, **neero** general name, uncle; the relative names here are as follows: **neera, neeru, neerone,** sing miy, your, his uncle, pl **neerowa, neerowu, neerogi;** our, your, their uncles; the relative which are not close but still come from the same clan, are called: **neeriwa, neeriwu, neerigi,** our, your, their uncles.

neero *n* uncle, see **neera**

ni, *conj* that; **atammo ni abicitto,** I think that I will go;

niya or ni nyo *conj* that it might, that perhaps; **atammo ni nyo bicitto,**

I think that perhaps he will go or I thought that perhaps he will go.

niaŋ *vt.* understand, enough, (ample) properly; 1 **en tikka niaŋ lok ma gititte,** does he really understand what he has been told? **niaŋ i lok ber,** understanding in the matter is very good; 2 enough; **kwiny bur oniaŋ,** dig the hole deep enough. 3 observe; **nen oniaŋ i waŋŋi,** look at it properly or observe it carefully, 4 not getting better; **twoone pudi oniaŋ i komme,** the disease is still with him no sign of improvement.

niaŋ *v* to understand, perceive, conceive; **niaŋ gin ma gititi maber ma pudi peya idok iye,** do understand very well what you are told before answering;

nid *v* **nid tolle matek,** tie the rope very tightly.

nidde *vi* to become / becoming thin circumferentially, to become / becoming constricted; **pyerre tye ka nidde,** his waist is becoming thin; 2 tight, **twee tol onidde matek,** tie the rope very tightly.

niddo *vt* to narrow by tying round, to become constricted; **ogul niddo bad dano woko,** the armlet does narrow the arm, or the arm where the armlet is worn becomes small.

nik *adj* quite, very; **col li nik,** quite or very dark or pitch dark.

niki-niki *adv* to and from; **yen ma gitweyo ma gitiŋŋo i wic yeŋŋe ni niki niki,** the tied pieces of wood carried on the head shakes to and fro.

nim *adv.* to be in great number or quantity; **dano gucokke ni nim i tee kanica,** a large number of people assembled under the church.

nimoniya *n Eng* pneumonia; **lacooni tye ka twoyo nimoniya ma rac twatwal,** the man is suffering very much from pneumonia.

nino *vi* to sleep; **tye ka nino,** is sleeping; **nino tye ka makko waŋŋe,** he is feeling sleepy.

nino *n* day; **nino ducu,** every day; **nino me abic,** the fifth day; **bin i nino abic,** come in five days / **bin i nino me abic,** come on Friday.

niŋa *n.* small black long-haired monkey (spoken by the east Acholi people).

niŋ−niŋ? *adv* 1 how? **opotto niŋniŋ?** how did it fall? 2 *adj* What; **komme obeddo niŋniŋ?** what is the colour of its body?

niŋŋe *v* . unwillingness, taking time to do something; **gicwalli ni icitti piŋo pud i tye ka niŋŋe kany? cit oyotoyot,** you were sent to go there, why are you still wasting time here, go quickly; see, **dokke, dwalle, galle, ŋinynye etc**

niŋ *v* close one eye; **niŋ waŋŋi ka inen maber,** close one eye and then see well.

niŋŋe *adj* closed; **waŋi oniŋŋe,** one of your eyes is closed.

niŋŋo *vt* to close / closing; **niŋŋo waŋ, to** close / closing one eye. 3 **niŋŋo lok,** speaking almost in an inaudible voice.

ni ŋoo? *vt inj* what is it?

nirro *vt* to brood / brooding, indulging in thought; **nirro tee lok,** to brood on old questions or matter.

nobbe *vi* weakened, ruined; **pi cam mabecco mape omiyo, latin ma yaŋ koŋ owotto maber, onobbe woko,** for lack of good food the child who was at first walking very well, became weak and unable to walk

nobbo *vt* to weaken; **twoone onobbo komme woko,** the disease has weakened his body.

Nobwemba *n* November, the eleventh months of the year.

nok *adj* not enough, small quantity, few; **kello dek manok,** not bringing enough food; **tye ruc ma nok.,** there is a small quantity of rice; **tye cupa cak manok,** there is a few bottle of milk.

nono *adv* without cause, without reason, for nothing, to no purpose; **onekke nono,** he killed him for no reason, for nothing; **odaa nono laboŋo tyen lok mo,** he quarrelled for nothing without any reason.

noŋ *v* find; discover, get; 1 find; **noŋ kalam wek icoo kwede,** find a pen so that you may write with it; 2 get; **noŋ koŋ waraga me peny meeri ka doŋ ibin,** get your examination certificate and then come; 3 get married; **myero doŋ inoŋ ot,** you should get a house but here it may mean also get married; 4 discover; **myero koŋ inoŋ gin mo manyen ka doŋ ibin,** you should discover a new thing and then come.

noŋŋe *vi* can be found; **caa ne tikka twerro noŋŋe kany?,** can the watch really be found here?

noŋŋo *vt* to find / finding; to discover / discovering, to detect / detecting; to get / getting; **noŋŋo tic pe yot,** to find /finding a job or work is not easy; **noŋŋo yat manyen pe yot,** to discover / discovering a new drug is not easy; **noŋŋo ot,** to find / finding a house, here it means to get / getting married or finding a wife. **noŋŋo twoo,** to get / getting disease.

not *n* Eng. nought, zero, nothing.

not *v* kiss; **not dakoni,** kiss your wife; **not latinni,** kiss your child, *see* **dot.**

nota *n* depression, valley; **nota kulu,** valley; **tye nota i wii got,** there is a depression on top of the mountain.

notte *vi* 1 to be united. (spoken very much by Langi); **gunotte kacel me konynyo luwotgi,** they united themselves to help their friends. 2 *vn* kissing; **gitye ka notte,** they are kissing (each other).

notto *vt* to suck / sucking; **notto muyembe,** to suck / sucking the mangoes. 2 to kiss / kissing; **notto lem latin,** to kiss / kissing the child's cheek; **notto lem dakone,** to kiss / kissing his wife's cheek. c/f **dotto, cwiiyo.**

notto *vt* 1 to make / making impression, to dent / denting, to imprint / imprinting; **notto agulu mapud dyak ma gitye ka cweyone,** to dent / denting or to imprint / imprinting the wet pot which is being made with a pattern.

nucu *A n* half; **omiyo nucu mugati keken,** he gave half a loaf only.

numu *adj* raw, unripe; **paipai pud numu,** the paw-paw is still unripe; **ocammo boo ma numu,** he ate raw vegetables.

nud *v* stir; make; **nud nyuka ki latin,** make porridge or gruel for the child.

nudde *vi* be worn out, wearied; **komme onudde,** he is worn out; **ticce miyo kom dano nudde oyot oyot mada,** the work wears out the people very quickly; can be stirred, made into gruel; **moko man tika twerro nudde me nyuka?** can this flour be stirred or made into gruel?

nuddo *vt* 1 to stir / stirring continuously; **nuddo nyuka,** to stir / stirring the porridge or gruel continuously while boiling, 2 **nuddo poto,** tilling the field again when it was tilled before; 3 wearing; **tukko ŋwec nuddo kom dano ma komgi wac,** athletics wears out those who are lazy.

nukuta *n Lug* letter **nukuta a.b.c.** Letters a.b.c.; some call it **nyukuta,**

nunno *vt* to annoy / annoying, to oppress / oppressing by repeating the same words or argument on one; **gununnogi ki lok mape doŋ gitwerro lok,** they repeated the same words over and over to them in such a way that they were unable to talk.

nuŋ *v* entertain; **nuŋ lok ki dano,** entertain the people by talk

nuŋŋo *vt* to speak / speaking humorously, entertainingly; **nuŋŋo lok mada,** speaks very humorously.

nuŋŋo *vi* to lick / licking and to move / moving; **nuŋŋo dog,** to lick / licking the lips and to move / moving the mouth with satisfaction (for eating good tasting food).

nur *vt* heavy, **wae tye ka nur,** he is feeling sleepy.

nurro *vt* 1 to weigh down, press down; **gunia cukari pek, nurro latin,** a bag of sugar is too heavy for the child to carry.

nurru *vi* feel sleepy; **nino nurru waŋŋe,** he is feeling sleepy.

nwaŋ *adj* tenacious, tough and courageous; **cwinynye nwaŋ,** he is courageous and brave; **boŋone nwaŋ,** the cloth is of a good material and is quite tough.

nweŋ 1 *v* climb; **nweŋ yat we ipwon muyembe,** climb the mango tree and pick up the mango fruits; 2 vi be emaciated; **latinne on weŋ mada,** the child's emaciated.

nweŋ *vi* getting small; **cam ma nok miyo latin nweŋ,** little food makes the child very small;

nweŋŋe *vi* can be climbed with dexterity; **yatti twero nweŋŋe,** with dexterity, this tree can be climbed.

nweŋŋe *vi* flat and small; **latin ma ŋwinynye onweŋŋe,** child with flat buttocks.

nweŋŋo *vt* to climb / climbing a tree with dexterity; **ŋeyo nweŋŋo yat mada,** he knows how to climb the tree very well.

nwoo *v* do again; **goo dok inwoo,** beat and beat again; **nwoo lwokko boŋone doki aye,** rewash the clothes or wash the clothes again.

nwoone *vi* repeated; **boŋoni tika twerro nwoone me lwokkone dok aye?** can this clothes be washed again?

nwoyo *vt* 1 to repeat / repeating the action; **nwoyo reggo nyim,** to grind / grinding the simsim paste over again. 2 **nwoyo lee,** to spear / spearing an animal the second time.

ŋ ŋ

ŋaa? *Int prn* **ŋaa?** who? whom?, whose? whom; **pa ŋaa?** whose? **ŋaa ma obinno?** who has come?; **jami pa ŋaa?** whose things are these? **gicwallo ki ŋaa?,** to whom was it sent?

ŋaa *adj.* stubborn, obstinate; **latinne laŋaa mada,** the child is very stubborn.

ŋaa *v* put lying on the back with face upwards; **ŋaa latin i wii kitanda ka doŋ irukki,** put the child on his back and then dress; see **ŋac, ŋayo.**

ŋaane *vt* lying or sitting on an inclined chair; **ŋaane i wii kom,** sat comfortably on the inclined chair facing upwards; see **ŋayo.**

ŋab *v* hang; **ŋab boŋo i wii tol,** hang the clothes on the rope.

ŋabbe *vi* can be hung; **boŋone twerro ŋabbe,** the clothes can be hung up.

ŋabbe *adv* 1 worrying; **cwinye tye ka ŋabbe pi lok ma gititte,** he is worrying about what he was told.

ŋabbo *vt* to hang / hanging up on; **ŋabbo boŋo i wii tol,** to hang / hanging the clothes on the line (rope); **ŋabbo boŋ i wii yat,** to hang / hanging the beehive on the (fork of a) tree.

ŋaca *adv* on one's back, careless posture. 1 **obutto ataro ni ŋaca,** he lied carelessly free on his back. 2 **twon jubi obutto caa ni ŋaca,** the big buffalo is lying there stretched out on the ground. see **ŋaa, ŋayo.**

ŋacaka *adv* lying down anyhow; **opotto li ŋacaka,** he fell down flat with his arms and legs lying anyhow.

ŋad *v¹* trim; 1 **ŋad wii cell woko,** trim the edges of the fence.

ŋad *v²* stretch; **ŋad ŋutti ka wek inen,** stretch your neck up in order to see.

ŋada-ŋada *adv* long and slender; **rii wotto ni ŋada-ŋada,** the giraffe walks with the body moving up and down because of its long legs.

ŋadde *vi* to stretch / stretching onself; **ŋadde matek wek ipwon mayembe ira,** stretch up hard and pick for me the mangoes.

ŋaddo *vt* to trim / trimming; 1 **ŋaddo lwet pe tek,** to trim / trimming the nails is not difficult; 2 **ŋaddo ŋet cuka,** to trim / trimming the edge of the sheet; **ŋaddo wii cel,** to trim / trimming the edges of the fence.

ŋaddo *vt* 1 to stretch; **oŋaddo ŋutte matek ka oweko oneno,** he stretched his neck very much to enable him to see. 2 to contract the muscle, to pull up the muscle; **oŋaddo iye matek,** he pulled up his belly muscles tightly or he coniracted tightly the muscles of his abdomen

ŋadi *indf prn* so and so, certain person; **ŋadi ocitto kwene?** where has so and so gone? **ŋadi munyo,** so and so or such and such a person.

ŋak *v* turn away; **ŋak idok gaŋ,** turn and go home.

ŋaki ŋaki *prd* coarse, rough; **pi gweŋ ma gionynyo i yoo omiyo obeddo ŋaki ŋaki,** for the stones which have been poured on the road made it coarse or rough.

ŋakko *vt* 1 to do / doing something roughly or coarsely; **ŋakko ŋor,** to grind / grinding the cow peas roughly; 2 **ŋakko lok,** to talk in a rude / rough manner.

ŋakko *vi* to mislead; **lok ma ŋakko dano,** the words that mislead people; **pe wutit lok marac ma biŋakko litino,** do not preach bad words that will mislead the children.

ŋal *v* tease, make fun, ridicule; **ŋal lawotti ni ma tek wek oniaŋ,** tease or ridicule very much your friend to make him understand.

ŋalle *vi* contesting in making fun, or ridiculing, of one another.

ŋallo *vt* to tease / teasing, to make / making fun of 1 **ŋallo laremme,** to tease / teasing or to make / making fun of his friend; 2 ridiculing; **ŋallo lokke aŋalla,** ridiculing his words.

ŋallo *vt* to cork / corking the gun; **ŋallo luduku me acella,** to cork / corking the gun ready to fire.

ŋallo *vi* to sprain / spraining; **ŋallo ŋut tyenne,** to sprain / spraining his ankle.

ŋallo *vi* to despise / despising something badly done; **ŋallo dek mape giteddo maber,** to despise / despising the sauce which was not well cooked.

ŋallo *vi* to eat / eating **kwon** without the sauce; **tye ka ŋallo kwon,** he is eating **kwon** without the sauce.

ŋammo *vt* 1 to yawn / yawning; **en dok ŋammo twatwal,** he yawns too much; 2 to open /opening, **ŋammo dog,** to open / opening the mouth.

ŋammo *vn* to blossom / blossoming; **tur yat doŋ oŋammo,** the flowers of the trees have opened up, about to blossom.

ŋan *v* take a handful; **ŋan kwon i ciŋŋi,** take a handful of **kwon** in your hand

ŋanno *vt* to take up a handful of food; **oŋanno kwon poŋ ciŋŋe,** he took a large amount of **kwon** in his hand.

ŋaŋ *adv* very, exceedingly, great quantity; 1 **tek ni ŋaŋ,** it is exceedingly hard. 2 stuck fast; **omokko ni ŋaŋ,** it is stuck fast. 3 *adv* great quantity; **mucumar obeddo ni ŋaŋ,** the nails are in great quantity or in a mass everywhere.

ŋaŋ *adv* crack, split; **bao ne oŋaŋ woko,** the board is cracked or split

ŋaŋŋo *vn/vt* rude talking / talk **ŋaŋŋo**

lak ki dano per bec, talking rudely to the people is not good

ŋany *v* waddle off; **ŋany oyot oyot,** waddle quickly; see **ŋanynyo.**

ŋanya-ŋanya, *adv* walking not quite well, waddle; **wotto ni ŋanya ŋanya calo gin mo tye i kin emme,** he walks with difficulty, with the buttocks shaking as though there is something between her thighs.

ŋanynyo *vn* to waddle as one having sores between the legs, because of this the word is regarded as an abusive word; **Otto ŋanynyo aŋanynya,** Otto waddles when walking; **wotto ŋanynyo aŋanynya calo bur tye i ŋwinynye,** walks as if being prevented by sore in the perineum.

ŋara-ŋara *adv.* coarse, rough surface; **ŋee nyaŋ obeddo ŋara-ŋara,** the back of the crocodile is rough.

ŋaro *n* visible light colour stripes on the skin (*striae cutis distensae, striae gravidarum*).

ŋaro-ŋaro *adj* not fully ripe, not well cooked; **layatane obeddo ŋaro ŋaro,** the potatoes was not well cooked because it was still hard.

ŋat *vt* 1 to show / showing off (with clothe etc.) to boast / boasting. **wotto ŋat kwede ki kotine ni,** to walk / walking showing off with his coat.

ŋat *prn* one or single, first; **ŋat acel,** one person; **ŋat mukwoŋo,** the first person; **ŋat maber,** a good person or a good one; **ŋat mukene,** another one or another person.

ŋat ŋat *adv* swaggering; **wotto ni ŋat ŋat,** walks swaggering.

ŋati *prn* someone, somebody; **ŋati**

okwallo boŋone, someone has stolen his clothes.

ŋatte *vr* to show / showing off. see **nyatte; awobini dok laŋatte mada,** this boy always is showing off; **ŋatte laboŋo gin mo ma itye kwede pe konynyo,** showing off without having anything is useless.

ŋawo *adj* brittle, easily breakable; **yatte ŋawo mada,** the tree is very brittle, easily breakable, see **ŋayo.**

ŋayo *adj* brittle, breakable; **pur nyolle ŋayo,** the handle of the hammer is breakable or brittle, see **ŋawo.**

ŋayo *vt* surpass ones power or ability; **ticce oŋayo woko,** the work is too much for him or the work is above his ability.

ŋayo *vt* to place with face upwards / placing the child on his back; 1 **ŋayo latin i wii kitanda,** to place / placing a child on the bed (with face upwards); 2 **ŋayo latwoo i wii kitanda,** to place / placing the patient, with face upwards or supine.

ŋayo *vt* to sleep / sleeping sexually with; **ŋayo dako piny,** to sleep / sleeping with a woman sexually. see **ŋaa, ŋac**

ŋee *v* know, understand; **ŋee likke maber,** know or understand the case or matter very well.

ŋec *n* knowledge; **en tye ki ŋec mada me yubbo cawa,** he has much knowledge in repairing watches; **pe tye ki ŋec mo,** he knows nothing or he has no knowledge of anything, see **ŋee, ŋeyo**

ŋec *n* alligator; **ŋec obollo toŋe kany,** the alligator has laid it's eggs here; **ŋec**

marro makko gweni, the alligator is fond of catching chicken.

ŋec *n* 1. dregs, what is left over after straining or filtering ; **ŋec koŋo (tiŋ),** dregs of the beer left behind after it has been strained; **ŋec moo, kic etc,** what is left after oil, honey etc have been strained away.

ŋec pii *n* the dirt that is left behind after the water has been filtered or strained.

ŋec *n* back; **latin myero gibyel i ŋec,** the child should be carried on the back.

ŋedi *n.* pain which is felt with advanced pregnancy; **ŋedi cammo iye mot mot,** there is a slight pain in the abdomen (preceding labour).

ŋee *v* know, understand, **ŋee tee lokke maber,** understand or know the meaning of the words well; see **ŋec, ŋeyo.**

ŋee *prp* **1** after or back; **obinno ki i ŋee Atoo,** he came after Atoo had left; **2 cit i ŋee ot,** go behind the house; **3 it malo i ŋee kana,** climb up on the back of a donkey

ŋeene *vi* recognisable; **dano ma ŋeene,** a well known person; **gin giŋeene,** they know each other; **tim gin ma ŋeene,** do what is known.

ŋek-ŋek *adv* emaciated, badly wasted; **dyel pa aŋaa ma ojony ni ŋek ŋek-ki?** whose goat which is quite emaciated?

ŋello *vt* inclining, giving slant; **yamo oŋello dero woko,** the wind has tilted the granary.

ŋem *v* take a large quantity, **ŋem pul madwoŋ,** take a large amount of groundnuts.

ŋemmo *vt* to take / taking up too much against the convention; **ŋemmo cukari dok madwoŋ twatwal,** takes too much sugar. (in his hand)

ŋen *v* roll; **ŋen kwon i kado ka doŋ icam,** roll **kwon** in salt and then eat it.

ŋenne *vi* to roll; **litino gitye ka ŋenne i kweyo,** the children are rolling in the sand; **opego gitye ka ŋenne i daba,** the pigs are rolling in the mud, that is, they are taking their bath in the mud.

ŋenno *vt* rolling along; **latinni ŋenno boŋone i daba,** this child rolls his clothes in the mud; **ŋenno mugati i kic ka doŋ cammo,** rolls the bread in honey and then eats it.

ŋeŋ *vi* open; **ŋeŋ doggi wek awiny ci inenno,** open your mouh for me to hear and you will see, in other words, he does not want him to speak.

ŋeŋŋo *vt¹* contesting or arguing with great noise; **ŋeŋŋo dog,** to say or speak something.

ŋeŋŋo *vt²* surprising; **lok oŋeŋŋo ladit woko,** the speech took the gentleman by surprise or the gentleman was so surprised that he could not speak.

ŋeny *v* open, **ŋeny lakki,** (open your mouth and) show your teeth.

ŋenynyo *vt* to open / opening, to spil / splitting; **1 ŋenynyo lak,** to open / opening the mouth to show teeth; **2 ŋenynyo got,** to break / breaking the stone or to crack / cracking the stone; here **ŋinynyo got** is preferred by some people; **ceŋ oŋenynyo lakke,** the sun has shone a little.

ŋer *vn* to swell up; **cak pa min latin tye ka ŋer, i tuno;** the breast of the child's mother is distending with milk.

ŋerro *vt* 1 to irritate / Irritating; **ŋerro**

dwan dano, irritates the throat (inflammation taking place). 2 **kiniga ŋerro junne,** anger his throat. 3 **lokke ŋerro ic,** the matter is annoying; 4 distension; **cak tye ka ŋerro,** the milk is distending the breast.

ŋet *n* side, flank, near; **ŋet doggola,** near or side of the door; **ŋet poto, ŋet waŋ,** side of the field, tail of the eye; **ŋet meja,** near the table.

ŋet *n* 1 worn out; **ŋet kweri,** worn out hoe; 2 **ŋet** is annoyance and provocation; **ŋet iye,** annoy and provoke him.

ŋet-ŋet ata, *excl.* angry phase used for refusing someone's claim.

ŋetto *vt* to provoke, to irritate, annoying; **lokke ŋetto iye mada,** the matter annoys him very much; **pe parro ŋetto cwiny luwotgi,** does not care annoying their companions; **lokko lok me ŋetto ic wek gidaa iye,** saying provocative words so that quarrel may take place / so tht they may quarrel.

ŋeyo *vt* 1 to know / knowing; **ŋeyo kwan,** to know / knowing how to read; 2 understanding; **ŋeyo tee lokke tek,** to understand / understanding it's meaning is difficult; 3 aware of; **en ŋeyo gin ducu ma gitimo i pacone,** he is aware of what has been done in his home; see **ŋee, ŋec.**

ŋib *v* bite bit by bit , take small pieces at a time.

ŋibbo *vt.* to bite / biting in small amount, to cut / cutting or to take / taking off small amount; gnawing; **oyoo ŋibbo tyen dano,** the rats gnaw the feet of people.

ŋic *n* cold, cool, chill; **piny tin ŋic,** the weather is cold today; **wacammo**

riŋo ma ŋic, we ate a chilled beef.

ŋic *adv* experience, used to; **en doŋ tye ki ŋic me ŋico,** he has got the experience of the cold; see **ŋii, ŋiyo.**

ŋic *vi* inspecting, **tye ka ŋic me odi,** he is inspecting houses, see **ŋii, ŋiyo.**

ŋic *adj* not acative, weak; **danone ŋic pe twerro loc,** he is weak, he cannot rule.

ŋid *vt* cut into small pieces; **ŋid riŋo man ka wek icel,** cut this meat into small pieces and then fry.

ŋidde *vn* can be cut into pieces; **riŋone twero ŋidde maber,** the meat can be easily cut very well into pieces.

ŋide *n* pieces; **man doŋ ŋide keken aye odoŋ,** only pieces which are remaining.

ŋidi-ŋidi *n* crumbs, pieces; **ŋidi-ŋidi riŋo,** pieces of meat; **ŋidi-ŋidi mugati,** crumbs of bread; see **ŋido ŋido,** this is the one that is normally spoken

ŋidi-ŋidi *adv* limping, hobbling; **kommo ni ŋidi-ŋidi,** he hobbles about.

ŋiddo *vt* to cut into pieces; **ŋiddo riŋo,** to cut meat into pieces for stew. (cooking).

ŋido ŋido *n* crumbs, pieces; **ŋido ŋido mugati en aye doŋ odoŋ,** only crumbs or pieces of broken bread which is remaining.

ŋii *v* get used to, experience; **ŋii kommi ki koyo,** get used to cold; experience; **ŋii ki tiyo tic kama rac,** get the experience of workung in a dangerous place, see **ŋic, ŋiyo.**

ŋii *v* 1 inspect; **ŋii kace pulle gibecco,** inspect if the groundnuts are good; 2 find out; **ŋii gin aŋoo matye ka yello**

latinni, find out what is bothering the child; 3 examine; **ŋii wiye maber ka tye iye nyugi,** examine the head carefully if there are lice in the hair, see **ŋic, ŋiyo.**

ŋiine *n vi* inspection, inspecting; examining; **gucitto ka ŋiine,** they went to be examined; **ŋiine me odi tin tye i gaŋ lai pa lupolici,** housing inspection today, is in the police line.

ŋik-ŋik *adv,* heavily; **wotto ni ŋik-ŋik,** walks with heavy sound on the ground.

ŋil *v* roll; **ŋil kidi man cen,** roll the stone away.

ŋil *vn* used to, not wonder to, acquiesce, design to; many people use **diŋ** in it's place; **litino kwan doŋ guŋil ki daa pa ladit cukul,** the students are used to the quarrel of the headmaster and don't care about it; **kome doŋ oŋil woko ki koyo,** he is now used to or acclimatized to the cold.

ŋili *n* large tuber of a climbing plant used as a target for children to spear while it is being dragged away or to shoot with arrows.

ŋiliri *n* aluminum ear rings; **ŋilirine doŋ ocokko cilo keken,** her aluminium ear rings are full of dirt.

ŋille *vi* being short and stout; **dano ma oŋille,** a short stout person.

ŋille *vi* can be rolled; **kidi man twerro ŋille,** the stone can be rolled away.

ŋillo *vt* to roll along; **ŋillo kidi madit mapek,** to roll a big heavy stone.

ŋimmo *vt* to bite / biting lightly with the points of the teeth; see **ŋibbo.**

ŋin *v* clean; **ŋin wii kidi reggo nyim ki laŋin,** clean the grinding stones urface

for grinding simsim by rolling the simsim dreg on it.

ŋini-ŋini *n* very small black ants; **ŋini ŋini tiŋŋo ter mapek makato pekgi,** the small black ants carry loads which are heavier than their own weights.

ŋinne *vi* can be cleaned; **wii kidine twerro ŋinne maleŋ,** the top of the grinding stone can be cleaned very well.

ŋinne *vi* assembled; **dano guŋinne i ot piddo,** the people assembled in the court house; 3 collected together; **acut guŋinne i kom lee ma otoo,** the vultures collected in large number on a dead animal.

ŋinno *vt* 1. to roll / rolling up on something; **ŋinno wii kidi nyim,** to roll / rolling up the surface of the simsim grinding stone with the dregs of simsim as a means of cleaning it; **ŋinno lobo agulu,** to roll / rolling up clay for pottery; **ŋinno kwon maber,** shapping the **kwon** very well into balls; **kwadeŋe ŋinno cet muluŋŋe ka en aye doŋ lorro,** the beetle moulds the feaces or dung into a shape of a ball which it rolls about.

ŋiny *v* to rub / rubbing with hands to break off shells of seeds; **ŋiny geya,** rub sorghum in your hands in order to remove the seeds from the husks and chaff from it.

ŋiny *v* break into pieces; **ŋiny pado agulu magi ducu,** break into pieces all these broken earthen pots.

ŋinyi-ŋinyi *adv* in pieces into splinters; **ogoyo agulu ma i ot oŋinynyo gi woko ŋinyi-ŋinyi,** he beat all the pots in the house and broke them completely into pieces.

ŋinynye *vi* 1 can be broken to pieces. 2 struggling with; 3 **boo ma otwoo twerro ŋinynye maber,** dried cowpeas leaves can be broken into small pieces by rubbing it.

ŋinynye *vi* delay; **ŋadi miŋ ŋinynye ki twoo twatwal pe mitto citto ka nenno daktar,** so and so is foolish, always delays with illness, and does not want to see a doctor.

ŋinynyo *vt* to destroy / destroying completely into pieces; **ŋinynyo kikopo,** to destroy / destroying the cups into pieces,

ŋinynyo *vt* 1 to rub / rubbing the eyes with the hands; **ŋinynyo waŋ twatwal kello lit waŋ,** to rub / rubbing the eyes frequently with the hand causes eye illness; 2 **ŋinynyo boo madyak ki ma otwoo,** to rub / rubbing fresh cowpeas leaves (and folding them into small balls) and dried leaves to break them into small pieces.

ŋir *vn* insist obstinately, persist; **dako man laŋir lok twatwal,** this is a woman who insists obstinately.

ŋirro *vt* to be persistent, inflexible in one's demand; **dako ma ŋirro lok twatwal ka mitto gin mo,** the woman who persistently asks for something when she wants something, (drives one mad by her persistence in asking for something); see **ŋwirro.**

ŋit *vn* soft, pulpy; **gioddo pul i pany doŋ oŋit maber,** the groundnuts have been pounded in a mortar and is now soft or like a pulp.

ŋitto *vn* to dizzle / drizzling; **kot tye ka ŋitto,** the rain is drizzling; see **kot tye ka woo.**

ŋiyo *vt* 1 to inspect; **ocitto ka ŋiyo acikari kama gitye ka dorre iye,** he went to inspect the police where they are drilling. 2 to select; **ocitto ka ŋiyo leela me awilla,** he went to select a bicycle for buying.

ŋiyo *vi* getting used to something; **pe ber latin me ŋiyo ki odoo,** it is not good for the child to get used to beating; **latin doŋ oŋiyo woko ki odoo,** the child is now used to beating, he does not fear it any more; see **ŋii, ŋic.**

ŋob *v* alternate; **ŋob raŋi makwaar ki ma ocwak ocwak,** alternate the red and the yellow colours; **ŋob dyel ki romi,** interchange goats with the sheep.

ŋobbe *vi* to alternate / alternating, to interchange / interchanging; **raŋi ma pat pat mere twerro ŋobbe,** various colours can be mixed or interchanged

ŋobbo *vt* to interchange / interchanging, mixing, to alternate / alternating things of various qualities or types; **ŋobbo raŋi ma pat pat,** to alternate / alternating different colours, interchange different colours; see **rubbo.**

ŋoc *vn* leaving, overlooking; **igi ocwer mada pi ŋoc ma giŋoyogi kwede,** they were very annoyed for the way in which they were left behind; see **ŋoo, ŋoyo.**

ŋod *v* pull in (contract); **ŋod ii ka wek itwee palini maber,** pull in your abdomen (abdominal muscles) in order that you may tie your trousers.

ŋodde *vi* can be pulled in or contracted; **iye mere twerro ŋodde maber,** his abdomen can be easily contracted or pulled in.

ŋoddo *vt* to stretch / stretching;

ŋoddo ŋutte ka neno winyo i ŋee ot, stretching his neck to see the bird behind the house; **ŋoddo iye ka nyutoni cam pee i iye,** contracts his abdomen to show that his stomach is empty.

ŋoddo-ŋoddo *adv* varying in thickness; **tolle giwiyo ŋoddo-ŋoddo,** the rope has been twisted in varying thickness, some parts thick and others thin.

ŋok *vn* 1 vomit; **latin tye ka ŋok,** the child is vomiting.

ŋok *vi* 1 bringing forth; **anyogi tye ka ŋok,** the maize is bringing forth it's seeds; 2 blooming, flowering; **kal doŋ tye ka ŋok,** the millet is blooming or flowering; 3 **lee laworo oŋok mapol mada,** a lot of game came out yesterday.

ŋoki-ŋoki *prd* coarse, uneven, rough; **yoone rac mada obeddo ŋoki ŋoki,** the road is too rough, full of stones, **ŋaki ŋaki** is the word that is now in common use.

ŋokko *vt* vomiting; **latin ŋokko gin aŋoo?** what is the child vomiting? **yatte ŋokko dano,** the medicine makes people vomit or it causes vomiting.

ŋol *vn* 1 maim, cripple, deformity; **ŋadi doŋ tyenne oŋol woko,** so and so's leg is now maimed; 2 cripple; **ŋadi doŋ oŋol woko ki i badde,** so and so is crippled in the arm;

ŋol *v* cut; **ŋol tyenne woko,** cut his leg off; **ŋol boŋo me akwoya,** cut the cloth for tailoring.

ŋolle *vi* capable of being cut; **bao ni en twero ŋolle iye aryo,** this sheet of wood can be cut into two; 2 attack suddenly; **oŋolle ka lweny i komme i yoo,** he suddenly attacked him on the way.

ŋollo *vn* 1 crippling condition; **ŋollo gin marac mada, geŋŋi tiyo jami mapol,** being crippled is a very bad thing, it prevents you from doing any things. 2 cutting across; **ŋollo yoo ari,** cutting across the road.

ŋollo *vi* to welcome / welcoming; **gucitto ka ŋollo wii lapwonygi,** they went to welcome their teacher.

ŋollo *vt* to judge, convict; **ŋollo kop pa Onen tye tin,** the judgment of one's case is today **giŋollo kop oloye,** he was convicted, or he was found guilty.

ŋollo *vi* prevent; **kot oŋollo wiye woko ka binno kuno,** the rain prevented him from coming there.

ŋollo *vi* cutting; **paala man lake oluu, pe ŋollo gin mo,** this knife is blunt, it does not cut anything; see **odiŋ, oligo.**

ŋolo-ŋolo *prd* very big or very large; **waŋŋe obeddo ni ŋolo-ŋolo,** his eyes are very large and big.

ŋom *n* earth, land, soil, ground; 1 **giyikko i ŋom,** he was buried in the earth. 2 **man ŋom meera,** this is my land. 3 **ŋom ma kany cekko cam mada,** the soil here makes the food grow well, or the soil here produces much food. 4 to sit / sitting down; **bed piny i ŋom,** sit down on the ground.

ŋoo-ne *vt* remaining behind, withdrawing from something (fear, cowardice); **ŋat ma ŋoone doŋ paco noŋo lalworro,** the one who remains at home is a coward.

ŋon *n* well bread, good manner; **en ŋon,** he is well bred; **iye ŋon,** he has a clean heart.

ŋon *vi* to tell off, boo; **ŋat ma lacoor mitto ŋon,** an impositor or a daring person needs to be told off; **en lokko twatwal, a malo iŋon ka wek oliŋ,** he talks too much, get up and tell him off to silence him.

ŋonne *vi* to be booed for telling lies

ŋonno *vt* to tell off, boo; **wacitu ka ŋonno Orac pi goba ne,** let us go to boo Orac and tell him off for his lies; **tin giŋonno mada,** today he was told off and booed very much.

ŋonno *n* smartness, pleasing deportment, clean in every way; **dako ma laŋonno,** a woman who is well behaved, clean and of pleasing deportment and keeps all things in her house in order.

ŋoŋe *n* otter (animal)

ŋoŋ-ŋoŋ *inj* sneering expression that "I don't care".

ŋoŋŋo *vt* to peep, strain the eyes to see something; **oŋoŋŋo waŋŋe ki waŋ dirica ci onenno woko,** he peeped through the window and saw it.

ŋoo? *Intj* what?, **ki ŋoo,** with what? **iwaci ŋoo?** what do you say?

ŋoo *vi* 1 melting, becoming watery; **cak doŋ oŋoo woko,** the milk has become watery, that is, the milk has curdled; **nyuka oŋoo woko,** the gruel has become watery; 2 **pig waŋŋe oŋoo woko,** he was about to shed tears; dripping, running; **pig waŋŋe tye ka ŋoo,** tears are dripping or running from his eyes; 3 feeling sick, loss of appetite; **cam ŋoo woko ki i dogge ka tye ka cam,** he feels sick when eating.

ŋoo *v* leave; **ŋoo cam mogo odoŋ ki litino,** leave some food for the children.

ŋoo *vi* 1 fear, fright, give up; melt away; **pe iŋoo kommi, wan ducu warom kwedgi,** do not fear or be discouraged, we are the same as they are; 2 melt; **moo dyaŋ ka giketto kama lyet ci ŋoo woko,** if butter is put in a warm place, it melts away.

ŋor *n* cowpeas. varieties; **ŋor alegi,** one which creeps; **ŋor lwoo,** the big type; **ŋor kilaŋ,** black peas; **ŋor amuli.** gives many branches while creeping.

ŋoro-ŋoro *adv* full of nice big fruits; **ŋor onyak ŋoro-ŋoro,** the peas have produced forth big pods with big peas inside; **kedo kom dako onyak ŋoro-ŋoro,** the woman's body is full of large tattoo or scarifying marks.

ŋot *n* sexual intercourse, coitus, canal knowledge (legal).

ŋotte *vi* having sexual intercourse, **gitye ka ŋotte,** they are having sexual intercourse (this is the language of not well bred people).

ŋotto *vt* to have / having coitus, to have / having sexual intercourse; having canal knowledge; this word **ŋotto** is normally not used, it is thought to be indecent or shameful word, therefore, **butto ki dako,** sleeping with a woman is used instead and it is the language of the well-bred people.

ŋoyi-ŋoyi *prd* watery; **moo ne ŋoyi ŋoyi,** the oil is watery i.e. butter or shea nut oil has partially melted.

ŋoyo *vt* to make / leaving back, to abandon / abandoning; **oterro jo mukene ento oŋoyowa woko,** he took some other people but he left us behind.

ŋoyo *vt* to make / making it watery; 1.

pii maŋic ka gionyo i dek ci ŋoyo woko, if cold water is added to the sauce, it makes it watery.

ŋoyo *vt* enervate, impair; **lworro ŋoyo kom woko me tiyo gin mo,** fear paralyses or enervates the body to do something; see **ŋoo, ŋoc.**

ŋubu-ŋubu *adv* sound made by goats when munching or eating potatoes or dried cassava.

ŋudde *vt vn* movement of waist during sexual intercourse.

ŋudi-ŋudi *n* crumbs, bits, scraps, fragments; **layata mabecco doŋ giyerro woko odoŋ ŋudi-ŋudi ne keken,** the good potatoes have all been selected except the small ones only which are remaining.

ŋukko *vt* coming unexpectedly, surprising; **kot koni ŋukko woko ka pe imoyo kalli kombedi,** if you do not pu out your millet to dry now, the rain may come unexpectedly and prevents it; **giŋukko lukwoo ka kwoo,** the thieves were taken by surprise stealing; **dako ma ŋukko nywal,** the woman who gets pregnancy before weaning the preceding child.

ŋuk-ŋuk *adv* sound made by a foot of a big man when walking

ŋul *v* spit; **ŋul aona woko,** spit out the sputum.

ŋullo *vi* to spit / spitting; **ŋullo remo,** to spit / spitting blood; **ŋullo laa atata kit marac,** spitting saliva anywhere is a very bad habit.

ŋun *v* divide; **ŋun dul dano man gucit i poto, mukene gucit i kullo,** divide some of the people to go into the field and some to the river.

ŋun *v* cut; **tal man bor twatwal ŋun woko,** this pole is too tall cut it off; **yen man bor twatwal ŋun woko,** this log is too long, cut it off.

ŋuna *n* lie, deception, **laŋuna,** a liar, a deceiver, see **lagoba.**

ŋunne *vi* can be divided, can be cut; **talli twerro ŋunne,** this pole can be cut.

ŋunno *vt* to cut / cutting off; **dobo ŋunno ciŋ danno,** leprosy cuts off fingers.

ŋunno *vt* telling lies; **en marra ŋunno lok me goba mada,** he likes to tell lies very much. **oŋunno ki wan lok me goba kany laworo,** he told us a pack of lies yesterday.

ŋuny *n* disappear; **oyoo ŋuny woko i odde / otte,** the rat disappears into it's hole.

ŋunya-ŋunya *adv* the movement of large caterpillars (worm).

ŋunynyo *vt* to withdraw; **opuk ŋunynyo wiye woko i pokke,** the tortoise withdraws it's head into its shell.

ŋur *n* to wear; **pur i poto ma gweŋ tye iye miyo lak kweri ŋur oyot oyot,** cultivating in a field where there are rocks makes the hoe blades wear out very quickly.

ŋur *vn* making noise, muttering, grumbling; **labwor ŋur,** the lion roars.

ŋurre *vi* wearing out; **lak kweri doŋ oŋurre woko,** the blade of the hoe is worn out.

ŋurro *vt* to suspect / suspecting one, murmuring against one; **dano gitye ka ŋurrone ni Okwera en aye ma** okwallo, people are murmuring that Okwera was the one who stole.

ŋurro *vi* to stone, throw; **oŋurro Ogwal ki lakidi,** he threw a stone at Ogwal.

ŋuru-ŋuru *adv* 1 not properly cooked, some parts feel hard or not properly ripe. e.g. banana 2 **ŋuru ŋuru cogo,** cartilage.

ŋut *n* 1 neck, 2 **ŋut ciŋ**, wrist, 3 **ŋut tyen**, ankle, **ŋut odoo, kweri, toŋ**, neck of stick, hoe, spear.

ŋut *vn* repent, regret; **doŋ oŋut pe doki bitimmone aye,** he has repented, he will not do it again.

ŋuu *n* predator animals, wild beasts **(lion, leopard, hyena, tiger etc).**

ŋuu-bar *n* man turning into a predator and eating man, this used to be a belief in those days that there were some people who used to change into man eating animals.

ŋwak *adv* light biting; **gwok okaye ni ŋwak,** the dog snapped at him.

ŋwaka ŋwaka *prd* covered with variegated colours (especially black and white); **kom kwac obeddo ŋwaka-ŋwaka,** the leopard's skin is spotted black and white.

ŋwala-ŋwala *prd* the same as above.

ŋwarro *vt* copy, imitate, mimic.

ŋwec *n* smell; **ŋwec cakke rac,** the milk smells badly; **ŋwec ŋoo makur twatwal li?** what is it that is smelling pleasantly? see **ŋwee, ŋweyo.**

ŋwec *n* running, flight, race; **gucitto ka tukko ŋwec,** they went for a running game; **ŋwec me lweny doŋ oromogi woko,** they are tired of running from war danger.

ŋwec *vn* running fast; **ŋwec matek mada,** he ran off or took off at a very high speed or he showed a clean pair of heels.

ŋwed *v* pluck the vegetables; **ŋwed boo i kel,** pluck the cowpeas' leaves and bring.

ŋwedde *vi* can be plucked; **pot boo ma odoŋ pud ŋwedde,** the remaining leaves of cowpeas can still be plucked.

ŋweddo *vt* to pluck or gather vegetables; **gucitto ka ŋweddo boo,** they went to pluck cowpeas's leaves.

ŋwee *v* smell, **ŋwee dekke ka pud peya okwok,** smell the food if it has not yet gone bad.

ŋwee *n* chronic ulcer on the toe, this usually smells very badly, that is, where it derived its name **ŋwee.**

ŋwee *adj* smells badly, stinks; **riŋo otop ŋwee mada,** the meat is rotten and it stinks or smells badly; **doge ŋwee twatwal,** his mouth smells very badly; **ŋwee li tuny,** smells very badly; see **ŋwec, ŋweyo.**

ŋwek *v* decorate; **ŋwek kom agwata man maber,** decorate this calabash bowel by making small cuts on it.

ŋwek *v* 1 divide; **ŋwek riŋo iye aryo,** divide the meat into two portions; 2 cut; **ŋwek gi woko matino tino,** cut them into very small portions.

ŋwekke *vt* can be cut or be divided into parts; **riŋone pe twerro ŋwekke,** the meat cannot be divided or cut into very small portions.

ŋweke ŋweke *adv* various design or colour; **boŋone komme ŋweke - ŋweke maber mada,** the clothes is of good design, with various colours and pattern.

ŋwekko *vt* 1 to cut /cutting into small pieces. 2 to make / making designs.

ŋwel *v* open widely; **ŋwel waŋŋi** open your eyes widely.

ŋwello *vt* to stare with wide open eyes; **marro ŋwello waŋŋe ka lokko,** likes to open his eyes widely when speaking; (people who always open their eyes when speaking are regarded as cowards) see **deŋŋo, collo ki dello waŋ.**

ŋwello *vt* to swallow / swallowing in a hurry a big piece of food (**kwon**); **kec tin onekke twatwal oweko oŋwello kwon matek caa abicel,** he was so hungry today, that he had to eat the food in a hurry at twelve.

ŋwello cet *vt* passing a large stool, defaecating a large stool; **ŋati moni oŋwello twon cet kany,** somebody passed a large stool here.

ŋwen *n* termites (white ants) - usually make a hill known as ant hill, there are many varieties of them and comes out in swarms; **ŋwen aribu,** comes out at dawn; **ŋwen agoro comes around** 8 pm - 12 mid-night; **ŋwen matino, okuba** comes at 6-7 pm; **naka,** 2 pm; **amiŋ amiŋ** 6-7 pm; **oyala** 5- 6 pm. etc.

ŋweny 1 *v* pinch, **ŋweny butte,** pinch his side; 2 tweak, **ŋweny umme,** tweak his nose; 3 scratch; **ŋweny kama yil,** scratch where it is itching; 4 pinch ; **lamar ŋweny,** one who likes pinching; some people call it **ŋwiny,** this could be confused with anus (**ŋwiny**)

ŋweny *v* take a portion with one's fingers; **ŋweny kwon i cam,** take a portion of **kwon** with your fingers and eat it.

ŋwenynye *vi* pincing one another; **ŋwnynye meno gin pa litino pe pa ludito,** pinching is the thing only for children not for adults.

ŋwenynyo *vt* to pinch, tweaking, scratch, twitch, 1 to scratch; **tye ka ŋwenynyo komme,** is scratching his body.; 2 taking a large portion of; **ŋwenynyo kwon madit,** taking a large portion of **kwon;** 3 pinching; **ŋwenynyo but lawotte,** pinching the side of his friend; 4 tweaking; **ŋwenynyo um,** tweaking the nose; see **ŋwinynyo.**

ŋwereke *prd* very short; **boŋone obeddo ni ŋwereke,** his dress is very short.

ŋwer *v* cut into small pieces; **ŋwer boo man me atteda,** cut this cowpeas leaves into pieces for cooking.

ŋwerre *vi* can be cut into pieces; **otigoni twerro ŋwerre maber,** the lady fingers (okra) can be well cut into pieces.

ŋwerro *vi* 1 to cut / cutting into small pieces or slices, to thread / threading into small pieces; **ŋwerro pot dek,** to thread / threading the vegetables into small bits or pieces. 2 to score, or cut skin and furrow on the skin, to make deep impression on the skin with string; **ŋwerro tyen ki tol ma onoŋo gitweyo iye matek,** making a furrow or deep impression with a string which was tied tightly on the leg.

ŋwerre *vi* can be cut, can have deep impression (on skin etc).

ŋwet-ŋwet *adv* sound which a person makes on the ground when walking quickly. 2 pace taken when walking quickly.

ŋwette *vi* to try to do a thing which one is not able to do; **ŋwette me dwoyo motoka kun kono peya opwonyo dwoyone,** trying to drive the car when he has not yet been taught how to drive.

ŋweyo *vt* to smell / smelling; **gwok ŋweyo oyot oyot kama bura tye iye,** the dog smells quickly where the cat is; see **ŋwee, ŋwec.**

ŋwid *vt* talk excessively; **ŋwid lok botte,** talk excessively to him; **dakone laywid lok,** the woman talks too much.

ŋwiddo *vt* talking over incessantly, causing annoyance; **dakoni dok ŋwiddo lok twatwal ma kello kiniga,** this woman complains incessantly causing anger or annoyance; **ŋwiddo lok put put,** incessantly talking; see **ŋwirro lok,** of the two, the latter is better.

ŋwil *v* look partially through a gap; **ŋwil waŋŋi ki i dirica ka wek inen,** peep through the window so that you may see.

ŋwillo *vt* being slightly open, slightly visible; **waŋ kwac oŋwillo** (metaph) small hole in a cloth which makes the body seen.

ŋwillo-ŋwillo *adv* a longing look; **piŋo ineno waŋŋa ni ŋwilo ŋwilo, dek oaa botwu kuno,** why are you having a longing look at me, the food came from your home.

ŋwiny *v* pinch; **ŋwiny matek wek okok,** pinch so hard that he may cry.

ŋwiny *n* anus, commonly named as **ŋwiny cet.** anus through which feaces pass; well bred people talk of vagina as **ŋwiny** or **nyim.**

ŋwinynyo *n* pinching, tweaking; **ŋwinynyo litino pe ber,** pinching the children is not good; see **ŋweny, ŋwenynyo**

ŋwir *v* insist, persist; **ciŋwir lok bot wooru,** go and insist talking to your father.

ŋwirro *vt* to insist / insisting obstinately on otherwise settled questions; **lacooni dok ŋwirro lok twatwal i kom gin ma doŋ gityekko,** this man insist obstinately on matter which has already been settled; **ŋwirro lok put put,** persisting incessantly on talking; see **ŋwiddo lok, ŋiddo lok, ŋirro lok.**

NY ny

nyaa *n* daughter; **nyaa pa rwot,** daughter of a chief; **nyaara,** my daughter. **nyaari,** your daughter etc.but it is written as **nyara, nyari.**

nyaa *vn* spread, abound, be plentiful, increase; **two anyoo nyaa oyot oyot mada ka litino pe gigwerrogi,** measles spread very quickly if the children are not immunised; **oyoo nyaa mada i ot ka cam tye madwoŋ ma pe giummo wiggi,** the rats flourish in the house if there are plenty of food which are not covered; slang, sometimes a girl is called **nyaa dyaŋ,** here it may mean a daughter of the cattle but actually it means increase the cattle because women were married with cattle and therefore once you have a girl it means you have heads of cattle; **nyaa dyaŋ** also means udder of a cow; see **nyac, nyayo**

nyaani *n* not in use now, it comes from the word **"nyaa"** daughter, **nyaani** should mean this daughter; it is a word used by girls to draw attention to one another if one wants to speak to another, but now the girls also use **"jal"** which used to be used by boys only; **nyaani** is a good word which girls should use.

nyaar *n* pubic region, the name is used usually for female private part; **nyaar** means cut and the hair in the pubic regions is usually cut, hence **nyaar**; **nyaar anyira ma dito tye iye yer, ento i pa litino anyira yer pe iye,** there are hairs in the pubic region of the big girls but none in the pubic regions of the little girls; **nyaar yaŋ con giputto aputta ci onynyo, en onynyone ni aye giwacci gin maber mada,** long time ago the pubic hairs used to be plucked and small pimples ensued, these pimples were regarded as signs of beauty.

nyaar *n* udder; **nyaar dyaŋ**, udder of a cow.

nyaar *v* cut, slash; **nyaar nyim wukel gaŋ,** cut the simsim and bring home

nyaarre *vi* can be cut or trimmed; **wii cel man twerro nyarre maber mada,** the edge of this fence can be well trimmed; **nyimmi twerro nyaarre maber mada,** the simsim can be cut very well.

nyaarro *vt* to cut / cutting; **nyaarro wic ki magac,** cutting or trimming the hair with scissors; **nyaarro boo,** cutting the cowpeas's leaves into small pieces or slides for cooking; **nyaarro**

kwon, taking a large amount of **kwon; nyaarro lum ki nyarro nyim,** slashing / cutting the grass and cutting simsim

nyab *adj* lazy, some people call it **nyap** both mean the same thing; **dano ma nyab,** a lazy person.

nyabbe *vi* to become lazy; **nyabbe pa kom pe gin maber,** laziness is not a good thing, **latinni doŋ komme onyabbe woko,** this child has now become lazy.

nyabbo *n* laziness, **nyabbo rac,** laziness is bad. **lanyabbo,** a lazy fellow, idler.

nyac *n* yaws or syphilis.

nyac *vt* to increase / increasing, multiplication; **ŋaa ma ŋeyo nyac,** who knows how to increase or to multiply? this is not commonly spoken; see **nyaa, nyayo.**

Nyaga *n* a female name.

nyaga *n* 1 a poetical name for **(kwac)** leopard; *prov* **kadi ibed ber calo kwac nyaga wek wakke,** even if you are as beautiful as a leopard, do not boast; 2 sometimes civet cat is also called **nyaga** by some people.

nyak *vt* 1 bring forth fruits, produce fruits, bear fruits; **muyembe man nyak mada,** this mango tree produces much fruits. 2 **mon mitto keddo kom ma nyak maber,** the women want the tattoo marks or the beauty's scar marks which are prominent. 3 **keddo kom nyak maber ka pe odoko bur,** the tattoo marks or the beauty's scar marks developed well if it is not infected.

nyak nyak *adv* limpingly; **oturro emme woko oweko doŋ wotto ni nyak nyak,** he broke his thigh bone that is why he limps when walking.

nyakabuko *n Lug* a skirt used to be made from pieces of old clothes; the old dress which is torn is cut and made into skirt; this was the dress that women used to wear before dresses were easily available.

nyako *n* 1 a girl (*pl.* anyira).

nyakko *vt* to produce / producing fruits; **muyembe man dok nyakko nyigge madoŋo mada,** this mango tree produces big mango fruits.

nyal *n* rust; **nyal omakko lak toŋ woko,** the edge of the spear has become rusty.

nyala-nyala *adv* full of worms; **riŋo ne otop woko opoŋ ki kwidi ma beddo iye ni nyala-nyala,** the meat is rotten and full of weevils' and flies.' larvae which move about in it.

nyalu-nyalu *prd* 1 tasteless, unappetizing, insipid. 2 **cammo ni nyalu- nyalu,** eats as though he wants to throw the food.

nyamagata *n* a kind of big antelope among which female has pronged horns (found in Agoro county).

nyammo *vt* to chew / chewing; **nyammo tyaŋ,** to chew / chewing the sugar cane.

nyammo lok *vn* to discuss; **gitye pud ka nyammo lokke,** they are still discussing the case / matter; **gitye ka nyammo koŋo,** they are drinking (slang).

nyampara *n* headman; **nyampara me tic meewu tye kwene?** where is your headman for work?

nyamucuna *Lug n* chicken pox (Acholi calls it **gwok-iguda).**

nyaŋ *n* crocodile; **nyaŋ yabbo dogge malac nio ka doŋ opoŋ ki lwaŋi ci**

miyo munynyogi woko, a crocodile opens it's mouth wide and waits until it is full of flies and then swallows them all.

nyaŋa-nyaŋa *prd/adv* open and bleeding or weeping serous fluid; **waŋ burre cwer beddi nyaŋa-nyaŋa,** the wound is open and weeping serous fluid.

nyaŋo *n* the morning sunshine (7-8 am.), **nyaŋo lagwe,** at about 7 am.

nyany *adv* 1 large quantity or volume; **latin opyello cet ni nyany i dye ot,** the child has passed a large faeces on the floor of the house. 2. sit comfortably on a chair; **obeddo li nyany i wii kom caa,** he sat there comfortably on the chair; **obutto ni nyany,** he is lying there comfortably.

nyany *vi* become blunt; **lak kweri nyany woko ka i purro kwede i kor got,** the edge of the hoe will become blunt if you use it for cultivating a stony field.

nyany *v* blunt; **nyany lak paala ne woko,** blunt the edge of the knife.

nyany *vt* part; **nyany lum wek kora yoo obed malac,** part the grass away by trampling on them to clear the way.

nyanynya *Lug n* tomatoes; **nyanynya ber mada me acamma ma numo,** tomatoes are very nice to be eaten raw.

nyanya nyanya *adv* in great number; **obinno ni nyanya nyanya,** came in great numbers.

nyanynye *vi* 1 being flattened or blunted. 2 being large and broad; **pe ipur kama obeddo got got miyo lak kweri nyanynye woko,** do not cultivate in a stony area because it will make the edge of the hoe blunt.

nyanynyo *vt* to trample down, treade upon; **nyanynyo lum me yabbo korra yoo,** trampling down the grass in order to make a path.

nyanynyo *vt* 1 blunting, making the edge not sharp; **got nyanynyo lak kweri woko ka itoŋŋo kwede,** the stone will blunt the hoe if you cut it with it; 2 sitting comfortably; **nyanynyo ŋwiny wii kom,** sitting comfortably on the chair, (this is not a good word, but vulgar language); **tye onyanynyo ŋwinnye i ŋom caa,** there he is sitting down on the ground

nyap *adj* lazy; **komme nyap,** he is lazy. See **nyab.**

nyara-bok *n* part of the grass thatching which reaches the top of a round hut on which a proper top is fixed.

nyat, *v* 1 do several times; **nyat ki toŋ matek,** spear several times; 2 *n* boast and showing off.

nyatte *vn* boasting, swaggering with something, being proud; **nyatte meeri ni nyayo nyerro ki dano,** your boasting makes people laugh at you or look down upon you; **tye ka nyatte,** he is boasting; see **wakke, butte.**

nyatto *vt* 1 to do over and over; **gunyatto labwor ki toŋ matek mada,** they speared the lion over and over. 2 speaking over and over, or again and again; **nyatto** lok, speaking incessantly about something. 3 do over and over; **gwok onyatto cet kany mada,** the dog has passed many of it's droppings here; **laďit tye ka nyatto lok mada pi jami ne,** the old man is complaining very much for his things.

nyayo *vt* to increase / increasing, to multiply / multiplying, to cause / causing to abound; **nyayo lok pe ber,** spreading or making the matter worse is not good; **aryo ginyayo waŋ adek doko abicel,** two increased three times becomes six; this is spoken by the people from the Catholic schools, the one commonly used is **aryo tyen adek doko abicel,** two times three becomes six. **nyaa, nyac**

nye *inj* (to call attention) listen, hark; **nye bin kany,** hi! or you! come here.

nyeb *v* familiarize, used to, interested; **nyeb bura ni mot mot wek gimak,** familiarize the cat slowly so that it may be caught.

nyebbe *n* be familiarized, be interested, be used to; **nyebbe ki matto koŋo biterri i can,** getting used to drinking will one day, take you to trouble; **nyebbe ki lwii ki i cukul,** getting used to escaping from the school; **nyebbe ki lapwony,** becoming familiar with the teacher, or becoming used to the teacher; **nyebbe ka beddo ki joo ma piny ceŋ mo bibolli i pekko,** familiarising yourself with low people, will one day throw you into great trouble.

nyebbo *vt* to interest / interesting, to acquaint / acquainting, to familiarize / familiarizing; **nyebbo litino marac ki cammo riŋo keken,** familiarizing children badly in eating only meat.

nyed *v* talk arrogantly, sarcastic talk; balance something on the head; **cit ici nyed lok botgi kuno,** go and talk to them arrogantly; **nyed agulu pii i wii wek wanen ka itwerro,** carry the water pot and balance it on your head, if you can, for us to see.

nyedde *vi* sitting aloof there not caring; **gimitti kany ento in inyedde meeri**

teŋŋe kwica, you are wanted here but you are sitting aloof there without caring.

nyeddo *vt* to talk / talking sarcastically, be arrogant, angry and offending retorts; cit ka nyeddo lok ki jo ma gitamoni gidito twatwal, go and talk sarcastically to those who think that they are very important people; tye ka nyeddo lok tin mada, -is talking too much arrogantly or sarcastically today.

nyeddo *vt* to touch / touching with tips or points of, write; wotto ma nyeddo tyenne anyedda, walks with the tips of her toes.

2 to balance / balancing something on the head; pe noŋo nyeddo agulu i wiye gin matek, finds no difficulty in balancing or carrying the pot on the head without holding it.

nyek *n* 1 jealous, envy; nyek pe ber, jealous is not good. 2 co-wife; nyek maa, my step mother or the co-wife of my father. .

nyeke-nyeke *adv.* continuously and slowly; anyeri cammo kal ni nyeke nyeke, the edible rats gnaw or eat the growing millet slowly and continuously.

nyekke *prn* her co-wife.

nyekko *n* jealousy, envy; nyekko pe gin maber, jealousy is not a good thing; nyekko omakke, he is full of jealousy; nyekko yelle, nyo nyekko nekke, he is jealous or full of jealousy or he is envious or full of envies.

nyel *v* cut round; nyel twok meja ne woko, cut or trim the sharp end of the table.

nyelle *vn* can be cut round or trimmed, dog boŋo man twerro nyelle maber,

the edge of this cloth can be well trimmed.

nyello *vt* revolving , turning over and over; nyello cam, eating like a sick person in turning the food over and over in the mouth, in Central Acholi prefer to call it nyallo.

nyello *vt* trimming the brim or side of a thing neat and tidy; nyello dog bao wek orom doggola, trimming the edge of the board so that it can fit the door; litino tye ka nyello tee gaŋ wek mac pe owaŋ odi, children are cutting round the boundary of the home so that the houes may be prevented from being burnt.

nyelo *n* python; nyelo goyo lee ci riine i komme matek nio waŋ ma otoo ka doŋ cakko munynyo ne, the python strikes down an animal and then winds tightly round it until it is dead and then swallows it.

nyem *adv* assembled and gathered in large number; dano opoŋ i bar odilo ni nyem, people have assembled in large number in the football field; *vt* moro onyem i doggola mape wacce, the soldier ants have amassed themselves so much at the door.

nyeme-nyeme *prd* very soft, watery, not well cooked; kwonne obeddo nyeme nyeme, the kwon is not well cooked, still too soft, cannot be shaped for scooping sauce.

nyeme nyeme *adj* dyaŋine bedo ni nyeme nyeme, his cattle are too many.

nyem-nyem *adv* slowly, unsteadily; ladit doŋ ocitto ki nyem nyem i wii kot, the old man walked away slowly during the rain; latin pudi wotto nyem nyem, the baby still walks unsteadily and slowly.

nyen *adj* new; **buk manyen,** a new book; *adv.* recently, newly; **gikello pud nyen,** been newly or recently brought.

nyenye *n* cockroach; **nyenye nyaa mada i ot kace cam oo i dye ot, mape giyweyo, dok wii cam bene pe giummo,** the cockroaches flourish easily in a house where lots of pieces of food drop on the floor and are not swept and where food are not covered.

nyenynye *vi* smouldering, increasing; **mac wii odur pud tye ka nyenynye anyenynya,** the fire in the rubbish heap is still smouldering on slowly; see **nyanynye anyanynya.**

nyee *prn* certain individual, somebody; **nyee moni,** a certain individual; **nyee mo,** somebody; **nyee cuŋ koŋ,** you stop for a moment

nyeer *v* laugh; **nyeer koŋ awiny,** laugh so that I may hear.

nyeere *vn prn* 1 laughing at; **gitye ka nyeerre ken gi,** they are laughing at themselves; 2 he; **nyeerre tye kwene?** where is he? **nyeeri,** you; **nyeeri icitto kwene?** where are you going?

nyeerro *vt[1]* laughing at; **nyeerro dano pe ber,** laughing at people is not good; 2 *n* laughter; **laworo lagoga omiyo nyerro mada ki dano,** yesterday the clown or comedian caused a lot of laughter to the people.

Nyero *n* a male name (lit. means laughter).

nyet *v[2]* spit; **nyet laa,** spit the spittle. 2 milk; **nyet lak** milk.

nyette *vi* leaping, jumping; bouncing; **ladeb nyette anyetta ka wotto,** the flea moves by jumping about; **onyette opye i loka gudu tuŋ caa,** he leaped over the other side of the road; **odilo**

ka gibollo piny ci nyette dok malo, when the ball is thrown down, it bounces upwards.

nyetto *vt* to milk / milking; **nyetto dyaŋ,** to milk / milking the cow; **nyetto laa,** to spit / spitting the spittle.

nyib *v* cut; **nyib yer wiye mabocco woko,** trim off his long hair, c/f **ŋib.**

nyibbo *vt* to cut / cutting; **nyibbo ŋet boŋo ma pe tye atir,** to cut off the edge of the cloth which is not straight.

nyig *n* seeds, grains, fruits; 1 **nyig kal,** millet grains; **nyig pul,** groundnuts; 2 **nyig tyen nyo nyig ciŋ,** toes or fingers; 3 **nyig man,** testicles; 4 **nyig atero,** arrows; 5 **nyig lak,** teeth; 6 **nyig waŋ,** eyeball; 7 **nyig luduko,** bullets or cartridges; 8 **nyig kidi,** small stone for grinding; 8 **nyig kic,** bees; 9 **nyig bul,** small drums or the little drums.

nyig *v* write finely small; **nyig waraga maber,** write a letter in a fine handwriting.

nyigi-nyigi *adv* closely; t. **gipito yatte nyigi-nyigi dok twatwal,** the trees were planted too closely together.

nyiggo *vt* closely together; doing something very finely or nicely; **nyiggo waraga maber mada,** writes very fine and neat letter; **nyiggo coc,** writes very fine small letters.

nyik *v* move slightly in some direction; **nyik kuca or kwica,** move there; **nyik cok kany,** move or draw near here; it can also be said that **nyikke kany nyo nyikke teŋŋe,** draw near or withdraw or move slightly away; see **dirre.**

nyiki-nyiki *adv* minutely, very small; **coyo matino nyiki-nyiki,** writes in very small letters.

nyikke *vn* move, draw; **nyikke teŋŋe,** move away, **nyikke cok kany,** draw near here.

nyikko *n* drawing near; **citto ka nyikko i kanica,** going for holy communion in the church.

nyim *n* simsim; kind of simsim: **nyim lajimo** (small stalk sown in September), **nyim ladoŋo** (big stalk sown in July-august), **nyim reŋe nyo latyen ayweri** (red simsim sown in August).

nyim *n* face, front side, private part (decent term instead of **tuun**); **tuur nyim,** front part of the face; **bur tye i nyim latin,** there is an ulcer over the child's private part; **giketto cam i nyim Owot,** food has been placed before **Owot**; **en okwoŋo citto anyim,** he went in advance or before.

nyimi-nyimi *adj* beset all over with marks, or dots; **boŋone komme obeddo nyimi nyimi,** the cloth is full of colour dots.

nyiŋ *n* name; 1 **nyiŋ doggola,** surname (in the past when a new child is being named, the one naming the child first knocks at the door and asks whether the child in the house has been named and then gives a name to the babe; that is why it is called **nyiŋ doggola.** 2 **nyiŋ mwoc or nyiŋ twon,** male pet name or warrior name. 3 **nyiŋ twat** or **nyiŋ deyo,** female pet name, or **nyiŋ deyo, nyiŋ me kwan,** honour name or Christian name; **nyiŋ tekko me nekko merok nyo lee mager,** heroes name, usually it has "**moi**" added to what one has done, e.g. **Bwormoi** one who has killed a lion, **Bwaŋamoi** or simply **Abwaŋ,** one who has killed an enemy; **Mayomoi** or simply **Amaya,** one who

has taken something by force from an enemy.

nyiri-nyiri *adj* same as **nyimi nyimi,** minutely and finely spotted or finely rough.

nyirro *vn* coming in dots, beads; **kwok tye ka nyirro i nyimme,** beads of sweat are coming out over his face. **kwok onyirro i nyimme,** he has beads of sweats forming on his face.

nyo *conj* 1 or **Okot nyo Otto, Okot** or **Otto**. 2 perhaps, **gwok nyo bibino diki,** perhaps he might come tomorrow.

nyoc *vn* bending, curving; **tyen litino pe tur woko nikup nyo nitap ento nyoc anyocca,** the children's legs do not break completely but only bend, that is a *green-stick fracture.*

nyocco *vt* to bend / bending, to curve / curving; **yat potto ci ogoyo onyocco cogo tyenne,** a tree fell and struck his leg and causing green stick fracture of the bone of his leg / bended his leg bone.

nyodo pei iye, she is barren; **nyodo ber,** having a child is good; **ot nyodo,** womb; **lanyodo pa Ocan,** parent of Ocan.

nyok *n* male; he goat or sheep; **nyok dyel,** he goat; **nyok romo,** ram.

nyok *adv* strong; **lacoone nyok mada,** the man is very strong, or courageous usually this is spoken in relation to sex.

nyol *n* hammer; **kel nyol me gurro mucumar eno,** bring the hammer for nailing.

nyom *v* marry; **nyom dako wek giworri,** marry so that you may be respected.

nyom *n* marriage; **nyom pa litinoni bibeddo diki**, the marriage of the children will be tomorrow.

nyomme *vn* marriage, marry; **waecitto ka nyomme pa Okelogi,** we are going for the marriage or weddng of Okello; **nyomme mere gin me deyo,** marriage or wedding is an honourable thing.

nyommo *vt* to marry / marrying, to take / taking a wife; **awabe nyommo anyira,** the boys marry girls, **oenyommo nyaa pa Otto,** he is marrying Otto's daughter; **pud peya onyommo,** he has not yet married or he is not yet married.

nyon *v* step on, trample with feet; **nyon tyenne ,** step on his foot.

nyonne *vi* 1 can be stepped on with feet. 2 kicking one another / fighting one another; **tin gitye ka nyonne mada;** they are kicking /fighting one another badly today.

nyonno *vt* to trample / trampling on with feet; **nyonno kal i dero,** pressing down the unthreshed millet in the grannary by trampling on it with feet.

nyoŋ *v¹* squat; **nyoŋ piny ka wek inen,** squat down in order to see; **nyoŋ piny ka wek i kwany,** squat in order to pick it.

nyoŋ *v²* rumple or crumple; **nyoŋ laa,** rumple or crumble the leather.

nyoŋ *adv* unfairly, for nothing; **kadi bed iyetta, ento acammo cam meeri nyoŋ,** even though you abused me, but I have eaten your food for nothing.

nyoŋ kom *vn* weakness, inability to move, *paralysis*; lifeless, weakness.

nyoŋŋe *v* weaken, enervate, inability to move; **komme nyoŋŋe woko oyot**

oyot ka otiyo tic mo manok, his body weakens easily after a short work.

nyoŋŋe *vi* can be rumpled and tanned; **laa ne twerro nyoŋŋe maber mada,** the leather can be rumpled, crumpled and tanned very well.

nyoŋŋo *vn* 1 squatting, crouching **labwor, kwac, ka gwok gin ginyoŋŋo anyoŋŋa,** the lion, leopard and dog do sit by squatting or crouching.

nyoŋŋo *n* residence; **ka nyoŋŋo pa Okot eno,** here is Okot's residence. **Okotgi doŋ nyoŋŋo kwene?** where is Okot's residence, or where has he settled?

nyoŋŋo *vt* to rumple / rumpling and to crumple / crumpling leather; **nyoŋŋo laa,** to crumple / crumpling, and to crumple / crumpling until the leather becomes soft.

nyony *n* sinking down slowly.

nyonynye *vi* sinking down slowly; **ocuŋ twatwal wii ceŋ omiyo ocakko onyonynye ci opotto piny,** he stood too long in the sun that made him sink down slowly and collapsed on the ground.

nyonyo *n* iron.

nyonyo *n* skin disease, ring worm. (*tinea*) due to *fungus* infections.

nyoo *v* sell; **nyoo jami meri,** sell your things (archaic)

nyor *n* chain; **nyor cawa,** watch's chain.

nyot *v* crush, mash, quash; **nyot layata ka imii ki latin,** mash the potatoes and then give it to the child.

nyot *n* tiredness, weakness, **nyot pa kom,** tiredness and weakness of body.

nyotte *vi* can be crashed, squashed, mashed; 1 **labolo ka giteddo ocek twetwal ci nyotte woko,** if plantation is over cooked it is squashed. the plantain has been over cooked and so it is squashed. 2 **tic me tiŋŋo ter ma pek miyo kom nyotte woko,** the work of carrying heavy loads weakens the body.

nyotto *vt[1]* to crush / crushing, to smash / smashing, to beat / beating into pulp, squashing, mashing; 1 **nyotto layata me nyubbo ki cak,** to mash / mashing the potatoes for mixing with milk 2 **ginnyotto wii twol woko ki odoo,** they beat the snakes head to a pulp with a stick. 3. **tic me tiŋŋo ter nyotto kom dano mada,** carrying heavy loads weakens the body very much.

nyoyo *vt[1]* to sell / selling; **citto ka nyoyo jami,** to go / going to sell things. (archaic) spoken mainly by Luo of Kenya.

nyoyo *vt[2]* to give / giving up; or get discouraged **tye ka nyoyo komme woko pien pe mitto medde ki kwan,** is giving up because he does not want to continue with study; 2 discouraged; **lok ma owinynyo omiyo onyoyo komme woko pe doŋ bicitto ka pyem me doŋŋe,** the news which he heard discouraged him, therefore he will not be going for the boxing contest.

nyub *v* mix; **nyub cak ki kwon,** mix milk with **kwon.**

nyubbe *vi* 1 can be mixed; **kic twerro nyubbe ki ŋwen,** honey can be mixed with ground white ants; 2 get or be soiled, dirty with; **tyenne onyubbe ki remo, daba nyo cet gweno,** his leg was stained with blood, or soiled with mud or chicken's droppings; **jamine onyubbe woko,** the things are mixed up or his things are mixed up.

nyubbo *vt* to mix / mixing different materials together; **nyubbo cak ki layata,** mixes mashed potatoes with milk; **nyubbo lok,** mix or evidence; **nyubbo komme ki latuk,** to soil / soiling himself with soot (from the kitchen); **onyubbo warre ki daba,** soiled his shoes with mud.

nyubo-nyubo *adv* mixing or massing together; **oluk pa ogwal beddi nyubo nyubo i pii,** there are masses of frog's tadpoles which are swimming about in the water.

nyugi *n* louse *pl.* lice; **boŋone opoŋ ki nyugi keken,** his clothe is full of lice.

nyuka *n* gruel, porridge; **litino myero gumat nyuka kal wek gubed mateggo,** children must drink a lot of millet porridge so as to be very strong.

nyul *adv* to come / coming out unexpectedly; **oyoo okatto ni nyul ki i ococce ci oriŋo woko,** the rat came out unexpectedly from its hole and ran away.

nyulle *vi* projecting, coming out, protruding; **cin dyel ma gicubbo ni tye ka nyulle woko ,** the bowel / intestine of the goat that has been speared is coming out

nyuny *v* build; **nyuny latin otti mo kany,** build your small hut here. see **cuny.**

nyunynyo *vt* to build / building a small thing; **nyunynyo odi,** to build / building a small huts; **nyunynyo cet,** to pass / passing small stool; **latin man kitte rac nyunynyo cet i kabedo**

ma pat pat, this child has bad habit of passings small faeces every where.

nyur *vi* germinate; bel nyar, the corn germinates bel doŋ onyur woko, the corn has germinated.

nyurro *vn* springing or shooting up, germinating; muraŋa doŋ tye ka nyurro, the shooting up of the beans; nyurro pa mwonaŋane yommo cwinnya, the shooting up of the beans pleases me. see obiiro.

nyut *v* show, point, indicate; nyut ciŋŋi, show your hand; nyut yoo ki dano caa, show the way to the people there.

nyutte *vi¹* can be shown, calle twerro nyutte, the picture can be shown; show; nyutte yoo, show him the way.

nyutto *vt²* to show / showing, to point / pointing at, to indicate / indicating, to introduce / introducing; nyutto cal ki dano, to show / showing picture to the people.

nywa-nywa *prd* fluctuating of shining light, e.g. switching on and off. macce lyel ni nywa-nywa, the light flickers.

nywak *v* accompany, going together; nywak ki latinni kacel kace iecitto Kampala, go together with this child if you are going to Kampala or go with your child if you are going to Kampala.

nywakko *vt* to accompany, to go together, to do something jointly with; 1 nywakko yoo ki ŋati mo; to accompany or to go with somebody; 2 wanywakko yoo ki wonne; we went together with his father. 3 rwot nywakko yoo ki askamme, the chief was accompanied by his policeman.

nywakko yoo ki ŋati nno, to accampany or to go together with somebody.

nywal *n* bearing, giving birth, delivery; prov. dako nywal ki nyekke, a co-wife is assisted by a co-wife when she is delivering; dakone nywal maber nino ducu, she always has normal deliveries.

nywalle *n* delivery, giving birth; dakone nywalle rac mada, the woman always gets a lot of problem during her delivery or giving birth.

nywallo *n* giving birth, bearing, delivering; nywallo jok, bearing twins or any deformed baby; nywallo latin, giving birth to a child or delivering a child or bearing a child.

nywan *v¹* confuse, confound; nywan lokgi woko, confuse their case or evidence; *n²* confusion nywan me lok man ocakke ning ning? how did the confusion in this case start?

nywanne *vi* be entangled, confused, mixed up; tye ka nywanne ki tam moni i cwinynye, is being confused with some ideas in his mind; gubeddo ka nywanne ki lokke laboŋo noŋŋo teere, they got entangled with the case without finding out the solution; lokke nywanne i kingi gin aryo, the matter is mixed up between two of them.

nywanno *vi* 1 to confuse / confusing, to confound / confounding, mix up; nywanno lok woko ki i kot, to mix / mixing up evidence in court; gunywanno Otto ki lok ma pol omiyo pe doŋ otitto lok maber i kot, they confused Otto with many words that made him unable to give good evidence in court. 2 mixes up things; gu nywanno boŋŋine woko atata, they mixed up his clothes anyhow.

nywaŋ *v* knead; nywaŋ moko me mugati, knead the flour for bread.

nywaŋŋe *vi* can be kneaded, **moko mungati ne twerro nywaŋŋe,** the flour for the bread can be kneaded.

nywaŋŋo *vt* to knead / kneading, to mould / moulding; **nywaŋŋo mugati, lobo etc,** to knead / kneading dough for bread, clay for pottery etc.

nywar *v* abuse, scorn; **nywar Jon wek koni i nen gin ma aa iye,** abuse or scorn Jon and see what will come out of it.

nywarro *vt* to abuse / abusing, to scorn / scorning, To deride / deriding, to mock / mocking; **nywarro dano pe ber,** to abuse / abusing or to scorn / scorning people is not good; **man lok me nywarro dano ,** this is a matter for mocking or abusing the people.

nywe nywe *prd* 1 moving in and out; **dogge beddo ni nywe nywe,** his mouth moves in and out as though he wants to smile; 2 flickering; **mac tarane doŋ beddi nywe nywe, t**he light from the lamp is flickering as though it is about to go off or vanish.

nywi *adv* slightly visible, very small; **macce owil i waŋŋa gicel keken, ni nywi;** the light flickered only once in my eyes.

O o

o - *prefix* to any word, the word becomes 3rd *pronoun* and past *tense*. e.g. **teddo,** cooking, once **o** is placed before it, it becomes 3rd pronoun and past tense, **oteddo,** he cooked; **ocitto,** he went; **ocammo,** he ate.

o *vn* arrival, reaching; **otyekko o gaŋ kuno,** he has already arrived at home there; **o ne gaŋ kuno yommo**

cwinynya,** his arrival at home please me.

oo *v* pour out; **oo pii woko,** pour the water out; see **oc, oyo.**

o o *vi* 1 poured out; **kal o o piny,** the millet poured down. 2 cleared; **odyer doŋ o o woko ki i komme,** the rashes of small pox on the body has now cleared, he is now cured of small pox. 3 aborted; **iye o o woko,** she has aborted or miscarried; 4 shed; **pot yat o o piny madwoŋ mada,** too much leaves have been shed; 5 fallen; **lak latin doŋ o o woko,** the child's teeth have fallen out; 6 wasted; **kom Okello o o mada,** Okello is much wasted.

oa *vt* has arisen, left; **doŋ oa woko ki kany,** he has left here.

ob *v* make fire; **ob mac ki ludito wek guoo,** make fire for the elders to warm themdelves with; **ob mac kany,** make fire here.

mac kany,** make fire here.

obaa *n* hamster, a kind of a large rat; it is known for it's power of stealing things from the house, such as knives and other things. **obaa kwalo paala,** hamsters steal knives.

obabbe *vi* he is confused; **dano ma doŋ obabbe woko pe ŋeyo gin mo obeddo macalo latin,** a person who is completly confused and does not know anything, he is just like a child; see **obaŋŋe, babbe.**

obaca *A n* corporal.(archaic), it is now called **kopolo.**

Obala *n* male name. (*lit.* stunted person.)

obala *n* a short person like somebody suffering from rickets; **obala macon dag doŋo,** an old dwarf who is unable to grow.

obalo *n* the two back neck tendons. **obalo ŋute okwot,** the neck tendons are swollens.

obaŋŋe *vi* confused, unstable in mind; **man dano ma obaŋŋe mape myero imii ni otimmi gin mo;** this is a person of unstable mind whom you should not give anything to do for you; see **obabbe; see baŋŋe.**

obar *vi* cracked; **bao ne obar woko,** the board is cracked or split; see **okak, otyer.**

obato *n* yams; see also, **mwodo, opelo ka aboce.**

obaya *n* 1 large papyrus mat for lying on.

obayo *vi* he threw away; **obayo kikopo woko,** he threw away the cup or he threw out the cup; see **bayo.**

obee *n* a kind of fish found in river Nile which sometimes jumps up out of the water.

obee *n* a bird which is similar to *whidah* bird with long tail.

obeer *n* 1. mosquito.

obeer *n* a tree which it's bark is thrown into the water to make fish stupefy; see **lurogo, larwece, obucu.**

obeno *n* leather made for carrying the baby at the back.

obibi *n* an imaginary giant, a man eating monster, some with one eye and others with eyes ranging from one to ten; the skin is hairy and with long nails; in the mouth there are two long canines; the word is used very much in fables.

obice *n* mouse; **oyo obice,** shrew mouse, has pointed nose and has very bad strong smell. It is believed that, if it crosses a path, it dies at once.

obiir *vi* beginning to germinate; **kal me tobi doŋ obiir woko,** the millet for liven is germinating.

obiku *n* grass tube - is used as tube for sucking or drinking beer.

obiŋa *n* chisel for iron; saw for cutting iron.

obiri *n* swelling due to injury to the body; **gigoyo ma komme ducu obiri woko,** he was beaten so much that all the body is swollen; *bruises and contusions. see* **biri.**

Obita *n* male name. (*lit.* he enticed me).

obiya *n* sword-like grass, commonly found and used very much for thatching.

Obiya *n* male name, (*lit.* means grass).

obbo *vt* to make a fire; **cit ka obbo mac,** go to make a fire.

oboke *n* leaf. *pl.* leaves, **pot oboke,** leaf; **kel pot oboke ium ki wii cak wek lwaŋi pe gupot iye,** bring the leaves for covering the milk in order to prevent flies from falling into it.

obokko *vt* 1 he has beaten thoroughly and flattened; **obokko pok yat odokko boŋo,** he has beaten thoroughly the bark of a tree to become a cloth. 2 half cooking; **obokko ŋwen laworo mada;** she half cooked a lot of the white ants (termites) yesterday. see **Obokko**

oboko *n* a crushed and dried shell of cucumber **"oboko okwer".** Okwer is round, the seeds usually removed and the skin allowed to dry, it is this skin which is cooked and eaten; the skin is called **"oboko"** the seed is **"okwer".**

obollo *vi* he threw; 2 **obollo woko,** he threw away or he threw out.

obolo 1 *n* cow with white face.

oboŋ *n* hoof; **oboŋ tyen dyaŋ**, the hoof of a cattle.

oboo *n* lung

oboro *n* 1 covering, envelop; **oboro toŋ gweno nyo pok toŋ gweno,** egg shell. 2 **oboro twol, nyo roc twol,** the shed skin of snakes; 3 **oboro nyo obworo pyen** *n* spider; **obworo pyen** is the one which is preferred.

oborro *adv* cooked until very soft; **giteddo layata ma doŋ oborro ni kwak,** the potatoes was cooked until it was very soft and splitting itself.

oboropyen / obworopyen *n* cob-web made by spider

Obot *n* male name.

obot *n* hollow reed stalks, used for sucking.

obot *n* 1 foot print, foot mark; **obot tyen lyec okatto kany,** the elephant's foot prints have passed here.

obot *n* left over, remain; **obot dek,** the sauce left over from yesterday; **gitye ka cammo obot dek,** they are eating the food left over yesterday.

obucu *n* 1 creeper with big tuberous roots which is crushed and thrown into water to stupefy fish, see **obeer, lurogo, larwece.**

obuccu *vt* he plucked; **obuccu gweno,** he plucked a chicken.

obuga *n* small plants, used as vegetables.

obuko *n* a kind of a grass.

obuko *n* cooked cow peas, **obuko ŋor** usually first cooked in water and then the water is drained away and put

aside to dry and then later used for say journey.

obul *n* tree with soft white wood.

obun *n Eng.* oven.

obur *n* old disserted site of a village.

obut *vt* slipped; **obut ki i ciŋŋe ci opotto piny,** its lipped from his hand and fell down. See **obuc, but**

obute *n* horn (of some kinds) used for dancing or during hunting.

obwoo *n* net, **obwoo lee,** net for hunting animal.

obwol *n* mushroom; there are many kinds, the eatable ones are **obwol oruka,** (from agoro termite hills) **obwol laguti** (in freshly cultivated field and during early wet season), **obwol okinyo** (very small and very many grouped in one place)**, obwol oket keny, obwol tuk, obwol tyen dyaŋ;** the non eatable ones, **obwol too, obwol otel, obwol yat. etc; obwol oruka** could be very big up to the size of a hat, grows from the "**agoro**" ant hill, very good for eating.

obwol mon *n* 1 blind worm; a certain kind of lizards which when looked at for the first time, it looks like a snake and it is taken for snake; 2 brief period of sun shine; **ceŋ obwol mon,** certain sunshine which comes suddenly during the dull day and then disappears soon after and deceives women for time of drying their millet.

obwollo *vt* he deceived; **obwollo Nyeko nono me miine cente,** he deceived Nyeko for nothing that he would give him money

Obwolo *n* a male name; (*lit* means he deceived).

obwolo *n* middle sized tree, used for production of fire, by rubbing it hard.

Obwona *n* a male name; (*lit* he thought that I was not enough)

obwonna *vt* he thought I was not enough for his purpose.

obwonno *vi* he thought it was not enough; **obwonno cam ma gimiine,** he thought that the food given to him was not enough.

obwotta *vt* he left or deserted me.

obwotto *vt* he left; **obwotto ticce woko,** he left his work; **obwotto dakone woko,** he left or deserted his wife; see **bwonna.**

Obwoya *n* a male name; (*lit* means he defeated me)

obwoya *vt* he defeated me; **obwoya woko i tuko me doŋŋe,** he defeated me in boxing.

oc *vn* 1 warming; **joo mamito oc me mac otyeno, gucit gukel yen,** those who want to warm themseve in the evening, let them bring the firewood.

oc *vn* aborting; **oc me ic en aye gin marac mada,** aborting is a very bad thing.

oc *vn* watering; **ŋaa ma ŋeyo oc me pii i poto ature?** Who knows watering the flower garden? these words are not commonly spoken; **oo, oyo.**

Oceco *n* Hill/Rock on which Samuel Baker camped in Patiko in 1862.

oceco *n* black medium sized bird.

oceke *n* 1 small long woody tube used for drinking local beer from a pot.

2 **oceke latek,** pipe handle.

ocene *n* green grasshoppers which usually come in large numbers at night; many people like them for eating. Some people call it lacene; see **awiny awiny, apededede, labaa, lakaibona, obaŋ cet, ajot jot, bonyo.**

oceyo *n* a grass like plant which roots produce small hard red covered fruits in the ground; the fruits are eatable and is sour like lemon used very much for mixing with gruel or porridge; *(Amomum Korarium Den).*

oci *n* a wild beast, flesh eating animal; some people refer to lion as **oci** some to civet cat as **oci.**

oci *n* curse, antenna placed on a village, which is supposed to hinder girls of a certain family from being married by man of the accursed village.

ococ *n* 1 porcupine, the name comes from the deep round holes which it makes which is called **ococ;** see **coo.**

ococ *n* deep round holes made by termites, burrows of rats, porcupine etc.

ocok *n* small thorny shrub with yellow inedible fruits; c/f **jagi.**

ocone *n* spoiled sorghum which is usually black and stuck together as one solid thing; children like to eat them.

ocoŋe *n* a field weed.

ocot *adv* has reached puberty; **awobini doŋ ocot,** the boy has now reached puberty as characterized by: 1 he has started having monthly emission of discarge from his penis, 2 his testes also has become pendulous and 3 there is a change in his voice; c/f **otuur** for female, see **cot.**

ocoyo-coyo *adj* stripped; **komme ocoyo-coyo,** its body is stripped.

ocuc n very small; **latin ot ocuc,** very small hut; **ocunyo latin at ocuc mo eno,** he build a small hut there.

ocuga *n* a kind of edible vegetables with small black fruits or berries which are edible.

ocuga *n* a tree with edible black berries. *(Carissa edulies)*; see **kano, olemo, olok, oduro, oywelo, etc.**

oculi *n* a small carnivore; it pretends to be dead and opens its anus which looks red, at which the hens come to peck when their heads are suddenly shut in and get caught. see also: **kak, cwiiny, kworo, giliri, too.**

ocun usually **pa ocu** *n* place of one's wife.

ocuur *n* an eagle, much bigger than a hawk or falcon, many of them are crested; **see olwit, oluri, okwata nyo okwateŋ.**

ocwak *n* sometimes called **acwak,** pole which is planted in the ground on which the net are tied for trapping animals.

ocwak *n* a yellow weaver bird *(plocerus auriantius) c/f* **aribe.**

ocwak ocwak *adj* yellow; **boŋone obeddo ocwak-ocwak,** the cloth is yellow.

ocwii *n* a rotten, watery insipid found on trees.

ocwici *n* young shoot of borassus palm which comes from it's kernel; it is edible; when it is cooked it remains hard, people who do not know about it, think that it is not yet cooked and so they add on more firewood, hence the proverb **"gin ma ikwiya darri yen"** it means, "what you don't know will finish all the firewood cooking it."

ocwiny *vi* dried up, **pii doŋ ocwiny,** the water has dried up. see **cwiny.**

ocwiny *adj* mature and strong; **latin ma ocwiny,** a mature and strong child.

ocwinynyo *prd* thinly spotted, speckled; **kom aweno ocwinynyo ma kwici kwici,** guinea fowl has fine spotted feather of black and white.

oda *n* beer left from the previous day; **oda koŋo.**

odaa *vi* quarrelled; **odaa mada ki cwarre,** she quarrelled very much with her husband, see **daa.**

odal um *n* dry mucus from the nose, **odal-um** crust from the nose; see **um.**

odaŋ kidi *n* centipede; see **bul apwoyo okolok.**

odaŋ kwon *n* uvula.

oddo *vt* to pound / pounding; **oddo kal i pany,** to pound / pounding the millet in a motar or to thresh / threshing the unshelled millet in a motar.

odeba *n* child stunted in growth, malnourished child; see **put.**

odec *n* abdominal swelling usually due to enlarged spleen which in turn due to repeated attacks of malaria.

odeke *n* boils which could be multiple around the buttocks, groins and armpits.

odeŋŋe *n* childish behaviour; **porro odeŋŋe,** behaving childishly like the children, behaving like a child.

oderu *n* winnowing container for winnowing millet which has been threshed.

odeyo *n* hard crust, corn flakes

odeyo-kwon *n* hard crust of **kwon** which are stuck on the inside of the cooking pot, corn flakes.

odii *n* ground simsim paste; **odii ŋwen,** roasted and ground white ants or termites paste; **odii pul,** ground groundnuts paste.

odi-odi *inj* a call from outside to let the people know that one is outside;

odiciŋ *n* plant used very much as charm, usually prescribed by a witch.

odiko *n* morning; **odiko con,** early morning.

odille *n* a game where a round ball of a hard wood is struck like in a game of hocky; **litino gitye ka tukko tuko odille i bar,** the children are playing the game of **odille** in the field.

odilo *n* ball; **litino gitye ka gweyo odilo,** the children are kicking the ball, in other words, the children are playing footbal.

odilo tyen *n* protruding round bones one on outer side of ankle and another on the inner side of the ankle *(the lateral and medial maleoli)*

odin *n* full of; **gaŋ odin mada,** the home is full of grass, it is bushy.

odini *n* a leech; **odini beddo i pii ci ka dano mo olutto tyenne i pii, ci kayo mokko iye ka doŋ cwiiyo remone,** the leech lives in water, it bites and sucks the blood from the person who has dipped his feet in water.

odiŋ *vn* stubborn, obstinate, not afraid any more, used to beating or quarrelling and does not mind about it any more; **latin ma odiŋ mape parro odoo,** a stubborn child who does not care about being beaten. See **oŋil, oŋiyo.**

odiŋ *n* nose bleeding; **odiŋ tye ka cwer i umme,** he is bleeding through the nose or having nose bleeding.

odiŋ *n* a trap for catching squirrel and birds; see **layutta.**

odiŋ diŋ *n* swelling on neck or armpit of calves, usually proves fatal.

odir *n* a field or compound cricket; it makes a lot of noise in the evening, eaten by children.

Odiya *n* male name (*lit* I am pressed or it is pressing me)

Odoc *n* a male name, name given to breech delivery child.

odocco *adv* again; **kella dok odocco,** bring it to me again; **mat yatte dok odocco,** take the medicine again; **nwoo lokke odocco,** renew the matter again.

odocco *v* confounding, confusing; **odocco lawotte mada,** he confused his friend very much.

ododo *n* fable, story which teaches children good manners and behaviours.

odok *n* resin, glue, juice, from the trees except **odok kic,** bees wax; **odok it,** ear wax

odok *vi* replied; **odok iye ni myero ibin,** he replied that you should come, see **dok.**

odon *n* **odon tyen,** crease, line or pit behind the knee joint above the calf.

Odoŋ *n* a male name. (second child that comes after twin); the first male child after twin is **Okello.**

odoŋ *n* remain; **odoŋ dek,** the food which has remained, or has been left over.

Odonga (Odoŋa) a male name, (*lit.* who is remaining there).

odoo *n* a stick; **kelle odoo me goyo gwok,** bring for him a stick for beating the dog

oduggu *vt* it is swelling; this is the swelling which comes after insect bites, like bees, wasp and even mosquitoes in some people; see **dugga.**

odugu *n* a hard tree which is good firewood tree; it's fire last for a long time.

Oduka *n* a male name (*lit* a small animal of the squirrel family).

oduka *n* kind of hill rat which belongs to squirrel family, *hyrax.*

oduny *vt* come out or fly out; **ŋwen oduny, yito oduny,** smoke came out, termites flew out, see **duny.**

Oduny *n* male name, (*lit* flew out).

odunyo *n* **jo mukene gilwoŋŋo ni otok** kind of grass which in the past used to be twisted and tied around the waist by youth; **otok** is the common name.

odur *n* place where wastes and garbages from the homes are poured forming a big heap, this big heap is called "**odur**".

Odur *n* male name (*lit* wastes heap).

odure *adv* 1 raining continuously without stoppage. 2 a man who spends much of his time with his wife or a boy with his mother - tied to his mother's apron or to his wife's apron; there is a song to discourage such people. **Odure kati woko wen keno - wen keno waŋo cunni,** Odure come out from near the fireplace, the fireplace will burn your penis.

oduro *n* an alarm made by mouth or sounded by mouth; **oduro kok caa,** the alarm is being sounded there; alarm for minor problem is different from that for wild beast or for attack by the enemies; **wululululu,** an alarm for ordinary danger; **wuk wuk wuk,** an alarm for serious danger such as enemy or wild beast; in this alarm people usually in the past.come out of their houses armed with spears.

oduro *n* become pregnant; it is uaually spoken of animal, **min dyelli doŋ oduro,** the goat is now pregnant or has become pregnant.

oduru *n* a big tree with edible fruit which is yellow similar to wild figs see **ocuga, olemo, olok, oywelo, kano etc.**

oduru pii *n* fine dust or soil deposited at the bottom of water in a water pot.

oduu *n* fleshy part of, pulpy covering of shea butter nut kernel; **oduu yaa,** pulp of the shea butter nut. It is sweet and eatable.

oduu *n* poorly developed; **oduu pul nyo oduu layata,** poorly developed groundnuts or potatoes.

odwel *n* dried hides of cattle and big game for sleeping on.

odwoŋ *n* a big tree, its wood is used for furniture.

odye nyo odye odye *adv* again, anew; **lok man doŋ dwokowa odye mada,** this matter now takes us back to the beginning to start all over again.

odyeer *n* small piece of leather of small animals cut for youth to wear on the buttocks during dance.

odyek *n Lang* hyena; Acholi call it **lalur nyo laŋudi.**

Odyek *n* male name (*lit.* means hyena).

odyer *n.* small pox.

ogaa *n* 1 water used for cleaning the strainer, which later poured on the dregs of beer. 2 **ogaa cak, n.** butter milk. i.e. milk from which butter has been removed.

ogali *n* 1 a big tree which is eaten very much by camels; the fibrous bark of its roots used for dressing the arrows; **pok ler ogali en aye giriyo ki tee nyo dog atero,** the fibrous bark of the roots of **ogali** is used for tying the end and upper part of the arrows. 2 **twol ogali, n.** a very poisonous snake which is brown and long. cobra.

ogele *n* a big full grown male for breeding; **twon ogele,** a big young bull, **nyok romo ogele,** a big young ram. 2 old dried hide.

ogitgit *n* a split or hangnail or split skin under the nail.

ogil *n* another name for **giliri,** civet cat, some people call it **nyaga.**

ogilo *n* a small bird when singing, male and female sing alternately.

ogilo lak *n* canine tooth;

ogodo *n* women's round dance; **myel ogodo, ogodo** dance.

ogodo *n* 1 wax; **ogodo it,** accumulated wax in the ear. 2. **ogodo um,** hard crust in the nose.

ogom *adv* bent; **yatte ogom woko pe atir,** the pole is bent not straight.

Ogom *n* part of Payira clan.

ogony-laa *prn* for removal of hide dress; **dek me ogony laa,** *fig.* the food given to the husband at night by the wife when he is about to lie down and sleep, in other words, the food that a woman gives to coddle her husband.

ogoo nyo ogoo yat *n* hole or opening, in the tree, or hollow space in an old rotten tree; into which, sometimes, bees make their honey; some people call it **ogor** or **ogor yat;** see **ojaŋ.**

ogore *n* a crab.

ogoro *n* a grey heron (bird).

ogoyo goyo *prd.* variegated colour.

ogul nyo ogul mola *n* a big brass wristlet, armlet and ankle ring or arm, ankle and wrist bracelets.

oguro ŋec *n* backbone (*thoracic spine*);

oguro *n* gizzards, stomach of birds, **oguro gweno,** gizzards of a chicken.

ogwa *n* a special kind of basket made for fishing, or catching fish.

ogwal *n* frog. There are various types, **ogwal pok,** ordinary frog. **ogwal til,** the frog which jumps and almost flies, **ogwal ore,** frog which makes noises at night from the river or pond

Ogwal *n* male name. (*lit.* frog).

ogwal-bad *n* muscle of the arm; *biceps* muscles of the human arm.

ogwaŋ *n* generic name for smaller carnivora of all kinds, e.g. **bura,** wild cat, **kworo,** serval cat; **giliri,** civet cat, **kak, oculi, cwiiny** (all these are mongoose family), **too,** fox or jackal.

ogwari *n* thorny impenetrable shrub growing in all directions.

ogwec *n* concave; **ogwec me piyo dek nyo gurro ŋor,** a stick which one end is enlarged, rounded and shaped like a bean used for smashing or mashing cooked cowpeas. and for mixing simsim pastewith water; **dwe pudi tye ogwec,** the moon is still in the concave shape.

ogwec *n* spur; **ogwec gweno,** spur of a chicken.

ogwec *vi* vt dislocated; **waŋ coŋŋe ogwec woko,** his knee is dislocated.

ogwil *n* a long rope for tying goats and sheep or cattle.

ogwit *n* clitoris (words used for insulting one another); **ogwit pa menni,** your mother has long clitoris; this is an abusive language and not spoken by well bred people.

Oitino *n* stream or small river coming from Gulu and flowing into Onyama river. **Oitino** *lit.* means river where children get drowned because they cannot cross it.

ojony pyer *n* work which causes tiredness of the lumber region; **cul me ojony pyer,** payment or indemnity for hard work.

ojaa *n* 1 plant with tuberous roots produces very strong glue used for joining woods. 2 a tree that its bark make strong fibres.

ojaŋ *n* kind of small bees which live in tree holes which produce honey, they have no stings see also **ojibu.**

Ojara *n* a person born with surplus fingers or toes.

ojee *n* small kind of termites which do not build ant hill but cause great damages to houses and furniture.

ojede *n* young locusts without wings, another name for it is **adwek.**

oji *n* grief, dejection; **oji too pud tye i komme,** he is still filled with grief after death; not commonly spoken now.

ojibu *n* small kind of insects living in holes of termite hill and produce honey

there, these do not sting people. see **ojaŋ**.

ojiga *n* mane, **ojiga pa labwor,** mane of a lion.

Ojiga *n* name; male name, (*lit* mane)

ojiri *n* small cricket.(insect), the same family as **odir** but are smaller.

ojoga *n* 1. intestinal worms; **ojoga nyakaboli,** tapeworms; 2. *prov* **yom cwiny a i ojoga,** generosity comes from the stomach, e.g. if you give me something, I shall also be pleased to give you something.

Ojok *n* male name, **Ajok** a female name, name given to children born with some deformities of some kind.

Ojoone *n* is a name; it is supposed to be a name of a legendary female king, who in all questions would decide against women, hence the exclamation of women in trouble "**aya ojoone**" (ha there you are again, **ojoone).**

ojula-wic nyo ojuny wic *n* tuft of hair on the occiput of man.

ojul *n* waxbills (birds).

ojul *vt* he is annoyed or he is sulky.

Ojul *n* male name. (*lit* sulky, annoyed)

ojul *n* a kind of creeping plant which it's pollen when it touches anybody especially those who are sensitive to it, causes much irritation and itching of the body and so makes the sufferer to scratch his body very much.

ojuŋ *adv* contracted, reduced in size; **boŋone ojuŋ woko pien gilwokkogi i pii maŋic,** the clothe has contracted because of washing it with a cold water

195

ojuu *n* small flies, fruit flies, always found on rotten fruits such as bananas, mangoes and so on and on dregs of beer.

ojwar *adj* very tall; **yatte ojwar mada,** the tree is very tall; **nyaanne ojwar mada,** the girl is very tall.

ojwayo *vt* 1 rubbed off, polished, wiped off; **ojwayo wii meja maleŋ mada,** he polished the top of the table very well; 2 **ojwayo moo ma oo i wii meja,** he rubbed off the oil that was spilt on the top of the table; 3 **ojwayo coc ma onoŋo tye i kom bao me coyo coc,** he wiped off the writing which was on the black board. see **jwayo.**

ojwee *n* a trace, foot mark; **ojwee labwor okatto kany,** the foot marks of a lion has passed along here. see **obot.**

ojwii -yat *n* juice or fluid that oozes or comes out from wet or green wood.

ojwiny-dyaŋ *n* male widah or widow bird.

ojwiny jwiny nyo ojwijwiny *n* white wagtail (bird).

okado *n* sun bird, bee-eater and nectar eater; they belong to the family of small birds and have many species but the distinctive thing about them are that they all have slender long and curved bills and in most species male have brilliant metallic green or blue feathers; they all visit flowers for the nectar

okak *n* a tree with edible fruits.

okak *vn* it is split; **baone okak woko,** the board is split; see **obar, otyer, kak.**

okal *n* caries of teeth.

okani *adv* peculiar; **danone kite obeddo okani,** the person has a peculiar manner or he is queer.

Okaŋ *n* male name (*lit* barren)

okaŋ *vt* she is barren; **dakone okaŋ woko,** the woman is barren or his wife is barren.

okaŋ *n* a field abandoned in order that it may have humus for cultivation the following year.

okaŋo *n* a small tree, which is very hard and not eaten by termites hence used very much as shrine poles.

okar *n* a piece of a wood with a fork on one end used very much for building.

okarre *adv* sits with the legs astride; **obeddo okarre i doggolane,** he sat with his leg astride at his door.

okarra *vi* a dilemma, divided in mind, wants to do this or to do that e.g; **lokke doŋ okarra woko, pe aŋeyo gin aŋoo ma ati,** I am in a dilemma, I do not know what to do.

okatto *vt* he has passed; **okatto ki i waŋ nak** *prov* passed through the gape in the teeth, means slip of the tongue, see **harre**.

Okebo *n* tribe in West of Lake Albert (Zaire) with different language.

Okec *n* a male name, (name given to children borne during famine)

okego *n.* 1 thick phlegm of throat, 2 mucus accompanying spermatozoa.

okelee *n* sharp smelling secretion of a skunk or civet cat (**giliri).** civet cat scent.

okelokoko *n* a messanger who used to carry letters fixed in a split piece of a twig, this was done when there was no way of posting the letters but to be carried in that way by people who did not know how to read; the word **okelokoko** *lit.* means it brought problems.

oken *n* a professional hunter.

okene *n* part of a liver

Okene *n* male name (*lit.* means himself, alone).

okeŋ *n* the ear of an animal killed which is cut off and tied to the arm of the killer.

okeŋ *vt* missed it or did not get it; **okeŋ cammo riŋo,** he missed eating meat, see **keŋ.**

okero *n* special hut for goats or sheep.

okeyo *n* my nephew, the son of my sister; **okeyo,** a nephew, a general name; the order in this relation is as follows: *sing* **okeya, okeyu, okeyone,** my, your, his nephew; *pl* **okeyowa, okeyowu, okeyogi,** our, your, their nephews; nephew which is not closely related but from the same clan, is called as follows:**okeyiwa, okeyiwu, okeyigi,** our, your, their nephews, this is not commonly spoken.

okito *n* placenta, (afterbirth of animals). see **byero, pel, kitogo.**

okoc *n* an old, big males of animals driven away from herd and lives separately.

okoco *n* a small tortoise shell tied around the arm as an ornament but used for rattling during dancing. Others call it **okoto.**

okodo *n.* ticks. Some people call it **okwodo;** central Acholi prefer **okodo.**

okok *n* fish with pointed fins

okok *n* 1 the small worker termites. 2 *vt* he has cried.

okok *n* egret (bird) they are white and usually fly in groups.

okokko apil *vt* he appealed or applied for appeal; **apil,** is adistortion of the English word appeal, see **kokko.**

okokori *n* tree ants.

okokori *n* a white and black coloured ostrich feather.

okol *n* a clog tied to the leg of a prisoner.

okolok *n* millipede; see **odaŋ kidi.**

okom *n* a stump of wood in the ground on which frequently people knock their toes; *prov.* **Okom oyokko laŋwec,** meaning, one who was already running makes excuses that he knocked his foot against the stump.

okono *n* a pumpkin; **okono man dyaŋ,** an oblong type; **okono nyakabwoli,** a small round kind of pumpkin.

okoŋ *n* a pangolin, a scaly ant-eater.

okoŋo *n* a bird of the size of a raven, its head is white, with black, body, and red wings, it eats banana; plantain eater *(Turocos). (Turocos - Musophaga Roasse).*

okoro *n* a snail, snail shell.

okoro *n* cartilage.

okoto wic *n* skull.

Oktoba *n* October, the tenth months of the year.

okuba *n* white ants which comes out at 6-7 p.m.; see **ŋwen**

okuk *n* coccyx.

okulat *n* a handbag - usually refers to the bags of the soldiers.

okuma *n* a black water tortoise, much bigger than the ones seen on land; turtle.

Okuma *n* a name of a person. (male) (*lit.* means **opuk.**)

okuro *n* young dog, puppy; in a slang a young child also is called **okuro** e.g. **okuroni tye niŋniŋ**? how is your child?

okuto *n* thorn; types of :**okuto oryaŋ, okuto laŋo, okuto oŋono, okuto lacari**

Okuto *n* a male name. (*lit.* means thorns).

okwac or okwaca *n* a bird which warns people against danger of wild beast, bees, snake etc.

okwara *prd* brown something; **dyaŋ okwara,** brown cow, goat etc.

okwata nyo okwateŋ *n.* kite; see **ocuur, olwit lwit, oluri.**

okwer *n* a pear shaped or round fruit like cucumber but yellow; its hard skin is eaten after the seeds have been removed and cooked; children do frequently eat them raw like cucmber; see **oboko kwer.**

Okwera *n* a male name, (*lit* means he rejected me).

okwik *n* a bird which picks ticks from the cattle, or ox-pecker. *widah*

okwil *n* kind of caterpillars which come from time to time in very large numbers and destroy grass or small plants.

Okwir *n* a name of a male person, (lit. bitter like poison).

okwiri nyo opit adj, an intelligent person, capable person.

okwodo *n* used by some people but "**okodo**" is the standard word for tick.

okwotto *vt* he passed flatus, broke the air, **okwotto cet,** he passed the wind or flatus, that is a crude word, good word for it is , **ocwallo nyo oywayo yamo,** see **kwotto.**

Ola *n* a path which is used regularly by smaller animals; **ola pa oyoo,** path of rats beneath the grass, sometimes children also make "**ola**" under the grass where they hide.

olam *n* sycamore or fig tree.

olaŋ *n* a bell[2], kidney; 1 **goo olaŋ, cawa doŋ orommo,** it is time, ring the bell; 2 **olaŋ ber mada me acamma,** the kidney is very good for eating.

olany *n* a common grasshopper; see, **labaa, awiny awiny, apededee etc.**

Olanya *n* a male name, **Alanyo** n. a female name given to the child by mother who feels abandoned by her husband.

olar wic *n* skull.

olayo nyo parat nyo lukille *n* a stick with axe, small pick-axe used for ornament and seldom as weapon, carried mainly by young men.

ola *n* path regularly used especially by animals.

olek *n* a stick with some kind of knob at one end, used for walking as ornament.

oleke ŋut *n* a necklace with iron beads joined behind by gourd handle.

olel *n* simsim sauce, simsim soup; **en mitto cammo olel,** he wants to eat simsim sauce.

olem or lalem *prd* hornless cow, goat etc.

olemo *n* a tree with yellow-brown fruit, the pulp of the fruit is edible and agreeably sour; *(ximenia americana),* see other fruits, **olok, ocuga, oduru, oywelo, pwomo, kano etc.**

olet *n* pasture where cattle go to graze; **dyaŋi tye i olet,** the cattle are in the pasture or in the grazing ground.

Olet *n* a male name used very much by Langi; (*lit* grazing field for cattle)

oli *n* kind of tomatoes.

olidi *n* a water bug.

oligo *prd* blunt; **lyedi ni lakke oligo,** this razor blade is blunt, or the edge of this razor blade is blunt.

olik *n* a bat; **olik cammo dyewor, ginino dyeceŋ,** bats eat during the night and sleep during the day time.

olik olik *adj* dark brown; **boŋone obedo olik olik,** the cloth is dark brown.

olili *n* 1 epilepsy, a disease which is characterised by the patient suddenly falling and shaking all over with froth in the mouth and later becoming unconscious 2 east coast disease of chicken which kills them in hundreds unless they are vaccinated against it.

olim *n* a big tree with large leaves.

ollo *n* 1 tiredness; **ticce doŋ orommo ollo,** the work is tiredsome now. 2 boring; **jal li ollowa ki lokke mape mit,** he bores us with his useless talks; 3 tiring somebody with work or talk; **ollowa ki temmo tukko man nono,** tiring us with this play or exercises for nothing.

ollo *vt* 1 clearing, emptying; **ollo waŋ pii obed maleŋ,** clearing the spring water to make it clean.

olo *adv* finally, in the end, at last, inspite of all, nevertheless, all the same, **olo ocitto,** at last he went, **olo ocammo,** at last he ate; **kadi beddi gikwerro ni pe ocitti, ento lacen olo ocitto,** even though he was refused to go, in the end he went; **kadi beddi pe okatto peny, olo ducu oyommo cwinynye me temmone,** even though, or inspite of the fact that, he did not pass the examination, he was all the same happy for trying it.

olobbi or **olobbo** *prd.* became soft, fluctuant, blistered; **akwotta man doŋ ocek olobi,** the swelling is now ready, that is now soft, fluctuant and pointing, see **lobbi.**

ologi *n* a climber with poisonous fruits, it looks like **ooko** which is edible.

ologo or **ologo lac** *n* bladder; **ologone goro, layo teretere twatwal,** he has poor bladder, he passes urine too frequently.

olok *n* wild grapes; see **olemo, ocuga, oduru, oywelo, kano, koŋo ogwal etc.**

olokoro or **olukoro** *n* trachea.

oloto *n* a stick; **oloto bul,** a drum stick; **oloto me goyo bul,** the stick for beating the drum.

olugo or **okummo** *vi* depressed, having grief, mourning, ill disposed.

oluk *n* tadpoles (frog).

oluma or **twon oluma** *n* chief, very big. 1. **twon oluma lyec,** a very big elephant; 2. **cogi oluma keken gin aye ma gudonyo i ot,** very important people only who entered the house.

oluma *n* very important **oluma mapol mada tin gubinno ka legga,** very many important people came to prayers. see **abembem.**

oluŋ cet *n* anus; here it means that it moulds the faeces into shapes; see **ŋwiny cet** (which cuts the feaces)

oluri *n* normally refer to it as **olwit oluri** *n* falcon or hawk; see **ocuur, okwata ka olwit.**

oluro *n* mouse bird (*colius striatus*), long thick-tailed brownish bird, crested, with speckled chest, it's face looks like that of a mouse.

olut *n* stick for walking .

oluta kwon *n* a special stick with flattened one end used for stirring **kwon".**

oluto *prd* without; **odoo la wiye oluto,** the stick without knob at the end.

oluu *adj* blunt, **lakke oluu,** its edge is blunt; **leb atero oluu,** the tip of the arrow is blunt, see **odiŋ, oligo.**

oluu *adv* entirely, wholly, completely; **cam pud tye oluu,** the food is not yet touched; **otiŋo guniya me cukari oluu ocitto kwede,** he took the whole bag of sugar and went with it.

olwa *n* a tree, - mivule, Lug. (African oak tree).

olwar *vi* collected just enough; **tikka moo yaa ma gitye ka teddone doŋ oton olwar i tee agulo?** is the shea butter nut oil, which is being distilled, reasonably collected at the bottom of the pot? see **loar**

olwedo *n* a tree; twigs or leaves of this tree are used in wishing good luck or success by the elders to the young people who are going to hunt or to war; the elders spit on the leaves and brush them over the spears to bless them and to wish them luck in front of the ancestral shrine.

olwet or **burugi** *n* A a bugle; **i cukul gigutto olwet odiko me coyo litino kwan,** in school the bugle is sounded or blown to wake up the pupils.

olwinyo *n* hookworms, thread worms, other small intestinal worms.

olwiro *n* **twol olwiro,** a snake which normally strikes the people but does not bite.

olwit-lwit *n* a hawk. or falcon; **olwit lwit oceyo latin gweno acel woko,** the hawk has taken (snatched) away a chick.

omak-wic *n* a small shrub which it's seeds stick on ones head or clothes.

omal *adv* lost, vagabond, wanderer; **latinne doŋ omal woko i tim,** the child is now a vagabond, roaming about outside the country; see **mal.**

omar *n* fresh grass grown up after first grass burning. others call it **lum ma buru buru.**

Omara *n* a male name given by the witch (ajwaka) possessing a spirit of that name.

omaarra, comes from the word **maar,** love; hence **omaarra** *n* my cousin; **omaarro** or **lamaarro,** male or female cousin, these are general names; the names are as follows: *sing.* **omaarra, omaarru, omaarrone,** my, your, his cousin; *pl* **omaarrowa, omaarrowu, omaarrogi,** our, your, their cousins; cousins which are not closely related but of the same clan are called as follows: **omaarriwa, omaarriwu, omaarrigi,** our, your, their cousins; **omarro me nyom,** brothers or sisters- in-law due to marrying in the same family.

omat *n.* fondness, infatuation; **omat me mutoka ma Okot owillo doŋ mitto nekke woko,** the pride of having a car is almost killing him. (lit the fondness of having bought a car is almost killing him); it is a word which is now not much spoken.

omeera *n* (comes from the word **mee,** love each other) hence **omeera,** my brother; **omeego,** *n* a brother, a general name; the order for this relation is as follows: *sing* **omeera, omeeru, omeerone,** my, your, his brother; *pl* **omeerowa, omeerowu, omeerogi,** our, your, their brothers; but some people say **ominwa, ominwu, omin-gi;** brothers which are not closely related but of the same clan is as follows: sing. **omeega, omeegu, omeege;** or **omeegina, omeegini, omeegine;** *pl* **omeegiwa, omeegiwu, omeegigi;** my, your, his; *pl* our, your and their brothers; **utumeega,** my brethren; **utumeego,** brethren.

omel *n* fish which is usually found in small rivers and lagoons.

omemelo *n* ring worm, characterised by itching round spot which has small pimples; it affects the head and causes round patches of loss of hair; see **mida, comogo, onaŋ melo.**

omen *n* 1 coffee. (in Acoli **omen** is found grown wild in the forest). 2 cud, **dyel nyammo omen,** the goat ruminates.

omin ŋadi *n* a brother of so and so; **omin ŋadi dwoggo diki,** so and so's brother will come tomorrow.

Omiro *n* nickname given to the Lango by Acoli; (not liked by Langi).

omiya, ajoŋa omiya n mbwa fly. *(simulium damnosuni)* the fly that carries filariasis which cause disease *onchocerciasis* which leads to river blindness and bad skin conditions, hanging groins, lichenoid skins etc.

ommo *vt* 1 to fetch / fetching. 2 to tempt / tempting; **oommo cwinynye ka twerro citto,** he tempted him if he can go.

omme *vi* 1 tempted, urged; **cwinynye omme ni myerro elweny,** he feels like fighting or urged to fight. 2 can be brought; **jami ne twerro omme,** the things can be brought; see **yutte, tiŋŋe, wet-wet.**

omukutiru or lomuk *n A* an old disabled person. this is now archaic, no longer spoken.

omuŋi kiyata *n* potatoes planted at the end of the rain season, at the river bank or marshy land; they become ready for eating at the beginning of the next rain season, properly called **leyata omuŋi.**

omuya *n* starling, a bird with a brilliant metallic greenish blue feathers, underparts, chin to belly and tail covered with metallic violet and coppery feathers, *(lamprotornis spendidus);* there are other species also.

omwom bye *n* a creeping plant on an ant hill, the bark of it's roots taste a bit like pepper,- is used as medicine for many conditions, such as stomach, eyes etc.

onaŋ melo *n* ring worms of the head, causing loss of the hair at the site affected in a circular manner usually; see **mida, omemelo, comogo.**

onaŋ melo *n* a gecko, common name for gecko is **laromo ot** or **gek.**

onee yat *n* a tree squirrel, c/f **aita.**

oniŋŋe *vt* half shut; **waŋŋe oniŋŋe,** his eyes are half shut see **niŋŋe**

onioŋo *adj* very dirty; **boŋone doŋ onioŋo mada,** the clothe is very dirty.

oŋaru *n* a praising or poetical name for leopard.

oŋato *n* a praising or poetical name for lion.

oŋele *prd* with pieces broken off; **dog can doŋ oŋele,** one part of the brim of the plate is broken.

oŋera *n* a grivet monkey, grey monkey; see **ayom, dolo, gunya, bim, puno.**

oŋol ŋol *n* an emergency; an hindrance or obstacle (unforeseen).

oŋon *n* prescriptive right, code of law that came by usage, legal norms which were laid down in the past in public prosecution by the elders which regulate public life. **Patiko, Payira ka Alero gitye ki oŋon acel; Puranga ka Koro oŋon gi pat; Patiko, Payira and Alero** have the same code of laws; **Koc, Puranga** and **Koro** follow a different code of laws.

oŋoo *n* grass patch preserved or left from burning for cultivation.

oŋoro *n* adenoids.

oŋot-togo *n* otter.

oŋullo *vt* he spat out; **oŋullo laa piny i dyee ot,** he spat the saliva on the floor.

oŋullo *vt* he revealed a bit of the case; **oŋullo manok lokke botwa,** he told us or revealed to us a bit of the case; see **ŋallo.**

oŋwek *n* a finger ring (not used now).

ony *v* 1 pour; **ony bel i aduko,** pour corn into the basket 2 put into, **ony cukari i cai,** put sugar into the tea, 3 fill; **ony pii opoŋ agulu man,** fill this pot with water.

Onyama *n* a river coming from Gulu and flowing into Nile near Nimule.

onyee *adv* closely together; **latin man doŋ konynye onyee i dye ot kany;** the child is defaecating every where in the house, and the house is covered with it.

Onyiŋe *n* a male name as well as female name.

onyo, onyoni *prep* at about this time, such and such a time; **onyo ki otyeno noŋo doŋ watye kacam;** we will be eating in the evening at this time.

onynyo *vt* to pour, fill, to throw out (pass urine); 1 **ocitto ka onynyo pii,** he went to pour out water, but *lit* it means he went to pass urine. 3 **onynyo cam ki gweno,** giving food to the chicken. 4 **gitye ka onynyo koŋo,** they are brewing beer. 5 **gwinyo oonynyo i komme,** he has got scabies. 6 **guonynyo odoo matek i kom Ocan,** they thoroughly beat Ocan.

onyoŋ - nyoŋ *n* weakness, fright, panic, terror; **en tye ka twoyo twoo me onyoŋ nyoŋ,** he is suffering from general weakness; **.pi onyoŋ nyoŋ ma onekko komme woko omiyo pe doŋ otukko tukko me doŋne,** because of panic, he did not take part in the boxing competition.

onyoŋ - nyoŋ *n* West Nile fever

onyubbo lapena or **muraŋa,** *n* pigeon peas or beans cooked and mixed with simsim paste and water.

onyuny *prd/adj* very small; 1. **omiine onyuny riŋo mo,** he gave him a very small piece of meat.

oo *v* warm; **oo mac caa,** warm yourself there. **bed piny ioo mac,** sit down and warm yourself with fire.

oo *v¹* pour, **oo pii i poto ature,** pour water in the flower garden or water the flower garden; 2 come out; **iye oo woko,** she has aborted; see **oc, oyo.**

oo *v* reach, arrive; **en oo paco nino ducu** he comes/reaches home always.

ooko *n* a climber which is both wild and cultivated, has truncated fruits, which it produces as it climbs up the trees and when the fruits are cooked, they taste like English potatoes; see **ologi.**

Oola *n* a male name, given to 3rd child from twins, means I am tired.

o oo *vp* he has arrived or it has poured out; 1 **en doŋ o oo paco,** he has arrived at home; 2 **pii o oo woko,** the water has poured out; see **oo.**

ono *vn* to cough; **en ono mada,** he coughs too much

opac *n* ejaculated sperms after coitus; **opac pa ŋwiny meni!** an insult, not used now.

opac *vn* disobedient, not caring anymore, unruly; **danone doŋ opac woko pe parro ŋati mo,** the man does not care for anybody, he is disobedient; see **odiŋ, oŋil,**

opal *n* an oyster-shell.

opalle *vt* squinted; **waŋŋe opalle,** he has a squint in his eye / his eye is squinted see **palle.**

opam *n* shot block of wood for threshing millet.

opany *n* palm of the hand and sole of the foot.

opec *prd* abound, plentiful; **lee opec mada kany,** there are many animals here or the animals are plenty here.

opego *n* a pig, wild or domestic; **opego lwokke i daba,** the pigs take birth in the mud.

opelo *n* a short plant with large leaves, it's tubers are edible like yams; see **mwodo ki obato.**

openo *n* turaco *(schalawi)* a bird with a crest on its head; **openo marro cammo labolo ma ocek,** the turaco likes eating ripe banana.

opici *n Eng* office; **tye i opici,** he is in the office.

opii *n* slave captured during the war; see **guci** (male), **aŋeca** (female), **lamiru, jane** (male)

Opii *n* a male name, (lit. means slave).

opilo *n* a small pointed stick for digging potatoes or cassava.

opilo-pilo *prd* striped; **kom lagwar obeddo opilo-pilo,** the zebra's body is striped; **dyaŋŋi ma-komgi obedo opilo pilo pe gimiyo me nyom,** the striped cattle are not given for marriage.

opilo pilo *adv* only by way of rumours; **lokke pud winynye opilo pilo,** the matter is as yet a mere rumour.

opir bul *n* medium sized drum; see **bul.**

opiro *n* 1 a large leather bag. 2 a child coming forth together with membrane covering it. 3 a kind of grass.

opit *n* a grass with hollow stem used by children for sucking.

opit *prd* an extraordinarily intelligent, and enterprising, energetic person.

opit or **opittu** *vn* matured; **nyakone doŋ opit,** the girl is now matured as characterised by presence of menses, well developed breasts and the peculiar smell of girls; see **otik, poŋ** or **opoŋ.**

opiyo piyo *adv* quickly, swiftly, speedily; **tiyo opiyo piyo,** work quickly.

opiyo aona (aona opiyo) *n* tuberculosis. (consumption).

Opiyo *n* **male, Apiyo female.** proper name for first born of twins, a male and a female baby.

Opobo *n* a male name; (*lit* means **opobo** tree)

opobo *n* a tree with good rods used very much for building and sometimes as sticks for beating the people.

opok *n* a big hardwood tree which is a popular firewood and a building wood; it is not easily eaten by the termites.

opok *n* a short flat fish, small head and a large body, the bones mainly on the spine.

Opok *n* a male name (born under the wood **opok).**

opok *prd* inconsiderate and thoughtless of others; **cwarre opok,** her husband considers only his stomach in matter of food.

opoko *n* the emptied and dried gourd with hole at the top / gourd bottle / calabash bottle. 2 **opoko lac,** bladder. 3 **opoko toŋ,** the open socket of the spear where the shaft of the spear is slotted.

opoko-yok *adv.* laughing-stock, but for teasing and ridicule; **odoko opoko-yok pa dano,** he has become a laughing stock for the people.

opol *n.* oar for propelling boat; **opol lakwaŋ yeya,** oar for propelling the boat

opolok *n* a shrub, which by twisting the bark several times the wood inside can be pulled out leaving a hollow tube which the children use as guns; by putting two balls of chewed "**ogali**" roots one at the end and another some distances apart and then pushing it at high pressure, the one ball at the end will shoot out with a loud sound like that of a gun.

opoŋ *adv* fully grown up, mature; **nyakone doŋ opoŋ,** the girl is now fully grown up and mature, see **opit nyo opittu,** see **poŋ.**

opotino *n* a person behaving like a child.

opotino *n* a vest, an old name; **kella boŋo opotino me kor,** bring for me the vest, not spoken now.

opuk *n* a tortoise.

opuny *n* heel; **twol otoŋŋo opuny tyenne,** he has been bitten on the heel by the snake.

oput *n* a tree, which barks of its roots are used as medicine for malaria etc.; it is also used as a drug which is drunk by two enemies as a sign of reconciliation. e.g. **matto tee oput,** drinking the root of **oput**

opuyu *n* black soil used for plastering the floor.

opyen *n* a spider, other peole called it **obworopyen.**

or *v* send; **or latin ocikel kom,** send the child to bring the chair.

or *n* an errand, message, commission; *prov* **or bwoŋ dyel,** means taking message is good luck

or *v* remove; **or kweri ki i kom purre,**. remove the hoe from it's shaft

or *n* a sister's husband, brother in law; **orra, orri, orre** (sing), my brother in law, your and his brother in law. (*pl*) **occa, occi, occe,** ours, yours theirs brothers in law but here **pa** must be added to it as **pa occa, pa occi, pa occe.**

ora *n* depression in a country, valley; **pii tye ka mol citto i ora,** the water is running down the valley.

oraa *n* long grass used for covering roofs of houses and for grass torch at night.

orada *prd* flat; empty; **ii latin obeddo orada caa,** the child is there with empty stomach, he is hungry.

orada *adv* burning sun; **ceŋ oryeny orada laworo otwoyo gin ma wapitto woko,** the sun was very hot yesterday and it burnt off what we planted; see **oryada** which is preferable.

oran *n* failure to grow, thrive, prosper; **yat man odoŋo oran ki iyo pe twerro medde weki onyak,** this tree has failed to grow and cannot grow any more in order to produce some fruits; see **ran.**

oree *n* joke, fun, jest; **loko lok oree,** he makes fun or jest; **lok oree,** jokes, entertainment talks; *prov* **lok oree ketto latin i ic,** that is , joking (with a woman) sometimes results in pregnancy of the woman.

oree *n* epidemics of infectious diseases, **oree gweno,** *east coast disease* of fowls, **oree dyaŋ**, rinderpest.

orini *prd* solid, compact, massive; **gin ma iye orini,** compact thing; **danone orini,** he is very strong and solid person.

oro *n* dry season Dec. - March.

orobo *n* strong, vigorous youth; **orobo nam pai,** group of youth number five; this was a distortion of English.

oroc twol *n* snake's shaded skin.

orok *n* trap for rats. (mud tube into which strings are arranged); see **layutta, odiŋ**.

orok *n* hoes with pointed end and tied on a straight shaft not bent ones; used now mainly by Langi.

ororo *n* 1 spittle snake, **twol ororo.** 2 **ororo me cam** or **koŋo** lover of food or beer.

ororo ayom *n* large tree with thorny stem; **layom pe ito,** a circumcised person cannot climb it presumably, thorns

on the stem will scratch or prick the exposed glands penis.

orro *nt* sending, delegating, commissioning, **orro dano mape genne pe ber,** sending an untrustyworthy person is not good.

orro *vt* removing ; **orro kweri ki i kom purre,** removing the hoe from its shaft.

orro *v* entertaining talk, or speaking entertainingly; **orro lok,** entertaining talk.

oruc nyo odoo ma wiye dit *n* a heavy cudgel or club for defence.

orudi *n* a wild dog, wolf; **orudi gimaarro wotto abicel abicel i dul acel,** the wolves always go about in a group of six.

oruka - obwol oruka *n* mushroom that grows on **agoro** ant-hill, usually grows to a very large size to that of a hat; see other **obwol .**

orukko *prd* densely covered with cutaneous eruption; **wii ŋadi orukko ki bur,** so and so's head is covered all over with infection, that is erupted all over.

orukko *vi* to germinate; **obwol orukko,** the mushrooms have germinated.

oruŋo bel *prd* wrinkled; **waŋŋe doŋ oruŋo bel,** his face is wrinkled, he is an old man, see **ruŋŋo.**

orup or **orup kweri** *n* the worn out hoe which is quite small, which is used for digging holes.

oruta or **carama** *n* long leather strings of loin wear hanging from the right hip, mostly adorned with beads.

oruta *n* a girl who had born a child at home without being married; such a girl would wear the above apparel.

orwoo *n* thirst, **orwoo pii,** thirst for water.

orwoo *n* a shrub with their soft sticks or poles used for making bee-hives.

orwoo *vt* gave up; **orwoo woko me citto ka doŋŋe,** he gave up going for boxing, see **nwoo.**

orwo *adv.* the following day; **odwoggo orwo,** he came the following day.

orya *intj* let us do it; **orya doŋ wacittu ka myel,** let us go to dance now.

oryada *prd* sharp, intense, severe, to (senses); **ceŋ oryeny oryada,** the sun was very hot; some people call it **orada** but the former is preferred.

oryaŋ *n* a tree which it's roots is a medicine for diarrhoea; the ashes from it make good alkali salt. **okuto oryaŋ** *q.v.*

Oryaŋ *n* name (lit tree's name)

ot *pl* **odi** *n* huts, houses; **ot apamma,** a house made of mud and wattle; **ot gony,** rest house; **ot okol, ot buc, or ot jeru,** prison.

otac *n* a round pad made of grass or cloth for protecting the head and supporting pots and other loads carried on the head.

otaci *n* gonorhoea. (not used by the Acholi) but by Langi.

otako *n* low, wide open earthen bath, used specially for washing babies.

otalaa *adv* frankly; **otitte woko otalaa,** he told him frankly.

otamo-tamo *prd* covered with big spots of some kind; **rii komme obeddo otamo-tamo,** the giraffe is covered with black spots on white ground.

otaŋ wic *n* hat; **otaŋ wiye dit kattto wiye,** he has an oversized hat, see **tok**

otara *n* a white (cow), a white (man);

muni otara gin aye gukeliwa pekku, the white people are the ones who brought us trouble.

oteka *n* a brave person.

oteka lawii mony *n* a commander of the fighting forces, general.

otel tok *n* cerebrospinal meningitis, see **adoŋi.**

oteŋ *adv* stubborn, obstinate, disobedient; **latinne doŋ oteŋ woko,** the child is now obstinate and disobedient, see **teŋ**.

otetel *n* woodpecker.

otigo *n* lady fingers, okra. *(hibiscus sativus)*

otiko *n* beads as necklace for womenit is called also **tiko** see **kiteyi teyi ki gagi.**

otini *n* a rope trap for game, a rope for snaring game.

otini *n* a tree which has small seeds but grows into a big tree.

otira *n* earthquake.

Otira *n* legendary, a mysterious person, who came sometimes ago and left marks of foot on stone, after which river or hills are called in Gulu district.

otira *n* a short person who is stunted, sometimes named **Obala.**

otir-ŋoor *n* king fisher.

otit *n* firefly, normally emits light intermittently; **otit meny ki dyer wor,** the firefly glows at night.

otit *n* palm which is normally found along the river bank or marshy area. *(Palmyra Palm),* used very much for making mats.

otit dud *n* coccyx, the last bones of the spinal column; **opotto piny ki i wii dudde ci oturro otit dudde woko,** he fell down on his buttock and broke his coccyx.

otogo *n* 1 small hut for boys or youth who are not yet married 2 temporary hut for a sick person or for hunting.

otok *n* a grass which in the old days used to be twisted into strings and tied around the waist as a kind of ornament.

otole *n* a painless soft swelling at the joints and prominent bony parts where pressure is likely to occur, *bursa*, the swelling is caused by continuous pressure.

otole *n* war dance, where people dance with spears and shield.

oton *n* scorpion; see **it.**

oton *n* trigger, cock; **oton me luduko,** a cock of a gun.

oton *vt* annoyed and angererd; **cwinynye oton mada i kommi,** he was very much annoyed with you, see **ton.**

oton-ton *n* tsetse fly; it is the fly that transmits sleeping sickness disease, *trypanosomiasis*

otto dano *vt* asking people to come for special purpose such as for hunting, for dancing, for war, for communal work in one's field etc. see **dwareti.**

otuk *vt* 1 he has flown away. 2 got loosen, trap came out; **kwakala ma gicikko me makko oyoo otuk woko ma ononyo oyoo pudi pekke,** the trap sat did not catch the rat, because it came off before the rat was there; **en doŋ otuk ocitto woko,** he has already flown away, see **tud.**

otul *n* drain, culvert, gutter, channel, **waŋ otul,** drain, channel.

otuur *adv* she has reached puberty;

nyaani doŋ otuur, this girl has now reahed puberty as characterized by her having monthly bleeding per vagina, that is, having monthly menstruation; c/f **ocot** in male; see **opoŋ, opit, otik,** see **twur. otwaŋ** *n* big narrow; **awal otwaŋ**, a big narrow calabash bowl for beer.

otwaŋ *n* big fish which has feelers on its mouth.

otweŋ *n* elbow; **otole i otweŋŋe,** there is a bursa on his elbow; **otale lot i oteŋ,** the bush developed in the elbou.

otwilo *n* kind of shrub full of thorns all over; it is burnt by women for it's alkaline salt or lye which is obtained from the ashes. It is usually cultivated. (*Hygrophila spinosa*).

otwol kot *n* earthworm.

otwoŋ koŋo *n* the same as **otwaŋ koŋo,** the former is better. **awal otwoŋ** *n* very small gourd bowel, used for ceremony, e.g. **me goyo taŋa,** for blessing arms for / good luck for hunting or fighting.

otwoŋo *n* grasshoppers; **awiny awiny, apededede, labaa, lakaibona, ajot jot, obaŋ cet, ocene ka bonyo**

otyeno *adv* evening; **obinno otyeno,** he came in the evening.

ouya *vn* it choked me; **piine ouya,** the water chocked me, see **uya.**

owaa *n* a fatal cattle disease affecting liver and bile, see **oree.**

owaca *prd* watery, spongy and rotten; **tyaŋŋe owaca,** the sugarcane is spongy, it has no juice and not sweet.

owacca *vt* he told me; **owacca ni en diki ebibino,** he told me that he will be coming tomorrow, see **wac, wacca.**

owaŋo *n* saddle-billed stork. (bird), some people call this **arum.**

owelu *n* crested crane or the crown bird, symbol of Uganda.

owelo *n* a high stemmed red flower, its tuberous root and leaves are used as medicine for enlarged spleen.

owic *n* small string trap for rats; see **layutta, odiŋ.**

owir pii *n* water spider.

owoo *n* leaf of borassus palm; **owoo tugo, goŋo owoo,** borassus palm leaves.

Owor *n* male name. *Lit* means born at night.

owor *n* . glutton, greedy, miser; **danne owor mada, cammo mere kene,** the man is very greedy, he eats alone, see **wor**.

oya *inj* exclamation of surprise, grief. **oya! latin mene ma okonynye kanynyi.?** alas! which child has defaecated here?

oyado *n* a plant *(cassin tora)* which is used as hedge, it's stem is very good for brushing teeth, the pulp covering seeds are eatable, it's seeds are used against scabies.

oyala *n* kind of white ants (termites) which swarms out about 5-6 p.m. see **ŋwen.**

oyee *vt* he has accepted or agreed; **oyee ni ebibino,** he accepted that he will come, see **yee.**

oyeŋ yeŋ *n* earthquake; **oyeŋ yeŋ otimme i Toro ma oturro odi madwoŋ mada kuno,** the earthquake took place in Toro and broke down many houses there; see **deer, otira.**

oyer *n* plant with edible bulb.

oyima *n* big black caterpillar of (butterfly)

oyo *vt* 1 to warm oneself. **oyo mac,** warming oneself at the fire; o**yo ceŋ, oyo nyaŋo,** warming oneself at, sun and morning sun.

oyo *vt* pouring, watering; **oyo pii i poto gin anena / ature,** pouring or watering the flower garden; see **oo, oc.**

oyo *vt* pouring, spilling out, throwing out. **oyo yugi,** throwing out rubbish.

oyo *vn* aborting; **oyo ic,** committing abortion.

oyolo *n* kind of beads.

oyoo n a mouse, rat; **oyoo ŋuu,** kind of shrew mice, has sharp pointed mouth; **oyoo adeŋ,** mouse, **oyoo ot me nino ducu,** rat; but there are bigger ones called *ratus ratus* which are responsible for carrying fleas which in turn responsible for the plagues.

oyoro *n* a tree which is made into horns.

oyoro *n* mane, long hair on head, neck as that of lion, back of sheep, hog.

oyot or **oyot-oyot** adv quick or quickly; **bin oyot oyot,** come quickly.

oyoyo mac *n* a black caterpillar with stiff hair which when touched causes strong burning pain and soreness.

oyutte-yutte *prd* at some distance from each other; **gaŋŋe doki tye oyutte yutte ki Kampala,** his home is some distance from Kampala.

oywec got *n* grass used for broom which are normally obtained from the mountanuos area.

oywec *n* broom. **oywec laywee ot,** broom for sweeping the house.

oywelo *n* a black plum *(Vitex cuneata)*

a big tree which produces black fruits which are edible; it's wood is soft, see **ocuga, oduru, olemo, olok, kano, koŋo ogwal, etc.**

P p

pa *prn* of. **latin pa Okot,** child of **Okot;** it indicates possessive genitive pronouns; when **pa** is placed before a proper noun as *prefix* e.g. **pa-Ayira** it means, of **Ayira,** normally is called **Payira,** one **a** is dropped instead of calling **Pa Ayira,** it is convenient to call it **Payira; Pa Atiko** becomes **Patiko.**

paa *v* make by means of carpentry work; **paa kom ki kitanda piwa,** make some chairs and beds for us; see, **pac, payo.**

paala *n* a red ochre - in the past **paala** was for smearing the girls hair and body

Pabo *n* clan of Acholi 24 miles North of Gulu.

pac *vn* carpentry, making furniture, beds, boxes; see **paa, payo**

pac *n* iron for ironing clothes.

pac *adv¹* sound made by a falling thing on the ground; **opotto ni pac,** it fell heavily with a sound on the ground. **ogoyo wiye woko ni pac,** he hit his head which lacerated it.

pac *n Eng* pass, permission to dissolve the marriage; in the past when a man wants to divorce his wife, he goes to the chief who gives him a letter of divorce and this letter was permission which the Acholi call **pac.**

pac *adv* partially shaved; **wii latin obutto ni pac pien pe gilyello otum,** the child's hair remained partially shaved because it was not completely done.

pac *vn* to be rubbed off; **tyen latin pac woko ka woto i ŋom malyet,** the child's foot becomes lacerated easily when he/she walks in a hot ground; **kin cekke opac woko ka wot,** skin between her thighs (inner side) is lacerated because of rubbing each other during walking;

pac-pac *adv* falling along; **owotto ki ooyo nyuka ni pac pac i dye ot,** he went on pouring the porridge along the floor.

pacco *vt* 1 taking up with hand a large amount; **pacco dek,** taking a good amount of food with fingers;

pacco *vt* peeling off; **pacco apoka yat,** peeling off the bark or a rind of a tree; 2 **ocubbo opacco apacca,** he speared it superficially. see **pokko, banynyo, wanynyo.**

paco *n* a home, village.

pad *v* flatten, mould; **pad lobo me cweyo agulu,** mould a flat clay which will be folded to make a pot.

padde *vi* can be folded; **lobone ber twerro padde me agulu,** the clay is good therefore it can be made or moulded for making pots.

paddo *vt* to flatten / flattening, to mould / moulding; **opaddo lobo me cweyo agulu,** he has flattened or moulded clay for making pots; **kel yat ma apadda me paddo lobo,** bring the flat wood for moulding the clay.

pado *n* fragment; **pado agulu, agwata etc.** fragments of broken pots, gourd etc.

pagi *n* main or chief; **pagi wir ot,** the chief or the main pole supporting the roof of the hut (round hut) i.e. the centre pole, see **wir.**

pai pai *n Eng.* paw paw. some call it
papai.

paipo *Eng n* a pipe.

Paito *n* a male name.

pak *vt* 1 praise; **pak Lubaŋa,** praise God.
nyiŋ pak, pet name, given to cattle,
girls, and women; in Bunyoro and Toro
it is given to both male and female.

pak *v* 1 sharpen; **pak lak paala man
ma bit,** sharpen the edge of this knife
very well. 2 sharpen; **pak lyedi,** whet or
sharpen the razor;

pakapaka *prd* large, broad; **latinne doki
itte obeddo pakapaka calo it olik,** the
child has very large ears like those of
bats, bat ears.

pakke *vi* can be made sharp or can
be sharpened; **lak paala man twerro
pakke maber mada;** the edge of this
knife can be sharpened very well.

pakko *vt* 1 to praise / praising, to adore
/ adoring, to extol / extolling; **pakko
Lubaŋa,** to praise / praising God. 2
pakko lyedi, to sharpen / sharpening,
whetts / whetting.

pal *prd* 1 emaciated, wasted, grown very
thin; **Okot doŋ tye ka pal apalla,**
Okot is getting thin and thin or Okot is
becoming more and more emaciated.

pal *v* slap; **pal lemme,** slap his cheek.

palaa *n* knife; **palaama lakke oluu nyo
oligo,** the edge of the knife is blunt / the
knife that is blunt.

pal cwiny *n* upper part of the abdomen
next to the angle where the ribs meet.
(epigastrium)

Palaro *n* a clan of Acholi N. East of Gulu
7 km.

pal gwok *n* shoulder; **tiŋ yen i wii
pal gwokki,** carry the wood on your
shoulder.

pali *n Lug* a trouser; **pali macek,** a pair
of short trousers; **pali mabor,** a pair of
long trousers, see **curuwal, ramatol.**

palle *vi¹* being elusive, taking another
direction, **dano ne marro palle mada,**
the man likes very much to be elusive; 2
waŋŋe opalle, he has got squint or has
cross eyes.

pal-pal *adj* brightly shining, beaming;
**dero ceŋ ma i kom madara ryeny
ni pal-pal,** the reflection of the sun's
rays from the mirror is dazzling or
blindfolding because of it's brightness.

pallo *vt* to slapp, **pallo lem dano,** slaps
a man's cheek with a hand (while **doŋŋo
lem dano** is boxing a man's cheek).

pallo *vt* gesticulate or move from side to
side; **pallo kwot,** gesticulating with the
shields as in fighting so that it glitters.

pallo *vt* blindfolding; **ceŋ pallo waŋŋe,**
the sun is blindfolding him or dazzling
him by it's bright shinning.

pam *n* a molar tooth; **pam lakke otwii
arii ci omiyo tye ka yelle ki arem,** his
molar tooth grew out across and that is
why it is troubling him with pain.

pam *v* plaster, add; **pam kom ot man ki
lobo,** plaster the walls of this house with
clay.

pama *s n* old name for cotton, **pamba,** is
now the new name for cotton.

Paminyai *n* locality about 11 kilometre
west of Gulu.

pammo *vt* to add / adding, side by side
or piling one on top of another; **pammo
lobo me ot,** to pile / piling up clay or
earth for building the hut; **pammo
lobo i kom ot,** to plaster / plastering the
house with the clay.

pamme *vi* united; **wucit ma kapamme
kacel,** go to unite.

pan *v* hide, conceal; **pan bukki woko kama dano mo pe twerro noŋŋone,** hide this book in a place where nobody can find it.

panne *vi* to hide / hiding, be hidden; **tye ka panne i ot,** he is hiding in the house; **panne doŋ apanna ki dano,** he avoids people.

panno *vt* to hide / hiding, to conceal / concealing, to keep / keeping secret; **en ŋeyo panno buk me lok ma pigi tek,** he knows how to hide away classified matters.

paŋ *v* turn aside, divert; **paŋ wiye woko,** turn him away.

paŋŋe *vi* 1 turning aside, diverting, **wii litino ma tino twerro paŋŋe oyot mada,** the mind of young children can easily be turned away; 2 being hopeless and roaming about; **tye ka paŋŋe ata,** he is just roaming about aimlessly with no job.

paŋŋo *vt* to turn off, diverting; 1 **paŋŋo wii mutokane woko ki i yoo matir,** turns off his car from the straight road; 2 diverting; **paŋŋo wii latin woko ki i kom dini,** diverting the child away from religion; 3 changed; **oo ki i court ci opaŋŋo dogge woko, i**n the court he changed his statements; **paŋŋo odilo,** to dodge / dodging the football.

paŋ-paŋ *adv* 1 walking aimlessly and does not know what to do; **latin pa ŋadi tye ka mal ni paŋ-paŋ i Kampala pe tye gin ma myero otii,** so and so's child is walking about aimlessly in Kampala and has no work to do.

pany *n* a mortar; **pany en aye gin me oddo bel, pany** is a motar for pounding cereals; **kal gioddo i pany,** millet is pounded in the motar.

Panyagira *n* a sub-clan of Patiko.

panyaka *adv* **nyo ni punyoko.** well nourished.

panycura *n* old name for Police of local administration (local government).

pany-pany *adv[1]* walks heavily with sound of foot on the ground (fat people).

pao pao *adj* very light = **yot ni pao pao.**

pao pao *adv* walking quickly and briskly (of a healthy person); **amarro dano ma wotto ni pao pao,** I like people who walk quickly and briskly.

pap *adv.* sound of a crack, smash, bang; **odilo omwoc ni pap,** the ball burst with a bang.

pap *n* side of;not commonly spoken.

pap got side of a mountain, c/f **tee got.**

pappe *vi* to flap / flapping the wings about (of a dying fowl or in danger). **gweno pappe katoo -** a chicken flaps its wings when dying.

par *n* . pondering, reflection; meditation, sorrow; **par pi latinne ma orweny tye ka nekke woko,** the sorrow for the loss of his child is killing him.

par *n s* empty cartridge; **lwak par tye kany mada,** there are many empty catridges here

par *v* think, meditate, consider, ponder; **par mada pi lok ma gitito i kanica,** ponder and meditate seriouely about what was preached in the church.

Paranca *n* **France; jo Paranca cammo opuk,** the France people eat tortoise.

parat *n* old name for **lukille,** ornamental axe carried on the shoulder.

parro *vi* to meditate / meditating, to worry / worrying, to mourn / mourning for or at; **parro mada gin aŋoo ma myero etim,** meditates / meditating very much as to what he hould do; 2 **parro mada pi rwenyo latinne,** mourns / mourning very much for the loss of his child; 3 worry about something; **parro mada ka latin tye ka kwan maber;** worries / worrying very much if the child is studying well. 4 cares, **pe parro,** he cares less

par tyen *n* back of a foot

pat *adj* different, separate, distinct; **kikopo man pat ki kikopo maca,** this cup is different from the other one there.

pat *adv* completely, perfectly; **ŋeyo ni pat nyo ŋeyo li weŋ,** he knows it all very well.

pata *n* flat rock on the ground, where women usually take their millet or sorghum to spread so as to make them dry; **mon guterro kalgi i wii pata ka twoo iye,** the women took their millet to the flat rock to dry them there; **anyira gitye ka dinno bel i wii pata,** the girls are threshing their millet on the flat rock.

pata *n s* door hinges, pieces of metal which hold the door and on which the door swings.

pata-pata *adv* dragging hurriedly all along; **giterre ni pata pata,** he was or taken hurriedy. see **kaba-kaba.**

patic *n Eng* puttee (a long band of cloth wound round the leg from ankle to the knee used to be worn by the Police of those days.

pat-pat *adj/adv* of different type, differently; **warre ducu pat pat,** all the shoes were different or it can be said **warre ducu ma kitgi pat pat,** all the show were of different type,

patte *vn* stuck, fixed; **odok opatte i kom boŋo;** the glue sticks on the clothe.

patto *vt* to throw / throwing mud; **gitye ka patto kom ot ki lobo,** they are building the house by throwing the mud or clay to cover the frabicated house; see **rwatto.**

Patiko *n* clan of Acholi living around Mt. **Ajulu.**

Pawel *n* clan of Acholi, 28 miles north of Gulu.

paya *n* channel or river bed - dry.

payi payi *n* same as **pai pai** = paw paw.

Payira *n* a big clan of Acholi living at **Awac , Atanga** and **Anaka.**

payo *vt* to trim / trimming, to whitle / whittling, to dress / dressing, further make smoother; **payo kom obwol,** he whittes the small round stool; see **paa, pac.**

pe *intj* no but when emphasis is needed then it could be written as **pee;** e.g. **pee kumeno,** no not like that

pec *vi* 1 act of pulling, dragging; **gitye i pec me dyaŋi,** they are in the act of pulling the cattle, this is not commonly spoken. 2 plentiful; **dyaŋi tye ma gupec kany mada,** the cattle are very plentiful here; see **pee, peyo.**

peca *n* old copper coin (used for cents).

ped *vt* open wide; **ped i recce wek otwoo,** open the fish widely to make it dry.

peda *n* large dry flat piece of something; **peda rec, kic, riŋo etc,** open dry fish, honeycomb, meat etc.

pedde *vi* can be opened widely; **rec man twerro pedde maber mada,** the fish can be cut and opened widely.

peddo *vt/vn* cutting and opening wide like open book.

peddo *vt* to open widely; **peddo**

ŋwinynye, she exposes her private parts, anyhow **dello, deŋŋo, danynyo waŋ**.

pee *n* hailstone; **kotte cweer ki pee**, it is raining with hailstones.

pee *v* pull along, drag; **pee dyel iter kama ginekko iye dyel**, pull along the goat to the slaughter house; see **pec, peyo.** *c/f* **ywaa.**

pee *intj* lazy; **komme pee**, he is lazy.

pee *intj* no no; **dek pee**, no there is no food. food

pek *adj* 1 heavy to carry. 2 Dense or thick; **guniya kado ne pek mada**, the salt bag is very heavy. 2 **nyukane pek pe matte**, the porridge is too thick, it cannot be drunk. 3 **dogge pek ka lok**, he cannot speak (*lit*. his mouth is heavy to speak). 4 **wiye pek**, he is slow in understanding, or taking action to do something; 5 **waŋŋe pek,** *fig*, he looks fierce, or has forbidding look, charismatic look. 6 **kome pek**-she is pregnant.

peki *n* provisions for safari such as roasted groundnuts, simsim and cow peas etc. **peki pul, nyim, ŋor** etc.

pe larre *adj* very, excellent; **gin marac mape larre**, a very bad thing indeed.

pelle *prd*. restless, young unruly child; **latin man lapelle mada**, this is a restless and unruly child; see **taŋgalo, tati, toŋtwe, abelu, gama; pelle okello, goc**, restless brought to him beating.

pel-pel *adv* quite small and light; **dakone doŋ pel pel mada**, the woman is very thin or his wife is very thin or much wasted.

pem *n* a bridge; **motoka opotto woko ki i wii pem pien pe gigerro maber**, the motor car fell off the bridge because the bridge was not well constructed.

pen *n* navel, umbilicus; **pen litino lukere ma gitweyo terro nino abic kadoŋ potto**, it takes five days for the stump of the neonate's umbilicus which was tied to fall off.

pen *prep* succeeding, being lucky; **ŋaa ma tin pen ki jubi**, who will be lucky to kill the buffalo? **open woko ki jubi tin ka dwar**, was lucky, he killed a buffalo for the first time; **jubi ma ginekkoni en open mere ki em**, he is lucky he got the thigh from the bufallo killed.

peny *n* questions, inquiry, interrogation; **litino gitye ka peny**, the children are in examinations.

peny *v* ask, question; **peny ka latin ŋeyo**, ask or question whether the child knows.

penynye *n* 1 the question; **penynye onoŋo pe atir**, the question was not right; 2 interrogated, questioned; **gupenynye mada**, they questioned or interrogated him very much.

penynyo *vt* to ask / asking, to question / questioning, to inqure / inquiring, to interrogate / interrogating; **ŋaa matye ka penynyo lakwooni?** who is interrogating the thief? **gupenynyo Okullo twatwal kace onoŋo ŋeyo gin ma otimme**, they interrogated Okullo thoroughly if he knew what happened.

pentikocte, *n* pentecost, the day when the holy spirit descended on the apostles of Jesus.

pep *adv* suddenly, unexpectedly; **otuc woko ni pep**, he appeared suddenly or arrived unexpectedly.

per *adv* talks too much; **per lok ki lacoone.** talk alot to the man; **lacoone laper lok mada**, the man talks too much.

pere-pere *adj* thinly, **guyarro belle i kolo pere pere wek otwoo oyot,** they spread the corn thinly on the papyrus mat to make it dry quickly.

pero *n* platform for drying corn etc. **terru kaal wii perro ka twoo iye,** take millet to the platform for drying there.

perre *adj* wide; **itte operre calo it olik,** his ears are wide as bat's ears.

perro *vt* to talk / talking too much; **obeddo ka perro lok owekko dek owaŋ woko i keno;** she was talking too much and left the food to burn.

pet *v* 1 spread; **pet pyen me beddo,** spread a hide for sitting on; 2 prepare; **pet kitanda me butto,** prepare the bed for sleeping, in other words spread the sheets and blanket on the bed for sleeping; 3 roaming about; **lapet piny nyo apetti,** a vagabond, a person who roams about aimlessly.

pette *vi* can be spread; **cukane twerro pette i wii kitanda,** the sheet can be spread on the bed.

petto *vt* to spread on the ground or something; **tye ka petto kolo me beddo ki welo,** she is spreading the papyrus mat for the visitors to sit on; **petto piny** *vt* roaming about; **tye ka petto piny pudi,** he is still roaming about.

peyo *vt* to trail, drag, draw behind with force or simply leading; **peyo dyaŋ ki uno,** trails a cow by means of a rope; **peyo lawaŋŋe otoo,** leads the blind man; see **pee, pec.**

pi *prp* on account of, the purpose of. **pi ŋoo?, pi lok aŋoo?** why? **pi aŋaa?** on whose account or on account of whom?

pi *n* concerning, affair, news about, for; **pi ladit kanica oywek kany mada,** the news about the clergy is well known here; **pi cakko nyiŋ i kanica mit mada,** for being baptized in the church is very much liked; **obinno pi lok moni ma otimme kanynyi,** he came for the trouble that has taken place here.

pic *vn* instigation, incitement, goad; **pic nac,** instigation is very bad. **en lapic mada,** he is the one that always incites or istigates fighting; see **pii, piyo**

pid, *v* plead, take case to court of law; **pid matek pi jamini ma giyakkoni,** plead seriously to the court for your things which were looted.

pida *n Eng* public works department, a distortion of p.w.d.

pidde *vi* can be pleaded for, can be taken to court; **lokke pe pidde i kot,** the matter cannot be settled in court or the case cannot be taken to court.

piddo *vt* to plead / pleading for a case, to advocate / advocating; **tye ka piddo i kot pi lawotte,** he is pleading in court for his friend; 1 **piddo banya,** asking for the debt to be paid; 2 **piddo banya i kot,** suing for payment of the debt before the court.

pig *n* water from; **pig waŋ,** tears; **pig keda,** bile; **pig riŋo,** watery blood from the meat; **pig pwomo, lemun, mucuŋgwa,** juices of passion fruit, lemon, oranges.

pii *v* incite, instigate, **pii litino ka lweny,** incite the children to fight **pe ipii litino ka lweny,** don't incite the children to fight.

pii *v* mix by stirring; **pii dek wek gicam,** mix the sauce (usually with simsim) so that it may be eaten.

pii *v* make fire by drilling or turning

round a stick at a high speed on a partcular wood, e.g. **pii mac i kom yat man,** make fire by drilling this wood (as explained above); see **pic** and **piyo.**

pii *n* water; **kel pii me amatta,** bring some water for drinkung.

pik *v* fill; **pik pii i agulo me amatta,** fill the pot with water for drinking; **pik pii i cupa,** fill the bottle with water; **pik tyen leela,** pump the bicycle tyre.

pikke *vi.* can be filled, can be closely planted, too big; **iye opikke,** he has a big abdomen; **cukari twerro pikke i kicaa man,** the sugar can be filled in

this bag; **anyogine gipitto opikke woko,** the maize was too closely planted.

piki-piki *n* motor cycle.

pikko *vt* 1 filling; **pikko latin ki cam pe ber,** stuffing the child with food is not good. 2 **pikko tyen leela,** pumping the bicycle tyre. 3 filling; **pikko pii i agulo me amatta,** filling the pot with water for drinking. 4 planting closely; **pe ber ka itye ka pitto pamba me pikko gi kacel twatwal,** it is not good to plant the cotton too closely.

pil *v* honour, respect; **pil wii worru,** give due respect and honour to your father.

pil *adv.*1 flashing; **kot ryeny ci wil ni pil,** lightning shines and flashes brightly.

pil *adv* passing through; **ocubbo lee toŋ okatto pil,** he speared the animal and the spear passed through the body.

pil *vn* arrogance, insolent to people; **litino man wigi pil mada i kom dano,** these children are very arrogant to the people.

pili *adv* completely, absolutely; **otum woko ni pili,** it is finished completely.

pilida *n Eng* pleader, one who pleads for a person in a court of law, a lawyer; **acitto bot pilidana wek okonya ki piddo,** I went to my pleader to help me with my case.

pille *vi* emerge, appear; **lakwoo opotto i kulu ci orweny woko, lacen doŋ opille wa loka tuŋ caa,** the thief fell into the water and disappeared, later he emerged on the other side of the river; 2 **lakwoo pille apilla i ot ka kwoo,** the thief was moving about freely in the house stealling.

pillo *vt* to polish / polishing, to make / making smooth and bright, **lillo** is much used than **pillo** both mean the same.

pillo *vt* 1 to be / being over indulgence with, spoil, pamper; **pillo wii latin nyo wii dako,** spoiling by over indulgence a child or the wife. 2 to recognise / recognising the importance of action or people by welcoming with ululation of happiness or with something; **gupillo wii awobe ma guloyo mupira ki kijira,** they welcomed the boys who, were victorious in the football match with ululation of joy. 3 honour; **wonne opillo wiye ki dyel i kare ma okatto peny.** his father honoured him by killing a goat when he passed his examinations.

pil macul *n Eng* field marshall, the highest military rank in the army, in infantry; the hierachy of the military rank is as follows; second lieutenant, lieutenant, captain, major, lieutenant colonel, colonel, brigadier, brigadier general, major general, lieutenant general, general, field marshall in the infantry.

pim *adv* in great quantity; **obakke ni pim,** it is heaped up or assembled in mass.

pim *v* 1 measure; **pim borre,** measure it's length;

pim *v* 2 aim; **pim maber ka wek icel,** aim well so that you may shoot.

pimme *vi* can be measured; **bor pa boŋone twerro pimme,** the length of the cloth can be measured.

pimmo *vt¹* to measure / measuring; **pimmo bor me waŋ lobo meegi,** to measure / measuring the boundaries of their land.

pimmo *vn* to aim / aiming; **pimmo lee ki luduku,** aiming at the animal with the gun.

pino *n* a hornet, wasp; **kac pa pino kec mada,** the stings of the hornet is very painful.

piny *n* 1. climate, weather; **piny lyet,** the weather is hot; **piny cwir,** rainy season; **piny oro,** dry season; 2 **piny oruu,** it is dawn; **kwar piny,** morning glow; **piny tin dyewor obuto mel,** it did not rain last night; **piny tin muttu,** therer is no moon shine today.

piny *adv* down, on ground; **bed piny,** sit down; **bed piny i ŋom,** sit down on the ground.

piny *n* ground; **piny pud dyak,** the ground is still wet.

piny ic *n* part of the body, the lower part of the belly or abdomen.

piny cwir *n* a black king fisher (bird).

pip *adv.* heavily (sound); **tugu potto ni pip,** the borassus palm fruit falls heavily to the ground.

pipa *S n* a barrel.

piir *adv* rashly saying. **lapoti piir,** rash imitator or rash counterfeiter - does not succeed.

piir *v* conspire, plot against, plan; **piir lok me makke,** plan to arrest him.

piir *v¹* fill up to the brim; **piir pii poŋ i agulu man,** fill this pot with water full to the brim; to fly / flying off, **winyo otuk woko ni piir,** the bird flew off

piirro *vt* 1 to fill / filling up to the brim; **opiirro nyim poŋ dero,** he filled up the barn up to it's brim / **piimo nyim poŋ dero** to fill up the granary with simsim up to its bim .

piirro *vt* to level / levelling, to make / making even the ground, road; **piirro yoo gudo,** levelling the road.

piirro *vt* to conspire / conspiring, to plot / plotting against; **gupiirro lok i komme,** they conspired or plotted against him; **piiro lok i kom daro ke bec,** plotting against the people is not good.

piri piri *adv* 1 flickering brightly; **odiko ma ceŋ pud katti ni piri-piri,** in the morning while the rising sun's rays was still flickering brightly.

piri piri *adv* flying all over; **bonyo tye ka tuk ni piri piri,** the locust are flying all over around; **dano gitye ka riŋŋo ni piri piri,** people are running away quickly; **lapwopwo gitye ka tuk ni piri piri,** the butterflies are flying all over around.

pit *v* 1 feed; **pit latin ki cak,** feed the child with milk; 2 plant; **pit yat,** plant the tree.

pit *adv.* unnoticed, unobserved; **Owot okatto woko li pit,** Owot disappeared unnoticed from here, or Owot went out unnoticed from here.

pit *n* feeding; upbringing; **pit tek mada,** feeding is very difficult, (costly).

piti *n* old overfilled waste heap, small sized hill, old rubbish heap

piti-piti *adv.* sound of feet of running people, **dano giriŋo ni piti-piti,** people running with quick movement of feet making noises on the ground

pit-pit *prd* covetous, longing for anything one sees, lustful, **waŋŋe beddo ni pit-pit. pit pit waŋ,** looking at thigns with great desire, lustful.

pitte *vi* can be planted, be fed; **anyogi twerro pitte kany,** the maize can be planted here; **gweni ni twerro pitte ki nyim,** the chicken can be fed with simsim

pitto *vt* 1 to plant / planting; **pitto yadi,** planting trees; 2 set up; **pitto gutti me gerro ot,** setting up wood for building (this is spoken by some people West of Gulu); the central people say **commo gutti me gerro ot.** 3 rear, breed (cattle); **pitto gweno ki pitto dyaŋ,** rear chicken and breeding cattle; 4 feeding children, nourishing baby, bringing up children; **pitto litino ki pitto latin lakere,** feeding the children and bringing them up and nourishing the baby.

pittu *vn/prd* having reached full puberty; being fully grown up; **nyakoni doŋ opittu,** this girl is now fully grown up (and having menses); **pittu,** is spoken of girls only; see **tik nyo otik, poŋ.**

piyo, piyo-piyo *adv* quickly, swiftly; see **oyot oyot** which is more commonly used now than **piyo-piyo** which should actually be **opiyo-piyo.**

piyo *vt* 1 persuading, urging, inducing or inciting one to; **ginpiyo latin caa ni ogoo lawotte,** they persuaded or incite the other child to beat his friend; **piyo me matto taa,** to persuade / persuading, to induce / inducing to smoke.

piyo *vt* 1 To bore / boring, to drill / drilling something; **piyo lapii wek mac**

opotti, to turn / turning the wood drill at high speed in a hole in the wood so that fire may be produced from it.

piyo *vn* stirring with a pestle; **piyo dek,** stirring the sauce with a pestle; see **pii, pic.**

poc *vn* remembering, recalling, recollecting; not normally spoken. see **poo, poyo.**

pogo (lak lyec) *n* ivory armlet.

poi or poyo *n* 1 youths of about sixteen; 2 **poyo gweno,** a well growing, middle sized fowls; all these words now archaic; see **awiya, bulu**

pok *adv* broad and wide; **yoo ocitto ni pok,** the road has gone on very wide and broad

pok *adv* sitting down anyhow, regardless of decency or propriety of the place; **obeddo ni pok,** he sat anyhow regardless of decency.

pok *n* bark of a tree, rind of fruits; scales of fishes, snakes, tortoises, pangolin; shell or husks of groundnuts, shea butter nuts etc.

pok *v* debark, peel; **pok kom yat man,** debark this tree, see **bany, wany.**

pok. *v* divide, separate, distribute; **pok dyel ki dyaŋi pat pat,** separate the goats from the cows; **pok kin joo ma gitye ka lweny,** separate the people who are fighting; **pok cam,** distribute the food.

pokke *vi vn* 1 *vn* separation, division; **pokke pa dano oa pi larro ŋom,** separation of the people (into tribes) came beause of the struggle for land; 2 *vi* can be divided; **cukari man twerro pokke ma rommo dano maber;** this sugar can be divided equally enough for every body.

217

pokko *vt* to give / giving, to seperate / separating, to divide / dividing up; **pokko gin man pe tek,** dividing this thing is not difficult or to distribute / distributing this thing is not difficult; **in pe iŋeyo pokko dano ki aryo aryo?** don't you know how to divide people in twos? **pokko dyel macol kikom matar,** separating black goats from the white ones; **pokko cam ki dano,** distributing food to the people.

pokko *vt* peel / peeling, to debark / debarking (tree); **pokko tol yat,** debarking the tree for it's fibre, **pokko labolo,** to remove / removing the rind of banana or peeling the rind of banana before eating; see **banynyo, wanynyo, daŋŋo.**

pol *adj* many, numerous; **jamine pol mada,** he has many things; **lok doŋ pol kany twatwal,** there are two many problems here

pol *n* meat part of the chest with foreleg = **pol bat.**

pol *n* clouds; **pol oummo waŋ ceŋ woko,** the clouds have hidden the sun.

polic *n Eng* a police; **polic gitye ka dorre,** the police are marching.

politik *n Eng* politics; **Godfrey doŋ owekko pwony woko odonynyo i politik,** Godfrey has left teaching and has joined polilitics.

polo *n* sky, heaven; **Lubaŋa tye i wii polo,** God is in heaven.

poŋ *v* fill up, make full; **poŋ kicaa man ki nyim,** fill this sack with simsim; *vi* **dano tin gupoŋ mada i bar,** the people filled up the field today.

poŋ *adv* fully grown, mature; **nyaanne doŋ opoŋ,** the girl is now fully grown up and mature; see **pittu, tik.**

poŋŋe *vi* sneaking about, pretending that one does not want yet one wants; **latinni tye ka poŋŋe mere nono ni pe emitto cam kun kono mitto,** this child is pretending that he does not want to eat and yet he wants to eat.

poŋŋo *vt* to fill / filling up, to make / making full; **poŋŋo wii pii ma orem,** filling up the water which is not yet full.

pony *n* a small hole or pit; **pony ŋwen,** small hole made at the foot of the termite hill where the white ants come and fall and from where they are then collected.

pony-pony *prd* uneven ground full of holes or cavities; **yoo matye pony pony,** the road which is uneven, full of pot holes.

poo *v* recall, remember, call to mind, recollect; **poo lok ma giwacci,** remember or recall what you have been told.; **poo wiye,** remind him.

poo *vn* startled, alarmed at; **latin opoo matek ki mwoc pa luduko,** the child gets startled by the shots of the gun. **latinni dok poo atata, atamoni komme lit,** this child startles very frequently, I think he is sick.

poo *vn* being mad; **lacooni doŋ cok ka poo woko,** the man is becoming mad; see **poc, poyo.**

poor *vn* elopement of a girl to her boy friend; **Akelo tin opoor woko,** Akelo has eloped today **Akelo mitto poor woko,** Akelo wants to elope.

poor *v* measure; **poor bor pa yatte,** measure the length of the pole.

poore *vi* can be measured; **bor pa gudone**

twerro poorre, the length of the road can be measured.

poorro vn 1 to elope /running away to a boy friend; 2 a man eloping away with a girl in order to marry her; **Otto opoorro nyako maber mada,** Otto has eloped with a beautiful girl; **poorro nyako,** eloping with a girl.

poorro vt 1 to try / trying; **mitto poorro boŋo ka romme,** wants to try the clothes if they fit him. 2 to compare; **mitto poorro war aryoni wek ekwany iye acel maber,** wants to compare the two shoes in order to take one of them. 3 to copy / copying, imitate / imitating; **poorro kit yoo ma ŋati mo timmo kwede,** copying or imitating the way how one does it. 4 **poorro gudo,** to measure / measuring the road; 5 pretend; **poorro twoo,** to pretend / pretending illness. 6 to discuss / discussing, to inform / informing, to narrate / narrating; **poorro lok ki laremme pi pekko matye kwede,** to discuss, inform or narrate the problem he has to his friend. 7 make plan; **opoorro ka odde laworo,** he made a plan for his house yesterday.

porre vi being perfect, complete, holy; **joo ma guporre,** the holy people, saints.

pot n leaf, foliage; **pot yat,** leaf; **pot oboke,** leaves of sprig.

pot v fall down; **pot piny,** fall down.

poto n field, garden, cultivated ground; **Lapene tye i poto ka doo,** Lapene is weeding in the field.

potte adj it's leaves. **pe amitto nyig malakwaŋ nyo kono potte keken,** I do not like the seeds of **malakwaŋ,** except it's leaves only.

potto vn 1 to fall / falling down, to tumble / tumbling, droping; **ladit ka potto pe ber,** it is not good for an elderly person to fall; 2 to break / breaking out; **mony cok ka potto i kin lobo caa,** the war is very near to break out between those countries. 3 sunset; **ceŋ potto cawa apar wiye aryo,** the sun sets at six.; 4 getting bad; **cak potto woko ka pe gimurro,** the milk coagulates if it is not boiled; 5 abortion; **potto pa iye oa pi twoo,** her abortion came as a result of illness; 6 to fall / falling into danger; **potto i bal,** to fall / falling into sin; 7 concentrated with; **pii potto oduru tworo ka agulone pe gilwokko jwi jwi,** the water becomes filled with concentrated algae if the pot is not frequently washed; 8 to borrow / borrowing; **ocitto ka potto banya bot lureme,** he went to ask for for a loan from his friends; **twoo dobo opotto i komme,** he is infected with leprosy. **potto cim,** he has an epilepsy or he suffers from epilepsy.

poyo vt 1 to remind / reminding one; **poyo wiye pi nino meere me wot,** to remind /reminding him of the day of his journey; **gin ma twerro poyo wiye me coyo waraga diki,** something that will remind him tomorrow to write the letter.

poyo vt startling, frightening; **mwoc pa luduko poyo kom dano,** the burst of the gun shot startles people; see **poo, poc.**

poyo n scar, cicatrices of ulcer.

puc vn plastering, smearing; **pu me kom ot ti pe ber,** their plasting of the walls of the house is not good; see **puu, puyo.**

puc n 1 wart; **Acoli wacci ka iribbo cam ki neru ci puc makki,** Acholi says that if you share food with your uncle, you get warts.

puc *n* 1 fillet (*psoas muscle*); **ladit mitto puc aye gikelle me acamma,** the old man wants fillet which should be brought to him for eating; 2 tendon; **tol aduŋu ki tol naŋa giwiyo puc,** the **aduŋu** girl's music instrument and **naŋa** strings are made of the fascia covering the *psoas muscle.*

pud *v* take a small portion, **pud mugati manok ci imii ki latin,** take a small portion of the bread and give it to the child.

pud *adv* not yet, still; **pud pe otum,** not yet finished.

pude-pude *adv* little at a time or little by little but repeatedly; **cam pude-pudeni kit marac,** eating food little by little is a bad manner; see **akuri akuri**

pudi *adv* not yet, still; **pudi peya ocitto,** not yet gone.

puddo *vt* to take / taking a very small amount; **puddo ŋet mugati manok ka imiyo ki latin pe ber,** to take / taking a small portion of the bread and then to give / giving it to the child is not good.

pugu or pugi *vt* nourishing well, making look well, fat; **latin doŋ tye ka pugu,** the child is gaining weight or putting on weight.

puk *vn* rising very early in the morning; **en puk con mada me citto ka tic,** he rises very early to go to work.

puk *v* pour, put; **puk kado i dek ento pe madwoŋ twatwal,** put some salt into the sauce but not too much.

puk *adv* tightly, hermetically; **olorro dogola li puk,** closed the door tightly.

puk cwiny *n* a violent inclination of passion, temptation urging one to do something.

pukke *vi* urge to do something; **cwinynye pukke me timmo gin mo,** there is a strong impelling feeling which seems to urge him to do something; see **yutte, tiŋŋe, omme cwiny.**

pukke *vn* couching down suddenly, fall down or throw onself down suddenly; **kono nene pe pukke piny kono gicelle woko,** if he did not fall down suddenly, he would have been short.

pukko *vt* 1 to do / doing something violently e.g. *prov.* **agwata matek mac aye pukko,** means a disobedient and stubborn child can be put right by getting the cane.

pukko *vt²* putting more; **pukko kado i dek,** putting excessive salt in the sauce.

pul *n* groundnuts, peanuts.

pule *n* a piece of earth removed from the tomb used by the witches or wizards to throw against somebody to injure him by its magic. (This was the old belief that, a stone or piece of earth from the tomb was dangerous).

pun *n* calf **pun dano,** calf of (a leg of) a man; **pun dano mape cammo maber beddo ma ojwer,** malnourished person has small calves.

pun coo *adv* not properly cooked. **riŋone ocek pun coo,** the meat cooked is not quite soft but firm like a man's calf.

pundi *S n* an artist, specialised worker, artisan; **ter leela bot pundi leela oyubi,** take your bicycle to the bicycle mechanic to repair it; **pundi layub caa tye kwene?** Where is the watch repairer? **pundi motoka,** motor mechanic.

puno *n* a name used by **Jo-pa-Lwo** for pig.

puno *n* a gorilla; **puno wotto ki tyenne**

aryo calo dano, nyonno ŋom ki ŋee ciŋŋe ma omiyo calo gunya, ka tye ka wot calo lee mukene ki tyenne aŋwen, a gorilla walks upright with two legs like human beings, but walks on the backs of the closed fingers like chimpanzee when walking like other animals on four legs; see **gunya, bim.**

punno *vn* cheating; **punno lawotti pe ber,** cheating your friend is not good.

punu *n* 1 a kind of clay with great content of salt where cattle go to leak or scrape with their teeth. 2 grazing place for cattle.

puŋ ŋuŋ *adv* flapping noise made by elephants ears.

puny *adv* noise made by something breaking loose.

puny *n* heel, **puny latin man okak mada,** the child's heel is very much cracked; sometimes called **opuny tyen.**

pur *n* a handle. **pur kweri,** a handle of a hoe; **pur latek,** a pipe's handle; c/f **bol.**

pur *v* cultivate, till the ground; **pur poto maber**, cultivate the field well.

pura *n* a hartebeest; see, **apoli, til,**

Puranga *n* name of Acholi sub-tribe South East of Gulu.

purre *vt* holding somebody suddenly; **lukwoo gupurre gumakko lacoomo ci guyakko jami woko liweŋ ki i komme,** the thieves jumped upon a person suddenly and robbed him of everything. 2 **kit purre me makko dano ni pe ber,** your way of suddenly arresting / holding the people is not good.

purre *n* its handle (of a hoe, a pipe)

puri *vi* grow mouldy; **layata opuri woko,** the potatoes have grown mouldy-rotten.

purro *vt* to till / tilling, to cultivate / cultivating; **gitye ka purro poto caa,** there they are cultivating the field.

puru puru *n* in great number; **winyo beddo ni puru puru ka cammo kaal,** the birds are flying all around eating millet; **lapwopwo gibeddi puru puru i kom ature,** the butterflies are flying all around the flowers.

put *n* malnutrition, under-nourished, weak; **latin put,** a malnourished child or an undernourished child, *kwashiokor.*

put *adv* in great quantity; **oŋollo riŋo ni put,** he cut a large piece of meat.

put *v* uproot, pull up; **put layata woko,** uproot the potatoes.

put-put *adv* **ŋwiddo lok ni put put,** talking persistently; see **ŋwirro lok.**

putte *vi* 1 can be uprooted; **yatte twero putte,** the tree can be uprooted; 2 coming out, **en oputte woko ki i kacokke kuno,** he walked out from the gathering; **oputte ki lok atta mape myero,** he burst out with an uncalled for words; 3 suddenly; **latinne doŋ oputte odoŋŋo odokko awobi,** the child has grown up suddenly to be a boy.

putto *vt* to uproot / uprooting, to pull / pulling up, **putto gwana,** to uproot / uprooting the cassava.

putu putu tyen dyaŋ, *n* roasted lower part of the leg of a cow after the legs have been de-hoofed.

puu *v* plaster, smear; **puu kom ot man tin,** plaster the house today. see **puc, puyo,**

puune *vi* can be plastered; **kom ot man twerro puune maber mada,** the walls of this house can be plastered very well.

puyo *vt* 1 to plaster / plastering, to smear / smearing; **puyo kom ot,** to plaster / plastering the house or to decorate / decorating the house; 2 rulling over; **puyo wii dano,** to rule / ruling over the people; see **puu, puc**

pwaa *v* stir, disturb; **pwaa winyo woko ki i poto kal,** stir or chase the birds off the millet field; **twar** is a better word for it; see **pwayo, pwac.**

pwac *vi* lacerating, abraising; **pwac tyen aa pi yokkone,** laceration of the foot comes as a result of knocking it. **oyokko tyenne ci tyenne opwac woko,** his foot got lacerated by knocking it / he knocked his foot and got lacerated.

pwac *adv* glaring, **kwar ni pwac,** glaringly red; **pac** is preferred to **pwac (kwar ni pac).**

pwaca-pwaca *adv* squelching sound on wet ground or in a watery place.

pwacco *vt* to scrape / scraping, to abrade / abrading, to lacerate / lacerating; **pwacco kom pe ber,** lacerating the body is not good; **lacere opotto ci opwacco coŋŋe,** **lacere** fell and got his knee abraded or lacerated; **pii malyet pwaces kom anno,** hot water lacerates the skin.

pwaka *adj* very wide, broad; **cukane lac ni pwaka,** the sheet is very wide.

pwako *adv* cracking and smacking; **lyec yabbo itte ni pwako,** the elephant open its ears with such noise.

pwa pwa *adv* overflowing with words; **dogge bedi pwa pwa,** his mouth is overflowing with talks.

Pwebwari *n* February, the second months of the year.

pwoc *vn* thankfulness, gratitude, thanksgiving; acknowledgement;

omiinigi pwoc madit pi kony ma gumiine, he thanked them very much for helping him; see **pwoo, pwoyo.**

pwod *v* beat, punish; **pwod latin pi gin ma en oballo,** cane the child for the bad thing he has done; **pwod pa Lubaŋa,** God's punishment.

pwodde *prd* plenty; **kabedo kama cam pwodde iye atta** the place where there is plenty of food; **cam opwodde ata,** there is plenty of food everywhere; **dano gupwodde tin mada,** the people beat themselves very badly today.

pwoddo *vt* beating, strike; **ginpwoddo ŋwiny lukwoo mada ki anino,** the thoroughly do beat the thieves' buttocks with hippopotamus hide.

pwoddo *vt* to drench; **kot tye ka pwoddo dano mada,** people are being drenched thoroughly by rain.

pwomo *n* passion fruits. *(granadilla).*

pwon *v* pluck up, pick up; **pwon mayembe kii kom yatte icam,** pluck up the mangoes from it's tree and eat.

pwonne *vi* can be plucked; **papai ne twerro pwonne,** the pawpaw can be plucked.

pwonno *vt* to pick / picking up, pluck up.

pwony *n* teaching, education, training; **pwony en aye tic maber ma myero dano mapol gukwany,** teaching is the best profession that many people should take.

pwony *v* teach, educate, train; **pwony litino maber,** teach the children well.

pwony *vi* **Otto tye ka pwony,** Otto is teaching.

pwonynye *vn* can be tought, learning; **otira macon pe doŋ gitwerro**

pwonynye, very old people cannot be taught; **pwonynye ber mada** being learned or educated is very good.

pwonynyo *vt* to teach / teaching, to educate / educating, to train / training; **pwonynyo litino maber** teaches the children well; **ŋeyo pwonynyo dano i tic me pac,** he knows training people in carpentry.

pwoo *v* give thanks, show gratitude, **pwoo pi tic maber ma en otiyo,** thank him for his good work; see **pwoc, pwoyo.**

pwoo *v* churn; **pwoo cak,** churn the milk.

pwoone *vi* be pleased, rejoice, be thankful

pwoone *vi* 1 can be churned; **dano tye ka pwoone ki cak mada,** people today are preoccupied with churning milk. 2 **gupwoone tin ki cak mada,** they churned the milk very much today.

pwor *v* sprinkle; put; **pwor kado i dek,** put some salt into the sauce; **pwor mo manok,** give some or give a little.

pworre *vi* can be sprinkled / put a little; **kado twerro pworre,** the salt can be sprinkled / put a little.

pworro *vt* to sprinkle / sprinkling, **pworro kado i dek,** sprinkling / to put a little salt in the sauce.

pwot *adj* 1 slippery; **pwot li lyolyo,** very slippery. 2 viscus; **otigu pwot,** okra or lady fingers is viscus and slimy. 3 smooth; **wii meja gijwayo mapwot mada,** the top of the table has been highly polished and very smooth.

pwot *adj.* slender, and tall, slim; **nyakone bor ci pwot,** the girl is tall and slender **nyako mabor mapwot la iye onat,** a tall slender girl with flat abdomen.

pwot *adj* fine; **moko mapwot,** this is fine flour.

pwotte *adj* 1 it's smoothness; **mokone tika pwot? pe aboŋo ka kit pwotte,** is the flour smooth? no I did not feel it's smoothness; 2 slenderness; **nyakone pwot,? pe aneno ka kit pwotte,** is the girl slender? no I did not notice her slenderness.

pwoyo *n* to churn /churning the milk; **pwoyo cak wek moo opotti,** to churn / churning the milk in order that the butter may form.

pwoyo *vt* 1 to thank / thanking, to like / liking , be pleased with, be thankful; **pwoyo tic ma en otiyo,** to thank / thanking for the good work which he did; 2 to agree / agreeing, to accept / accepting; **apwoyo lok meri ,** I agree with what you said; see **pwoo, pwoc.**

pyee *v* 1 jump from a high place; **pyee piny,** jump down; 2 *n* high and long jump games, **litino gitye ka tukko pyee malo ki pyee piny mabor,** the children are in high jump and long jump games; 3 *v* hop, leap; **pyee kit macalo ogwal pyee kwede,** jump as the frog does, that is hop, leap and hop; 3 *vi* alight and perch; **winyo pyee i wii yat,** birds alight and perch on the trees; 4 settle, calm down; **yamo doŋ opyee,** the wind has calmed down; 5 compose oneself; **ywee wek cwinynyi koŋ opyee,** rest until you have composed yourself; 6 jump from one to another, **pe ipyee apyeya i tic,** do not jump from one work to another.

pyec-pyec *adv* noise caused by whetting or sharpening knife.

pyed *vn* improper behaviour that is contrary to the tradition or custom.

pyeddo *vt.* to behave / behaving improperly, the behaviour that is contrary to the tradition which normally requires sacrificial of a hen, goat or sheep for atonement.

pyel *v* lay down, spread, **pyel latin i wii kitanda,** lay the child on the bed.

pyel *v* pass the stool or defaecate; **pyel kany,** pass the stool here, this is the crude word for it; civilized word for it is, **konynye kany,** help yourself here or ease yourself here.

pyelle *vi* can be laid; **latin twerro pyelle kany;** the child can be laid here.

pyello *vt* to lay / laying down to rest, to spread / spreading on the ground or on something; **pyello latin piny wii kitanda ka nino;** to lay / laying the child on the bed to sleep; **otyekko pyello odwel i dye ot ki welo,** she has already laid down the hides on the ground for the guests.

pyello *vt/vn.* to defaecate / defaecating, to open / opening the bowel, voiding, **gweno pyello i ot,** the chicken pass their droppings in the house. **latin opyello cet wii kabuto,** the child has defaecated on the bed;

pyem *vt/n* 1 protest, objection, disapproval, dispute, competition; contest, competition, **opyem ni en pe labal**, he protested his innocence; **opyem ni pe en aye ma ekwallo,** he objected that he was the one who stole. 2 contest, competition;

pyem *vt/n* 1 **pyem ŋwec, odilo etc;** athletic and football competitions etc. protest, objection, disapproval, dispute, competition; **opyem ni en pe labal,** he protested his innocence; **opyem ni pe en aye ma ekwallo,** he objected that he was the one who stole. 2 contest, competition;

pyen *n* hide on which usually people lie or sit; **pyen jubi yubbe me kwot maber mada,** the buffalo's hide can be made into very good shield.

pyer *n* loin, waist; **dano mogo marro pyer mon ma tino,** some people like women's narrow waist; **pyer ma opete,** gynaecoid pelvis.

pyer *n* number in tens; **pyer-aryo = pyeraryo,** twenty; **pyeradek,** thirty.

pyet *vn* winnow, blow through; **pyet nyim man maleŋ,** winnow this simsim, that is, by turning it round and round in **odero** and then throwing it up, to let the wind blow through it to blow away the chaffs.

pyette *vi* can be winnowed; **kalle twerro pyette,** the millet can be winnowed.

pyette *vi* yearning, desiring; **cwinygi onoŋo tye ka pyette me cammo nyig yat meno,** they were yearning to eat the fruits; central Acoli say, **kee cammo nyig yat meno onoŋo nekkogi mada.**

pyetto *vn* winnowing, **pyetto nyim,** winnowing the simsim.

pyetto *n* winnowing; **pyetto pe gin ma yot ki litino anyira,** winnowing is not an easy thing for the young girls.

R r

raa *n* a hippopotamus.

raa. *n* a bulrush millet (**durra**); a main cereal in Sudan

raa *v* collect, gather; **citti iraa yen matitino ikel me moko mac,** go and collect twigs and bring them for lighting the fire; **rac, rayo.**

raane *vi* can be collected; **jami ma oket**

i dyee ot ata ni twerro raane, things which are scattered all over the floor can be collected. *C/f* cokke,

rab *v* go round; rab ki ŋee ot, go round the house; rab ki ŋet kulu, poto ki gaŋ, go along the river, field's, and outside the home.

raba *adv* exhausted, tired and flabby; ool obutto piny ni raba, he is extremely tired and lied down flabbily.

raba-raba *adv* thinly and sparsely; kot cwer ni raba raba, it rains sparsely and unevenly.

rabbe *vi* going round; yoone wotto rabbe ki i ŋet kanica, the road passes round the church wuwot mot mot ka wuwotto wurabbe ki i ŋet gaŋ, go slowly when walking round the home.

rabbo *vt* to flank / flanking something, to go / going round something; gurabbo dog kulu, they went along the river bank; rabbo tok gaŋ, passing round behind the village; atero orabbo lee arabba, the arrow glances past the game.

rac *adj* bad, ugly, distasteful, wicked; cam man rac, this food; dano ma kitte rac, a bad person; a bad mannered person; a person with bad behaviour etc; lokke rac, his words are bad or the word is bad; dogge rac pe mitto cam, he has no appetite or he does not like food; waar marac, bad shoes are bad.

rac *adv* very. ber marac, very good; bor marac, very far. marac is superalive when 'ma' is joined with rac then it becomes excellent or very good.

rac *vn* gathering, collecting; (not commonly spoken) see raa, rayo.

racac *A n* a bullet.

Racia *n* Russia; dano me Racia yaŋ gubeddo kommwuniciti, the Russian people were at one time communists.

rad *v* 1 throw; rad kom ot ki coka, throw all over the house. 2 kill all; rad oyoo ma gupoŋ i ot tin, kill all the rats today which have filled this house,

radde *adv* 1 scutter all over, gitye ka radde ki lee caa, they are killing there the animals indiscriminately. cok jami ma oradde idyee ot, collect all the things which are scuttered sll over the floor; 2. tin waŋŋi guradde mada ki lee, this time they killed the animals indiscriminately.

raddo *vt* 1 to throw / hrowing all over; raddo lobo i kom ot, throwing mud all over the wall of the house; raddo jami ata i dyee ot, throwing things all over the floor. 2 to do something without consideration; guraddo lee mape wacce; they killed many animals indiscriminately 3 litino guraddo cet kany, the children have defaecated all over here.

raddo *vt* to speak / speaking indiscriminately; raddo lok aradda, speaking indiscriminately and angrily bad words. see rwaddo, datto. nyatto.

rag *v* make roughly, rag latin aduku mo me muyembe, roughly make a basket for the mangoes.

ragaraga *adv* roughly, clumsily, awkwardly; ocweyo adukone ragaraga, he made a rough basket, or coarse basket.

ragge *vn* force oneself on; intrude, obtrude upon; ragge araga i kom dano, forces himself upon the people; oragge araga i komwa ki i kanica, he forced himself upon us in the church.

raggo *vt* to make / making temporarily, to

make / making badly; **raggo dog kika ne aragga,** make the door roughly or clumsily.

raka-raka *prd/adv* quickly, all direction; **gukatto ni raka raka,** they passed quickly in all direction.

raku-raku *adv* with greediness, relish; **orammo riŋo ni raku raku,** he ate the meat with great greediness.

ram *v* eat raw vegetables, meat; **ram letac man ma pe giteddo,** eat this raw lettuce.

ramme *vi* eaten raw; **boo ramme ma numo,** cow peas leaves are eaten raw

rammo *vt* 1 to eat / eating uncooked or raw vegetables or tender uncooked cowpeas pods. 2 to eat / eating something that is not meant for eating; **dyel rammo boŋo woko** the goat eats the clothes **dyel orammo boŋona woko,** the goat has eaten my clothes.

ramtol *A n* long trousers; see **curuwal, pali.**

ran *vn* stunted, left undone; **ceŋ malyet miyo kall ran wokko,** hot sun stunts / makes the millet become stunted **lokke oran ki iyo,** the case never materialized. **ticce oran woko,** the work did not take place.

ranno *vt* 1 stunting something in its growth; **ceŋ ranno bel woko,** the sun stunts the corn in its growth, or makes the corn remained short; 2 to prevent / preventing; **yamo ranno kot woko,** the wind prevents the rain from falling.

raŋi *n* colour; **tye raŋi ma pat pat macalo magi,** there are many varieties of colours like thse: **ma kwaar,** red; **ma taar,** white; **ma ocwak ocwak,** yellow; **ma atworo,** green; **ma kibworo,** brownish or tawny; **ma col,** black; **ma**

obeddo aciri aciri, stipled black and white, **ma bururu,** blue and so on.

raŋ-raŋ *adv* transparent, having (small multiple holes or perforation)

rany *n* scornful speaking; **rany lok kany ci wagoyi cut,** speak scornfully here then we beat you straigh away. **danone larany lok,** he is a man who always speaks scornfully and sarcastically.

ranynye *vt* making fun or fool; **laworo guranynye mada,** yesterday they made fun or fool of each other; **gin ranynye mada** they make full or fun of each other very much see **lanynye.**

ranynyo *vt* to speak or retort scornfully; **dano ma ranynyo lok beddo kwede tek mada,** it is difficult to stay with a man who always speaks scornfully and sarcastically.

rap-rap *adv* clapping of the hands sound; **doŋo ciŋ ni rap rap,** clapping the hands and making the sound "rap rap".

ratili *n S* weight; **ratili adi me kado matye i gunia man,** how much weight of salt is in this bag?

rau *vt* collect or harvest stems altogether and then cut, **nyarro nyim ni rau,** collecting the stems of the simsim together and cut them.

rayo vt to collect bit by bit especially by going round the people; **gin rayo moko me teddo welo,** they collect millet flour for cooking for the guests; **gurayo yen madwoŋ me teddo,** they collected plenty of firewoods for cooking; see **raa, rac.**

ree *v* smear; **ree paala i kom latin,** smear the body of the child with red ochre.

rec *n* a fish.

red *v* shout; **red matek ka wek guwiny,** shout very hard to make them hear; see **daŋŋe.**

redde *vn* shouting, making noise; **redde pe ber,** shoutring is not good; **redde i wii litino baŋogi woko gidoko miŋ;** shouting at the children, makes them lose confidence in themselves and so become foolish.

reddo *vt* to shout / shouting, to speak / speaking loudly with much noises, to prevent / preventing others to speak, to scream / screaming, to shout / shouting; **reddo wii dano,** to scream / screaming / to shout / shouting at people.

ree *v* smear, paint; **ree kom bao man ki raŋi ma atworo,** smear or paint this timber with green colour; **ree dog latin ki raŋi makwar,** smear the childs' lips with the red colour.

reene *vi* smear onself; **latin tye ka reene mada ki moo i komme,** the child is smearing himself very much with the oil.

reeno *vt* to smear / smearing; **reeno paala i wic,** smearing the hair with red ochre.

reg *v* grind; **reg bil ene,** grind this corn; **cit ireg bell,** go and grind the millet.

regge *vn* 1 bent / bending down; **regge dok piny okonynye,** bending down helped him to duck; **oregge odok piny,** he ducked down in order to escape being hurt or seen; 2 can be grinded; **anyogine twerro regge,** the maize can be ground.

reggo *vt* to grind / grinding, **reggo bel,** to grind / grinding millet. -**ocitto ka reggo,** -gone to grind.

rek *n* a line, row; **rek pa litino, a** line of children **acikari guryeyo rek aryo,** the soldiers stood in two lines.

rek *adv* to go round investigating or getting information; **wotto ni rek rek i kin dano ka yenynyo lok,** going round the people looking for information. or other matters.

rem *vn* 1 insufficient, inadequate, not enough. **riŋo orem pe rommo dano;** the meat will not be enough for the people or insufficient for the people.

rem *vi* pain; **coŋŋe tye ka rem mada,** his knee is paining very much or he is having much pain in his knee. **korre tye ka rem mada, geŋŋe tiŋo jami mapek,** he is having much pain in his chest and prevents him from carrying heavy things; **lakke rem mada,** he is having very bad toothache or his tooth is aching very much.

remme *vt* deprive him, not enough; **obinno ka remme ki cam,** he came to take away part of his food; **cammi remme,** the food is not enough for him.

rem nyac *n* literally it should mean yaws pain, but usually they refer to eruption or rashes due to syphilis, usually of secondary stage.

remmo *vn* 1 not enough. **remmo ki cam,** making the food not enough by sharing. 2 **cam pe remmo dano,** food is never insufficient for the people.

remmo *vt* to do / doing something big (which normally is not good); **remmo lok me muŋ i nyim kacokke,** to let / letting out or blurting out a very important secret to the assembly. 2 to throw / throwing something big; **remmo kidi madit i yoo me geŋo dano wok kenyo,** to roll / rolling a big stone on the road to prevent people passing along the road or path.

remo *n* blood.

renno *vt* 1 to condon / condoning, to overcook / overlooking; **renno wii dakone,** to condon / condoning what his wife does or overlooks what his wife does good or bad.

reŋe *n* colour (a tree from which red dye is found).

rep *adj* thin, 1. **boŋo ma rep,** a thin cloth.

rep *vn* talkative; **dogge rep ka lok,** he is very talkative.

rep *adj* watery; **olel ma rep,** watery sauce. (simsim).

ret *vn* wound, injury; **ŋadi olimmo ret,** so and so has been hurt or injured.

ret *v* 1 throw (down); **ret piny i ŋom,** throw down to the ground; 2 **tiŋ latin ci ento pe iret piny,** take the child but do not throw him down.

rette *vn* wrestling; **ŋeyo tukko me rette mada,** he knows very well the game of wrestling.

retto *vt* to throw (to the ground); **en retto dano mada,** alway throws people down.

reyo *vt* 1 to smear / smearing; **reyo remo i dogge,** smears bllod on his lips **oreyo remo i dogge,** he smeared blood on his lips. 2 wipe off, clear; **gwok cammo ci reyo dogge i ŋom,** a dog eats and then cleans its mouth on the ground.

reyo *vt* to impute / imputing, to implicate / implicating; **reyo lok i kom ŋat mukene,** to impute / imputing or implicating another person with the matter, see **weyo.**

rib *v* join, add, unite, reconcile; **rib jami man ducu ci ititta welle,** add these things and let me know the result; **rib joo matye ka daani,** reconcile those who are quarrelling.

ribbe *vi* to join / joining, to reconcile / reconciling; **ribbe ber omiyo pe doŋ gidaa,** reconciliation is good, that is why they do not quarrel **yaŋ gidaa mada kombedi doŋ guribbe pe doŋ gidaa,** they used to quarrel very much but now they have reconciled and there is no quarrel; **guribbe ka lweny kom Woko,** they joined to fight **Woko.**

ribi ribi *adj* shining indistinctly; **obinno ma piny ribi ribi,** he came at dusk.

ribi ribi *adj* full; **aduko opoŋ ni ribi ribi,** the basket is full to the brim.

ribbo *vt* to join / joining, to unite / uniting, to share / sharing, to reconcile / reconciling; **ribbo wego acel,** to share / sharing the same father; **ribbo cam ki ominne,** shares the food with his brother or sharing the food with his brother; **ribbo yoo kwede,** coming / to come together with him.

ric *vn* 1. urging, insisting or pushing; **en pe mitto ric i dog tic,** he does not want pushing or to be pushed to work.

ric *vn* tying round and round; **ric pa tolle pe ber,** the tying of the rope was not properly done.

rid *v* insist; **rid lokki matek wek in bene inoŋ,** insist on your case so that you may also get.

rid *v* push; **rid tyenni matek i war ci donyo,** push hard your foot into the shoe and it will enter.

ridde *vi* pushing through with force, entering a place when one should not; **latin matidi me ridde i kin ludito pe ber,** a young child pushing or intruding among the elders is not good; **dano onoŋo ocullo doggola ento en obinno oridde odonynyo,** the door was blocked by people but he came and pushed himself through with force into the house; **oridde i kom dyaŋ mape mere,** he persisted in claiming the cow which was not his.

riddo *vt* to persist / persisting, to insist / insisting; **riddo lok,** insisting in the matter; **riddo keny,** insisting / to insist in the marriage; **riddo agit i ciŋ,** to force / forcing the ring into the finger.

riddo *vt* to tie / tying in big bundles; **riddo yen, riddo lum,** tying a big bundle of wood, to tie / tying a big bundle of grass.

ridi *n* narrow passage of a fence; **waŋ ridi,** narrow door or passage or entrance, see **apidiŋ**

rido *n* dry twigs of trees (gathered by women for cooking); **cittu wucikel**

rido yen me mokko mac, go and get twigs of trees for lighting the fire.

rii *n* giraffe; **rii ŋutte bor mada,** a giraffe has a very long neck.

rii *vn* staying at a place for a long time; **rii ka matto koŋo,** stays drinking beer, **orii botta laworo,** he stayed with me for a long time yesterday; **orii kec,** he remained without food, he fasted, he starved himself / **rii kec,** fasting.

rii *v* tie round; **rii tol i ŋut dyel,** tie the rope round the neck of the goat.

rii *v* put across; **rii tal woko i korayo,** put a pole across the road.

rik *v* to fill / filling up; **rik ot maber ka doŋ imwon,** fill up the gaps between the big poles with the small ones and tie them and then plaster it with mud.

rik rik *adv* jerking excitedly; frightened; **komme poo nirik rik,** his body jerks excitedly.

rikke *vt* to ward / warding off when fencing (with shield when fighting with spears), parrying e.g. **rikke ki kwot,** to ward / warding off with shield, to evade /evading.

rikko *vt* to fill / filling up gaps between the poles with small poles or twigs of wood e.g. **rikko ot ki yadi matino ka wek omwonne maber,** to fill / filling up the

gaps between the poles with small ones so that it can be covered well with mud or clay.

rim *adv* in large number, quantity; **dyegi gubakke ni rim i poto,** a large number of goats gathered in the field.

riine *vn* coil round, twining; **nyelo oriine i kom apwoyo,** python coiled round the hare. **Nyelo riine i kom lee me nekkone,** python coils round the animal to kill it.

riŋ *v* run; **riŋ matek,** run very fast.

riŋo *n* meat; flesh, game.

riŋŋo *vt* to run / running, to avoid / avoiding or to escape / escaping from; **riŋŋo tic ciŋ woko,** running away from manual labour; **riŋŋo tiŋŋo teer,** to escape / escaping or to avoid / avoiding carrying load; **riŋŋo ma dwir mada,** runs very fast.

riŋ-riŋ *n* mucous stool or faeces, diarrhoea mixed with mucus; **caddo riŋ riŋ ki remo,** has dysentery.

ripot *Eng n* report; **an doŋ anoŋŋo repot mera,** I have already received my report.

rit *adv* 1 far off; **onyetto laa ni rit,** he spat the saliva far off; **pii nyette ni rit rit,** the water spurts intermittently. 2 tightly or closely; **otweyo yen ni rit,** he tied the wood tightly.

rit *n* the rib of a *borassus* palm leaves. e.g. **rit owor.**

rit *n* tonsillitis, **dwanne lit ki rit,** he has tonsillitis.

ritto *vt* not cutting only pressing; **lyedi oluu ritto wic aritta,** the razor is blunt, it presses the hair without cutting them; **latin matidi ritto ciŋ aritta ki wokke,** the child bites the fingers with his toothless jaw.

riu *adv* passe swiftly away e.g. **okatto ni riu,** passes swiftly away.

riyo *vt* 1 to wind /winding round, to wrap / wrapping round; **riyo tol i ŋut dyel,** to wind / winding a rope round the goat's neck.

riyo *vt* to put / putting across; **riyo yat madit i yoo,** to put / putting a big log of wood across the road.

robbo *vt* to peel / peeling, off; **yatte robbo kom dano ka iwirro,** the medicine makes the body peel off if you smear, causing blisters of skin or ulceration; **aburo robbo dog dano,** severe cold in the head causes eruption and ulceration of lips.

robbo *vt* 1 to provoke / provoking, **pe icit ka robbo dogge,** do not go to provoke him. 2 **lok me robbo dog dano,** a case for provoking the people.

roc *v* spoil; **roc lokke woko,** spoil the case.

roc *vn* mistake; **obakko dogge pi roc ma otimmo,** he begged for forgiveness for his mistake.

roc *vn* pushing in, putting something into, grilling, (not commonly spoken) see **roo, royo.**

roc *n* 1 shocks, stockings, gloves, condoms; **amitto roc me aruka ka wek doŋ aruk war,** I want shocks to put on so that I may put on my shoes; **ginne rac twatwal, ruk roc i ciŋŋi ka wek imak kwede,** the thing is very dirty, put on the gloves so that you may handle it; **coo mukene girukko roc wek ogeŋ gin noŋŋo twoo nyo yacco dako mo ka gibutto kwedgi,** some men wear or put on condoms in order to prevent them from getting infections or impregnating any woman when they sleep with them.

roc *v* renovate; **roc ot meeri wek odok maber.** renovate your house to make it very good.

rocce *vi* can be spoiled, **lokke twerro rocce,** the case can be spoiled; **tic tin orocce,** today he failed to do his normal share of work or the work could not be done.

rocco *vt* to renovate / renovating; **rocco ot ma otii,** to renovate / renovating an old house; to recultivate / recultivating; **rocco poto,** to recultivate / recultivating a field which was cultivated before; to repair / repairing; **rocco leela,** to repair / repairing the bicycle; to restore / restoring, to revive / reviving, **rocco wer,** to revive / reviving an old song; to revive / reviving; **rocco tee kwoor macon,** to revive / reviving an old enmity or to reopen / reoppening the old enmity

rocco *vt/n* 1 to spoil / spoiling, to corrupt / corrupting; **rocco lok,** the meaning of this sentence depends upon how you pronounce it; it may mean spoiling the evidence of the matter or it may mean revizing the evidence; **iroco ka tiyo kit eno,** you were wrong or mistake to do that way; **piny rocco dano,** people always make mistake.

rod *v* pile; **rod buk man i wii lawotte,** pile this book on top of the other; see **dod, dwod.**

rodde *vi* can be piled; **agulune twerro rodde i wii lawotte**, the pot can be piled on top of another.

roddo *vt* to pile / piling up; **roddo agulu**, piling up pots on top of one another; see **doddo, dwoddo**

roddo *adv.* tired, **guol gubeddo ni roddo**, they were tired and sitting entirely exhausted; see **roggo.**

rok *n* tribe, race, sub tribe; **rok Acoli**, Acholi tribe; **larok**, a foreigner; **rokke**, his tribe

rok *v* hollow out the wood, make a hole through it; **rok i yat man**, hollow out this wood.

rokke *vi* can be hollowed; **iye orokke**, it is hollow inside. **twenno rokke**, can be hollowed.

rokko *vt* 1 to excavate / excavating, to hollow / hollowing out; **rokko yat me bul**, to hollow / hollowing a piece of wood for a drum. 2 push a stick into a hole to force what is there to come out; **rokko oyoo ki i ococce wek okat woko**, to push / pushing a stick into the rat's hole to make it come out.

rokko *vt* to provoke / provoking; **rokko dog dano**, to provoke / provoking somebody to do something; see also **robbo.**

rokko *vt* to stab over and over; **rokko lyec ki toŋ yot**, stabbing the elephant with a spear over and over is easy.

gurokko lyec ki toŋ mape wacce, they speared the elephants over and over with spears.

rom *adj* equal, the same; **boŋowa rom**, our clothes are the same; **bocogi rom**, their lengths are equal; **warom**, we are the same.

romme *vi* unexpected meeting; **romme meegi ni i Rom obeddo me gum mada**, their.meeting in Rome was of a great luck indeed.

rommo *vn* 1 to meet / meeting with; **wutwerro ommo i Kampala**, you can meet in Kampala

gurommo ki kot i yoo, they met with rain on the way.

rommo *vt* started, to stage; **gucako rommo ka lweny**, they started fighting for no reason;

rommo marac *vi* meeting with bad sign / bad omen, e.g. it is a belief among the people that if your first born child is a boy, then when you are travelling and the first person to meet is a boy, that is a bad sign, you should meet a girl to be a good sign but to meet / meeting a black cat or snake etc. all bad signs.

rommo *vn* being sufficient, being enough; **cam matye rommo litino maber**, the food which is there is enough or sufficient for the children. 2 sufficiently developed.

rommo *vi* fully developed; **labolo doŋ oteggi rommo atoŋŋa**, the banana is fully developed and ready for harvesting.

rommo *vi* to be tired or enough; **wer maraccu rommo dano oyot**, bad songs make people tired quickly. **wer doŋ oromma**, I have enough of singing, I am tired of singing.

romo *n* sheep.

rony *vn* making fun; **rony pe ber**, making fun is not good; **danone larony luwadigi**, he is a man who always makes fun of his companion **pe ber me rony**, making fun is not good.

ronynye *vn* making fun of somebody; **dano ma kitte ber pe ŋeyo ronynye**, a good man does not know how to make fun.

ronynye *vt* sexual relation; **dako ma ronynye ki coo,** a woman who goes about with men; this is archaic, now not very much spoken.

ronynyo *vt* to make / making fun of a person in his presence, pretending to speak of somebody else; **tye ka ronynyo lawotte,** he is making fun of his friend.

ronynyo *vt* to have / having an illicit sexual intercourse; **en ronynyo nyaa pa Otto,** he sleeps with the daughter of Otto.

ronynyo *vi* to glance / glancing; **ronynyo waŋŋe ki i waŋ dinica ka neno** he glances his eyes through the window in order to see. **oronynyo waŋŋe i ot ki i waŋ dirica,** he glanced into the house through the window.

roo *v* insert, put into; **roo i a gulu,** put into the pot; **roo tol i libira,** thread the needle; **roo tyeni I waar,** push your foot into the shoe.

roo *v* grill, broil; **roo riŋo me amwodda,** grill the meat for eating; see **roc, royo.**

roone *vi* can be grilled; **riŋo man biroone maber mada,** this meat can be broiled or grilled well.

roone *vi* can be inserted; **tyenni twerro roone i waarre,** your foot can be pushed into the shoe.

roone *vi* can be threaded; **tol twerro roone i libirane,** threads can be threaded into the needle.

roone *vi* being irritated; **dogge tye ka roone ki kalara,** his mouth is being irritated by red pepper.

roro *n* treachery, lying, deceitfulness. **lok roro rac,** treachery talks are bad.

roro roro *adv* dripping; **laa cwer ki**

i dogge ni roro roro, saliva drips / dripping from his mouth continuously.

rot *v* look for or tract; **rot kama lee cammo iye,** find out look for or trace where the animals graze.

rot *adv* track left by trampling; **kor lee ocitto ni rot kwica,** the track trampled by the animal has passed through here to make and gone forward.

rotte *vi* can be tracked; **kor lee** twerro **rotte,** the track of the animal can be tracked.

rotto *vt* to search / searching for, to track / tracking, to explore / exploring; **rotto piny,** to spy / spying, to explore / exploring the country; **rotto lee,** to track / tracking the animal.

roya *n* heifer.

royo *vt* to grill / grilling, to broil / broiling; **royo riŋo,** to grill / grilling or to broil / broiling the meat.

royo *vt* to irritate / irritating; **kamlara royo dog dano,** the hot pepper irritates people's mouth.

royo *vt* clean by burning; **royo ŋet gaŋ,** firing grass round the home to prevent fire burning the home; see **roo, roc**

royo *vt* 1 to insert / inserting; **royo tol ma gituddo i ŋutte,** to insert / inserting his head into a noose of rope; 2 to thread / hreading; **royo tol i libira nyo i kinyo,** threading the needle; 3 to push / pushing; **royo tyenne i waar,** to push / pushing his foot into the shoe; see **roo, roc.**

rub *v* mix; **rub yat,** mix the medicine.

rubbe *vi* can be mixed, **yatte twerro rubbe maber,** the medicine can be mixed very well.

rubbo *vt/n* to mix / mixing, to stir / stirring; **rubbo kic ki nyuka,** to mix / mixing honey with gruel of millet; **rubbo cukari i cai,** to stir / stirring sugar in a cup of tea.

rubbo *vt* to cause / causing confusion; **rubbo lok i kin dano,** to cause / causing confusion among the people.

rubia *n* (old, not used now) the value of two shillings, used in 1920s.

rubu-rubu *adv* 1 not hard, sandy like; **ŋomme obeddo rubu rubu,** the ground is coarsely soft like sand. 2 in great number; passing in great number; **dyaŋi gitye ka mol ni rubu rubu,** the cattle are passing by in great number.

rubuku *adv.* falling down; collapse; **opotoni rubuku,** he fell down on his knees and hands.

ruc *vt* to hurry / hurrying or compel somebody to do something; **en tiyo ki ruc matek mada i kom luticce,** he uses alot of hurry on his workers; see **ruu ki ruyo.**

ruc *v* wipe out; **ruc coc woko ki i kom bao,** wipe out writings from the black board.

ruc *n* rice; **wel ruc kombedi rac twatwal,** at the present time the price of rice is very bad.

rucce *vi* can be wiped off, rubed off; **coc ma i kom bao ni rucce maber, the** writing on the board can can easily be wiped off; **coc ma gicoyo ki bwino pe rucce,** letters written with ink cannot be wiped off.

ruccu *vt* 1 to rub / rubing out, effacing, wiping out; **ruccu bao,** rubbing out the black board; 2 to embezzle / embezzling goods, swindling; **ruccu lim**

pa lawotte, embezzling or swindling his friend's money.

rucu rucu *adv.* superficially, hurriedly; **gerro ot rucu rucu,** building the house hurriedly (not very well); **cwerro bao rucu rucu ,** planes / planning the board hurriedly, not very well.

rud *v* rub; **rud ŋee latin maleŋ,** rub the child's back clean or well.

ruda *n* bushbuck. See also **lajwa, abur.**

rudde *vi* can be rubed; **ŋeye twerro rudde ki ciŋ,** his bacck can be rubbed with hand.

ruddo *vt* to rub / rubbing. to polish / polishing; **ruddo agulu maryeny mada,** to polish / polishing the pot very brightly or polishes the pot very brightly (depending how you read it).

ruk *n* a dress, attire; **ruk pa litino me cukul becco mada,** the dresses of the school children are very good.

ruk *v* dress or put on; **ruk boŋo,** dress or put on clothe.

ruk *v* dress; **ruk latin ki boŋo maleŋ,** dress the child in a clean dress.

ruk *v* stir; **ruk mac,** stir the burning ember.

rukca *A n* a permission, absence from work; **gimiye rukca me citto gaŋ,** he was given permission to go home.

rukke *vi* dressing; **oecitto ka rukke,** he is going to dress up.

rukko *vt* to dress / dressing up, to don / donning a clothe on, to put / putting on; **citto ka rukko boŋo,** going to put on a dress or going to don on clothes.

rukko *vt* to raise the earth upwards; **okok ŋwen rukko ŋom i yoo gi; the**

soldier termites raise upwards the earth along their tracks.

ruk mac *n* ash with ember underneath

rum *v* surround; **rum wiye i ot,** surround him in the house.

rum *v* kneel; **rum coŋŋi piny ka doŋ ileggi,** kneel down and then pray.

rum *adv* quite, definitely; **otop ni rum,** quite rotten, completely rotten

rumme *vi* can be surrounded; **lukwooni twerro rumme i ot,** these thieves can be surrounded in the house.

rumme *vi* engaged; **gurumme ka lweny i ot ken ken gi kuno,** they were engage in fighting in the house by themselves there.

rummo *vt* kneeling; **rummo coŋ,** kneeling on the knees.

rummo *vt* surrounding; **rummo dyaŋi,** surrounding the cattle.

ruŋ *n* wrinkle, crease, crumple; **geŋŋo boŋo ruŋ,** prevents the cloth from wringling or creasing.

ruŋŋe *vi* can shrink; **boŋone rac mada, ruŋŋe oyot ka gilutto i pii,** the cloth is not good, it shrinks easily.when put into water or deeped into water.

ruŋi-ruŋi *prd* unequal, unlevel; **gudo ne obeddo ruŋi ruŋi,** the road is rough and uneven.

ruŋŋo *vt* to crumple, rumple, crease, wrinkle; **pu kot ruŋŋo boŋona,** rain water wrinkles my clothes.

ruŋu-ruŋu *prd.* coarse and wringled, e.g. **komme obeddo ruŋu-ruŋu,** his skin is wrinkled and coarse.

ruru-ruru *adv* rumbling noise as that of dragging something on the floor. **ruru ruru** *vi* rises up; **yito duny ni ruru-ruru,** smoke rises up.

rut *v* pierce, make; **rut it latin me ketto ogwilo,** pierce the child's ear lobes for ear rings.

rut *v* instigate, incite; **pe irut lok kuno,** do not instigate or incite trouble there **rut lok wek gulweny,** incite trouble so that they may fight.

rut *pl* **rudi** *n* twin (of human beings it is said **onywallo rudi,** has given birth to twins or borne twins, but of the animals, **ogwarro rudi** or **ogoyo rudi).**

rutte *vi* 1 to crouch / crouching, to duck / ducking, to throw / throwing oneself down; **kono pe orutte kono ocello woko ki kidi,** if he did not duck, he would have hit him with a stone; **rutte ka donyonyo i ot,** duck the head when entering the house.

rutte *vi* can be pierced; **itte twerro rutte,** her ear can be pierced.

rutte *vi* to decay / decaying, become rotten; **papai otop orutte woko,** the pawpaw is completely rotten; **papai rutte oyot oyot,** the pawpaw rots very quickly.

rutto *vt* to instigate / instigating, to incite / inciting, **rutto lok i kom dano,** to instigate / instigating a case against a person.

rutto *vt/n* 1 *to sew* / sewing; **rutto boŋo,** to sew / sewing the clothes. (with hand); 2 to pierce / piercing; **rutto it,** to pierce / piercing the ear.

ruu *v* impel, urge, hurry; **ruu dano ka tic matek,** impel people to work hard;

ruu *n* dawn, day-break; **piny cok ruu,** it is about to dawn.

ruu piny, *n* dawn, daybreak; **ruu piny ki ruu piny,** day by day; see **ruc, ruyo.**

ruyo *vt/n* to hurry / hurrying, to urge / urging, impel; **ruyo dano ka tic,** impel or hurrying people to work; **ruyo citto ka coo,** hurries / hurrying to go to be married; **ruyo lok,** talks / talking too fast; see **ruu ki ruc.**

rwa-rwa *adv* the sound made by water when one walks through it, or drinking beer e.g. **matto koŋo ni rwarwa,** drinks beer with that noise.

rwac *v* throw; **rwac piny,** throw down.

rwacce *vi* to fall / falling down heavily to the ground; **koni rwacce piny nia ki i wii yat,** he will fall down very badly from the top of the tree.

rwacco *vt* to throw or fling down violently to the ground; **rwacco gwok matek twatwal i ŋom per ber,** flinging down the dog violently is not good. **Oneka orwacco Lacere matek mada iŋom,** Lacere was flung down by Oneka or violently thrown down by Oneka.

rwad *v* plaster; **rwad kom ot ki lobo,** plaster the walls of the house with mud. See **rad, rwat.**

rwadde *vi* can be plastered, **kom ot man twerro rwadde maber,** the walls of the house can be well plastered.

rwaddo *vt* to kill / killing in large numbers; **rwaddo lee mada,** to kill / killing many animals indiscriminately; see **raddo, nyatto.**

rwaddo *vt* plastering with mud; **rwaddo kom ot ki lobo,** plastering the walls of the house with mud.

rwak *v* insert into, push into; **rwak palaa i akura,** insert the knife in its sheath; **rwak tyenni i war,** push your foot into the shoe; see **roo, ruk.**

rwakke *vi* can be inserted, pushed; **tol twerro rwakke i libira meno,** this needle can be threaded; **tyenni twerro**

rwakke i waar man, your foot can be pushed into this shoe.

rwakko *vt* to insert / inserting, to fit / fitting in; **rwakko wii ot,** to fill / filling in the gaps on the roof with new grass; **rwakko toŋ i akurane, to insert** / inserting the blade of the spear in it's sheath.

rwanno *vt* to speak fluently; **rwanno dum,** speaks foreign language fluently. **rwanno kwan,** reads fluently; an archaic word not used now.

rwaŋ *v* crumple or crush; **rwaŋ cupiriane woko,** crush or crumple the sauce pan.

rwaŋŋe *vi* be crumpled or crooked; **cupuria ne rwaŋŋe woko,** the sauce pen dents or crumples easily.

rwaŋŋo *vt* to spoil / spoiling by bending, wrinkling or breaking.

rwany *v* turn inside out; **rwany cunni,** turn your prepuce inside out; **rwany i catini ka doŋ imoo otwoo,** turn inside out your shirt and then put it to dry; **rwany cin doŋo me dyel ka wek ilwok cette,** turn inside out the goat's large intestine and then wash it's droppings.

rwanynye *vi* can be turned inside out; **cunne twerro rwanynye,** the prepuce of his penis can be turned inside out

rwanynyo *vt* to turn / turning inside out; **rwanynyo cun,** to turn / turning inside out of the prepuce to show glans penis, **rwanynyo cin dyaŋ,** to turn / turning inside out the cattle's intestine for cleaning.

rwat *v* plaster; **rwat wunu kom ot ma gitaddoni tin,** plaster with mud today the house that has been fabricated; see **rad, rwad**

rwatte *vi* 1 to meet / meeting with; **obedo me yom cwiny, rwatte ki ominne i Kampala** meeting his brother in Kampala was a happy occasion 2 to accidentally killed or wounded; **ciŋŋe orwatte ki dano ka dwar,** when hunting he accidentally killed or wounded a person.

rwatto *vt* rough to cast / casting, to plaster / plastering (a wall); **rwatto ot nyo dero,** plastering the walls of hut or granary with clay; see **rwaddo.**

rwee *prd* hoarse; **kokko twatwal kello rwee dwan,** crying too much causes hoarse voice.

rwee *v* stretch, manipulate, massage; **rwee tyenne malit,** stretch or massage his painful leg, in other words, carry out *physiotherapy* on his painful leg.

rwee *adv* quietly and lost; **obeddo piny ni rwee,** he sat down quietly, silently, and completely lost; **i kare ma gijukke, obeddo piny oliŋ ni rwee,** when he was rebuked he sat down and became silent.

rweene *vi* 1 to stretch / stretching onself. 2 to take / taking a walk; **citto ka rweene i cuk,** to take / taking a walk to the market, or to go / going for a walk to the market; 3. **tyenne twerro rweene,** his leg can be stretched or manipulated.

rweny *vn* loss; **rweny pa dyaŋŋe,** loss of his cow or his cow went astray; **nino ducu rweny woko limany,** every day he gets lost completely to all knowledge.

rweny *vi* forget; **rweny ki nyiŋŋe,** forgets his name; **rweny kwede woko;** cannot remember him, or he forgets him, or he does not recognise him.

rwenynye *adj* bowed or stretched, **tyenne orwenynye,** his leg is bow legged.

rwenynyeke *adv* disorderly; **ocuŋ kwica ni rwenynyeke,** he stood there disorderly; **obeddo piny ni rwenynyeke,** he sat carelessly or in disorderly manner.

rwenynyo *vt* to lose / losing, to go / going astray, to forget / forgetting, being lost. 1 *n* **rwenynyo caa ne woko,** loses / losing his watch; 2 forget; **rwenynyo lok woko,** forget the matter or forgot the word.

rweyo *vt* 1 to ask / asking people to come, **rweyo dano ka tic, ka dwar nyo ka myel,** to go / going round asking or inviting people to come to or for work, hunting or dancing.

rweyo *vt/n* to massage / massaging, **rweyo tyen dano ma owil,** to massage / massaging a sprained or strained ankle.

rwi-rwi *adv* nystagmus opening and shutting, restless movement; **waŋŋe beddi rwi-rwi,** his eyes are restless, opening and shutting or closing.

rwic *v* crush or squash; **rwic ladep ki lwet ciŋŋi,** crush the flea with your finger nails.

rwicce *vt* can be crushed; **ladep twerro rwicce ki lwet ciŋ,** the flea can be crushed with finger nails.

rwicco *vt* to crush / crushing, to squash / squashing (usually between two fingers) **rwicco ladep ki lwet ciŋ;** to crush / crushing a flea with the finger nails.

rwid *v* tie, **rwid tol matek,** tie the rope tightly; see **rid.**

rwidde *vi* 1 to become / becoming tight; **tol tye ka rwidde woko ki i ŋut**

dyel, the rope is becoming tight on the goat's neck; 2 **twerro rwidde,** can be tightened.

rwiddo *vt* to tie / tying tightly; **rwiddo tol matek,** to tie / tying the rope tightly.

rwit *adv* firmly, fast, tightly, fixedly, **tweyo ni rwit,** tto tie / tying it firmly.

rwitte *vi* to be / being firmly bound or fixed; **tol rwitte woko i ŋut dyel,** the rope becomes tightened on the neck of the goat. (The above not very much used now) **rwidde** is a better word q.v

rwoo *vt* to give / giving up, to withdraw / withdrawing because of fear or cowardice from something; **rwoo woko i pyem me rette,** withdraw / withdrawing from the games of wrestling because of fear or cowardice.

rwok *adj Lang* very; **ber rwok,** very good.

rwom *n* ladder, rank; **kel rwom me itto wii ot,** bring the ladder for climbing up the roof.

rwom *n* a position; **en doŋ oo i rwom mene i mony?** what rank is he in the army?

rwom-nam or **rwom kulo** *n* confluence, junction of river or brook, where rivers meet.

rwot (*pl* **rwodi**) *n* king, chief, master, lord.

ryac *adv* sharp, jumping far; **kado dek bit ni ryac,** the salt in the sauce is too sharp or bitter; **ogwal pye ni ryac,** the frog jumps a long distance.

ryak *adv* cracking sound; **baro yen ni ryak,** splitting the log with a cracking sound.

ryal *n A* an aluminium or a tin.

ryam nyo ryem *v* chase, dismiss, drive away; **ryam woko ki i tic,** dismiss from the work; **ryam gwok woko ki i ot,** chase or drive away the dog from the house.

ryammo *vi* to chase / chasing away, to drive / driving away. Some people refer to it as **ryemmo,** to dismiss / dismissing, to send / sending away, to chase / chasing; **ryammo dano ki i waŋ tic,** to dismiss / dismissing a person from the work. **ryammo gwok woko ki i ot,** to chase / chasing or to drive / driving away the dog from the house.

ryaŋ *v* frighten, terrify; **ryaŋ cwinynye ki lok maraccu,** frighten him with bad news.

ryaŋ *adj* very bright and hot; **ceŋ oryeny ni ryeŋ** the sun shone very brightly and hot *see* **ryeny.**

ryaŋ-ryaŋ *adv* 1 terror stricken. frightened. 2 shining and fat; 1 **cwinynye beddi ryaŋ ryaŋ,** he is terror stricken or he is very frightened 2 **kom dyaŋ man bedi ryaŋ ryaŋ,** the cow is very fat with shining body.

ryaŋa-ryaŋa *prd.* soft swampy area which shakes under feet when walking on it; see **daga daga.**

ryaŋŋe *vi* being terrified, being alarmed or being frightened; **cwinynye tye ka ryaŋŋe,** he is very much frightened.

ryaŋŋo *vt* to terrify / terrifying, to alarm / alarming or to frighten / frightening; **lokke tye ka ryaŋŋo cwinynye,** the matter is alarming or terrifying him.

ryany *adj* very big; **twon em dyaŋ ni ryany,** a very big cows thigh; **obutto ni ryany caa, i**t is lying there broad and big.

ryany *adv* bright and hot; **ceŋ oryeny ni ryany,** the sun shone birghtly and hot, some use **ryaŋ** instead of **ryany**.

ryany *v* make a big something; **ryany kwon madit ki litino me acamma,** make a big **kwon** for the children to eat.

ryanynye *vi* can be made big; **kwon twerro ryanynye pi litino,** a big amount of **kwon** can be made for the children.

ryanynyo *vt* to make / making something big; **ryanyo kwon,** to make / making a big amount of **kwon.**

rya-rya *adj* lascivious, lust, loose; **dako ma waŋŋe bedi rya-rya,** a lascivious woman, a prostitute **rya-rya waŋ,** being lescivious.

ryeb v 1 turn upside down; **ryeb dog agulo pii piny,** turn the water pot upside down. 2 cover; **ryeb wii agulu dek eno,** cover that cooking pot.

ryebbe *vi* can be turned upside down, **aguluni twerro ryebbe piny,** the pot can be turned upside down; **latin obutto oryebbe piny caa;** the child is sleeping on his abdomen there.

ryebbo *vt* 1 to turn / turning upside down; **ryebbo dog agulo pii piny,** turning the water pot upside down. 2 to cover / covering; **ryebbo wii agulo dek,** to cover /covering the top of the cooking pot.

ryebbo *vt* put to rest or aside or into cold storage; **lokke pud doŋ gireybbo piny;** at the moment the matter has been put aside or to rest or into cold storage.

ryec *vn* straightening, making straight, lining; **ryec pa acikari pudi peya ber,** the lining up of the police is not yet good; see **ryee, ryeyo.**

ryee *v* line up; **ryee acikari i tyeŋ atir,** line up the police in a straight line; see **ryec, ryeyo.**

ryeene *vi* 1 can be lined up; **litino twerro ryeene kany,** children can be lined up here; 2 lying full length on bed or ground; **aecitto ka ryeene wii kitanda wek aywe,** I am going to lie down on the bed so that I may rest.

ryek *adj* wise, clever, prudent, intelligent, skilful; **ryek mada,** very clever, intelligent or skilful.

ryek *v* rip or cut open; **ryek i dyel caa,** rip open the goat's stomach.

ryekke *vi* 1 can be cut open; **i dyel man twerro ryekke,** the abdomen of this goat can be ripped open **cin dyaŋ madoŋo twerro ryekke,** the cattle's large intestine can be cut open; 2 his own effort; cleverness; **pi ryekke omiyo olwii woko ki i jero,** he escaped from jail for his own effort or for his cleverness.

ryekko *vi* to rip / ripping up, open; **ryekko i dyaŋ,** to open / opening the cow's abdomen.

ryeko *n* cunning, intelligence, cleverness, prudence; **en tye ki ryeko mada me yubbo caa,** he has much cleverness in repairing watches **ryeko omiyo ogerro ot madit,** intelligence made him build a big house.

ryem or ryam *v/vi* chase, drive away, dismiss or send away; **ryem woko ki i tic,** dismiss him from work. the central Acoli prefer **ryam**

ryemme or ryamme *vi* chasing, dismissing, sending away; **giryemme pi** kwoo, he was dismissed for theft;

laworo guryemme mada ki lakwoo, yesterday they were occupied with chasing the thief.

ryemmo *vi* to chase / chasing, to drive / driving away, to send / sending away, to dismiss / dismissing. c/f **ryammo.**

ryeny *vn* to shine, to be bright; **ryeny ni daŋ daŋ, ryak ryak, tai tai,** shines brightly; see also **lyak lyak.**

ryenynye *prn* it's shining; **kom motokani ryenynye carro waŋ dano,** the shining body of the motor car, dazzles the eyes.

ryeyo, ryeeno *vt* 1 to line / lining up, put in row or line; **ryeyogi ityeŋ,** lining up. 2 to stretch / stretching out; **ryeyo tyenne mot,** to strecth / stretching out her legs comfortably; **ryeyo boŋo wii tol,** to hang / hanging the clothes on the rope; see **ryee, ryec.**

T t

taa or tuba, or taba *Eng. n* tobacco.

taa *v* defeat, overpower, win; **taa Okello i tukko doŋŋe wek inoŋ mot,** defeat Okello in the boxing competition and get the prize; see **tac, tayo.**

taar *adj.* 1 white; **lak mataar,** white teeth; 2 lustful, looseness; **nyako ma waŋŋe taar,** a loose, lustful girl; **taar waŋ,** lustfulness, looseness.

taar *adv* hard; **oyokko wiye ni taar,** he knocked his head very hard against something.

taara *S n* lamp, in the past some people used to call it **tawaca.**

taarre *vi* to turn / turning aside, to withdraw / withdrawing from doing something; he

feels he is not fit for it, not commonly spoken now, *c/f* **caane**

taarre *adj* its brightness.

taarro *vi* to despise, take no notice of, take little or no care of; **lacoo ma taarro dakone,** a man who despises his wife and does not care about her, not commonly used now.

taba-taba nyo tabu tabu *prd* spotted, **rii komme obeddo tabu tabu,** the giraffe's body is regularly spotted.

taba taba *adv* unstable gait or unsteady walk; **omeer ma doŋ wotto ni taba taba,** he was so drunk that he walks unsteadily.

tac *adv* heavily, **agulu opotto piny ni tac ci otoo woko,** the pot fell down heavily and got broken to pieces; **pi kokko too, obolle kenne ni tac marac mada,** because of mourning the dead, she threw herself very badly on the ground.

tac *n* 1 hip, pocket; **ocuŋ omakko tacce,** he stood holding his hip, it is not commonly spoken now; 2 his pocket; **aketto i jeba tac,** I put it in my pocket; **ladit koŋ iboŋ tacci,** Sir just touch your hip-pocket, this is actually a request that he should give them some money; see **jepa.**

tac *vn* defeating, winning, (not commonly spoken) see **taa, tayo.**

taci *n* an old gun pattern (Winchester).

tad *v* construct; **tad wii dero,** construct a frame for the granary's.

tadde *vi* 1 being spread out; **ogwal nino ducu tadde wii pii,** the frog always lies spreading out on the surface of the water; 2 **wii ot twerro tadde ki yadi ma odoŋŋi,** the remaining poles are enough for the construction of the roof of the hut.

taddo *vt* to construct / constructing the wooden frame of a hut, roof or a granary; **taddo kom ot, wii dero, ot ŋwen, lyer nyim etc,** building or constructing the wall of the hut, roof or a granary, covering of an ant hill for termites, frame for drying simsim etc.

tag *v* move to and fro; **tag pii i agulu,** shake the water in the pot to move to and fro.

tagge *vi* to rise / rising and to fall / falling (waves in the water or sea) **wot maber pii tye ka tagge i wii i cupuria,** be careful, walk straight, the water is shaking in the saucepan on your head it might pour out; *prov.* **ot tagge,** in a marriage, there is usually some trouble which later is settled.

taggo *vt.* to cause / causing to move to and fro (waves in water); **yamo taggo yeya,** the wind moves the canoe up and down the water.

taga-taga *adv* moving of water to and fro (in a pot or saucepan) when it is being carried on the head; **pii yeŋŋe ni taga - taga,** the water moves to and fro.

tak *adv* precisely; **ladit oo i kom caa ki kome ni tak,** the big man arrived precisely at the exact time.

tak *v* remove, **tak wii koŋo manok imii ki dano,** remove a little of the beer and give it to the people.

tak *vn* magical removal; **ocitto ka tak bot ajwaka,** she went to the traditional healer to have the poison magically removed.

takke *vi* to walk / walking with an affectionate movement; **wotto takke,** walks with an affectation; see **wotto ma ŋatte, wotto ma jagge.**

takke *vi* flowing over the brim of something in small quantities; **pii takke ki i agulo ma gitwommo iye ci oo piny,** because of shaking, the water flows over the brim of the pot where it has been collected; **pii tagge** is better than **takke.**

takko *vt* to remove / removing by magic means; **takko awola,** to remove / removing by magical means the poison or anything which has been magically placed into body; **ocitto ka takko komme bot ajwaka,** he went to the traditional healer to have the poison magically removed from his body.

takko *vt* to pour / pouring or to rmove / removing small quantity; **takko wii koŋo me abila,** to pour / pouring or to remove / removing a small quantity of beer for tasting. 2 **takko wic teŋŋe,** moving the head aside as to avoid being hurt.

tako *n* spleen.

tal *v* roast usually meat until dry; smoke until dry, **tal rec magi maber,** smoke this fish well; **tal gwana me abaŋŋa,** roast the cassava for eating.

tal *n* charming, casting spell on somebody; **pe amitto lok me tal,** I do not want anything to do with charming or casting spell; **latal,** one who cast spell on people.

tal *n* 1 thin pole or a long stick like bamboo for fixing nets. 2 **tal agat,** a long stick which elders hold at sacrifices for ancestors or having serious talks to their clan members or expressing prayers of the clan.

tal *adj* bald; **tal wic,** baldness of the head; **wiye tal, medde ameda** his baldness is increasing **winye otal,** he is bald.

talle *vi* can be dried; **recce twerro talle ki yen matye ni,** the firewood which is present is enough for smoking it.

tallo *vt* to dry / drying over fire, to smoke / smoking or to broil / broiling meat or fish to become dry.

tallo *vt* to charm / charming, to cast / casting spell; **tallo dano pe ber,** casting spell is not good.

tam *v* think, consider, ponder; **tam lokke maber,** think about it carefully

tam *n* thought, idea, pondering, consideration, deliberation; **tam pe rac,** idea is not bad or pondering is not bad.

tam *adv* wide, broad; **mukeka ne lac ni tam,** the mat is very wide and broad.

tamciya *n A* an umbrella

tam-tam *adv* unsteadily; **wotto ni tam-tam calo ŋat ma omeer,** walks unsteadily or staggers like a drunkard.

tamme *vn* his idea, thought, opinion; **tamme tye kwene i kom lok man,** what is his opinion or where is his thought or idea on this matter?

tammo *vt* to think / thinking, to ponder / pondering over, to reflect / reflecting, to consider / considering, to meditate / meditating, to deliberate / deliberating; **itye ka tammo ŋoo?** what are you thinking about or pondering over or considering about? **tammo me dok gaŋ diki,** thinks / thinking of going home tomorrow; **tammo pi gin ma etimmo,** reflects / reflecting or ponders / pondering on what he did.

tandarua *n A a* mosquito net.

taŋ *v* deviate, turn away from the norm; **taŋ wiye woko wek pe otii gin ma en mitto tiyone,** turn him away from doing what he wants to do.

taŋ *adv* tightly, immovable. **omokko ni taŋ.** It stuck fast, cannot be removed.

taŋ *prd* disagreeable taste, taste like ash, alkaline salt.

taŋ *adv* indisciplined child who cannot listen to his father; the central people prefers **teŋ**; see **diŋ**

taŋa *n* a mixture of water and flour which is used for ritual sprinklings at the ancestral shrine; **gigoyo taŋa i wii lee ki i cwiny dano,** they sprinkle the mixture on the head of the animal killed and on the abdomen (*epigastrium*) of the people.

taŋauji *n* ginger, one of the spices used for cooking food to make it taste very good, some people use it in their tea; it is obtained from a tuber of a plant.

taŋŋe *vi* deviating, turning away; **tye ka taŋŋe caa pe mitto citto gaŋ,** is turning away, he does not want to go home. **otaŋŋe ocitto ka mukene,** he suddenly turned and went elsewhere;

taŋ ŋwiny, taŋ tee *n* buttocks.

taŋ laro *adv* in the open air, unprotected, defenceless; **latin odoŋ i taŋ laro, jo tugi doŋ gutoo woko, gipe,** the child is now left on his own because all his relatives have died.

taŋŋo *vt* to extend and supinate ones hand when begging for help; **taŋŋo ciŋŋe pi kony,** extends and supinates his hand for help.

taŋo *n* miracle, wonders, mystery; **man jami me taŋo mada,** this is a wonderful thing or this is a mysterious thing.

tany *vn* rage, be furious; **tany ka lweny,** furiously fighting, cannot be stopped; **otany i komme ki daa,** he sat upon him with furious quarrelling with him.

tanynye *vi* burst with rage; **danone marro tanynye ki daa made,** he liked buarsting out with rage of quarrlling **otanynye obinno ma lyet macalo mac tet,** he bursts out with rage and came out with force which is hot like a burning furnace.

tanynyo *vt* to uproot, lift the earth all over; **opego tanynyo piny,** the pig disarranges the ground all over; **yamo tanynyo wii dero woko,** the wind blows off the grass from the roof of a granary.

tanynyo *vt* to turn something inside out, push the chest forward; **wotto ma tanynyo korre atanynya,** pushes his chest forward, in a boastful manner while walking / walking out pushing his chest forward in a boastful manson.

tap *adv* at once, at one blow; **gutoŋŋo ŋut gweno ni tap,** they cut the fowl's neck at one blow.

tarabana = karakap *n.* wooden sandals or clogs.

tara-tara *adv* showy, with display; **wottoni tara tara ki waar tyenne,** walks with boastful display with shoes knocking the ground.

tat *v* investigate, inquire; **tat tee lokke maber,** investigate the matter carefully.

tatte *vi* capable of being investigated or scrutinized.

taun *n Eng* town; **aecitto i taun,** I am going to the town; see **boma.**

tatto *vt* investigating, inquiring, scrutinizing; **tye ka tatto lok me kwoo matye kany,** he is investigating the theft here.

taya *S n* rest camp; **muni gugerro taya i ŋet got,** the Europeans built a rest camp near the hill; **taya** seems to be a distortion from English word *tire.*

tayi *adv* brightly, shining, **mac lyel ni tayi,** the fire burns brightly.

tayi *n* Eng. necktie; **tayi ŋut,** neck tie; **tayi tye ma kitgi pat pat mada ma dano gitweyo i ŋutgi,** there are many varieties of ties which people wear or put on their necks.

tayo *vi* to defeat / defeating, to subdue / subduing, to conquer / conquering; **tayo i lweny,** conquering or defeating in war; **tayo i doŋŋe,** to win / winning or to defeat / defeating in boxing; **see taa, tac**

teblet *n Eng* tablets; **munynyo teblet tek,** it is difficult to swallow tablets.

tebo *n* night-jar. (bird) family of owls. also pronounced **tepo.**

ted *v* cook; **ted dek wek gicam,** cook the food so that it may be eaten.

tedde *vi* can be cooked; **riŋo man twerro tedde maber,** the meat can be well cooked.

teddo *vt* to cook / cooking; **lateddo,** a cook; **ŋaa matye ka teddo?** who is cooking?

tee *v* lightly cut, scarify. **tee tyenne ki yat,** lightly cut or scarify his leg and put medicine into it; **tee iye me deyo,** make small cutting for decoration of her abdominal wall; a form of tatooing; see **teyo.**

tee *prop* 1 under; **tee** has many meanings depending upon the words with which it is joined as a prefix ; **tee cwak,** angle of lower jaw; 2 **tee gaŋ,** neighbourhood, or near the village; **tee got,** at the bottom of the hill, **tee itte,** back of his ear; **tee kika,** at the bottom of the door shutter; **tee kwaro,** tradition, ancestrial history; **tee lok,** meaning of the word or matter; **tee ŋwiny,** in the anus; **tee odoo,** the lower end of a stick; **tee ot,** at the side of the wall of the house; **tee poto,** bottom boundary of the field; **tee tokke,** back of his neck; **tee yat,** under a tree; **tee ywaat,** under the armpit;

tee kwaaro n tradition, customs, history.

teer *n* load, **teer me kado,** load of salt.

teer *v* take, carry; **teer kom i ot,** take the chair into the house; **teer latin paco,** take the child home.

teer *v* set the trap; **teer owic maber,** set the trap (for rats) well and ready.

teer *n.* state of pregnancy; **ŋat ma tye ki teer myero pe obed ka tiŋŋo teer ma pek twatwal,** the one who is pregnant should not be carrying very heavy things. **teera** sometimes called **tuura** n. raised part of a country or elevated part of ground as opposed to low part.

teere *adv* throughout the night; **gumyello piny ni teere,** they danced throughout the night.

teerre *prn* the load; **teerre pek,** the load is heavy.

teerre *vi/n* 1 can be tuned; **naŋane twerro teere,** the harp can be tuned; 2 to take / taking onself; **teerre kenne ka tukko odilo,** to take / taking himself by his own means to the football match; **teerre kenni,** take / taking yourself, that is, go by your own means; **teerre ki coo,** to go / going to men (normally for sexual activities).

teerro *vt* 1 to adjust / adjusting properly, make straight or right. 2 **teerro it,** *(lit* set up ones ear) to listen, pay special attention to.

teerro *vt* to set / setting ready (something); **teerro owic,** to set / setting the trap or snare ready; **teerro kor,** to show / showing strength; **teerro**

naŋa or aduŋu, to tune the harp or other string musical instruments.

teerro *vt* to take / taking, to carry / carrying away; **teerro boŋo i ot,** to take / taking the cloth into the house; **teerro mon,** to take / taking women (for sex).

tee te *vt* words, said to a baby to encourage walking.

tee te *adv* tottering, unsteadily, unfirmly; **latin wotto tee-te ,** the baby walks unsteadily or tottering; see **teyo**

tee ywaat *n* under the armpit, other people say **tee ywet,** *axilla.*

teggo *vt* 1 to strengthen; **riŋo teggo kom,** meat strengthens the body; 2 to be strong, robust, sturdy; **latin doŋ oteggi,** the child is now fully grown up to look after himself; **nyig yat doŋ oteggi,** the fruit is fully developed and ripe for harvesting.

tei-tei *n* glass blue beads. (for neckless), normally called **kiteyi teyi.**

tek *v* give, distribute; **tek ka ciŋŋini,** give or distribute as before.

tek *v* stop, prevent; **tek litino pe gulweny,** stop the children from fighting.

tek *adj* 1 hard, strong, brave, courageous; **nyonyo tek,** the metal is hard. **dano man tek,** this man is strong; **cwinynye tek,** he is brave or courageous; 2 **lokke tek,** the matter is difficult. 3 rigid, stern; **tek me noŋŋo gin mo ki botte,** it is difficult to get anything from him, he is stingy; 4 **dogge tek,** he is stubborn and clever at talking; 5 **wiye tek,** he is frank, bold; **tek wic,** boldness, and frankness.

tek *n* force, vigour; **okwanynyo ki tek,** he took it by force; **tek okello buk cen ci pe doŋ gigoye,** once he brings the book, he will not be caned.

teke *n* small wooden pin or nail; **teke me guro laa nyo pyen,** pins or nails of wood for nailing and stretching hide.

tekko *vt* to separate / separating or to stop / stopping fighting parties; **tekko litino ma gitye ka lweny,** stopping the children who are fighting.

tekko *vt/n* to give / giving in equal proportion; **tekko waragi i gilac,** pouring waragi in glasses in equal proportion.

teko *vn* strength; **teko kom ber mada,** body strength is very good.

tel *v* 1 pull; **tel matek,** pull very hard; 2 *vt* **bin itel wiwa,** come and lead us or guide us; 3 *n* **latel wii dano,** leader. 4 *v* **tel wiwa,** lead us.

tele *n* **anyeeri tele,** reed rat, edible rat with long tail; c/f **anyeeri atuya.**

telle *n* pulling; **tukko me telle,** tug of war. *c/f* **ywaane.**

tello *vt* to pull / pulling, 2 to lead / leading, or to head / heading, to conduct / conducting or to guide / guiding.

tello *vn* to become / becoming erect; **tello cun,** erection of the penis; **cunne otello,** his penis is erected or his penis has become big, straight and rigid.

tem *v* try; **tem kwan matek,** try to read hard.

temme *vi* try yourself; **temme me kwan matek,** try yourself to read very hard.

temmo *vt* to try / trying, to attempt / attempting, experiment; 1 **temmo kwan matek,** tries to read very hard; 2 **temmo cuŋ ki tyenne acel,** tries or attempt / attempting to stand on one leg. 3 to test; **temmo motoka ka cakke,** tests / testing the car if it can start.

tem tem *adv* slightly better; **lokke dok temtem,** his speech is better or preferable; see **tworra tworra.**

ten *v* support; **ten wiye ki dul,** support his head with a pillow; **ten toŋ ki kwot wek pe opoti,** prop up the spear with the shield to prevent it from falling; **laten wic,** pillows (soft or hard, in the past people used a piece of log as pillow).

tenne *vi* to learn / leaning, to rest / resting against, or on; **ladit tye ka tenne ki kicaa pamba ma giketo iŋeye,** the old man is leaning on a bag of cotton placed behind him; **latwoo doŋ tenne tenne,** the patient now sits up, 2 to be in an isolated and visible place; **winyo otenne wii yat caa,** the bird visibly perching on a tree there alone; **dwe tin otenne kama leŋ,** today the moon is visibly clear in the sky.

tenno *vt* 1 supporting, sustaining; **tenno canduk ki kidi ma oketto i teere,** to support / supporting the box with a stone which he placed underneath. 2 to prop / propping, to prevent / preventing from falling.

teŋ *v* 1 dust, shake off; **teŋ apwa woko ki i kom bataniya,** dust the blanket by beating it with stick or shaking; 2 entice **teŋ wii dako woko,** entice the woman (away from her husband). 3 strike or cane **teŋ ŋwiny latin ki odoo,** strike the child's bottom with a stick.

teŋ *n* side; **teŋ meja,** side of a table; **teŋ waŋ,** corner of an eye.

teŋ *vn* to become stiff, rigid and crooked, or bent; **laa teŋ oyot ka giwekko orii wii ceŋ,** the hide becomes stiff if left in the sun for a long time; **laa otwoo oteŋ woko,** the hide dried and became stiff; **doggola oteŋ woko pe lorre,** the door is bent, and cannot be shut.

teŋ *vt* disobedient, turn away; **pe ber wiri latin me teŋ i kom wonne,** it is not good for the child to be disobedient to his father; **wii dako oteŋ woko i kom cwaare,** the wife has become disobedient to her husband.

teŋŋe *adv* sideways, aside; **ket ki teŋŋe,** put aside; **bed ki teŋŋe,** sit away or stay away or keep away.

teŋŋe *v /vi* be absent, or absent onself; **teŋŋe woko liweŋ i gaŋ,** living the home empty; **guteŋŋe woko liweŋ, gaŋ odoŋ kene,** all the people went away and the village was left empty.

teŋŋe *vi* fighting with sticks; **dano tin guteŋŋe mape wacce,** the people fight today each other very badly with sticks.

teŋŋo *vt* to turn / turning aside or off, to divert / diverting; **teŋŋo wii dano woko i komme,** diverting away the people from him.

teŋŋo *vt* to cane, beat with a stick; **teŋŋo ŋwiny litino ma wiigi ramm tin tye,** caning the disobidient children is today 1 **oteŋŋo ŋwiny latin pi rac wic,** he caned the child for being disobedient. 2 to thresh / threshing simsim from their pods, **guteŋo nyim aduko aboro,** they thresh the simsim filling up eight baskets; 3 to shake / shaking; **teŋŋo apwa woko ki i boŋo,** to shake / shaking the dust away from the clothes.

teny *v* dissert, abandon, leave alone; **teny litino gudoŋ paco,** leave the children to remain at home; **teny dakoni,** abandon your wife or dissert your wife; **teny tic,** abandon your work or leave your work.

tenynye *vi* can be deserted, abandoned, left alone; **tic man twerro tenynye,** the work can be left or abandoned.

tenynyo *vi* to leave / leaving alone, to dissert / disserting, to abandon / abandoning; **tenynyo dako,** to abandon / abandoning or to dissert / disserting a wife; **tenynyo tic,** to leave / leaving or to abadon / abadoning work.

tep *adv* sound of a broken thing especially gourd.

tet *v* forge; **tet kweri,** forge hoes; **cit ka tet,** go to forge.

tette *vi* can be forged, **nyonyo man tette,** this metal can be forged.

tetto *vt.* to forge / forging; **tetto kweri,** to forge / forging a hoe; **latet** *n* a blacksmith.

teyo *vn* walking unsteadily, **latin pudi teyo ateya,** the baby is still walking unsteadily; see **tee te.**

teyo *vt* to cut / cutting superficially usually for decoration of the body or for putting in medicine, tattooing, or scarifying (medicine); **gin teyo kama rem nyo okwot,** they cut or make superficial incision where it is painful or swollen, **latec,** the person who cuts the skin. see **tee.**

tic *vn* 1 working; **tye ka tic,** he is working; 2 pouring; **nen ka tic me pii i gin anena / ature tye maber,** see wether the pouring of water in the flowers is good; see **tii, tiyo.**

tic *n.* work, occupation, job; **tic en aye gin maber ki dano ducu,** work is something which is good for everybody. **latic,** a worker or an employee, **won tic,** an employer.

tic *adj* . moist, damp, little; **ciŋŋe tic,** his hand is moist, or he gives very little, in other words he is a miser.

tid *v* get little by little; **pii odwon woko**

tid doŋ atidda, the water has almost dried up, get a little by little. See **tod.**

tidde *vi* can be drawn little by little; **pii madoŋ odwon wokoni tika twerro tidde?** can the water which is almost dry, be drawn a little by little?

tidi *adj* small, little. **tidi mo,** very small; **miya matidi mo,** give me a little bit of it; **matidi mo kono inoŋŋe kany,** for a fraction of a minute you would have found him here.

tidu *n* mahogany tree.

tidu *n* numbness; **tidu odiŋo tyenne woko,** he has numbness of his leg; see **diŋ.**

tidu wic nyo cwiny wic *n* pit on head, seen usualy in children.

tigu *vt* coitus (animal), mounting; **nyok dyel tye ka tigu min dyel,** the he goat is having coition with the she goat or the he goat is mounting a she goat.

tii *vn* be old; **dano ma otii,** an old man of about 75+ years; **dano tii,** people get old.

tii *v* work, do; **tii tic ma gimiini maber,** do the work that you have been given well.

tii *v* pour; **tii pii i dek,** pour some water in the sauce; see **tic ki tiyo.**

tik *n vi* chin, **yer twii i tik,** the hair grows in the chin **yer tik,** beard; **yer tik myero gilyello teretere,** beard should be shaved frequently.

tik *v* follow; **tik yoo acel keken,** follow only one way; **tik tic meri keken,** concentrate on your own work only or occupy yourself with your work only.

tik *vn.* being fully grown (girl); **nyaane doŋ otik,** she is mature now or fully grown-up now (as judged by the smell of her body), see **opoŋ, otuur.**

tik *adj* sharp, pungent smell; **komme ŋwee tik,** she has a pungent smell.

tik *adv.* keep completely silent; **myero iliŋ ni tik,** you should keep completely silent.

tik *adv.* jumped and landed firmly; **opye ni tik i ŋom,** he jumped and landed firmly on the ground.

tika *adv* 1 is it, truly; **eno tika meeri,** is it yours? or is it truely yours? or is it really yours? 2 really; **en tika bicitto,** will he really go?; 3 should have; **tika acitto an ki komma,** I should go myself, *c /f* **tuka** is better; **tuka acitto an ki koma.**

tik-tik *n.* sound made by a turtle-dove and so name; **akuri tik tik nyo latik tik,** turtle dove; noted for its soft cooing

tiki-tiki *adv* 1 shaking about; **litino giyeŋŋo yat ni tiki-tiki,** the children are shaking the tree about. 2 truly; **abinno an ki komma ni tiki tiki,** truly I came myself personally.

tiki-tiki *Eng n* ticket; **tye ki tiki tiki me wot i dege,** he has an air ticket for travelling with the aeroplane.

tikko *vt/n* to follow, apply completely to one, concentrate; **lok man tikko in keken,** this matter concerns only you; **tikko yoo acel keken,** to follow / following only one way.

tiko *n* normally called **otiko,** beads. **tiko pyer,** beads worn round the waist

til *n* kob, gazelle, impala.

tim *v* do; **tim oyot oyot,** do it quickly.

tim *n* bush, jungle.

timme *vi/v* 1 to behave / behaving; **cit ento timme maber,** go but behave well. 2 to happen; **gin ma timme kuno ŋati moo pe ma ŋeyo,** nobody knows what happens there.

timme *vn* behaviuor, **timme, timmi rac,** his, your behaviour is bad,

timmo *vt* to do / doing, to make / making; **itye ka timmo ŋoo?** what are you doing. **timmo gwok nyo kir,** to do / doing something which is disgraceful, untraditional and regarded as a bad omen, which requires goat, sheep or chicken to be killed for atonement.

timo *n Lug* a thin long drum; this drum is common among the Baganda.

tin *v* sparingly, not all at once; **tin camme atinna,** eat the food sparingly.

tin *prp n* today; **obinno tin,** he came today.

tinne *vt* can be economized; **limme twerro tinne,** the money can be economized.

tinno *vt* to economize / economizing, **tinno lim** to economize / economizing the money i.e. take a little by little.

tino *n* childish manner, acting like a child; **lokko lok tino,** talks like a child, talks childishly or nonsense.

tiŋ *v* carry, lift; **tiŋ gunia man iteer kwica,** lift this bag and take it there.

tiŋ *n* drinks from the dregs of beer.

tiŋ *adv* fixed; **waŋŋe ocuŋ li tiŋ i komme,** he fixed his eyes on him; **ocello ki atero ni tiŋ,** he short and hit decisively with an arrow.

tiŋŋe *vi* can be carried, lifted, taken away; **yecci twerro tiŋŋe,** this load can be carried; **tiŋŋe ki i wii yat ci opotto piny,** came off from a tree and fell down.

tiŋŋe *vi* urging, hurrying; **cwinyne tiŋŋe ni myero etim gin mo,** he has an urge that he should do something; **otiŋŋe ki**

ŋwec, he took off in a hurry; see **yutte, omme, wet wet, pukke.**

tiŋŋo *vn* lifting, taking up, carrying; 1 **tiŋŋo yec malo i wic,** lifting the load up to the head; 2 **tiŋŋo latin,** carrying the baby; 3 **tiŋŋo lok terro i kot,** taking up the matter into the court; 4 **tiŋŋo lok,** getting involved in a case; 5 **tiŋŋo ali,** causing hostility, causing trouble or falling into trouble.

tiny *v* rub off; **tiny ŋor nyo pul,** rub off the pod from the cow peas or red skin from the groundnuts.

tinynye *vi* can be rubbed off; **pulle twerro tinynye,** the red skins on the groundnuts can be rubbed off.

tinynyo *vt/n* to rub / rubbing off the husks from seeds; 1 **tinynyo pul, kal, ŋor,** to rub / rubbing off red skin from groundnuts, husks from millet, pod from cow peas; 2 **tinynyo kidi ki cet nyim,** to rub / rubing off dirts from the grinding stone with dregs of simsim.

tipo *n* 1 shadow; shade; **tipo yat,** shade of a tree; 2 soul, spirit; **tipo dano,** soul or spirit of a man, 3 shade of a man, 4 ghost.

tir *v* make straight; **tir yoo man wek ocuŋ atir,** straighten this way to make it straight.

tir *adj* straight, right, just; **lapim bor piny tye atir,** ruler is straight; **lokke atir mada,** his story is quite right; **oŋollo lok atir,** he made a just judgement.

tir *n* long stick or rod used for playing game of circle / loop (**cubbo lawala**).

tirre *vi* can be made straight, straightened; **yoone twerro tirre,** the road can be straightened or made straight.

tirri *vi* becoming hard, hardening; **layata otirri woko dag cek,** the potatoes has become hard it cannot be cooked soft; **lokwu miyo ciŋŋe tirri woko ka coc,** your words make him unable to write; or your words discouraged him from writing 2 Stunted; **latinne tye ka tirri woko pe doŋo;** the child is becoming stunt, cannot grow; **Okot otira macon,** Okot is an old dwarf.

tirro *vn* to correct / correcting, to make / making better; **tirro lok,** to correct / correcting the words said; **tirro dano i tyeŋ,** to make / making people stand in a straight line.

tirro *vt* to put / putting up at, to stay / staying at; **Okello tirro kwene?** where does Okello go to stay? or at what place does Okello put up?

tiru *n* large grass patches over water, the "sudd" **rec tye madwoŋ i tee tiru,** there is plenty of fish under the patches of the grass over the water.

tit, *v* tell, explain; preach; **tit lok ki dano wek guniaŋ maber,** tell or explain to the people so that they may understand well or preach to the people so that they may understand well.

titte *vi* 1 can be explained or can be told; **lokke twerro titte,** the case can be explained, 2 tell; **titte wek oŋee,** tell him so that he may understand. 3 explain yourself, say who or what you are; **titte wek giŋeyi ni in aŋa,** say who or what you are so that the people may know you.

titto *vi* to explain / explaining, to preach / preaching; 1 **titto tee lok,** to explain / explaining the meaning of words; 2 **titto lok,** to preach / preaching; **titto lokke niaŋŋo dano mada,** his

preaching makes people understand well; **latit lok** *n* a preacher.

tiyo 1 *n* aging, getting old; **tiyo kello pekko,** getting old brings problems; 2 working, doing something; **tiyo tic matek yoggo kom dano,** hard work weakens the body; 3 pouring; **tiyo pii me lwokko ciŋ,** pouring the water for washing the hands; see **tii, tic.**

to *conj* normally placed after an appropriate pronoun; **en to** becomes **ento,** but; **giwacci icit Gulu ento in dok i icitto meri Kampala,** you were told to go to Gulu but you went to Kampala instead.

tobi *n* yeast, levean.

Toci *n* a river; **kulo Toci ocakke nia ki i kom got Keyo ka ocitto odonynyo i River Nile.** river Toci started from Mount Keyo and flowed into River Nile.

tocco *adj.* not fully developed, not ready for harvesting, tender, delicate; **anyogi pud tocco,** the maize is not yet ready for harvesting or it is still tender.

tod *v* draw water in small quantity; **tod pii ki i waŋ it kadi doŋ tye ka cwiny woko,** draw the water in small quantity from the well even though it is drying up; see **tid.**

todde *vi* can be drawn in small quantity; **pii ma doŋ odwon woko tika twerro todde?** can the water which is almost dry, be drawn in a small quantity?

toddo *vt* to draw water in small quantity from a well which is drying up.

togo *n* papyrus; **togo gicubbo doko kolo,** papyrus is made into a kind of a"mat"

tok *v* dish up; **tok cam ki dano wek gucam,** dish up the food for people to eat.

tok *n* neck, back part of the head; **lokko tok botte,** he turns his back to him, means he does not want to see him; **lok meno doŋ gi winynyo ki tee tok,** the matter can be heard with the back of the head, (which means he does not want to hear it or he dislikes it); **ocitto i tok ot,** he went behind the house, sometimes it means he has gone to the toilet.

tok *n* swelling of the knee, (*synovitis, septic arthritis,* effusion in the knee which may be blood or *sympathetic effusion*); see **took.**

tokke *vi* can be dished; **camme doŋ twerro tokke,** the food can now be dished.

tokke poss *adj* his hat; **teer tokke wek orukki,** take his hat to wear (on his head).

toki **(nyig malakwaŋ)** *n* seeds of a plant or vegetable called **malakwaŋ**; seeds are ground into paste which then made into sauce; the leaves of the plant taste sour but a delicacy to the people of the Acholi also called **toke** in some parts of Acoli.

tokko *vt.* 1 to hatch eggs; **gwenone pe tokko maber,** the hen does not hatch well. 2 *n* apportioning, distributing food, or serving food, dishing; **tokko cam ki dano me acamma,** dishing food for the people to eat.

tokko kom *vt* ulcerating the skin; **twoone tokko kom dano woko atokka, the disease** causes ulceration of the body; **twoo marac ma tokko kom woko,** a very bad disease which causes sores or ulcers all over the body.

toko *n* swelling; **toko okwot i ŋut ciŋŋe,** his wrist is swollen due to *synovitis* of his wrist joint, see **tok** of knee.

tokoloŋ *n* male a big lizard with red head and tail.

tol *n* a thread, string, rope.

ton *v* 1 drop or pour a little; **ton moo i dek,** drop some oil in the food. 2 to dilute / diluting; **ton pii i nyuka wek obed maliyo,** pour little water into thick porridge to make it more fluid.

ton *vi* droping; **pii tye ka ton,** the water is droping.

tonne *vi* can be dropped into; **yat twerro tonne i waŋ latin,** the medicine can be dropped into the child's eyes.

tonno *vt* 1 to speak / speaking scornfully, arrogantly or bitingly; **dakone rac tonno lok twatwal,** she is a bad woman, she always speaks scornfully and arrogantly; 2 posing ones head; **tonno ŋutte caa,** she poses her neck there, she stretches her neck there; **ŋutte otonne,** she has a long nice neck.

tonno *vt.* to pour drop by drop; **gitye ka tonno yat i waŋŋe,** the medicine is being dropped into his eyes.

tonno *vt* to grieve, or annoy, offend; **lokke tonno cwinynye mada,** the matter grieves him very much, or annoys or offends him very much.

tonno *vt* drips; **agulu pii ne tonno pii,** the water pot drips water.

toŋ *v* cut; **toŋ yat maca woko,** cut that tree down.

toŋ *n* Eggs; **toŋ gweno, winyo, twol, nyelo, udo, ki nyaŋ,** Eggs of chicken, fowls, birds, snakes, python, ostrich and crocodile

toŋ *n* 1 spear, *pl* **toŋŋi,** spears; there are many kinds of **toŋŋi; toŋ agara,** spear with long blade; **toŋ alwici or alwiro,** spears with short blade but long neck; **toŋ-kaba,** spears with broad blade but short neck; **toŋ-atum,** spear with broad blade but without mid rib; **toŋ-lore,** small spear; **toŋ-jok,** spirit spear, that is, the blade and shaft forming one iron piece.

toŋ-jok *n* painful swelling of the pulp of the fingers, *whitlow.*

toŋ ogwal *n* frog's eggs, **toŋ ogwal,** eggs of frogs;

toŋ–waŋ, toŋ-man *n* eyeball, testicle.

toŋŋe *n* real, model, type, pattern; **leb Patiko ki Payira en aye toŋŋe Acoli,** Patiko and Payira language is the real or standard Acholi; **en aye toŋŋe latin atika ma ŋeyo lok ma kunno,** he is the real child who knows what is there.

toŋŋo *vt* to cut / cutting, to fell / felling, to chop / chopping; 1 **toŋŋo yat,** to fell / felling a tree or to cut / cutting a tree; 2 false accusation, to slander / slandering, calumniate; **toŋŋo dano nono,** false accusation of a person; 3 to bite / biting; **twol otoŋŋe,** he was bitten by snake; 4 dig; **toŋŋo layata ki pul,** to dig / digging up potatoes and groundnuts. 5 to peck / pecking; **gweno tye ka toŋŋo kal,** chicken are pecking millet. 6 to start / starting home; **toŋŋo gaŋ,** starting a new home in a new place. 7 to break / breaking out; **toŋŋo twon nyero,** to break / breaking out into a fit of laughter; 8 *n* eating with; **toŋŋo kiteya,** eating with the children; e.g. **min gweno bene toŋŋo kiteya i kin litino,** the hand also eats the food which the chicks are eating.

toŋŋo *adj* 1 unbaked, unburnt; **agulu man**

toŋŋo, this is an unbaked pot, or pot which is not yet fired or burned. 2 not roasted; **moko koŋŋo man toŋŋo,** this unroasted flour for beer, not commonly spoken.

toŋŋo keny *vn* marriage without the consent of the girl.

toŋ pur *n* a kind of cuckoo (bird) that is the sound of how it sings or cries.

toŋ twok *n* a spear fixed on heavy clog and suspended over the passage of elephants as a kind of snare or trap; see **toŋ.**

too *v* deflate, reduce in size; **too mupira / odilo woko,** deflate the football. see **joo.**

too *adv.* even when stopped; **en olokko too,** he spoke even when he was prevented. (spoken mostly in Pabo, Pawel etc.)

too *n* a tree, from which oil can be obtained.

too *n* a Jackal, fox.

too *vn* becoming small, shrivelling, shrinking up, deflating, decreasing; **odilo doŋ tye ka too woko,** the football is becoming deflated; **akwotta ma i emme doŋ tye ka too woko,** the swelling in his thigh is decreasing.

too *n* 1 death, dying, becoming useless, expiring; **too pa litino gin marac mada,** the deaths of children are very bad; 2 *vi* **en doŋ cok ka too,** he is about to die; **otoo ni lwee,** he died peacefully.

topino *n* big brown fierce species of wasp.

top *vn* rot, putrefy, decay; **top pa riŋo a pi gwok marac,** rotting of meat comes as a result of poor preservation. **labolone otop,** the banana is rotten;

toppo *vt.* causing to rot, decaying, putrefying; **cukari toppo lak woko,** sugar causes decay of teeth or causes teeth decay.

tor *v* block, fill; **tor ot oyoo man,** block this rat's hole by filling it with earth.

torre *vi.* be filled up, be collected, assembled or massed in number; **dano torre i ot lukiko,** people have assembled in the court room; **umme otorre,** his nose is blocked (cold in the head); **itte otorre,** he is deaf.

Toro *n* a clan found in Gulu District as well as in Western Region.

torro *vt* 1 to cover / covering, to fill / filling, to block / blocking; **torro ot oyo,** to fill / filling in or to block / blocking the rat's hole; **otorro itte,** he decided not to hear or listen. 2. to gather; collect, **gutorro nyim i dero,** they collected sesame and put in the granary.

tot *v* gather, take, collect; **tot kic ki i boŋ maca,** take or collect honey from that beehive.

totto *n.* gathering. **totto kic,** gathering honey; **gitye ka totto kic,** they are gathering or taking honey, 2 straining; **litino toto waŋgi ka neno dano matye kalega,** the children strain their eyes to see the people who are praying.

toyo *n* dew; **toyo odyakko komme woko,** he was wet all over with dew.

toyo *vt* 1 to release, vent, reduce; **toyo kiniga i kom ominne,** he vents his anger on his brother. 2 to relieve; **ocitto ka tukko me toyo iye,** he went to play to relieve his fullness from eating food. 3 deflation; **otoyo odilo woko,** he deflated the ball.

tub *v* provoke, incite, **tub kic ci gikayo dano,** distub or provoke the bees and they will sting the people.

tuba *n Eng* tobacco; see **taba.**

tubbe *vi* to fall out; **dano tye ka tubbe ka lweny matek mada i bar odilo,** people are falling out into fierce fighting in the football field.

tubbo *n* inciting, instigating; **en aye ma tubbo dano miyo aa iye lweny,** he is the instigater of the peope which results in fighting; **tubbo kic miyo gikayo dano,** inciting the bees make them sting people; **tubbo lee ito** incite the animals.

tuc *v* 1 pierce, perforate; **tuc it latinni,** pierce the ears (lobes) of your child; 2 reveal; **tuc lok ma iwinynyo,** reveal what you heard, 3 confess; **tuc bal meeri,** confess your sin; **pe i tuc tyen leela,** don't pierce the bicycle tyre; 4 *vn* to arrive suddenly; **wonne otuc mapudi peya gucakko cam,** the father arrived suddenly before they have started lunch; **ceŋ otuc,** the sun has risen. 5 a lesson; **ka pe doŋ itti otuc ci ibinenno,** if you don't listen you will see (this must be a lesson to you, if you have not yet learnt you will see).

tucce *vi* can be pierced; **awal man twerro tucce,** the gourd plate can be pierced; **ocitto ka tucce i ot yat,** he went to have an injection in the hospital.

tucco *vt/vn* to pierce / piercing, to perforate / perforating; **tucco it,** to pierce / piercing the ear lobes; 1 **tucco pii,** to drill / drilling for the water; **tucco waŋ it,** to excavate / excavatng a well. 2 confess; **tucco balle,** to confess / confessing his guilt. 3 betraying; **tucco gin ma dano moo otiyo pe ber,** betraying somebody for what he has done is not good; **tuccu kerro / pil,** to pierce through.

tud *v* knot; **tud tol aryo eno wek obed mabor,** knot the two ropes to make it long; **tud tol kany,** knot the string here; **tud uno i ŋut dyel,** knot the rope around the neck of the goat.

tudde *vi* 1 can be tied; **tol aryo man twerro tudde,** these two ropes can be tied; 2 united; **gutudde kacel i komme,** they united together against him; 3 filled or full of; **ot otudde ki yito,** the house was filled with smoke.

tuddo *vt/vn* to knot / knotting up, entangle / entagling, get into a knot, connect; **tuddo tol,** knotting the ropes. 2 to join / joining, make common state; **tuddo dog woko,** to join / joining together against.

tug *n* home village; **yoo tug gaŋwa eni,** here is the way to our home **tug tye kwene?** where is the home / village of those people?

tug *v* stir, instigate, incite; **tug lweny,** stir people to fight, instigate people to fight; **tug lee wek gubin ci wacubgi,** stir the animals so that they may come for us to spear them.

tuga *n* bunch; **tuga labolo,** bunch of banana or plantain, also **tug labdo.**

tugge *vi* can be stirred, **lweny twerro tugge oyot ka gilarro waŋ poto,** fighting can be started easily if they continue to dispute about the boundary of the field; **gutugge ka lweny nono,** they started fighting for nothing.

tuggi *n* their home, village; **tuggi tye Kitgum,** their home is at Kitgum.

tuggo *vt* to stir / stirring up, to incite / inciting, to instigate / instigating, to frighten / frightening; **tuggo lee woko ki i dog kulo,** to stir / stirring or to frighten / frightening off the animal from the river; 2 **tuggo lweny,** to stir / stirring or to instigate / instigating people to fight. 3 to release / releasing or to set / setting off; **tuggo owic woko,** to set / setting off the snare.

tugu *n* borassus palm; **tugu muno,** pawpaw.

tuk *vn* flying; 1 **tuk ki degge ber mada,** flying with an aeroplane is very good. 2 to start, take off; **otuk ki kany,** left from here; **otuk ki ŋwec cut i kare ma owinynyo lokke,** he took off at once on hearing the news. 3 to come to nought; **lok me kenynye tuk woko,** his marriage affairs has broken off. 4. to strain or sprain; **pyere otuk woko,** he sprained his back and now having pain in it.

tuk *n* small ant-hill; **mon marro tuk mada me torro dye ot,** women like the earth from the small ant-hill for making strong the floor of the house.

tuk-keno *n* fireplace which consist of lumps of clay or stones (three) used as support for pots;

tukke *prp* flying (time); **tukke ki kany bibeddo aweene?,** when will his flying time be? when will it fly from here?

tukkeno *n* place beside the fireplace, some call it **tukeno.**

tuk-tuk *adv* 1 sound of a motor cycle. 2 soap foaming make similar noise **tuk-tuk.**

tuko *vn* play, games, sport; **tuko ŋwec,** athletic; **tuko odilone tye niŋniŋ?** how is the football play or match going on? *vi* to play, **cittu ka tukko woko,** go to play outside;

tukko *vt* threading; **tukko otiko / tiko,** threading beads on a string.

tukko *vt* to force somebody to do something; **otukko Ocan me ŋwec kun onoŋo pe mitto,** he forces Ocan to run though he does not want to run.

tuko-lum *n* remain of bases of grass that have been burnt off.

tul *v* 1 open wide; **tul waŋŋi,** open wide your eyes; see **deŋŋo waŋ, tullo, nyullu waŋ, danynyo waŋ;** 2 project backward; **tul duddi,** project your buttock backwards.

tula *n* an owl; **tula cammo dye wor,** an owl eats at night.

tullo *vt* 1 to cause to project, open wide; 2 to project / projecting backwards; **tullo dud,** to project / projecting buttocks backwards. **otullo waŋŋe i komme,** he gazed at him with wide open eyes (usually in anger);

tum *n* straight wooden horn.e.g. flutes, oboes and some trumpets etc.

tum *vi* finish; **tum kwan bicakke i ceŋ abic,** the end of study will begin on Friday. **tic otum,** the work is finishes;

tum *v* sacrifice, cut; **tum romo man me abila,** sacrifice this sheep for the atonement.

tummo *vn* sacrificing; **tummo romo,** sacrificing sheep by killing it.

tun *v* sell; **tun jami magi woko,** sell all these things (not very much spoken now) see **cat.**

tunno *vi* to sell / selling; **tye ka tunno jamine i cuk,** she is selling her things in the market, (not very much spoken now) except by people from west of Gulu.

tuno *n* breast; **tuno dyaŋ,** udder; shapes of breasts: **tuno nya romo,** big conical breast with wide base; **tuno yago or**

tuno lut, a breast which has already drooped, a long suspended or pendulous breast; **tuno opiro,** small conical breast which becomes very small in old age; **tuno kiluka,** breast with thin neck and big head (usually droops down quickly).

tuŋ *n* horn; **tuŋ dyaŋ, dyel,** etc., cattle's and goat's horn; **tuŋ kwot,** pointed corners of the shield.

tuŋ *n* direction, side, part or region; **tuŋ ku nyaŋo,** East; **tuŋ kupiny, nyo tuŋ potto ceŋ,** West; when looking East; **tuŋ lacuc,** South; **tuŋ lacam,** North; **odok tuŋ kwenne?** which direction has he gone? **dwog tuŋkany,** come this side; **gin gitye tuŋ potto ceŋ me boma nyo taun,** they are on the West side of the town.

tuŋ *vi* to suffocate, choke, suppress; 1 **tuŋ ki yito,** suffocates or chokes with smoke; 2 to drown; **en opotto i pii ci otuŋ iye kuno,** he fell into the water and drowned there; **tuŋ ki cam,** choking on food.

tuŋŋo *vt* 1 to suffocate, suppress; **yito tuŋŋo dano,** smoke suffocates people; 2 **tuŋŋo lokke woko ci pe doŋ lokko gin mo,** he suppresses his thoughts and therefore he did not say anything; **lokke otuŋŋo woko,** he was overwhelmed by the words or matter; 3 pump with many words; **tuŋŋo dano ki lok twatwal,** to talk / talking too much and at frequent intervals; 4 to stuff, **tuŋŋo latin ki cam,** to stuff / stuffing the child with food.

tuny *v* uproot, **tuny layata,** uproot the potatoes.

tunynye *vi* can be uprooted, **layatane twerro tunynye,** the potatoes can be uprooted.

tunynyo *vt* to uproot / uprooting,
tunynyo layata, to uproot / uprooting
potatoes.

tunyo-tunyo prd. softish and loosely
coherent (cooked egg yolk).

tup *adv* at once, at one stroke; **otoŋo
ŋutte woko ni tup,** he cut the neck with
one stroke.

tut *n* beetle, there are many type of
beetles, tree beetle is the one that makes
holes in the tree while other beetles eat
beens, peas and leaves of vegetables
and by doing so make holes in them.

tut *n* pus; **bur okwotto emme, gibarro
ci tut omol madwoŋ mada,** he had
swelling in the thigh which was incised
and a lot of pus came out.

tutte *v* endure, strive, struggle with it
alone; **tutte kwede kumeno, ibinoŋo
berre lacen,** strive or struggle with
it like that, you will reap the benefit
later; **latutte mada,** indefatigable hard
worker, or an enduring person.

tutu *n copper sulphate,* medicine for the
treatment of the ulcers and eyes disease
(*trachoma*); now not much used.

tutu *n* a pot with pierced bottom for
straining alkali or lye salt from ashes.

tutuu *n* a bird which makes the same
sound of crying, they are *turacos* family.

tutuuno *adv* for the present, for the
moment, for the time being, in the
meanwhile; **mak man koŋ pi tutuuno,**
take this one for the moment; **koŋ ibed
kenyo pi tutuunu,** sit there for the time
being; **aecito woko, in koŋ ikura
kany pi tutuuno,** I am going out, in the
meanwhile, wait for me here.

tutuuno *n* small heaps of earth made for
planting sweet potatoes; it is named so
beause it resembles breast.

tuun *n* vagina, a female external opening
of the genital organ; **dog tuun,** vulva;
dog tuun tye iye aryo, ma woko, *labia
majora,* **ma i iye,** *labia minora* **(en
aye kare mukene katti woko i tuun
mon mogo ma gilwoŋŋo ni lyeer,** it
is the one which sometimes comes out
of vagina in some women and is called
lyeer); the *labia minora* is the one that
swells during intercourse and the one
that is called **ladeŋ.**

tuur *v* break; **tuur odoo man woko,**
break this stick.

tuur *vn* 1 fracture, breaking; **tuur tyen
latin obedo rac,** the breaking of the
child's leg was bad.

tuur *vi* reaching puberty; **anyira tuur ka
oromo mwaka apar wiyi abic,** girls
reach puberty when they are fifteen;
**anyakani doŋ tuur, pien doŋ nenno
dwee,** this girl has reached puberty
because she is now having monthly
bleeding, that is, she has monthly
menses now, see **poŋ, tik.** c/f **cot**

tuur *n* raised ground; **cittu wii tuur malo
ka wek wunen maber,** go up to the high
ground so that you may see well.

tuur *n* 1 flowers; **tuur yat man becco
mada,** this tree's flowers are very
beautiful.

tuur *n* face; **tuur nyim,** forehead;
tuur waŋ, eyebrow.

tuura *n* raised ground on side of river;
**cittu wii tuura ka wek wupyee maber
i pii,** go up the raised river bank so that
you may jump well into the river

tuure *vn* can be broken; **odoone twerro
tuure,** the stick can be broken;

turre *vi* suddenly started something;
tuure ka lweny pi lok mo ma titidi mo,
suddenly started to fight for a very small

thing; *vi* a sudden start; fighting; **lweny otuure oyot oyot mada laworo i duka,** fighting broke out suddenly yesterday in the shops.

tuurro *vi* blossoming, flowering; **yat tye ka tuurro,** the trees are flowering or blossoming. 2 *vn* blossoming, flowering; or blossoming of this tree **tuurro pa yat man yomo cwinyany,** the flowering blossoming pleases me.

tuurro *vt* to break / breaking, 1 **turro yat,** to break / breaking the tree. 2 to show / showing ungratefulness; *fig.* **kadi bed lawotte otimme maber ento pud tuuro yat i ŋwiny lawotte,** even though his friend treated him well, he still showed his ungratefulness by slandering him; 3 to defeat / defeating, to subdue / subduing; **muno otuuro lupyem woko,** the whites broke down the dissidents. 4 levying; **gutuuro cul madit i wiye,** they levied a heavy fine on his head or he was heavily fined.

tuurro *vt* to come / coming upon, to arrive / arriving unexpectedly, to take / taking by surprise; **marro turro dano mada ka gitye ko cam,** likes very much to come unexpectually upon the people when they are eating; **ladit otuurowa atuura,** the big man took us by surprise, **gutuuro makke ni kwic,** they seized him suddenly or he was suddenly seized.

tuut *adj* deep; **burre tuut mada,** the hole is very deep; this has given the above words **tu(u)t,** beetle, **tu(u)t,** pus, because beetle makes deep hole in the tree, and pus comes from a deep hole, hence they are all named **tut,** they can only be differentiated by how you pronounce them.

tuwa, tuwu, tugi poss *prn* our, your, their homes.

twac *v* throw down; **twac piny kenyo,** throw down there or hurl down there.

twac, twaca-twaca *intj* 1 exclamation of anger; **twac, wac kombedi wek watyek woko,** yes, tell me now so that we may settle it (usually in a fight).

twaca twaca *adv* turning about, writhing or twisting about; **rec bolle ni twaca twaca ka tye woko i wii teera,** fish twists or turns about when out of the water.

twacce *vi* falling heavily to the ground; **otwacce piny ni but nia ki i wii yat,** he fell down heavily from the tree; this is spoken mostly by Langi.

twacco *vt* 1 to hurl, throw to the ground with anger or vehemence; **makko lawotte ci twacco i ŋom marac mada,** takes his friend and hurls him down badly with anger; 2 to tell / telling (*lit* throwing big words); **twacco lok,** to telll / telling serious lies which is likely to cause problems; see **twac, remmo lok.**

twak *v* shout at; **twak litinoni gucit woko ki kenyo,** shout at the children to go away from there;

twak *v* boil, cook for a long time; **twak del raa man me acamma koni otyeno,** boil or cook this hippo's hide for a long time for eating in the evening.

twak *vn* 1 to boil / boiling, to bubble / bubbling; **dek tye ka twak i agulo,** the sauce is boiling in the cooking pot, being cooked; **kiyata tye ka twak,** the potatoes are boiling on the fire and making loud noise. 2 *vn* boiling, bublling; **twak pa dek i agulu,** the boiling or bubbling of food in the pot.

twakke *vi* to shout / shouting; *vi* **twakke matek kom litino wek guriŋ woko,** to shout very loudly at the children to make them run away.

twakko *vt* 1 to boil / boiling for a long time on the fire; **twakko riŋo ma otwoo nyo del raa,** to cook / cooking for a long time dried meat or hippopotamus hide. 2 to scold / scolding, to reprimand / reprimanding; **twakko litino matye ka ballo pii,** to scold / scolding the children who are spoiling water.

twal *adv* for ever; **ocitto matwal pe doŋ odwogo,** he went for ever, he did not return.

twala *adv* with long tail and menacing; **gin aŋoo ma okatto piny kany ni twala twala?** what has passed here with menacing long tail?

twatwal *adv* very, quite, very much; **ber twatwal,** very good or very nice, or very beautiful; some people say **tutwal, totwal, nyo twal twal,** but the central people speak, **twatwal.**

twaŋŋo *vt.* to strike one with stick; **twaŋŋo ŋee lawotte ki odoo,** to strike the back of his friend with a stick. (this word is used mainly by Langi).

twany *v* turn inside out; **twany del waŋŋe ka wek i nen maber,** turn the eyelid inside out in order to examine well.

twany-twany *adv* intermittently; **otit ryeny ni twany-twany,** the firefly shines or glows intermittently; **matto taa ki yitone ni twany twany,** smokes with the smoke rising out by each puff.

twanynye *vi* turned inside out; **del waŋŋe twanynye maber,** his eyelid turned inside out easily.

twanynyo *vt* 1 to turn / turning inside out, to reverst / reversing, turn up; **twanynyo tee waŋ,** to turn / turning inside out of eyelids; **twanynyo ciŋ,** to turn / turning the fingers backward.

2 **twanynyo lok,** to involve / involving in serious problems or argument.

twar *v* drive away, disperse; **twar dyegi ki i poto woko,** drive away the goats from the field.

twarre *vi* flown away, **aweno twarre woko mapudi peya wao,** the guinea fowls fly away before our arrival.

twarro *vi*[1] to snore; **ŋadi twarro twatwal ka onino,** so and so snores too much when asleep. 2 snore, **twaro rac,** snoring is bad.

twarro *vt* to drive away, disperse,; **dano ma wotto twarro aweno woko ci pe doŋ wacello mo,** passersby, drive away the guinea fowls and so we do not shoot any.

twat *n* pet name, for girls or women (usually the names of famous people or chiefs). c/f **nyiŋ twon.**

twec *vn* imprisioning, tying, binding; **dano myero gulwor twec i jero,** people should be afraid of being imprisoned in the jail; **twee, tweyo.**

twee *v* tie, imprison, bind; **twee ciŋŋe,** tie his hand; **twee i jero,** imprison him; **twee boŋŋi maggi,** bind these clothes; see **twec, tweyo.**

twek *v* send, transmit from person to person by words; **twek lok ocit gaŋ,** send words home; *vt* **yeny yoo mo wek itwek lok ocit bot nerru,** find means of sending words to your uncle.

twekke *vi* be transmittable, be transmitted; **lokke twerro twekke,** the news can be sent or transmitted from hand to hand.

twekko *vt* 1 to send / sending, or to transmit / transmitting; 2 **twekko lok,** to send / sending news, information;

that is, from one person to another until it arrives.

tweŋ *vt* speak with versatility, cleverness; **dogge bedi tweŋ-tweŋ**, to speak / speaking non stop without reasoning (usually in quarrelling).

tweŋŋo *vt* 1 to speak / speaking with versatility, cleverness; **lacoone tweŋŋo leb Raciya mape wacce,** the man speaks Russian fluently and with great versatility; chatter; **latin man tweŋŋo lok mada,** this child speaks very well (though very young);; quarrelling; **tweŋŋo lok myero ki mon ma doggi beddi tweŋ tweŋ laboŋŋo gik ento pe ber ki coo,** talking too much belongs to women who go on talking non stop but not good for men.

tweny *vn* straighten, make straight; **bao ne mitto tweny ka wek gicwer me doggola,** the wood plank needs to be straightened in order to be planed for the door.

tweny *v* straighten, make straight; **tweny bol toŋ,** straighten the shaft of the spear; **tweny latin obed maber,** straighten the child to his senses to be a good child.

tweny, nyo twany *adv* suddenly, at once; **otuc ni tweny,** he arrived suddenly, unexpectedly; here **twany** is preferred.

twenynye *vi* to stretch; **ladit aa malo ci twenynye,** the old man gets up and stretches himself; 2 can be straightened; **odoone twerro twenynye,** the stick can be straightened.

twenynyo *vt* 1 to straighten / straightening; **twenynyo bol toŋ,** to straighten / straightening the shaft of the spear; 2 **twenynyo dano.** to set / setting right, bringing a person to his senses or reason by some punishment; 3 to stretch.

twer *vn* power, capability, strength, ability; **tye ki twer me makki,** has the power to arrest you.

twer *n* power, strength, ability, capacity, right; **twer ma en tye kwede oa ki bot Lubaŋa,** the power which he has, has come from God; **en tye ki twer me makkowu,** he has the power to arrest you, **en tye ki twer me beddo i ot kany,** he has the right to stay in this house.

twerre *vi* can be done, **twerre tikka me gerro otti ?** can this house be constructed? **gerro otte twerre,** the house can be constructed.

twerro *aux v* can, capable, able; **twerro kelone,** can bring it; **twerro tiŋone,** can lift it, or capable of lifting it; **twerro citto,** can go.

tweyo *vt* to tie / tying, bind / binding, fasten / fastening, fetter, chain; **tweyo dyel,** to tie the goat; **tweyo yen,** to bind / binding the wood together; **tweyo tol waar,** to fasten / fastening the shoe; **tweyo tyen dano ki nyor,** to fetter / fettering the legs of people with chain; **tweyo ŋut dano ki nyor,** chains / chaining the people together by their necks; **tweyo i mabuc,** jails / jailing in the prison; see **twee, twec.**

twii *vn* to germinate / germination, to sprout / sprouting, shoot forth; **muraŋa twii oyot oyot mada,** the beans germinate easily and quickly; germinating; **anyogi tye ka twii,** the maize is germinating. 2 *vn* germination, sprouting, **twii pa muraŋa yot,** the germination of beans is easy.

twii *adv* in a thin column; **yito katto ni twii ki i wii ot,** the smoke rises up in a thin column from the house.

twic *adv* instant, trice, swiftly; **winyo odonynyo woko ni twic i odde,** the bird entered its nest in an instant.

twil *vi* emaciated, loose weight, lean; **danone doŋ twil atwilla** the man is getting thin and thin or becoming emaciated *see* **nweŋ**.

twillo *vi* to waste / wasting, to emaciate / emaciating, weakening; **twone twillo kom latin atwilla,** the illness makes the child thin and thin or the illness is wasting away the child's body.

twiny *v* blow the nose; **twiny ummi matek,** blow your nose very hard.

twinynye *vi* can be blown; **ogodo umme otwoo mape doŋ twerro twinynye,** the crust of mucus in his nose is so hard that it cannot be blown out.

twinynyo *vt* to blow / blowing (the nose); **twinynyo um,** to blow / blowing the nose.

twiyo *vi* to produce, bring forth; **ŋomme twiyo anyogi maber mada,** the maize germinates very well in the soil; see **twii** above.

twod *v* build in a form of a circle.; **twod latin ot mo,** build a small round hut.

twodde *vi* can be made round, be made in the form of a circle; **gin ma otwodde, twerro twodde,** a circular thing; can be made round.

twoddo *vt* to draw / drawing round, to encicle / encircling; **twoddo dyegi woko i otgi ki odiko con,** to surround / surrounding the goats in their sleeping place early in the morning; **twoddo latin ot mo,** builds a small round hut;

twoddo *vt* to inquire / inquiring from; **twoddo ka tee lok,** to enquire / enquiring about the information (from the neighbourhood); **wek goba, ka terri doŋ gitwoddo woko,** don't tell lies, all information about you have been found by inquiry; see **tatto, kweddo**.

twok *n* corner e.g. of table, sheet of cloth's edge; **twok meja,** angle of the table.

twol *n* snake.

twolo *adj* open; **dog canduk twolo,** the box door is open; 2 **waŋŋe twolo,** he is awake. 3 hollow; **oceke iye twolo,** the pipe for beer is hollow.

twom *v* knock, butt; **twom wii romo ki twor,** knock the ram's head with a mallet.

twom *v* draw; **twom pii ci ikel kany,** draw the water and bring it here.

twomme *vi* to butt / butting each other; **romo ki dyel gitye ka twomme,** the ram and the he-goat are butting each other.

twomme *vi* can be drawn; **pii matye i it twerro twomme,** the water in the well can be drawn.

twommo *vt* knocking, butting; **twommo wic i kom ot,** knocking the head against the walls of a house; **twommo tyenne i kom ajut,** knocking his foot against the stump.

twommo *vt* 1 to draw / drawing; **twommo pii,** to draw / drawing water. 2 To scoop / scooping off; **twommo wii cukari woko ka doŋ opoŋŋo kicaa woko,** to scoop / scooping or to remove / removing some sugar from the sack when it is too full.

twon *n pl¹* **twoni** 1 male of most animals; **twon dyaŋ,** bull of cattle. **twon dyel,** he goat;. **twon gweno,** a cock, rooster etc; 2 big, **twon lacoo, twon nyako, twon dano,** big man, girl and person.

twon *v* refuse to give; **twon koŋo woko,** refuse to give (him) beer.

twon *v* strain, filter; **twon kado,** strain or filter the ash to get out salt, lye salt

twonne poss *prn* *adj* his bull, the big one; **okello twonne me anekka,** he brought his bull for slaughter; **tye twonne mo madit mada i kom twonni ma okello,** there is a very big bull among the bulls which he brought.

twonno *vt* to refuse to give; **twonno koŋo woko,** refuses to give (him) beer.

twonno *vi* to strain / straining or to filter / filtering alkali salt or lye-salt from the ash; **twono kado,** strains or filters alkali or salt from the ash.

twoŋ *n* curved, bent; **twoŋ bad a api twoo nyac,** curved arm comes as a result of yaws infection.

twoŋŋe *vi.* to be curved, distorted; **badde twoŋŋe,** his arm is deformed, (insult).

twoo *v* look after or take care of ; **twoo meenni pien twoo mada,** take care of your sick mother because she is very sick or ill; see **twoyo.**

twoo *vi* diseased, ill, sick; **en twoo twoo me cukari,** he is suffering from diabetes.

twoo *n* 1. sickness, illness, deseases; **twoo odyer,** small pox; **twoo otel tok,** cerebrospinal meningitis; **twoo anyoo,** measles; **twoo anino,** sleeping sikness; **twoo gwok igudda,** chicken pox, **twoo ma lokko waŋ nen calo binjali,** yellow fever and jaundice of other causes; **twoo abaji,** syphilis; **twoo lujiko,** gonorrhoea; **twoo dobo,** leprosy; **twoo maleriya,** malaria; **twoo lugaga,** osteomylitis; **twoo cukari,** diabetes; **twoo jonynyo, AIDS** disease; **twoo aona opiyo,** tuberculosis; **ki mukene ducu mapol,** and many others.

twoo *vi* to dry; **boŋo tye twoo,** the clothes are drying.

twoo *vi* to wait for a long time; **dano gubeddo ka twoo kunno niaa odiko nioo wa otyeno,** people have been there from morning up to the evening.

twoo *n* dryness; **twoo ki kec,** staying with dry mouth without any food.

twoor *n* mallet; **twoor gioddo ki lobo agulo me acweya,** the mallet is used for beating clay for pottery.

twoor *v* knock; **twoor but ot kama pe atir oo piny,** knock down the wall which is not straight.

twoorre *vi* 1 to strike / striking, to knock / knocking against. 2 can be struck, can be knocked against; **tworre ki meja i dye wor,** knocking against the table at night; **dano twero tworre kwede ki dye wor,** people can knock themselves against it at night.

twoorro *vt* to knock / knocking with a heavy thing; **twoorro wiye i kom ot,** to knock / knocks his head against the wall

twoorro *vt* to push / pushing, **gwogi gin aye ma twerro tworro agulu ma i ot,** the dogs are the only ones which can push/pushing down pots in the house. to knock / knocking down, casting down; 1 **latin twerro twoorro agulo woko,** the child can knock the pots down.; **mutoka otwoorro but ot omuko woko,** the car knocked down sides of a house. 2 to throw; **mutoka opotto i pii ci otwoorro nyim ma otiŋŋo i pii,** the car overturned and thrown all the simsim it was carrying into the water.

twora *adv* I wish or I should wish but; 1 **twora nene acitti man kono atye maber,** I wish I had gone, now I would be much better; 2 **mutoka meera yella mada, twora meeri dok giber ber,** my car is bothering me very much but yours is slightly better.

twora twora *adv* slightly better, preferable; see **tem tem.**

tworo *n algae,* moss, slippery green *cryptogenic* plants in water; **pii obeddo tworo-tworo,** the water is full of moss or *algae.*

tworo *n* sisal, used for making strong ropes.

twoyo *vt* suffering, to care / caring of a sick person; **twoyo ŋoo?** what is he suffering from? **tye ka twoyo minne,** she is caring or looking after her sick mother; see **twoo.**

twoyo *vt.* 1 drying; **ceŋ twoyo kal,** the sun dries the millett. 2 to silence, **lokke otwoyo dogwa woko,** the news silences us, or we were silenced by the news.

tyak-tyak *adv* shining brightly; **kot will ni tyak-tyak,** rain flashes; **diamond wil ni tyak tyak,** diamond shines brightly or sparkles brightly.

tyaŋ *adv* very bright; **taar ni tyaŋ,** very white, snow-white.

tyaŋ *n* 1 sugar cane. 2 sweet sorghum stalk.

tye *vi* present, exist, greetings; 1 **en tye ningning?** how is he? the answer, **en tye maber,** he is quite well. 2 **en tye i ot,** he is in the house; see **mot.**

tyek *v* finish, complete, be over; **tyek dek ma i nyimmi,** finish all the food before you; **tyek tic mudoŋ manok-ki,** complete the remaining work.

tyekke *vi* can be completed or fished; **gerro otte tyekke diki,** building the house will be completed or finished tomorrow.

tyekko *vt* to finish / finishing, to complete / completing; **tyekko cam,** to finish / finishing to eat or finishing eating; **tyekko tic,** to complete / completing the work or finished working.

tyel *v* 1 support; **tyel kitanda wek pe oyeŋŋe,** prop up the bed so that it does not shake; 2 *n* **tyel me ot man tye kwene?** where is the support for the house?

tyelle *vi* supporting one another; **dano myero tyelle i tic ka gimitto doŋŋo anyim,** people must support one another, in work, if the want to succeed.

tyello *vi* to support / supporting; **tyello dano ma onoŋo tye ki pekko,** to support / supporting somebody who has trouble.

tyelo *n* inner room in a hut which is usually separated by a wall partition normally it is called **kutyelo.**

tyen *n* 1 leg, foot; **tyen myerro gilwokko maleŋ nino ducu,** feet or legs should be washed clean daily; **nyig tyen,** toes; **lwet tyen,** toe nails; **opuny tyen,** heels of the feet; **dye tyen,** sole of the foot; prn **tyenne ojweer,** he has small legs; **opuny tyenne okak,** the heels of his legs are cracked; **tyen ma okwot waar pe rukke iye,** shoes cannot be worn in a swollen leg; 2 cause; **tyen lok,** cause of the problem or meaning of the word. 3 **tyen mapol,** many times; 4 **tyen dyaŋ** *n fig.* **cammo tyen dyaŋ,** wedding feast provided by the bride's parent immediately after registration.

tyeŋ *v* to make rough; **tyeŋ kidi me reggo,** rough the stone for grinding by knocking with another hard stone to make it rough.

tyeŋ *n* row, line; **cittu ka ryeyo i tyeŋ,** go to line up.

tyeŋŋe *vi* can be made roughen; **kidi reggone twerro tyeŋŋe,** the grinding stone can be made roughn / can be roughened.

tyeŋŋo *vt* to make rough; **tyeŋŋo kidi,** to roughen the stone; **tyeŋŋo kidi reggo,** to roughen the grinding stone by knocking with another hard stone to make it rough so as to make it grind.

tyer *v* crack, split; **tyer got man,** split this stone.

tyer *v¹* present, gift, offer; **tyer twon dyaŋ ki cukul,** present the school with a big bull;

tyer *n* offering; **tyer mewu tye kwene?,** where is your offering **miyo tyer me dyel,** offering a goat?

tyerre *vi* can be split, cracked, **nyig yat man twerro tyerre,** this seed or nut can be cracked or split.

tyerro *vt* to split, crack, cause to crack; **ceŋ tyerro meja woko,** the sun makes the table crack or split. 2 to split; **tyerro kikopo woko,** breaks up the cup.

tyerro *vt* 1 to present or serve a person with something; **tyerro atabo dek ki lwak,** offering or laying before the people dishes (usually meat) to eat; it is done during ceremonies. 2 to offer / offering meat from animal killed by anybody to the chief according to the custom; **tyerro riŋo ki rwot,** to offer / offering or to present / presenting meat to the chief.

tyet *n* prophecy, divination, consultation with; **kany pe kabeddo me tyet,** this is not a place for devination or prophecy.

tyetto *vt* to consult / consulting with "**jok**" by the witch ("**Ajwaka**") so as to predict, or prophesy and to devine.

U u

uc *vn* exhibition of sham fighting with shield; **latinni pe ŋeyo uc,** this child does not know how to fight with shield; **cittu wunu ka uc,** go to carry out exercises of fighting with shield.

uc *vn* choking; **latinne dok limmo uc twatwal,** the child does get frequent attacks of choking; not frequently spoken, see **uu, uyo.**

uci *n s* thread (cotton) for sewing cloth; **mitto uci me kwoyo boŋone ma oyec,** wants thread for sewing or mending her torn clothes; some call it **wuci.**

ucu *n* crumpled grass, wood shavings.

udu *n* Ostrich.

uk *v* to rinse (mouth); **uk doggi,** rinse your mouth.

uk *v* pour to empty; **uk kal piny,** pour down the millet; **uk jami ma i canduk i wii meja,** pour all the things in the box on the table.

ukke *vi* 1 falling or running out; **nyim tye ka ukke woko ki i kicaa,** the simsim is pouring out from the sack. 2 poured or fall upon; **dano guukke i kom lakwoo ci gugoyo gunekko woko,** the people fell upon the thief and beat him to death; covered, **kic oukke i komme,** the bees fell upon him and covered him.

ukko *vt* to rinse especially the mouth; **tye ka ukko dogge,** he is rinsing his mouth. 2 to pour / pouring, to spill /spilling; **ukko bel woko liweŋ i ŋom,** to pour / pouring all the millet to the ground; 3 to empty; **ocitto ka ukko tutu,** he went to empty the dregs of lye.

uk-uk *n* alarm made with mouth by people calling for help for great danger (lion, enemy). **wuk wuk** is preferred.

ul *n* 1 *v* move; **ul pamba ma i dyee ot odok tuŋ cel wek owek ka beddo ki dano,** move all the cotton on the floor to one side in order to leave room for sitting of the people. 2 have too much; **guul tin ki cam mada,** they ate too much food today.

Ulaya *n S* Europe.

ulle *vi* move to one side; *v.* **ulle wudok tuŋ caa,** move to the other side. **dano ducu guulle gudok tuŋ cel,** all the people moved from one side to the other.

ulle *vi* feeling sick, **cwinynye ulle,** he feels sick; he feels like vomiting; he has *nausea.*

ullo *vt* to upset; **cam ma ocammo ni ullo cwinynye,** the food that he has eaten has upset him and making him want to vomit; *nausea;* **ullo cwiny,** nauseating, feeling sick, see **lemmo cwiny.**

ullo *vt* 1 to stir up, push; **raa ullo pii,** the hippopotamus stirs the water by pushing it about; 2 moving away; **ullo pamba odok tuŋ cel ki i dye ot,** move / moving the cotton to one side from the floor of the houise.

um *n* nose; **um ma ŋwee,** smelling nose; **um ma obab,** flat nose; *prov* **laber umme ŋwee,** a beautiful girl has smelling nose, it means that the one who is beautiful has some bad things (character, manner behaviour etc) therefore don't look only at the beauty of the girl; **ogodo um,** crusts from the infected dry nose; **um latin oluk,** the child has thick mucus coming out of his nose, **ummi okoŋŋe,** you nose is hooked or aquiline.

um *v* 1 cover; **um komme woko,** cover him up; 2 covering; **boŋo um tye kwene?** where is the cloth for covering? 3 lid cover; **laum agulo,** pot's cover,

um *vi* to pride and be happy; **Otto um ki lim ma ocammo aram,** Otto is proud and happy of the money which he fraudulently obtained.

um coŋ *n* knee cap; **otale twii i wii um coŋ,** the bursa develope on the knee cap. **opotto ci opwacco um coŋŋe woko,** he fell and got laceration of his knee.

umme *vi* 1 be cold towards somebody; **waŋŋe umme woko i komme,** he becomes jealous of him, or he becomes cold towards him. 2 to cover; **guumme ki bataniya ma giwillo laworo ni,** they covered themselves with the blanket bought yesterday.

umme *prn* his nose; **umme odiŋ woko,** his nose is blocked; **umme tye ka mol,** his nose is running; **umme tye ka cwer,** his nose is bleeding.

ummo *vt* 1 to cover / covering; **ummo kom ki boŋo,** to cover / covering the body with cloth; **ummo wii agulo ki ŋoo?** with what does he cover the pot? **oummo wii cak kiŋoo?** with what has he covered the milk? 2 to hide the truth; **gin ummo lokke woko,** they keep the affair secret.

un *n* over usage, over work, torture; **un me tic geŋŋogi cweyo,** overwork prevents them from being fat; **lumabuc gilimmo un twatwal,** the prisioners suffered very much from torture.

unne *vi* to suffer / suffering, **unne me pitto litinone kene,** to suffer / suffering to feed his children alone; **unne me**

gerro otte kene, to suffer / suffering to build his house alone.

unno *vt* 1 to over-use. **unno dano pe gin mober,** over-using a person is not a good thing. **guunno latinni mada,** they over worked the child very much, (that is they gave the child too much work to do, which he could hardly do). 2 to torment, torture; **guunno lumabuc mape wacce,** they tortured the prisoners very much.

uno *n* rope; **gam uno ene me tweyo dyel,** get the rope here for tying the goat.

ur *n* wonder, amazement, astonishment; **gin me ur,** a thing of wonder.

urra *n* wondering. **gin me urra,** a wonderful thing, a thing to be wondered at; **gin me aurra** is the proper sentence for the above.

urro *vt* to wonder at, gaze with amazement or astonishment; **gin urro tukku me rette mada,** they admire the game of wrestling very much.

urulee *n A* an adjutant (a soldier) to somebody.

uru-uru (uuru uuru) *prd* distended or swollen with gas, that is why it makes that sound.

utte *vi* urge to do something, other people say **yutte,** this is the one that is spoken by the central people; **cwinynya utte ni myero atim gin mo**—I feel an urge to do something; see , **yutte, tiŋŋe, omme, pukke.**

utumega *n* my brethren; **utumego,** brethren.

utuwora *n* my fathers; **utuwego,** fathers.

uu *n* chocking; **latinne dok marro uu twatwal ki cam,** the child chokes frequently with food or the child gets frequent attacks of chocking with food; this is not commonly spoken.

uyo *vi* choking, **cam dok uyo twatwal,** always gets frequent attacks of choking with food; see **uu, uc.**

uyu *n* puff - adder, viper, very poisonous snake.

W w

wa *prs prn prf* means we; **wa** *pref* to other words, e.g. **neno** becomes **waneno,** we see, or we saw; **wacammo,** we ate; **wakwanno,** we read.

wa *prs, prn. sff* means us, our, e.g. **kelwa,** bring us or bring for us, **otwa,** our house; **dwokwa gaŋ,** return us home.

wa *adv* even, as far as; **oriŋŋo wa Gulu,** he ran to as far as Gulu; **ocitto wa ki latin bene,** he went even with the child.

waa *adv* with much noise; **giwotto ki kokko beddi waa,** they were walking with much noise of crying.

waa *vt* bring taste, bring appetite, **waa doggi ki lemun mvan,** stimulate your taste and appetite with this lemon. **naŋ cwaa man wek owaa doggi,** suck this tamarind so that it may produce good taste in your mouth or good appetite; see **wac, wayo.**

wa a *prs vi* we rose, come from; **wa a odiko ki Gulu ,** we rose early in the morning from Gulu; **wa a ki Kampala laworo,** we came from Kampala yesterday.

waar *n* 1 shoe, boot; **waar tyen,** shoe; **del waar,** leather straps. 2 re- marrying somebody else's wife; **pe i kel kop me waar kany,** don't bring the case of remarrying other peoples' wives here.

waar *vt* remove **waar moo ma i wii cak woko,** remove the cream from the top of the milk

waaro *n* cotton; see **pamba**

waarre *vi* 1 to clear up; **piny doŋ tye ka waare** the weather is clearing up. **piny doŋ waarre,** the weather has cleared up or sky has cleared up; 2 disperse, withdraw; **wuwaarre woko ki kany wucit cen,** clear away from here and go away or elsewhere.

waarro *vt* to refund a husband by the person who has taken his wife, the dowry that the husband paid to the woman's father for marrying her.

waarro *vt* to skim / skimming or to take / taking from surface; **waarro moo ki iwii cak,** skimming the cream from the milk; **waarro jami woko ki i ot,** removing things from the house; not commonly spoken now.

waat *n* relative; **danone waat ki wan,** he is our relative; **waat macon,** old relative.

waat nyo wao waat *n.* landing place, drinking place for animals or watering place for animals.

waaya *n* sister of the father and sister of the husband, **waaya,** my aunt; **waayo,** aunt, a general name; the relations here are as follows: *sing* **waaya, waayu, waayone,** my, your, his aunt; pl **waayowa, waayowu, waayogi,** our, your, their aunt or aunts; **waayo** which is not closely related but from the same clan, they are as follows: **waacciwa, waaciwu, waacigi,** our, your, their aunts. **waayo** *pl* **waacci** *n* aunt (father's sister) (or husbands sister).

wac *vn* sour tasting like lemon, used as an appetizer; **dog ma kec mitto gin ma wac macalo lemun,** bad taste in the mouth requires sour tasting thing like lemon to produce good taste, that is, good appetite; see **waa, wayo.**

wac *adj.* 1. sour; **cwaa wac,** tamarind is sour; **gin ma wac yubbo dog kello mit dog ka icammo,** sour things bring appetite and good taste if you eat it.

wac *adj* lazy, indolent; **komme wac,** he is lazy or indolent.

wac kom *n* laziness, indolence, idleness.

wac *n* 1 news, **wac aŋoo?** what news? (**lok aŋoo** is preferred); 2 v say, tell; **wac weki awiny,** say so that I may hear, or tell me so that I may hear or listen; **lok** is preferred to **wac** and the one which is in common use now.

waca waca *prd.* spongy; **kiyata iye obedo waca-waca,** the potatoes are bad because they are spongy and watery.

wacce *vi* 1 capable of being pronounced or said; **lokke pe wacce,** the literal translation word cannot be pronounced or said. 2 **wacce,** his words or statement (not commonly used now); 3 **wacce,** tell him; c/f **titte.** (3) **wacce,** very; **ber mape wacce,** very good.

wacco *vt* to say, tell, mention the name; **enwacco ni ŋoo nyo wacci ŋoo?** what does he say? **owacca lok mo marac mada;** he told me a very bad news; **owacco nyiŋŋi bot rwot,** he mentioned your name to the chief.

wad *v* remove; **wad lum ki jami mukene ma ocullo waŋ it woko,** remove the grass and other things that have blocked the well; see **gwad, cot.**

waadi *pl* **of waat** *n* relatives; **gin waadi,** they are relatives; **joo man gin aye waadi pa Otto,** these are the relatives of Otto.

wadde *vi* can be removed; **daba ma i waŋ pii twero wadde woko,** the mud from the well can be removed.

waddo *vt.* to remove / removing with hands, (mud, thick gruel etc); **waddo waŋ it tye diki,** to remove / removing of mud away from the water well is tomorrow, **guwaddo lobo woko ki i waŋ pii,** they removed the mud away from the water well.

wai *inj* I say, word to draw attention, comes from **awacci; latinni wai pe mitto cam,** really or in truth this child does not want to eat.

wai *adv* really covered; **remo obeddi wai i dye ot,** the floor was really covered all over with blood.

waka *adv* dry, arid; **guwekko cogo odoŋ ni waka kenyo ma gucammo,** they left the dry bones scattered all over there from the meat which they ate.

wakke *vt* pride, showing off; **lacoo ne wakke mada;** the man is very proud or boastful; **lawakke,** a proud person, a boaster. 2 *n* pride, **wakke pe ber,** being proud is not good.

wakko *vt* -inviting people for collective work or action; **wakko dano ka dwar, myel, pur, ki mon ka kac,** -to invite / inviting people to come for hunting, dancing, caltivation and women for harvesting.(custom of Acholi).

wako-wako *adv* flapping wings; **arum tuk ki bwomme ni wako wako,** the ground horn-bill fly with flapping wings.

wal *v* collect or gather and remove, **wal lum ma i dyekal,** gather and remove all the grass in the compound.

walle *vi* can be gathered off; **yugi ma i ŋee otti twerro walle woko maber,** the rubbish behind the house can be well gathered away.

wallo *vt* 1 to gather / gathering; **wallo yugi,** to gather / gathering rubbish; **wallo lum ki i poto,** to gather / gathering grass from the field; **wallo lum ma i waŋ pii,** to gathere / gathering and to remove / removing the grass form the water well; 2 take off; **wallo boŋo woko ki i komme,** takes off part of the clothe from his body

wallo *vi.* boiling;. **pii tye ka wallo i agulo i wii keno,** the water is boiling in a pot on the hearth.

wan *prs prn* we, us. **wan kenwa,** we ourselves; **kel ki wan bene,** bring for us also.

wanno *Lang vt* hurting; **wanno tyenne,** he hurtshis foot.

waŋ *n* eye, 1. **yer waŋ,** eyelashes; **toŋ waŋ or nyig waŋ,** eye balls; ; **del waŋ,** eyelids; **waŋne odwet,** he has a weeping eyes;.*v* **ton yat i waŋ latin,** drop medicine into the child's eyes; *v* **rwany del waŋne ka inen,** evert the eyelids in order to see; **yat waŋ,** eye medicine; 2 look, appearance; **waŋne leŋ mada,** she is very beautiful, attractive; **waŋ latin pe leŋ,** child's face is not clean; **waŋne ogollo,** he has sunken eyes; **waŋne col,** he is unfriendly and has cold look; **waŋne tek,** he is smart, cannot be deceived, cunning, subtle, clear sighted; **waŋne ŋic,** he is still young, inexperienced, dull, sluggish; **en lworo waŋ dano,** he is shy, timid; **ocekko waŋne i komme,** he looked at him with anger and hatred, he directed his anger on him; **nenne rac ki i waŋne,** he hates him; 3 sight; **waŋ ceŋ,** sight of the sun; **pol oummo waŋ ceŋ,** the clouds has covered the sun's sight;.4 opening ; **waŋ-ot**, window; **waŋ-cel**, small hole through a fence or a hedge. 5 passage; **waŋŋa-yoo**, path; **waŋ-kor**, track; **waŋ-waat**, port, landing place (i.e. sea port); **waŋ-coo poto**, field's boundary 6 place, position, opportunity, need, requirement; **waŋ tic**, place for work; **waŋ lokke tye**, there is a reason (for discussion); **waŋ it**, source of water; spring, water well; **waŋ mac oo**, fireplace for warming; **waŋ bur**, sore, ulcer; **lawaŋ rwot**, confidant of the chief, **lawaŋ gabumente**, ambassador, representative; **ŋaa ma bicammo waŋ ker pa wonne**, who will be the successor or heir to his fathers kingship?; **waŋ kwanynyo cip** (*fig.* it means, it exposes the private part to the eyes to see), part of women's loin dress (no longer used); 7 time, moment, period; **waŋ otyeno**, in the evening; **waŋ tino**, childhood, childish, in the early age; **diki waŋ caa**, next year; **tin waŋi**, this time; 8 once, when; **waŋ mo** *cnj*, one day or once upon a time; **waŋ giryo**, twice.

waŋ *n*. 1 burning; **waŋ me ot pe ber**, burning of a house is not good. **duka acel tin owaŋ mada**, one shop burnt to ashes today.

waŋ *v* burn; **waŋ yugi man woko**, burn this rubbish.

waŋŋe *vn* burning; **waŋŋe ki peterol rac mada**, burning onself with petrol is terrible. **latin owaŋŋe marac mada**, the child burnt himself very badly.

waŋŋo *vt* burning; **waŋŋo buk dokocakke niŋniŋ?** how did burning of the books start?.

wany *n*. longing, burning desire, yearning; **lawany riŋo**, yearns or longs for meat; **wany kic nekke mada**, he yearns very

much for honey; **lawany, lakee**, eager, burning desire person. (for meat).

wany *vt* peel; **wany pok labolone ka doŋ icam**, peel the skin off the banana and then eat. See **bany, pok**.

wanynye *vi* 1 can be peeled; **pok yat man twerro wanynye**, the bark of this wood can be peeled; 2 *vn* yearning for, **pi wanynye me cammo kic ma omiyo obeddo i ŋet ot, omiyo gionynyo pii macol i waŋŋe**, because of yarning for eating honey, which caused him to sit at the side of the house, made it possible for the dirty water to be poured upon his face.

wanynyo *vt* to long / longing or to yearn / yearning for something; **wanynyo rec**, yearning for fish.

Wanynyo *vt* to peel / peeling, bark or remove the skin of something; **wanynyo pok labolo**, to remove / removing the thick skin of banana; **wanynyo waŋ bur**, removing off dressing on the sore or ulcer; **piny doŋ owanynye**, the weather has cleared out.

waraga *A. n.* paper, letter, epistle, *c/f* **karatac**

wau *adv* grown quickly very tall and large e.g. palm tree.

wau-wau *adv* looks big in appearance but light.

wayo *v* war dance before the ancestral shrine in thanksgiving (for having killed an enemy or a fierce wild beast).

wayo *vt* to eate something to bring appetite; **wayo dog ki gin mamit,** to eat either sweetened or nice sour taste to bring appetite to a sick person.; see **waa, wac**.

wec *vn* imputing, attributing, turning

away; **wec me bal i kom dano mukene gin marac mada,** imputing the fault to a man is very bad; **wec me wii leelani okonyi mada,** turning away of your bicycle saved you; see **wee, weyo.**

wec *prd.* 1. fully grown or developed for the purpose or expectation; **pe aŋeyo ka lee tin wec botwa,** I do not know whether we shall have plenty of animals **latin doŋ cok ka wec maber,** the child is now about to be fully grows-up and to care for himself. 2 according to expectation; **lee tin doŋ owec mape wacce,** there is plenty of animal according to our expectation today; **kare tin doŋ owec ki botwa,** there is favourable chance for us today. 3 suitable opportunity or chance; **kare pud peya owec ki botta,** I do not yet found a suitable opportunity or *lit* there ` is still no suitable opportunity for me.

wece *vi* rustle; **ŋoo ma beddo ni wece - wece i tee lummi?;** what is it that is rustling under the grass?

wed *vn[1]* careless talk; **lawed lok,** one who talks carelessly. 2. to talk carelessly, **wed lok,** talk carelessly.

weddo *vt* to act / acting or to do / doing something which is contrary to custom or good manner; 1 **weddo lok,** to speak / speaking carelessly or thoughtlessly; 2 carelessly or indecently; **beddo awedda,** seating carelessly and indecently.

wee *v* turn away, impute, attribute, 1 **wee wii motoka odok tuŋ lacam,** turn the motor car to the left; 2 **wee i wiye ni en aye ma okwallo,** attribute or impute to him the theft; see **wec, weyo.**

wee *n,* 1 contents of stomach; **wee dyaŋ,** content of stomach of cattle. 2 fresh cow dung, used for plastering floor.

wee! *inj* exclamation of surprise of (disapproval).**in wee, wek lokke obeddi,** you leave the case alone.

weene *vt* to duck aside, turning aside avoiding danger, **komme gum pi weene woko oyot oyot kono toŋ ocubbe,** he was lucky to duck away quickly to avoid being speared / or he would have been speared.

wee-wee *n* whispering secretly without arousing suspicion.

wego *n* fathers, owners

wek nyo weki *v* leave, let go, forgive, release; **wek ocitti,** let him go or release him; **wek anen,** let me see; **wek pe ocul,** leave him not to pay; **kadi beddi oballo wekke,** although he has made a mistake, forgive him.

wekko *vt* 1 to leave alone. forgive, release. 2 allowing, 3 be responsible for, cause; **wekko banyane,** to forgive / forgiving his debt, **wekko citto,** to let / letting him go; **boŋo ka gilwokko teretere wekko tii oyot oyot,** when the cloth is washed frequently, it gets old quickly.

wel *n* amount, sum total; **wel me willo guniya me kado ni adi?** what is the total amount of value of the sacks of salt?

wele *adv* easily at once, immediately; **yatte oputte ni wele,** the tree was pulled out easily without difficulty.

welle *adj its* cost, price; **gwenoni welle adi?,** what is the price of this chicken?

welo *n.* guests; **welo adi ma obinno tin?** how many guests arrived today?

wen *n* neck, **wen keno,** 1.the projected part of a small calabash or gourd. 2. fireplace usually made with three

projections and one of these is called
"wen keno".

weŋ *adv* completely, wholly, entirely;
cukari otum woko li weŋ, the sugar is
completely finished.

wenye *adv* sit or lie sprawling out;
**nyako ma caar beddo mere ni wenye
nyo liwenye**, a loose girl sits with
the legs opening wide or sprawling
out without care or sits indecently or
ungracefully.

wenye-wenye *prd*. not well prepared or
cooked and therefore unappetizing;
kwonne obeddo wenye wenye, the
kwon is not well prepared and therefore
watery and softish.

wenynyo *vt* to lie / lying with legs wide
open in an indecent way or sitting
sprawling out.

weer *n* wooden dish, oval in shape;
**weer en aye gijollo ki odii ka gitye ka
reggo nyim**, weer is used as a receiver
for simsim paste when the simsim is
being ground.

wer *v* paint or decorate; **wer kom ot man
ki raŋŋi ma obeddo ocwak-ocwak**,
paint or redecorate this house with
yellow paint.

wer *v sing* **wer wek wawiny**, sing so that
we may hear. **cittu ka wer**, go to sing;
joo mene ma gitye ka wer, who are
singing?

wer *vn* singing, songs, hymns; **wer me
pakko Lubaŋa**, hymn or songs for
praising God.

were *vi*. sound made by stirring or rustling
grass. **oyoo were kany**, the rat is making
a rustling sound here.

were-were *adv*. well flavoured, seasoned;
kadone were-were, the salt is very nice

and palatable; **pulle gicello were were**,
the groundnuts were roasted very well
with salt to make it palatable.

werro *vt* making slight noise by moving
something.

werro *vn* singing; **werro wer**, sing
songs.

werro *vt* 1 to colour / colouring, to dye
/ dying, to ting / tinging, to decorate
/ decorating; **werro ot ki reŋŋe**, to
plaster / plastering or to decorate /
decorating the house with colour;
werro wic macol, dying the hair black.
2 to season / seasoning; **werro kado
mamit i dek**, to season / seasoning the
sauce very well. 3 to stir / stirring or to
rustle / rustling grass.

wet-wet *prd*. hasty, rash, headlong;
cwinynye beddi wet-wet, his mind
is over anxious and excited to do
something; see **yutte, tiŋŋe, omme,
pukke, utte**.

weyo or weeno *vt* 1 to turn away; **ka pe
weyo wii leela maber ci yokko dano**, if
he does not turn well away the bicycle, he
will knock the people **ka nene pe oweyo
wii leela woko kono oyokko latin**, If he
did not turn the bicycle away, he would
have knocked the child.

wic *n* head; **wic ma otal nyo tal wic**,
bald headed, **lyello wic**, shaving the
hairs; **wic** means the flesh not inert thing
wheras **wii** means on top of or above
something e.g. **"wii meja,"** on top of
a table, it cannot be said **wic meja**,
because **meja** is innert; again it cannot
be said **"lyello wii**, but **"lyello wic"**.
when **wii** is used as adj. then it can be
said as **"lyello wii latin."**

wic *adv*. at once, quickly; **okatto woko ni
wic**, he went out at once unobserved.

wic *vn.* twisting thread and making string, spinning; See **wiyo, wii.**

wici-wici adv. quickly swiftly; **cam wunu ni wici-wici,** do eat quickly.

wid *v* cut round to make small; **wid tyen meja ki pinynye wek onen maber,** cut round the lower parts of the legs of a table, to make them look nice .

widde *vi* be thinned, narrowed; **pyer nyako widde woko,** the girls waist is narrowed or very small.

widi-widi *adv* very thin, small and narrowed; **pyerre widi widi calo pyer pino,** her waist is very small and narrowed like the wasp's waist.

widdo *vt.* to make thin round, reducing the size; **tyen meja ma en widdo nen maber mada,** the legs of the table which he has reduces in sizes look very nice.

wii *v* twist, spin; **wii pamba wek odok tol,** twist or spin the cotton into threads; **wii told pamba,** twist or make a cotton thread see **wic, wiyo**

wii *adj.* 1 head, top of something; **wii dano,** human head; **wii dero,** granary cover; **wii meja,** top of the table; 2 **wii mon,** leader of women, woman, leader, **wii lutic pamba,** headman of cotton workers. 3 descendant, ancestor; **wii kaka mewu oa ki kwene?** whence is your descendant from? 4 like at the level of; **odoŋo ka wii wonne,** he grew up to his fathers height. 5 boldness; quickness, agility, suppleness, nimbleness, frank; **wiye tek,** he is bold, frank; **wiye yot,** he is quick, agile and ready. 6 dullness, slowness; **wiye lik,** he is slow; **wiye pek,** he is dull, stupid; **otoo laboŋo wiye,** he died without any offspring or descendant, progenitor

wil *v* buy; **wil cukari ratili aryo,** buy two pounds of sugar.

wil *vi* flashes, lightens; **kot wil,** the rain lightens, or flashes; *adv.* **okatto ni wil,** he passed quickly like lightening.

wil *vn* to buy; **wacittu ka wil i cuk,** let us go to buy (something) in the market. .

wil tyen *vn* spraining; **wil tyen geŋŋo dano tukko odilo,** spraining of foot; prevents people from playing football; **tyenne wil woko ka tukko odilo,** his foot will be sprained if he plays football or his foot gets sprained when playing football; medically they call it *strain.*

wil wic *n* forgetfulness; **wil wic gin marac mada,** forgetfulness is a very bad thing); *vi* **wii owil woko i komme,** you have forgotten about him.

wille *adv* being bought; **jami pe tye ka wille maber,** things are not being well bought.

willo *vt* to sprain / spraining, to wrench / wrenching, to strain / straining, to dislocate / dislocating, to put / putting out of joint; **willo coŋ woko,** straining the knee; **pi willo coŋŋe woko omiyo pe doŋ ocitto,** he did not go because of straining his knee.

willo *vt* to buy, trade, **willo boŋo,** to buy / buying of clothes **willo boŋo,** he bought a cloth; **gucitto ka willo cam,** they went to buy some food.

willo *vn* make one to forget; **lok miŋo miŋo willo wii dano woko,** foolish talks make people to forget (being serious.)

wino *n* the hair of tails of; elephant, giraffe, cow, horses etc.; **wino kul,** bristles of warthog,

wino *n* cord of the placenta; **wino omakko dako woko,** the woman has failed to get rid of the cord of the placenta or part of it.

wiŋ *v* turn, deform, bend; **wiŋ wiye woko,** turn his head aside / turn his mind away.

wiŋŋe *vi* be bent, distorted, deformed, turned aside; **yatte wiŋŋe oyot oyot,** the wood bends easily **doggolane owiŋŋe woko,** the door shutter is bent.

wiŋŋo *vt* to distort, deform. **bur wiŋŋo dog litino woko,** the sore distorts the lips of the children to one side.

wiŋŋo vt. to spice / spicing, season / seasoning; **wiŋŋo dek ki kado wiŋ-wiŋ,** seasons the sauce with salt very much.

wiŋŋo *vt* to confuse / confusing, to derange / deranging someone's mind; **two wiŋŋo wii dano,** illness derange the mind; **twoo owiŋŋo wii latin woko omiyo oriŋŋo woko i lum,** the child's mind was deranged by the illness that made him ran to the jungle.

winy *v* listen, pay attention; **winy lok ma gilokki,** listen to what you have been told.

winyo *n* 1 bird, fowl. 2 **twoo giwinyo,** name for convulsions in children in cases of malaria and other causes. sometimes referred to as **gimalo; in** convulsion children usually look up and down, hence the name **gimalo or gin malo.**

winynye *vi* can be heard; **lokke winynye maber,** the word is audible, that is, it is heard well.

winynyo *vt* to hear, listen, understand, obey; **latin maber winynyo lok pa wonne,** a good child listens to his fathers words; **latin marac pe winynyo lapwony,** a bad child does not obey the teacher; **pe wiwiinynyo lok maber**

ma gipwonynye kwede, does not understand well what he is being taught.

wir *n* pillar, central pole of the hut; **wir ot,** central pole of the round hut.

wir *v* 1 smear, anoint; **wir wiye ki moo,** smear his head with oil; 2. turn; **wir wii mutoka odok tuŋ lacam,** turn the head of the motor car to the left

wirre *vn* 1 revolving, spinning round; **litino gitye ka tukko tukko me wirre,** the children are playing spinning round game.; *vi* to revolve / revolving; **tyen leela pe tye ka wirre maber,** the bicycle wheel is not revolving very well. 2 to go / going for something several times; **jali owirre mada pi waraga me wot i lobo ma woko,** that fellow came many times for his pass port. 3 giddiness, dizziness; **wiye wirre ci potto piny,** he feels giddy and falls down. 4. walking to and fro many times; **wirre ata,** walks anyhow, a tramp.

wirro *vt* to move / moving something round in a circle, or to turn / turning something round in a circle; **wirro tyen leela,** to turn / turning the wheel of a bicycle round and round.

wirro *vt* to annoint / annointing, to smear / smearing, to rub / rubbing in; **wirro rwot ki moo me ker,** to annoint / anointing the king with oil of kingship.

wit v fling, hurl; **wit latiŋdio ci ibaa wek ocel winyo,** swing your stone and fling it at the bird to stone it.

wit *n*. 1 ear of (corn); **wit geya, kal, ruc, etc.** the ears of sorghum, millet and rice etc; **wit kal ma widi,** the unthreshed millet. 2 *vt*. fling or hurl away; **wit lakidi ci ibol kwica,** swing the stone and hurl it there.

witte vt can be flung, hurled away, rebounded; **toŋ twerro witte i kom lec ci pe cubbo,** the spear can bounce from the animal, and does not spear it.

witto vt 1 flinging, hurl away **witto latiŋ dio atata cillo dano** flinging the stones about will stone the people; **latiŋ tiŋo latiŋ dio ci witto lakidi ma citto cello winyo nekko woko,** the child takes the stone and put it into the fling and flings it at the bird and hit it dead. 2 **makko twol ki yibbe ci witto woko wa i lum,** takes the snake by it's tail and hurls it into the grass. 3 swinging; **acikari giwotto ma giwitto badgi,** soldiers walk swinging their arms. 4 turning away; **owitto wiye woko oyot, kono kidi ocello wiye,** he turned his head away in time otherwise the stone would have struck his head. 5 jerking; **owitto rec ki goli,** he drew the fish with a jerk with the hook; **yutto ki goli** is prefered to **witto.**

wiu adv all at once, suddenly; **olwit, oyuto latin gweno ni wiu,** the eagle took away the young chick at a speed of lightening.

wiyo or wiino vt to spin / spinning thread, make / making string; **wiyo tol pamba,** to spin / spinning the cotton yarn; comes from **wii, wic.**

woc vn drying, putting out to dry; **woc pa boŋone pe doŋ okonyo,** it's drying did not help; see **woo, woyo.**

wod n / vn 1 son. 2 young; **wod dyaŋ,** male calf; **wod raa,** young male hippopotamus.

wok n 1 gap between teeth; **wok pe ber,** a gape in the teeth is not good 2 pass; **en owok ki kwene?** which way does he pass? **wok ki kwica,** passes over

there. 3 result; **peny owok niŋniŋ?** what is the result of the examinations? 4 manifest; **jok owok i komme,** the spirit manifested itself on him.

woko adv 1 out, outside; **ocitto woko,** he went out; **bin woko kany,** come outside here. 2 n universal spirit; **wek nyerro woko,** don't laugh at the crippled (which come as a result of misfortunes).

wol v 1 poison; **wol gwok,** poison the dog; **dakone lawol,** she is a person who always poisons people. 2 poisoning; **gitweyo pi wol,** he was jailed for poisoning.

wol n joint; **waŋ wol pyerre lit,** his hip joint is painful.

wolle prd poisoning; **wolle rac mada,** poisoning is very bad.

wollo vt to poison / poisoning; **wollo latin** to poison / poisoning the child

wolo-wolo prd loose, slack; **boŋone lac obeddo wolo-wolo,** his cloth is wide and loose.

won inj for my part, **en won pe ŋeyo gin ma watye ka timm one,** he does not know what we are doing.

won n 1 father of; **won latin,** the child's father. 2 owner of; **won leela ni tye kwene?,** where is the owner of the bicycle 3 employer; **won tic tye kwene?,** where is the employer? 4 **won ot,** husband or owner of the house; 5 **won ŋom,** land lord 6 **won paco,** headman of a village; **won lok,** plaintiff,

wonne, adv his father; **wonne tye kwene?** where is his father?; **otti wonne tye kwene?,** where is the owner of this house?

woŋ adv 1 very wide, large; **ot kanica ne lac ni woŋ,** the church is very wide or

271

large. 2 for good; **ocitto woko ni woŋ**, he went away for good.

woo *vi* dry on the surface (not completely); **boŋo woo i ceŋ** the clothes get partially dry in the sun. **piny doŋ cok ka woo**, the ground is nearly dry, **ket boŋo owoo i ceŋ**, put the clothes to partially dry in the sun; see **woc, woyo.**

woo *vi* 1 *n* noise, an uproaring, shouting; 2 making noise; **litino gitye ka woo**, the children are shouting or making noise. 3 *v* falling; **kot tye ka woo**, the rain is falling. (usually not very much but drizzling; 4 croak; **ogwal tye ka woo**, the frogs are croaking.

woo *vn* sprouting, germinating; **kal doŋ tye ka woo**, the millet is germinating or sprouting.

woor *n* 1 night; **woor kano ɗyaŋ matar**, night or darkness hides a white cow; **dyee woor**, at night or mid night. 2 greediness, selfishness; **dano ma woor**, a greedy person.

woor *n* respectful, well educated person; **dano ma woor**, an humble and respectable person.

woor *v.* respect, honour, esteem, obey; **woor meenni ki wooru**, obey and respect your mother and father.

woora *n* my father, *sing* **wego**, father, *pl* **wegi**, fathers; a general name; *sing* **woora, wooru, woone**, my, your, his father; *pl* one father with many children, the chidren refer to him as: **woonwa, woonwu, woongi**, our, your, their father; *pl* fathers with many children then they refer to them as **wegiwa, wegiwu, wegigi**, our, your, their fathers.

wooro *vt* to honour / honouring, to respect / respecting, to worship / worshipping, **latin myero wooro woonne ki minne**, the child should respect his father and mother; 2 *n* respecting, honouring, **wooro ludito gin maber**, respecting the elderly is a good thing.

wooro *n* greediness, gluttony, selfishness; **wooro pe ber**, greediness is not good. **gicammo ken-gi pi wooro ma gitye kwede**, they eat by themselves because of greediness of food. **gin luwooro mada**, they are very greedy and selfish people;

woro *n* dry cow dung; **mon waŋŋo woro dyaŋ me kado atwonna**, women burn the dry cow dung for alkali salt which is used for cooking vegetables.

woro-woro *adv* not solid or fully distended; **dako iye doŋ ocek woro-woro, pe doŋ katto tin mape onywal**, the lady's abdomen is greatly distended and full, it will not pass this night before she delivers.

wot *vi* travelling, **wot ata**, roving, and roaming aimlessly, a vagabond.

wot *v* pul out; **wot lum ot**, pull out grass from the roof of the house; **citti iwot yen acel ikel**, go and pull out one firewood and bring it.

wotte *prp* his journey; **wotte tye diki**, his journey is tomorrow.

wotto *vi* 1 to walk, travel **latin doŋ woto**, the child now walks; 2 pull out; **en wotto lum me cwinyo mac**, he pulls out the grass for lighting fire.

woyo *vt* partial drying; **giterro bel woko ka woyone**, the millet was taken out for partial drying it; see **woo, woc.**

wu *pref prs* you. **wubin kany** (you) come here **wucitti** (you) go - **wu** prns sff you, your. **mewu** - yours **meegiwu** your mother.

wuci, better spelling **uci** *N S* thread; **uci me kwoyo boŋo**, thread for sewing clothes.

wun *prs prn* you; **wun litino maracu,** you are bad children.

wunno *vi*. do, let; **wubin wunno con,** do come early; **wacit wunno ka cam ba,** please let us go to eat.

wurru *vt* to prepare / preparing large quantity; **wurru "kwon"** preparing a large amount of **kwon**; **min latin wurru kwon ki litino me acamma,** the mother prepares a large amount of **kwon** for the children to eat;

wuru-wuru, *adv* dull sound of hide which is being dragged on the floor; **latin tye ka ywayo pyen i dyee ot ni wuru wuru,** the child is dragging the dried hide on the floor with that dull sound.

Y y

ya *adv* yet; *suff* to **pe** becomes **pe ya** adv not yet; **pe ya odwogo,** not yet returned or come back; **pe ya ocitto,** not yet gone; really, *intj* **adaa do ya,** it is really true.

ya *inj*. with **a** as prff, becomes **aya** an exclamation e.g. **aya omeera in itimme niŋniŋ?** oh brother what are you doing? or oh brother what is becoming of you;. **aya do,** oh dear me (cry).

yaa *n* shea - butter nut tree. *(Butyrospermum parkii).* **moo yaa,** the butter of shea nut.

yaa *n* age mate or contemporary; **yaa**

lwakgi, their age mate or contemporary; **Jon en aye ŋat acel i kom yaa lwakwa ma wakwanno kwedgi Budo,** John is one of our contemporary with whom we studied at Budo.

yaani for **niya,** *conj* that, **en owacco yaani,** he said that, in a sarcastic way

yaar *v* spread out; **yaar kolo ki dano gubed iye,** spread the papyrus mat for people to sit on.

yaarre *vi* 1 being very proud; **dako wotto kun yaarre pien tye ki wodde,** the woman walks with pride beause she has a son; 2 behaving in a way which causes suspicion, rejoicing excessively; **yaarre i wii lyel pa nyekke calo en ma onekko nyekke,** full of happiness during the funeral of her co-wife as if she was the one who killed her co-wife; 3 get out to fight; **guyaarre ka lweny,** they got out to fight

yaarro *vt* to spread /spreading out; **yaarro kweyo, kal, ki nyim,** to spread / spreading out sand, millet and simsim.

yaarro *vt* ready to fight, **gijukkogi ki tek onoŋo doŋ guyaarro woko ka lweny,** they were about to fight when they were forcefully stopped.

yab *v*. open, unlock; **yab doggola,** open the door; **yab yoo me tic ki dano,** open the way for the people for work or job; **yab waŋwa,** open our eyes; **yab muŋ matye,** reveal any secrete.

yabbe *vi* can be opened, to open; **doggolane tweno yabbe,** the door can be opened; **waŋ ceng tin pe tye ka yabbe maber,** the sun is not shining / opening its rays, well **doggola oyabbe kene,** the door opened itself; **piny tin oyabbe maleŋ,** today it is bright, no rain or today the sky has cleared up;

yabbo *vt* to open / opening 1 **yabbo doggola,** to open / opening the door. 2 to commit / committing adultery; **yabbo wii dako pa ŋatimo,** to open the door of the wife of another person means to commit adultery with the wife of another person. 2 to uncover / uncovering; **yabbo kom latwoo,** uncovering the patient. 3 to give / giving birth; **dakone oyabbo waŋŋe tin,** his wife has given birth today. 4 to comfort / comforting , to encourage / encouraging; **yabbo waŋ latwoo,** comforting and encouraging the patient. 5 to comfort / comforting, to console / consoling; **yabbo waŋ latoo,** to comfort / comforting and to console / consoling a bereaved person.

yac *n /vn* pregnancy. **yac pa latin kwan pe ber,** the pregnancy of a student is not good. **oyac woko,** she is pregnant; **yac luk,** illegitimate pregnancy.

yacce *vn* her pregnancy; **dano pe gumeddi ŋeyo kit ka yacce,** people did not know about her pregnancy.

yacco, *vi* to impregnat / impregnating; **gimakke pi yacco nyaa pa Oto,** he was arrested for impregnating Oto's daughter. **en oyacco nyaa pa ŋadi,** he has impregnated so and so's daughter.

yacu *n* pregnancy.

yago *n* sausage tree; *prov* **labwor ka oyenynyo lee kwee ci mwoddo yago,** when the lion fails to find an animal, it eats the sausage tree, this means that if you cannot find what you realy want, you can do with an alternative.

yai *prd* frail, brittle, soft, poor quality; **latinne komme yai,** the child is frail; **kikopo ne yai,** the cup is brittle and breaks easily.

yak *n* robbery, plundering, enslaviing, looting; **gimakko dano apar kai yak laworo,** ten people were arrested yesterday for robbery; **layak,** a robber, plunderer, looter.

yaka *adv* then (spoken by people bordering Lango); central Aholi say , **ka doŋ**; **tye ka kurro lawotte obin yaka doŋ gicam,** the central Acholi says, **tye ka kurro lawotte obin ka doŋ gicam,** he is waiting for his companion to come so that they may eat.

yaka-yaka *adv* shaking; **wotto ma tuno kore yeŋŋe ni yaka-yaka,** walks with her turgid breasts shaking up and down.

yakke *vt* can be looted, robed; **dano tin gitya ka yakke ki jami ma pe larre,** people today looting many things.

yakko *vt* to rob / obbing, to plunder / plundering, to loot / looting; **gimakko luyak ka yakko beŋe,** the robbers were arrested while robbing the bank. **yakko dano pe gin maber,** robbing people is not good.

yal *n* presents given during process of marriage.

yal *v* give presents; **yal anyira keny,** give presents to the bridemaids.

yallo *vt* to give / giving presents. (connected with marriage; **yallo anyira keny,** to give / giving presents to the bridemaids, according to tradition, who accompanied the bride to her bridegroom's village before they accept any food.; there are many presents given for different purposes during the period. **ayalla,** the presents given.

yam *prd* long time ago; spoken by Acholi bordering Lango, the central group prefer **yaŋ**. see **yaŋ**.

yammo *vi* making jokes, fun, amusing,

entertaining, **.yammo ki ywere,** making jokes with his sister in law.

yammo *vi Lang* conversing with, flirting with a girl, courting a girl.

yamo *n* air, wind.

yaŋ *v* skin, operate; **yaŋ dyel man,** skin this goat; **cit ka yaŋ,** go to do operation.

yaŋ *n* 1 skinning of (animals). 2 operations on (human).

yaŋ *adv* this is the word preferred for **yam,** which means once upon a time, in the past, long ime ago; **yaŋ con,** long time ago, in the past; **yam con,** spoken mainly by the people bordering Lango, **Koro, Puranga etc.**

yaŋ-yaŋ *adv.* carrying something big; **otiŋo em dyaŋ obino kwede ni yaŋ yaŋ,** he carried the heavy thigh of a cow and came with it quite overloaded.

yaŋŋo *vt* to skin / skinning, cut / cutting up; **yaŋŋo dyel,** skins / skinning the goat.

yaŋo *v* to operate / operating, **yaŋŋo dano gin matek mada,** operating on the people is very difficult, *vn* 2 operation **yaŋŋo pe gin ma gitiyo aruya,** operation is not the thing that you do it hurriedly.

yany *adj* big; **otiŋŋo riŋo ni yany ocitto kwede kuno,** he carried a big portion of meat and went with it there.

yanynyo *vt* to make / making big; **yanynyo kwon,** to make / making big "kwon" in a plate *see* **wurru.**

yat (*pl* **yadi**) *n* a tree, wood, medicine; **latwoo omunynyo yat ma gimiye,** the sick person swallowed the medicine given to him; **tidu yat maber mada tidu** is a fine tree.

yau *adv* very light; **gwenone yot ni yau pe romo kit wel ma giŋollo pire,** the chicken is too light, it is not enough for the price given for it.

yec *n* load; **laye yec,** carrier; **en otiŋo yec ma pek mada,** he carried a very heavy load.

yec *n* 1 hair of; **yec winyo,** feathers of birds; 2 wings **yec bonyo, yec otwoŋo, yec ŋwen,** locusts, grasshoppers and termites' (wings, wings of insects);

yec *v* tear, be torn; **yec i boŋo wek odok aryo,** tear the cloth so that it becomes two **boŋone oyec woko,** the cloth is torn or his cloth is torn.

yec *vn* 1 acceptance, consent 2 carrying; **yec pa anyira nino ducu pe tye atir,** the consent of the girls are always not straight; 3 weight **yec ma pek turro kor litino,** heay loads break the children's back. See **yee, yeyo.**

yecce *vn* his load; **yecce tye caa, ma myero en otiŋ,** his load is there, that he should take.

yecce *vn* his acceptance, consent, agreement; **yecce me wekko wan me citto pudi peya walimmo,** we have not yet received his consent to allow us to go.

yecco *vt* to tear / tearing, rend / rending, split / splitting; **yecco boŋo,** tears / tearingthe clothes.

yee *vn* 1 belief; **joo ma yee lok pa Lubaŋa,** those who believe in God's word 2 consent, agree, obey; **yee ni gitucce ki yat,** consents to be injected with medicine. 3 assent; **rwot oyee ni lokke gitii kwede,** the king assented that the words be used or the king has given his assent for the use of the words. 4 tasting; **camme oyee dogge mada,** the food was very tasting to him. 5 acceptance; **en yee dano binno gaŋŋe,**

he is very good, accepts people to come to his home;see **yec, yeyo.**

yee *v* carry on head; **yee pii i cupuria iteer gaŋ**, carry the water in the aluminum saucepan on your head and take it home; see **yec, yeyo.**

yeene *vi* 1 can be accepted, can be believed, be consented to, assented to; **yeene matir pud peya walimmo,** we have not yet received his consent or acceptance. 2 can be carried; **piine twewrro yeene,** the water can be carried.

yeg *v* loosen, make it loose; **yeg tee yatte** shake the tree; **yeŋ wek oyeg tee yatte,** shake the pole so that it may loosen it.

yege-yege *prd* loose, shaky, infirm; **lakke yege-yege,** his tooth is loose.

yeggo *vt* to loose / loosening, to joggle / joggling or to jolt / jolting so as to make it loose; see **yoggo.**

yek *v* pick, separate; **yek ruc eno ma kweyo tye iye,** pick out stones and separate sand from the rice.

yekke *vi* can be separated, sifted; **lapenane twerro yekke nia ki kom nyim man,** the pigeon peas can be separated from the simsim. **wek ludito guyekke gudok tuŋ caa,** let the elders separate and move to the other side

yekko *vt* 1 to sift / sifting or to separate / separating something. 2 to select / selecting, to pick / picking the good ones. 3 to examine / examining and to pick / picking out the right words; **yekko lok,** to pick / picking out the right words; **yekko kal,** to winnow / winnowing and to pick / picking out the stones and chaff from the millet.

yel *v* trouble, bother, molest, torment; **yel lu - wac kom,** bother the lazy people **pe iyel litino,** do trouble the children;

dano ma layel pe mitte kany, a troublesome person is not wanted here.

yelle *vt* trying; **tye ka yelle mada me citto,** he is trying very much to go;

tye ka yelle ki lok me piddo-ne, preoccupied with his case in court..

yello *vn* troubling , bothering, worrying, tormenting, molesting; **yello litino gin marac mada,** troubling the children is a very bad thing; **yello lu mabuc pe ber,** molesting or tormenting the prisoners is not good.

yem-yem *prd* fringe; **dogge yem yem,** the fringed and ravelled edge that floats.

yen *n* wood for fire or for building; **gucitto ka tweyo yen,** they went to gather the firewood; **gimitto yen mabocco madoŋŋo me geddo,** they want tall big wood for building.

yeŋ *n* 1 an insect which when touched feigns death. 2 satisfied, full, satiated; **latin doŋ ocammo oyeŋ ki cam,** the child has eaten and is full and satisfied. **latin doŋ cammo yeŋ hi cam,** the child now eats and gets satisfied.

yeŋ *v* shake; **yeŋ cwaa wek nyigge opot piny,** shake the tamarind tree so that the fruits may drop down.

yeŋŋe *vi* -be shaken; **yat tye ka yeŋŋe ki yamo,** the tree is being shaken by the wind; **yatti twero yeŋŋe,** this tree can be shaken; **bedo mot pe yeŋŋe,** remains calm and does not shake.

yeŋŋo *vt.* to shake / shaking, ring; **tye ka yeŋŋo olaŋ,** is ringing the bell; **tye ka yeŋŋo ajaa,** is shaking the rattle to call the spirit to relieve the person who is obsessed by it; **yeŋŋo wiye pien pe mitto,** shakes his head in disapproval or shakes his head because he does not like it.

yeny *v* search for, look for, find, seek; **yeny kama caa tye iye,** look for where the watch is; **yeny adaa me lok man,** seek for the truth of this case; **yeny kama latin tye iye,** find out where the child is; **yeny tee kwarrowa,** search for our ancestry.

yenynye *vn* to look / looking for, to search / searching; **lim ma doŋ orweny pe tweno yennye;** the money which is lost cannot be looked for. **guyenynye mada me noŋŋo kama gikanno iye luduko,** they searched and searched to find out the place where the gun has been hidden.

yenynyo *vt* 1 to look / looking for, to seek / seeking, search for, to inquire / inquiring; **yenynyo buk me cura,** to look / looking for mathematic book; **yenynyo lok macon,** searching for old stories. 2 **yenynyo tyen lok ma okello jemmo,** inquiring into the cause of strike; provoking; **wek yenynyo alii obeddi,** do not provoke quarrel or anger or do not annoy.

yenynyo *vi.* 1 to boiling; **pii tye ka yenynyo,** the water is boiling. 2 to ferment. **koŋo kwete yenynyo maber mada,** kwete beer ferments very nicely. 3 to foam; **cak tye ka yenynyo bwoyo,** the milk is foaming 4 distend. **oboo yenynyo,** the lungs distends, 5 swelling (and ready to fight); **labwor tye ka yenynyo i tee lum,** the lion is swelling up under the grass and ready to fight.

yer *n* 1 hair; **yer wic,** hair on the head; 2 **yer tik** ,beard; 3 **yer dog,** whiskers, (animals) 4 **yer um,** moustache, 5 **yer waŋ,** eyelashes, eyebrows; 6 **yer tok kana,** mane of a donkey; 7 **yer ŋut labwor,** mane of a lion.

yer *n* 1 election, selection, choosing; **yer atyer,** general election for (Parliament); **gucitto ka yer atyer,** they went for general election or they went to choose or select.

yer *v* select, choose; **yer waar ma imitto,** select or choose the shoes you want.

yerre *vn* selected themselves; **Lubobi tin yerre gin keken,** today the Bobi clan will select themseves alone.

yerro *vt* 1 to select / selecting, to choose / choosing, or to elect / electing; **tye ka yerro gin ma en mitto,** he is choosing what he wants or selecting what he wants; 2 picking; **mon tye ka yerro muraŋa ma orubbe ki nyim,** the women are picking out the beans which were mixed with simsim; 3 pecking; **winyo tye ka yerro pul ma gipitoni woko,** the birds are pecking up the groundnuts which were planted.

yet *n* insult, abuse; **yet pe ber,** abusing or insulting is not good; **pe myero iyet ŋati mo,** do not abuse or insult anybody.

yet *v* abuse, insult; **yet matek wek pe dok odwog cen,** abuse or insult him very much so that he may not come back.

yet *v* sharpen; **yet yat magi me teke me guurro laa,** sharpen these pieces of wood into wooden nails for nailing the hide.

yette *vn* abused or insulted themselves; **yette pe gin maber,** an abuse or insult is not good; **tin gin guyette mada,** they abused or insulted themselves very much.

yette *vn* can be sharpened.

yetto *vt* insulting, abusing; **yetto dano pe ber,** abusing or insulting people is not good.

yetto *vt* to sharpen, cut to a point, **yetto teke me gurro laa,** to cut and shape the small woods to a point as wooden nails for pinning down a hide, see **mucumar.**

yeya *n* canoe, boat. ship *see* **mabur**

yeya *vt* helping to put on the head; **yeya ki agulo pii,** help me to put the water pot on my head.

yeyo *vn* accptance, agreeing; **yeyo pa danone pe genne,** his acceptance cannot be trusted; see **yec, yee.**

yeyo *vi* 1 **yeyo or yeeno,** to carry / carrying on head, to put / putting on head, to help / helping on lifting and placing on head; **yeyo yec,** carrying load; **bin iyeya,** come and help me to place it on my head. 2 be involved (in big problem); **oyeyo pekko mo madit mada i wiye,** he is involved in a big trouble or a big case; see **yee, yec.**

yib *n* tail; some people call it **ib** but the former is preferred; **yib ayom,** tail of a monkey; **yib ogwal peke,** the frog has no tail.

yik *n/vt* burial, **gucitto ka yik,** they went for a burial.

yik *v* bury; **yik gwok ma otoo ni,** bury the dead dog,

yikke *vi.* to hide / hiding under; **yikke i tee lum,** hides under the grass; *n* **yikke obeddo lok madit mada,** his burial was a very important matter or burial is a very important matter.

yiki-yiki *adv* to and fro; **kitanda yeŋŋe ni yiki-yiki,** the bed moves to and fro making the noise.

yikko *vt* burying; 1 **yikko dano ma otoo,** burying a dead person. 2 **yikko layata i buro malyet wek ocek iye,** burying a potato in a hot ash for roasting it.

yil *n* 1 troublesome, irritation or itching; **yil me jwinya,** troublesome irritation and itching of jiggers; 2 *adv* **latinne komme yil mada,** the child is restless and troublesome. 3 **gwenyo yil mada,** scabies do cause a lot of itching.

yim *adv* be densely, covered completely; **kom romo obeddo ni yim,** the sheep is covered with flowing hair; **dano gubakke i bar odilo ni yim,** the people assembled in a large number in the football field.

yimme *v* be in great quantity or number; **yimme pa dano i bar odilo pe oyommo cwiny Jon;** the gathering of a large nymber of people in the football field did not please John; **piny tin ye ka yimme** today the sky is heavily loaded with dark clouds, or today there is heavy overcast in the sky; **dano guyimme mada i bar odilo,** people gathered themselve in a large number in the football field (not commonly spoken now).

yimmo *vt* to do with great force, to overload; **oyimmo kor dakone ki adoŋ matek adada,** he gives a mighty blow to the chest of his wife; **yimmo ter i wii dano,** placing a heavy load on the head of a person. (spoken by Langi)

yir *n* bewitching, charming.

yirre *vi/ vn* be bewitched, charmed. **en ŋeyo lok me yirre mada,** he knows very much about bewitching and charming; **yirre pe tye** bewitching is not there.

yirro *vt* bewitching with evil eye; **yirro waŋ rac,** bewitching the eyes is bad. **giyirro waŋŋe woko ci waŋŋe otoo woko,** his eyes were bewitched and became blind; **oyirro riŋo woko ci**

giteddo kwee pe ocek, he bewitched the meat and the meat could not be cooked soft.

yiru *n* smoke or **yito** *n* smoke, the latter is preferred

yito *n* smoke, which some pewople call it **ito,** the former is preferred for smoke to avoid. it being confused with climbing; **yito tye ka duny ki i ot,** the smoke is coming out of the house or rising out from the house.

yoo *n* **nyo waŋayoo, korayoo,** path, tract, road, **yoo tye kwene?** where is, road, path, or tract?.

yog *v* loosen; **yog tol ma gitweyo ma tek i ŋut dyel woko,** loosen the tight rope on the goat's neck see **yeg.**

yogge *vi* loosen / loosening or make / making loose; **uno yogge woko ki iŋut dyel ma pe noŋo gitweyo matek;** the rope become loose from the goat's neck when it is not tight; **yogge woko,** becomes loose.

yoggo *vt* to loosen / loosening; **yoggo doggola,** to loose / loosening the door.

yogo-yogo *adv* loosely, not firmly; **gitweyo yogo-yogo,** tied loosely.

yok *v* knock, hit, butt; **yok doggola,** knock the door; **yok doggola ki tee luduku,** hit the door with the butt of the gun.

yokke *vi* to but, to knock / knocked against something, hit. **yokke ki mutoka,** to knock / knocking against the car; **oyokke ki ajut,** knocked himself against the stump.

yokke *vt* urinate, **acitto ka yokke,** I am going to pass urine, this is the civilized

way of saying it, like in English, among the well-bred people, they say I am going for a wash up.

yokke *vi* clash; **tin gitye ka yokke mada i kot,** they are clashing very badly in the court.

yokko *vt* to knock, but, hit; **yokko wiye i kom ot,** knocks his head against the wall of the house; **oyokko tyenne kom ajut,** knocks his foot against the stump, or strikes his foot against the stump; **yokko doggola,** knocks the door; **yokko wic ki tee luduku,** hits / butting the head with the butt of the gun.

yokko *vi* stopping; postponding, **yokko yoo ayokka ci dwoggo cen,** went and postponded the journey on the way and returned. **yokko yoo ayokka,** going and returning.

yom *n* without prepuce (naturally i.e. from birth); **layom,** is usually referred to the one who is borne without the prepuce.

yom *adj* soft; 1 **kiyata ne yom,** the potatoes are soft; 2 **koŋone yom,** the beer is not strong, it is soft; 3 **cwinynye yom,** he is happy, glad, satisfied, friendly and of pleasing character.

yom-cwiny *n* happiness, gladness, pleasure, contentment; **tic maber kello yom cwiny bot dano,** good work brings happiness to the people; *prov.* **yom cwiny aa i ojoga,** happiness comes from the stomach; that is, if you give me something then I will also be happy to give you something; **obeddo ki yom winy mada pi katto penynye,** he was very happy or pleased to pass his examination.

yomme *vn* winning in racing; **yomme i tuko me ŋwec gin me deyo mada,**

winning in a game of racing is a thing of great honour.

yomme *vt* to surpass / surpassing in running or overtake; **yommo luwotte i ŋwec,** surpass / surpassing his friends in running.

yon *v* move forwards and backwards; **yon ŋutti,** move your neck forwards and backwards.

yon *vi* disdain doing or receiving something; **yon dag cammo dek,** disdained eating the food; **yon i komme,** he treats him with disdain (refuses to accept anything from him, because he thinks it is below him); **wek yon obeddi,** leave being disdainful or do not be disdainful, see **lyerre.**

yonno *vt.* **yonno ŋut,** moving forwards and backwards of the neck.

yoŋ *v* add; **yoŋ kado i dek wek obed mamit,** add more salt in the sauce to make it taste nice.

yoŋ-kado *n* **obot kado,** second lye after the first lye has been drained off.

yoŋŋo *vt.* to add / adding more, augment / augomenting; **yoŋŋo wiye manok wek giwil,** adds a little more to it so that it may be bought; **oyoŋŋo wii kadone manok doki i kare madoŋ giwilo,** he added a little more to the salt after it had already been bought.

yoo *n* path, track, way, road; **yoo obeddo pony pony,** the road is full of pot holes. **yoo merac,** a bad road.

yoo *v* sprinkle, some people prefer to call it **yoor** or **yor** see below.

yor *v* add a little more; **yor nyimme imed manok i kom ma ipimmo wek giwil,** add some more simsim on the one

you have measured so that it may be bought, see **yoŋ.**

yor *v* sprinkle, wet by spraying and spattering; **yor pii i dye ot,** sprinkle the floor with water; **yor pii i tee ature wek pe otwoo,** spray the flowers with water to prevent it from drying; **yor pii i poto nyanya,** sprinkle or spray the tomatoes field with water, see **yoo.**

yorre *vt* add a little more; **yorre pul manok i kom ratili ma ipimmoni,** add to him a little more groundnuts to the ones that you have measured.

yorro *vt* 1 to sprinkle / sprinkling with water. 2 to half fill; **gitye ka yorro pii i dye ot,** they are sprinking the floor with water or spattering it with water; 3 draining; **moo ocwer oyorro tee atabo ayorra keken,** the oil only filled the bottom of the bowel after draining.

yorro or **yoono** *vt* to wet by spraying, spattering, sprinkling or squirting; **gitye ka yorro pii i tee yat ma gipitto wek pe otwoo,** they are spraying the water under the planted tree to prevent it from drying; **ginyorro pii i tiŋ wek otwakki,** they spatter the water in the beer dreg to make it effervesce or ferment more; **guyorro pii i wii latwoo ma owille wek ocoo,** they sprinkled or poured the water on the head of an unconscious patient so that he might gain his consciousness.

yoyo *vi* to sprinkle / sprinkling; **yoyo pii i poto nyanya,** to sprinkle / sprinkling the tomatoes field *see* **yorro.**

yot *adj* light, easy; 1 **gwenone yot,** the chicken is light; 2 **komme yot,** he is healthy; **cwinynye yot,** he is unreliable, cannot keep secret.

yub *v* repair, prepare, adjust, put right or set right, or in order; **yub leela oyot**

oyot, repair the bicycle quickly; **yub dwanni maber,** clear your throat; **yub lokki maber,** prepare well your words or speech; **yub cam oyot oyot,** prepare the food quickly.

yubbe *vi* 1 prepare yourself, be ready; **yubbe oyot oyot wek wacitti,** prepare yourself quickly so that we may go; 2 prepared; **litino tika doŋ guyubbe me peny?** are the children now ready or prepared for examinations? 3 repaired; **caa ne tika twerro yubbe?** can the watch be repaired? **yabbe wuno doŋ me pany** get ready for examination.

yubbo, *vt* to set / setting right or in order, to repair / repairing, to prepare / preparing, adjust; **ŋaa matye ka yubbo cam?** who is preparing the food? **cit ka yubbo kitanda pi welo,** go and make or prepare the bed for the visitor; **yoo doŋ gityekko yubbo maber mada,** the road has been well repaired; **caa doŋ gityekko yubbo maber,** the watch has now been well repaired.

yuc *vn* throwing; **yuc atata me lakidi kama pe ineno pe ber,** throwing stones where you do not see is not good.

yuc *vn* inhaling, breathing in; **pe twerro nino ka pe koŋ onoŋo yuc mo me taa,** he cannot sleep until he has inhaled or puffed at tobacco; see **yuu, yuyo.**

yuc *vn* plucking; **yuc me mayembe manunmu pe ber,** plucking unripe mangoes is not good.

yugi *n.* uprooted weeds, sweepings from the house or offices or compound.

yuk *adv* densely; **lum otwii ni yuk,** the grass has grown up; **yer kom gunya odin ni yuk,** the chimpanzee has dense long hair.

yuk *v*, dig up the ground; **yuk tee yat ma gipitoni wek pii odony iye,** dig up round the planted tree to make the water sink underneath.

yukku *vt* 1 to push up earth from beneath; **okok yukku yoogi ki i ŋom,** the termites push up the earth from beneath to make their way; **odir yukku ŋom ka gerro odde i ŋom,** the cricket pushes up the earth when making it's hole in the ground.

yul *v* pull; **yul lum ki i wii ot,** pull the grass off from the roof of a hut.

yullu *vt* to pull, spoil; **litino gubeddo ka yullu wii ot me mokko mac,** the children have been pulling off grass from the roof of the hut for making fire.

yuŋ *v* entertain, make jokes; **yuŋ lok ki wan wek oyom cwinywa,** entertain us with some jokes.

yuŋ *vi vn* humour, entertainment, interesting talk; a commedian. **yuŋ lok ki wan,** entertain us. **ŋaa ma layuŋ lok i kinwu?** who is the most humourous person among you? **layuŋ lok,** an entertainer, a humourous person in talk,

yunŋe *vi* swelling or increasing in size; **pol tye ka yuŋŋe nyo pinynye tye ka yuŋŋe,** the cloud is gathering up, that is, increasing.

yuŋŋo *vt* 1 being humourous; **danone yuŋŋo lok mada,** the man is very humourous in his talk; 2 tasteful, **dekke yuŋŋo lem,** the food is very tasteful.

yurre *vi* gliding down; **litino gitye ka yurre i kom bao me tukko meggi,** the children are gliding down on the board made for them for play.

yurru *vi* acting carelessly, indolently; **yurru tic ayurra,** working half heartedly, indolently without determination.

yut *v* snatch; **yut boŋo woko ki i ciŋŋe,** snatch away the cloth from his hand.

yutte *vi* urge; **cwinya yutte me lweny kwedde,** I feel like fighting him or I have an urge of fighting him, some people call it **utte.** see **omme, tiŋŋe, wet-wet, ille.**

yutto *vi.* 1 to jerk / jerking suddenly, pull suddenly; **yutto rec ki goli ki i pii,** jerking a fish with a hook from the water; **layutta,** a snare or a trap with a strong pole that jerks violently in the air on being released; **gucitto ka yuttu or yutto rec,** they went to fish with hooks. 2 to snatch / snatching; **yutto buk woko ki i ciŋŋe,** snatching away a book from his hand.

yutto *vi* 1 to become dark; 2 **yutto piny,** night fall; 3 feeling sleepy, **nino yuttu waŋŋe,** he feels sleepy; **piny oyutto,** it has become dark.

yuu *v* 1 inhale, take a puff at, breathe in; **yuu taane gicel keken,** inhale or take a puff at the tobacco once only; 2 throw; **yuu yugine odok tuŋ kupiny,** throw the rubbish towards the west; see **yuc ki yuyo.**

yuu *v* pluck; **yuu mayembe ma pud numo,** pluck the unripe mangoes; **pe iyuu lemun ma pud numu,** don't pluck the unripe lemons.

yuyo *vt* **yuuno;** lacerating, abrasing, rubbing off skin; **yuyu coŋŋe dok pwacco bene,** he abrades and lacerates his knee.

yuyo *vt* 1 to throw away; **tye ka yuyo kikebe macon i lum,** -is throwing away old tins into the grass. 2 **yuyu taa ki um,** sniffing the tobacco; **yuyo**

lakidi madit meno yuc me nek, throwing such a big stone is a throw for killing; see **yuu, yuc.**

yuyo *vi* to pluck; **tye ka yuyo mucuŋgwa mape ya ocek,** is plucking the unripe oranges.

ywaa *v.* drag, pull; **ywaa kom i kel cok kany,** pull the chair near here; **ywaa twon yen man i teer kwica,** drag this big log of wood and take it there; see **ywac, ywayo.**

ywaane *vi* 1 drawing near; **ywaane wuno kany,** draw near here; 2 tug of war; **dano adii ma gucitto ka ywaane?,** how many people went for the tug of war? See **telle, ywac.**.

ywaat *n* armpit or axilla, some people call it **yweet.**

ywac *n* dragging, trailing, tug of war; **wamitto dano me ywac,** we want people for tug of war; see **ywaa, ywaayo.**

ywayo *vt* 1 to drag / dragging, trail / trailing; **ywayo dul yat madit,** dragging a big log of wood. 2 enlarge; **ywayo twon ot mo madit mape wacce,** builds a very big house. 3 announcing, notifying, arranging publicly; **ywayo mony, myel, dwar,** declaring war, notifying for dancing and for hunting; see **ywaa, ywac.**

ywee *v* breathe, respire; **ywee matek wek anen,** take in deep breathing for me to see.

ywee *vi* 1 breathe, respire; **latin pe tye ka ywee maber,** the child is not breathing well. 2 rest; **i ol twatwal, cit koŋ iywee,** you are too tired, go and rest; 3 *vt* sweep; **ywee dye ot maleŋ,** sweep the floor very clean; see **ywec, yweyo ywec** *n* sweeping; **gin me ywec pe tye,** a thing for sweeping is not there;

ywec *n* breathing; **ywecce pe tye maber,** his breathing is not good; (this is not commonly spoken), **yweyone pe tye maber** is preferred; see, **ywee, yweyo**

ywek *vn* become famous, become known; **ywek pa nyiŋŋe oa pi nekko lyec,** his fame came from killing an elephant. **oywek mada pi nekko labwor,** he became very famous for killing a lion.

ywekka *n* fame, reputation, good name. **ywekka winynye wii lobo ducu,** fame is known all over the world.

ywekke *vi.* assembling, gathering, coming together from everywhere; **dano tye ka ywekke me citto ka ŋollô wii rwotgi,** the people are gathering to go to welcome their chief; **dano gitye ka ywekke me citto ka nenno odilo,** the people are gathing to go to see the football match.

ywekko *vt* to transport, collect; **ywekko yugi** to collect rubbish; **guywekko got doŋ orommo me geddo,** they have collected the stones which are enough for building.

yweer *n* 1 calf (back of leg of human).

yweer *n* sister or brother in law, **yweerra,** my sister- or brother-in-law; **ywecca,** of sisters or brothers of my sister-in-law or brother-in-law; **joo pa ywecca,** the people of my sister or brother in law.

yweer *v* clear the water; **yweer waŋ pii,** clear the water well; see **gwad, cot, wal.**

yweero *n* sister or brother in law.

yweerro *vt* 1 removing the water and wiping it away with hands; **yweerro pii ki i wii meja ki ciŋ,** removing the water from the table with hands; 2 clearing;

ywerro waŋ pii, clearing the water well so that it may run well.

yweyo *vt* 1 to sweep / sweeping; **cit ka yweyo ot,** go to sweep the house. 2 to rest / resting; **en tye ka yweyo nia ki i tic matek ma obeddo ka tiyone,** he is resting from the hard work that he has been doing; **cit ka yweyo i England,** go for a holiday to England.

yweyo *n* to breathe / breathing; **tye ka yweyo maber,** is breathing well.

ywic *vn* making small, running fast see **ywii ki ywiyo.**

ywii *v* 1 make small; **ywii kor odoo man wek odok matidi,** make the middle of the stick small. 2 run away fast; **ywii ŋwec matek,** run very fast, see **ywic, ywiyo.**

ywiin *v* make small; **ywiin tee odoone woko,** make the bottom of the stick small.

ywiino *vt* to make / making thin by cutting; **ywiino tyen meja,** cutting the table legs small; **kor odoone pudi peya oywinne** or **oywiine,** the stem of the stick is not yet thin; **med ywiinno ne,** continue with cutting it to be small.

ywiiyo *vt* 1 to make / making thin by cutting, **ywiinno** is preferred; 2 to run away very first; **ywiiyo** or **ywiine ki twon ŋwec mo matek mada,** he took off at a very high speed; see **ywic ki ywii. ywiiyo ŋwee matek twatwal,** running away very fast / taking off in a high speed.